MAGILL INDEX
TO
GREAT LIVES
FROM
HISTORY

MAGILL INDEX
TO
GREAT LIVES
FROM
HISTORY

With Additional Citations for the "Principal Personages"
Found in Great Events from History

Cumulative Indexes

1972–1995

SALEM PRESS

Pasadena, California   Englewood Cliffs, New Jersey

Library of Congress Cataloging-in-Publication Data
Magill index to Great lives from history : with additional
citations for the "principal personages" found in Great
events from history : cumulative indexes, 1972-1995.
    p. cm.
    ISBN 0-89356-891-0
    1. Biography—Indexes. 2. History—Indexes. 3. Great
lives from history—Indexes. 4. Great events from history—Indexes. I. Magill, Frank Northen, 1907-
Z5301.M35   1995
016.92002—dc20   94-47091
                                                         CIP

PUBLISHER'S NOTE

This index to Magill's *Great Lives from History* publications combines and collates the name indexes from those multivolume reference sets with the Principal Personages Indexes from the *Great Events from History* sets.

Launched in 1987, the *Great Lives from History* series began with a survey of influential figures in American history in the *American Series*. It was followed by a similar overview of prominent individuals from British history in the *British and Commonwealth Series*. The *Ancient and Medieval Series, Renaissance to 1900 Series, Twentieth Century Series*, and *American Women Series* examine the lives of historically significant individuals worldwide.

The *Great Events from History* series, which serves as a companion to *Great Lives from History*, provides a chronologically arranged survey of events which shaped civilization, beginning with the domestication of the horse in ancient times, continuing through the formation of modern Europe and the New World and into the 1990's. Each set in the Great Events series includes an index to the principal personages involved in those events, and those indexes are represented here.

The current, cumulative index offers, in one location, a guide to discussions of these men and women and the impact they had on their society. Entries are followed by a code indicating the series in which the discussion appears, which in turn is followed by the page or pages locating the discussion:

GE:A&C	Great Events from History II: Arts and Culture Series
GE:A&M	Great Events from History: Ancient and Medieval Series
GE:Am	Great Events from History: American Series
GE:B&C	Great Events from History II: Business and Commerce Series
GE:HR	Great Events from History II: Human Rights Series
GE:ME	Great Events from History: Modern European Series
GE:S&T	Great Events from History II: Science and Technology Series
GE:W20	Great Events from History: Worldwide 20th Century Series
GL:A&M	Great Lives from History: Ancient and Medieval Series
GL:Am	Great Lives from History: American Series
GL:AmW	Great Lives from History: American Women Series
GL:B&C	Great Lives from History: British and Commonwealth Series
GL:Ren	Great Lives from History: Renaissance to 1900 Series
GL:20	Great Lives from History: Twentieth Century Series

Alphabetization is by word rather than by letter. Common abbreviations such as "St." are alphabetized as though they were spelled out. The *Mc* particle in names such as McPherson is alphabetized as though it were spelled *Mac*. Surnames that are composed of more than one element are alphabetized as though one word; hence "De Klerck, Frederik Willem," is preceded by "Dekker, Wise."

Code System

GE:A&M   *Great Events from History*: Ancient and Medieval Series. 3 vols. Salem Press, Englewood Cliffs, N.J. 1972

GE:ME   *Great Events from History*: Modern European Series. 3 vols. Salem Press, Englewood Cliffs, N.J. 1973

GE:Am   *Great Events from History*: American Series. 3 vols. Salem Press, Englewood Cliffs, N.J. 1975

GE:W20   *Great Events from History*: Worldwide 20th Century Series. 3 vols. Salem Press, Englewood Cliffs, N.J. 1980

GL:Am   *Great Lives from History*: American Series. 5 vols. Salem Press, Englewood Cliffs, N.J., and Pasadena, Calif. 1987

GL:B&C   *Great Lives from History*: British and Commonwealth Series. 5 vols. Salem Press, Englewood Cliffs, N.J., and Pasadena, Calif. 1987

GL:A&M   *Great Lives from History*: Ancient and Medieval Series. 5 vols. Salem Press, Englewood Cliffs, N.J., and Pasadena, Calif. 1988

GL:Ren   *Great Lives from History*: Renaissance to 1900 Series. 5 vols. Salem Press, Englewood Cliffs, N.J., and Pasadena, Calif. 1989

GL:20   *Great Lives from History*: Twentieth Century Series. 5 vols. Salem Press, Englewood Cliffs, N.J., and Pasadena, Calif. 1990

GE:S&T   *Great Events from History II*: Science and Technology Series. 5 vols. Salem Press, Englewood Cliffs, N.J., and Pasadena, Calif. 1991

GE:HR   *Great Events from History II*: Human Rights Series. 5 vols. Salem Press, Englewood Cliffs, N.J., and Pasadena, Calif. 1992

GE:A&C   *Great Events from History II*: Arts and Culture Series. 5 vols. Salem Press, Englewood Cliffs, N.J., and Pasadena, Calif. 1993

GE:B&C   *Great Events from History II*: Business and Commerce Series. 5 vols. Salem Press, Englewood Cliffs, N.J., and Pasadena, Calif. 1994

GL:AmW   *Great Lives from History*: American Women Series. 5 vols. Salem Press, Englewood Cliffs, N.J., and Pasadena, Calif. 1995

MAGILL INDEX
TO
GREAT LIVES
FROM
HISTORY

A

Aalto, Aino Mario
  GE:A&C II-1067
Aalto, Alvar
  GE:A&C II-1067
  GL:20 I-1
Aaron
  GL:A&M I-1
Aarvik, Egil
  GE:HR V-2292
Abahai
  GL:Ren I-1
Abailard, Pierre. *See* Abelard, Peter
Abalkin, Leonid
  GE:B&C V-2022
Abano, Pietro d'
  GL:A&M I-6
Abarca y Bolea, Pedro Pablo. *See* De Aranda, Conde
ʿAbbās the Great
  GL:Ren I-6
Abbas, Ferhat
  GE:HR II-651, III-1155
  GE:ME III-1628
  GL:20 I-7
Abbey, Henry E.
  GE:Am II-1135
Abbott, Berenice
  GL:AmW I-1
Abbott, Grace
  GE:HR I-520
  GL:AmW I-6
Abbott, Henry
  GE:ME I-405
Abbott, H. L.
  GE:Am II-865
Abbott, Lyman
  GE:Am II-1161
Abboud, Ibrahim
  GE:HR II-941
ʿAbd al-Muʾmin
  GL:A&M I-10
ʿAbd al-Qādir. *See* Abdelkader
ʿAbd al-Rahman I
  GE:A&M II-1117, 1189
ʿAbd al-Rahman II
  GE:A&M II-1189
ʿAbd al-Rahman III al-Nasir
  GE:A&M II-1189
  GL:A&M I-15

Abdelkader
  GL:Ren I-11
ʿAbduh, Muhammad
  GL:Ren I-16
Abdul-Hamid II
  GE:HR I-98, 150
  GE:ME II-1133
  GE:W20 I-411
Abdullah, Farooq
  GE:HR V-2426
Abdullah, ibn-Husein
  GE:W20 I-494
Abdullah, Sheikh Mohammad
  GE:HR V-2426
Abeken, Heinrich
  GE:ME II-949
Abel, John Jacob
  GE:S&T I-16, II-512, IV-1459
Abel, Niels Henrik
  GL:Ren I-21
Abelard, Peter
  GE:A&M III-1313, 1329, 1400
  GL:A&M I-20
Abell, George Ogden
  GE:S&T IV-1454, V-2306
Abelson, Philip
  GE:S&T III-1181
Aberdeen, Countess of. *See* Godron, Ishabel M.
Aberdeen, Earl of Aberdeen (George Hamilton Gordon)
  GE:Am II-778
  GE:ME II-813
Abernathy, Ralph
  GE:HR II-947, 974, III-1257, 1419
  GE:W20 II-865
Abner
  GE:A&M I-90
Abrabanel, Isaac
  GE:A&M III-1752
Abraham
  GL:A&M I-27
Abraham Senior
  GE:A&M III-1752
Abraham, Nelson Ahlgren. *See* Algren, Nelson
Abraham bar Hiyya. *See* Bar Hiyya, Abraham
Abraham ben David. *See* Ben David, Abraham
Abraham ibn-Ezra. *See* Ibn-Ezra, Abraham
Abram. *See* Abraham

Abram, Morris B.
 GE:HR IV-2090
Abrams, Creighton Williams
 GE:W20 II-1083, III-1212
Abrial, Admiral Jean
 GE:ME III-1456
Abse, Leo
 GE:HR II-991
Abu ʿAbd Allah Muhammad ibn ʿAbd Allah
 al-Lawati al-Tanji. *See* Ibn Battutah
Abu ʿAbd Allah Muhammad ibn Jabir ibn Sinan
 al-Battani al-Harrani al-Sabi. *See* Battani, al-
Abu ʿAbd Allah Muhammad ibn Muhammad
 ʿAbd Allah ibn Idris al-ammudi al-Hasani
 al-Idrisi. *See* Idrisi, al-
Abu ʿAbd Allah Muhammad ibn ʿUmar ibn
 al-Husayn ibn ʿAli al-Imam Fakhr al-Din
 al-Razi. *See* Fakhr al-Din al-Razi
Abu al-Hasan ʿAli ibn Husain al-Masʿudi. *See*
 Masʿudi, al-
Abu al-Hasan Yehuda ben Shemuel ha-Levi. *See*
 Judah ha-Levi
Abu ʿAli Hasan ibn ʿAli. *See* Nizam al-Mulk
Abu al-Mughith al-Husayn ibn Mansur al-Hallaj.
 See Hallaj, al-
Abu al-Wafa. *See* Abul Wefa
Abu Bakr
 GE:A&M II-1075
Abu Bakr Muhammad ibn al-ʿArabi al-Hatimi
 al-Taʾi. *See* Ibn al-ʿArabi
Abu Bakr Muhammad ibn Zakariyaʾ al-Razi. *See*
 Razi, al-
Abu Hamid Muhammad ibn Muhammad al-Tusi
 al-Ghazzali. *See* Ghazzali, al-
Abu Hanifah
 GL:A&M I-32
Abu Muhammad al-Kumi. *See* ʿAbd al-Muʾmin
Abu Musa Jabir ibn Hayyan. *See* Jabir ibn Hayyan
Abu Saʿid ibn Abi al-Hasan Yasar al-Basri. *See*
 Hasan al-Basri, al-
Abu Talib
 GE:A&M II-1075
Abu ʿUthman ʿAmr ibn Bahr ibn Mahbub
 al-Jahiz. *See* Jahiz, al-
Abu Zayd ʿAbd al-Rahman ibn Khaldun. *See* Ibn
 Khaldun
Abul Qasim Mansur. *See* Firdusi
Abul Wefa
 GL:A&M I-38
Abu-Nuwas
 GE:A&M II-1142
Abū-ul-Fath Jahāl-ud-Din Muhammad Akbar. *See*
 Akbar

Abzug, Bella
 GE:HR III-1327
 GL:AmW I-11
Acacius
 GE:A&M II-989
Accursius
 GE:A&M II-784, III-1344, 1519
Achebe, Chinua
 GE:A&C IV-1763
 GL:20 I-13
Acheson, Barclay
 GE:B&C I-390
Acheson, Dean
 GE:Am III-1806
 GE:B&C III-902
 GE:HR II-771
 GE:W20 II-564
 GL:Am I-1
Acheson, Lila Bell
 GE:B&C I-390
Ackerman, Martin S.
 GE:B&C IV-1379
Ackley, Gardner
 GE:B&C III-1235, IV-1341
Açoka. *See* Aśoka the Great
Acton, Lord
 GE:W20 I-24
 GL:B&C I-1
Acuff, Roy
 GE:A&C II-675
Adalbert
 GE:A&M III-1210
Adam de la Halle
 GL:A&M I-42
Adam le Bossu. *See* Adam de la Halle
Adam of St. Victor
 GE:A&M III-1349
Adam, James, and Robert Adam
 GL:B&C I-8
Adamec, Ladislav
 GE:HR V-2570
Adamov, Arthur
 GE:A&C IV-1871
Adams, Abigail
 GL:AmW I-16
Adams, Ansel
 GE:B&C III-896
 GE:S&T III-1331
Adams, Carolyn
 GE:A&C III-1602
Adams, Charles Francis
 GE:Am II-1072

Adams, Henry
GE:Am II-1184
GL:Am I-8
Adams, John (composer)
GE:A&C V-2599
Adams, John (president)
GE:Am I-194, 231, 246, 256, 261, 300, 341,
350, 403, 408, 414, 426, 432, 437, 456
GL:Am I-14
Adams, John Quincy
GE:Am I-485, 522, 558, 593, 607, 631, II-673,
831
GL:Am I-20
Adams, Randall Dale
GE:HR V-2414
Adams, Samuel
GE:Am I-241, 246
GL:Am I-29
Adams, Samuel Hopkins
GE:HR I-64
Adams, Stanley
GE:B&C I-252
Adams, Thomas
GE:B&C II-579
Adams, Thomas S.
GE:B&C I-319, III-1035
Adams, Walter Sydney
GE:S&T II-645, 815, 948, III-1325, IV-1640
Adda(i)
GE:A&M II-807
Addams, Jane
GE:Am III-1369
GE:HR I-131
GL:Am I-36
GL:AmW I-21
Addison, Joseph
GL:B&C I-15
Adelard of Bath
GE:A&M III-1524
Adelbero of Rheims
GE:A&M III-1200
Adenauer, Konrad
GE:B&C III-981, III-1169
GE:HR II-795, III-1125
GE:ME III-1601, 1624, 1690
GE:W20 II-647, 690
GL:20 I-17
Ader, Clément
GE:S&T I-41
Adet, Pierre
GE:Am I-403
Adhemar de Monteil
GE:A&M III-1276
Adimantus
GE:A&M I-237

Adler, Alfred
GE:ME III-1310
GL:20 I-22
Adler, Lou
GE:A&C IV-2104
Adler, Mortimer J.
GE:A&C III-1351
Adler, Stella
GE:A&C II-874, 1006
Adoian, Vosdanig. See Gorky, Arshile
Adolf of Nassau
GE:A&M III-1603
Adoula, Cyrille
GE:ME III-1613
Adrian IV
GL:B&C I-20
Adrian of Utrecht
GE:ME I-40, 72
Adrian, Edgar Douglas
GE:S&T I-243, II-890
Aeken, Jeroen van. See Bosch, Hieronymus
Aemilianus, Scipio. See Scipio Aemilianus,
Publius Cornelius
Aemilius Lepidus, Marcus. See Lepidus, Marcus
Aemilius
Aeschylus
GE:A&M I-248
GL:A&M I-48
Aetius
GE:A&M II-975
Afghani, Sayyid Jamal od-Din al-
GE:HR I-52
Afonso I
GL:A&M I-54
Africanus, Scipio. See Scipio Africanus, Major,
Publius Cornelius
Africanus, Sextus Julius
GE:A&M II-789
Aga Khan III, Sir Mohammad Shah
GE:HR I-87
Agassiz, Elizabeth Cabot Cary
GL:AmW I-26
Agassiz, Louis
GL:Am I-42
Agesilaus II
GL:A&M I-59
Agnelli, Giovanni
GE:B&C III-1293
Agnew, Spiro T.
GE:Am III-1933
GE:HR III-1537
GE:W20 III-1188
Agramonte, Aristides
GE:S&T I-73

Agricola
  GE:A&M II-616
Agricola, Georgius
  GL:Ren I-26
Agrippa II, Herod. *See* Herod Agrippa II
Agrippa, Marcus Vipsanius
  GE:A&M I-551
  GL:A&M I-65
Agrippa, Menenius
  GE:A&M I-221
Aguinaldo, Emilio
  GE:Am II-1290
  GE:HR I-7
Ahidjo, Ahmadou
  GE:HR III-1491
Ahijah
  GE:A&M I-106
Ahlquist, Jon
  GE:S&T V-2267
Ahmad, Hocine Ait
  GE:HR III-1155
Ahmad, Ibrahim
  GE:HR II-1050
Ahmad ibn Hanbal
  GL:A&M I-70
Ahmad Khan, Sir Sayyid
  GL:Ren I-31
Ahmedzai, Najibullah
  GE:HR V-2449
Aidan
  GE:A&M II-1081
Aidit, Dipa Nusantara
  GE:HR III-1305
Aiello, Danny
  GE:A&C V-2641
Aikawa, Yoshisuke
  GE:B&C I-185
Aiken, George D.
  GE:HR I-555
Aiken, Howard Hathaway
  GE:S&T III-1396, IV-1593
Ailey, Alvin
  GE:A&C IV-1774, V-2521
Ain, Gregory
  GE:A&C III-1290
Aitken, William Maxwell. *See also* Beaverbrook,
  Lord
  GE:B&C I-174
Akalaitis, JoAnne
  GE:A&C V-2571
  GL:AmW I-31
Akbar
  GL:Ren I-36

Akers, John
  GE:B&C V-1809
Akhenaton
  GE:A&M I-64
  GL:A&M I-76
Akhmatova, Anna
  GL:20 I-27
Akhund, Iqbal Ahmad
  GE:HR IV-1841
Akiba ben Joseph
  GE:A&M II-702
  GL:A&M I-81
Akiyoshi, Toshiko
  GL:AmW I-36
Akoka, Henri
  GE:A&C III-1206
Akutagawa, Ryūnosuke
  GE:A&C III-1476
Al-. *See also* entry under family name
Alain. *See* Chartier, Alain
Alanbrooke, First Viscount
  GE:ME III-1467, 1477
  GE:W20 I-430
  GL:B&C I-25
Alaric
  GE:A&M II-935, 940
Alaric II
  GE:A&M II-1005
Al-ashraf al-Khalil
  GE:A&M III-1574
Albategnius. *See* Battani, al-
Albee, Edward
  GE:A&C IV-1903
Albert, Archduke of Austria
  GE:ME I-220
Albert Francis Charles Augustus Emmanuel of
    Saxe-Coburg-Gotha, Prince
  GE:ME II-799
Albert of Hapsburg
  GE:A&M III-1603
Albert of Saxony
  GE:A&M III-1614
Albert the Great
  GE:A&M III-1544
Albert, Friedrich Wilhelm Viktor. *See* William II
  (of Germany and Prussia)
Albert, Jacques Victor (Duc de Broglie)
  GE:ME II-974
Alberti, Leon Battista
  GE:A&M III-1665, 1691
  GL:Ren I-41
Albertus Magnus, Saint
  GL:A&M I-87

Albinus
  GE:A&M II-731
Albinus. *See* Alcuin
Albinus, Lucius
  GE:A&M I-221
Albrecht, Andreas
  GE:S&T V-2047, 2125
Albuquerque, Afonso de
  GL:Ren I-45
Alcibiades
  GE:A&M I-308, 318
  GL:A&M I-92
Alcimus. *See* Eliachim
Alcmaeon
  GE:A&M I-194, 302
  GL:A&M I-97
Alcmeon. *See* Alcmaeon
Alcott, Amos Bronson
  GE:Am I-654
Alcott, Louisa May
  GL:AmW I-40
Alcuin
  GE:A&M II-1136, 1146
  GL:A&M I-102
Alda, Alan
  GE:A&C V-2271
Aldington, Richard
  GE:A&C I-326
Aldrich, Nelson Wilmarth
  GE:Am II-1325, III-1390, 1415, 1432
  GE:B&C I-168
Aldrin, Edwin E. ("Buzz"), Jr.
  GE:Am III-1940
  GE:S&T V-1907
Alekseev, Eugeni Ivanovich
  GE:ME III-1148
Alekseyev, Konstantin Sergeyevich. *See*
  Stanislavsky, Konstantin
Aleksi
  GE:HR I-561
Alembert, Jean Le Rond d'
  GE:ME I-428
  GL:Ren I-50
Alençon, Duke of. *See* Francis, Duke of Anjou
Alessandri, Jorge
  GE:HR IV-1725
Alessandro Filipepi. *See* Botticelli, Sandro
Alexander I (of Russia)
  GE:Am I-593
  GE:ME II-568, 585, 598, 612, 623, 654
  GL:Ren I-56
Alexander II (of Russia)
  GE:Am II-1037
  GE:HR V-2298

  GE:ME II-813, 866, 886, 988, 1007, 1062
  GL:Ren I-61
Alexander III. *See* Alexander the Great
Alexander III, Pope
  GE:A&M III-1243, 1257, 1375, 1381
  GL:A&M I-107
Alexander III (of Russia)
  GE:ME II-1062, 1070
Alexander IV, Pope
  GE:A&M III-1528
Alexander VI, Pope
  GE:A&M III-1728
  GE:ME I-21, 26
  GL:Ren I-66
Alexander, Bishop of Alexandria
  GE:A&M II-867
Alexander Nevsky
  GL:A&M I-118
Alexander of Neckam. *See* Neckam, Alexander
Alexander of Villedieu
  GE:A&M II-1023
Alexander the Great
  GE:A&M I-338, 353, 358, 403
  GL:A&M I-113
Alexander, Ben
  GE:A&C III-1531
Alexander, Sir Harold Rupert Leofric George
  GE:ME III-1467
  GE:W20 I-457
Alexander, Sir Henry
  GE:ME III-1477
Alexander, James
  GE:Am I-188
Alexander, James Dallas
  GE:Am I-539
Alexandra
  GE:HR I-225
Alexius I Comnenus
  GE:A&M III-1276, 1354
Alexius III
  GE:A&M III-1436
Alexius IV
  GE:A&M III-1436
Al-Farabi
  GE:A&M III-1395
Alfasi, Isaac
  GE:A&M III-1334, 1391
Alfonsín, Raúl
  GE:HR IV-1864, V-2280
Alfonso X
  GE:A&M III-1524
  GL:A&M I-124
Alfonso XII
  GE:ME II-1003

Alfonso XIII
  GE:ME III-1368
Alfonso, Pedro
  GE:A&M III-1524
Alfonso, Perez
  GE:W20 II-912
Alfonzo, Juan Pablo Pérez
  GE:B&C I-385, III-1154
Alfred, Mother
  GE:Am II-1178
Alfred the Great
  GE:A&M II-1063
  GL:B&C I-30
Alger, Russell Alexander
  GE:Am II-1284
Al-Ghazzali. See Ghazzali, al-
Algren, Nelson
  GE:A&C III-1449
Al-Hakim II
  GE:A&M II-1189
Alhazen (Abu ʿAli al-Ḥasan ibn al-Haytham)
  GE:A&M III-1555
  GL:A&M I-129
Alhwini. See Alcuin
Ali
  GE:A&M II-1075
Ali, Maulana Muhammad
  GE:HR I-87
Ali, Muhammad
  GL:Am I-48
Ali, Uluch
  GE:ME I-180
Alia, Ramiz
  GE:HR V-2553
Alighieri, Dante. See Dante
Al-Khowarizmi. See Khwarismi, al-
Al-Kindi
  GE:A&M III-1395
Allegretti, Gus
  GE:A&C IV-1678
Allegri, Antonio. See Correggio
Allemane, Jean
  GE:ME II-1044
Allemann, Beda
  GE:A&C IV-2070
Allen, Fred
  GE:A&C II-828
Allen, Gracie
  GL:AmW I-45
Allen, James
  GE:HR IV-1817
Allen, Steve
  GE:A&C III-1623

Allen, Sture
  GE:A&C V-2668
Allen, William M.
  GE:B&C III-1112
  GE:S&T IV-1897
Allen, Woody
  GE:A&C V-2381
Allenby, Lord
  GL:B&C I-35
Allende, Salvador
  GE:B&C III-1207, IV-1527
  GE:HR IV-1725, 1747, 2186, 2204, V-2540
Allibone, T. E.
  GE:S&T III-978
Allison, Fran
  GE:A&C III-1400
Allison, William Boyd
  GE:Am II-1325
Al-Mansur
  GE:A&M II-1189
Alp Arslan
  GE:A&M III-1253
  GL:A&M I-135
Alphanus of Salerno
  GE:A&M III-1478
Alpher, Ralph Asher
  GE:S&T III-1309
Alphonse of Poitiers
  GE:A&M III-1496
Al-Rāzi, abū Bakr Muhammad ibn Zakarīyā. See Razi, al-
Alsberg, Henry
  GE:Am III-1632
Altgeld, John Peter
  GE:Am II-1237
  GL:Am I-53
Althorp, Viscount. See Spencer, George John, Viscount Althorp
Altizer, Thomas Jonathon Jackson
  GE:W20 I-507
Altmeyer, Arthur
  GE:B&C II-711
Alula, Ras
  GE:ME II-1094
Alva, Duke of
  GE:ME I-153
Alvarez
  GE:S&T II-491
Álvarez, Juan de Yepes y. See John of the Cross, Saint
Alvarez, Luis Echeverría. See Echeverría Alvarez, Luis

Alvarez, Luis W.
  GE:S&T IV-1470, V-2120
  GE:W20 II-683
Alvarez, Walter
  GE:S&T V-2120
Alyattes
  GE:A&M I-144
Amann, Max
  GE:W20 I-188
Amaral, Francisco Xavier Do
  GE:HR IV-1835
Amaziah
  GE:A&M I-125
Ambartsumian, Viktor A.
  GL:20 I-33
Ambedkar, Bhimrao Ramji
  GE:HR I-469, II-743
Ambiorix
  GE:A&M I-516
Ambrose, Saint
  GE:A&M II-852, 920
  GL:A&M I-143
Ambrose, James
  GE:S&T V-1961
Amenhopsis IV. *See* Akhenaton
Amenhotep III
  GE:A&M I-64
Amery, Julian
  GE:B&C IV-1606
Ames, Fisher
  GE:Am I-350, 356
Ames, Oakes
  GE:Am II-969, 1054
Ames, Oliver
  GE:Am II-969
Amherst, Lord
  GL:B&C I-43
Amherst, Jeffrey
  GE:Am I-200, 207
Amin, Hafizullah
  GE:HR IV-2062, V-2449
Amin, Idi
  GE:HR III-1600, IV-2136
Amirthalingam, Appapillai
  GE:HR IV-2068
Amis, Kingsley
  GE:A&C III-1454
Ammann, Othmar H.
  GE:S&T IV-1782
Amos
  GE:A&M I-125

"Amos 'n' Andy." *See also* Freeman Gosden and
  Charles Correll
  GE:A&C II-755
  GE:Am III-1501
Amphilochius
  GE:A&M II-893
Amsterdam, Anthony
  GE:HR III-1674
Amsterdam, Morey
  GE:A&C IV-1908
Amstutz, Dan
  GE:B&C V-1859
Amundsen, Roald
  GE:W20 I-63
  GL:20 I-38
Anable, Gloria Hollister
  GE:S&T III-1018
Anastasius I
  GE:A&M II-989
Anaxagoras
  GE:A&M I-270
  GL:A&M I-149
Anaximander
  GE:A&M I-173
  GL:A&M I-154
Anaximenes of Miletus
  GE:A&M I-173
  GL:A&M I-159
Ancel, Paul. *See* Celan, Paul
Andersch, Alfred
  GE:A&C III-1357
Andersen, Arthur E.
  GE:B&C I-319
Anderson, Al
  GE:A&C V-2344
Anderson, Carl David
  GE:S&T II-532, 694, III-983, IV-1470
Anderson, Charles W.
  GE:HR II-1038
Anderson, Clinton P.
  GE:B&C III-1248
Anderson, Herbert L.
  GE:S&T III-1198
  GL:Am I-58
Anderson, John W.
  GE:HR II-766
Anderson, Laurie
  GE:A&C V-2517
  GL:AmW I-50
Anderson, Marian
  GE:A&C III-1126
  GL:Am I-58
  GL:AmW I-55

Anderson, Robert
  GE:A&C III-1164
Anderson, Robert O.
  GE:B&C IV-1331, 1653
Anderson, Roberta Joan. *See* Mitchell, Joni
Anderson, Roger E.
  GE:B&C V-1870
Anderson, Thomas
  GE:ME II-935
Anderson, Warren M.
  GE:B&C V-1893
  GE:HR V-2238
Andersson, Johan Gunnar
  GE:S&T II-761, III-1096
Anderton, James
  GE:HR II-991
Andō Hiroshige. *See* Hiroshige
Andō Tokutarō. *See* Hiroshige
Andragoras
  GE:A&M I-427
Andrássy, Count Gyula
  GE:ME II-939, 988, 1007
André, Frederick
  GE:ME I-542
Andrea d'Agnolo. *See* Andrea del Sarto
Andrea de Pietro della Gondola. *See* Palladio,
  Andrea
Andrea del Sarto
  GL:Ren I-71
Andreotti, Giulio
Andrewes, Lancelot
  GE:ME I-241
  GL:B&C I-49
Andrews, Julie
  GE:A&C IV-2033
Andrews, Roy Chapman
  GE:HR IV-1988
  GE:S&T II-735
Andrews, Samuel
  GE:Am II-1116
Andropov, Yuri
  GE:HR V-2298
Andros, Sir Edmund
  GE:Am I-163
Angel, James Roger Prior
  GE:S&T V-2291
Angelico, Fra
  GL:Ren I-76
Angell, James Burrill
  GE:Am II-1077
Angell, Norman
  GL:B&C I-55
Angelo, Brother
  GE:A&M III-1447

Angelou, Maya
  GL:AmW I-60
Anglesey, Marquis of. *See* Paget, Henry William
Anhalt-Zerbst, Sophie Friederike Auguste von.
  See Catherine the Great
Anicius Manlius Severinus Boethius. *See* Boethius
Annas of Ananus
  GE:A&M II-601
Anne of Austria
  GE:ME I-278 324, 341, 349
Anne of Brittany
  GE:A&M III-1733
Anne of Cleves
  GE:ME I-123
Anne, Queen
  GE:ME I-385
  GL:B&C I-62
Annis, Martin
  GE:S&T IV-1708
Annunzio, Frank
  GE:B&C IV-1595
Anschütz-Kaempfe, Hermann
  GE:S&T I-303
Anselm, Saint
  GE:A&M III-1291
  GL:B&C I-68
Anson, Lord
  GL:B&C I-73
Antall, Jozsef
  GE:HR V-2421
Anthemius of Tralles
  GE:A&M II-1040
Anthony of Egypt, Saint
  GL:A&M I-163
Anthony of Padua, Saint
  GL:A&M I-168
Anthony, Susan B.
  GE:Am III-1513
  GE:HR I-339
  GL:Am I-63
  GL:AmW I-64
Antigonus I Monophthalmos
  GL:A&M I-173
Antiochus III
  GE:A&M I-427
Antiochus IV
  GE:A&M I-459
Antiochus the Great
  GL:A&M I-177
Antiphon the Sophist
  GE:A&M I-286
Antonelli, Cardinal Giacomo
  GE:ME II-770, 902, 978

Antonelli, Count Pietro
GE:ME II-1094
Antoninus Pius
GE:A&M II-616
Antoninus, Marcus Aurelius. *See* Marcus Aurelius
Antonio
GE:ME I-189
Antonio, Donato di Pascuccio d'. *See* Bramante, Donato
Antonio, Emile de
GE:A&C IV-2053
Antonioni, Michelangelo
GE:A&C III-1228
Antonius, Marcus. *See* Antony, Marc
Antonius Merenda, Titus. *See* Merenda, Titus Antonius
Antony, Marc
GE:A&M I-521, 541, 546, 551
GL:A&M I-182
Antschel, Paul. *See* Celan, Paul
Anyon, James T.
GE:B&C I-308
Anytus
GE:A&M I-318
Aoki, Shuzo
GE:HR I-81
Aosta, Duke of. *See* Di Savoia, Amadeo Ferdinando Maria
Apfelbaum, Hirsch. *See* Zinoviev, Grigori Evseevich
Apgar, Virginia
GL:AmW I-69
Apollinaire, Guillaume
GE:A&C I-337, IV-1812
GL:20 I-44
Apollonius
GE:A&M I-413
Apollonius of Chalcedon
GE:A&M II-725
Apollonius of Perga
GE:A&M I-422
GL:A&M I-187
Appel, Mike
GE:A&C V-2325
Appius Claudius. *See* Claudius, Appius
Appius Claudius Caudex. *See* Claudius Caudex, Appius
Appius Claudius Crassus Caecus. *See* Claudius Crassus, Appius
Appleton, Sir Edward Victor
GE:S&T I-174
Apponyi, Albert György
GE:W20 I-181
Aqiba ben Joseph. *See* Akiba ben Joseph

Aquila (biblical translator)
GE:A&M I-418
Aquila (christian convert)
GE:A&M II-632
Aquillius, Manlius
GE:A&M I-486
Aquinas, Saint Thomas. *See* Thomas Aquinas, Saint
Aquino, Benigno "Ninoy," Jr.
GE:HR IV-2198, V-2286
Aquino, Corazon
GE:HR IV-2198, V-2286
GL:20 I-49
Aquitaine, Duke of. *See* William the Pious
Arafat, Yasir (Mohammed Abed Ar'ouf Arafat)
GE:HR III-1241, IV-1685, 2003, 2164, V-2331
GE:W20 I-145, II-1028, III-1235
GL:20 I-54
Arago, Dominique François Jean
GE:ME II-649, 747
Aranda, Count of
GE:ME I-442
Arango, Doroteo. *See* Villa, Pancho
Araújo, Arnaldo Dos Reis
GE:HR IV-1835
Araújo, Arturo
GE:HR I-464
Arbuckle, Roscoe "Fatty"
GE:A&C I-230
Arbus, Diane
GL:AmW I-74
Arcesilaus
GE:A&M I-471
Archias
GE:A&M I-129
Archimedes
GE:A&M I-422
GL:A&M I-193
Archytas of Tarentum
GE:A&M I-194
Arden, Elizabeth
GL:AmW I-78
Arden, John
GE:A&C III-1454
Arden-Clark, Charles
GE:HR II-980
Ardrey, Robert
GE:S&T IV-1808
Areco, Jorge Pacheco
GE:HR IV-1715
Arendt, Hannah
GL:AmW I-83
Arendt, Walter
GE:B&C IV-1549

Aretaeus of Cappadocia
  GL:A&M I-200
Aretin, Baron
  GE:ME I-542
Arezzo, Guido d'. *See* Guido d'Arezzo
Argall, Sir Samuel
  GE:Am I-65
Arias Navarro, Carlos
  GE:W20 II-1043
Arias Sánchez, Oscar
  GE:HR V-2336
Arif, Abdul Rahman
  GE:HR II-1050
Arif, Abdul Salam
  GE:HR II-1050
Ariosto, Ludovico
  GL:Ren I-81
Arista, Mariano
  GE:Am II-825
Aristarchus of Samos
  GE:A&M I-398, II-712
Aristides
  GE:A&M I-226, 242
Aristides of Athens
  GE:A&M II-707
Aristo of Pella
  GE:A&M II-707
Aristonicus
  GE:A&M I-486
Aristophanes
  GE:A&M I-318
  GL:A&M I-206
Aristotle
  GE:A&M I-328, 343, 348 363, II-712
  GE:S&T IV-1751
  GL:A&M I-213
Aristoxenus
  GL:A&M I-218
Arius
  GE:A&M II-867
Arkwright, Richard
  GE:Am I-362, 371
  GL:B&C I-79
Arlin, Harold W.
  GE:A&C I-469
Armand, Jules. *See* De Polignac, Prince
Armas, Carlos Castillo
  GE:B&C III-1040
Armijo, Manuel
  GE:Am II-818
Arminius
  GE:A&M II-578, 584
Armour, Jonathan Ogden
  GE:HR I-46

Armour, Philip Danforth
  GE:B&C I-107
Armstrong, Edwin H.
  GE:Am III-1674
  GE:S&T II-939
  GL:Am I-69
Armstrong, Helen. *See* Melba, Nellie
Armstrong, Lillian Hardin
  GE:A&C II-670
  GL:AmW I-88
Armstrong, Louis
  GE:A&C I-480, II-670
  GL:Am I-73
Armstrong, Neil A.
  GE:Am III-1940
  GE:S&T V-1907
  GL:Am I-79
Armstrong, Samuel Chapman
  GE:Am II-1249
Arnard-Amalric
  GE:A&M III-1441
Arnaud de Villeneuve. *See* Arnold of Villanova
Arnaz, Desi
  GE:A&C III-1525
Arnaz y de Acha, Desiderio Alberto, III. *See* Arnaz, Desi
Arness, James
  GE:A&C IV-1668, 1768
Arno, Peter
  GE:A&C II-648
Arnold of Villanova
  GL:A&M I-222
Arnold, Benedict
  GE:Am I-277
  GL:Am I-85
Arnold, Harold D.
  GE:B&C II-470
  GE:S&T II-615
Arnold, Henry Harley (Hap)
  GE:S&T III-1187
  GE:W20 I-487
Arnold, Matthew
  GL:B&C I-86
Arnold, Thomas
  GL:B&C I-93
Arnolfo di Cambio
  GL:A&M I-227
Aron, Raymond
  GE:A&C III-1262
Aronson, Max
  GE:A&C I-74
Arouet, François-Marie. *See* Voltaire
Arp, Hans
  GE:A&C I-419

Arpino, Gerald
  GE:A&C IV-1694
Arrhenius, Svante August
  GE:S&T III-1118, IV-1840
  GL:20 I-60
Arsaces
  GE:A&M I-427
Artaud, Antonin
  GE:A&C IV-1812, 2005
Artaxerxes II
  GE:A&M I-313
Arteaga, Melchor
  GE:S&T II-491
Arthur, Chester A.
  GE:Am II-1123, 1128
  GL:Am I-90
Artin, Emil
  GE:S&T I-438
Artois, Count of. See Charles, Count of Artois
Arutyunyan, Suren
  GE:HR V-2348
Arvaleuk, James
  GE:HR IV-1876
Arwidsson, Adolf Ivar
  GE:HR I-212
Aryabhata
  GL:A&M I-233
Arzelà, Cesare
  GE:S&T I-325
Arzner, Dorothy
  GL:AmW I-93
Asaka, Prince Yasuhiko
  GE:HR I-539
Asaro, Frank
  GE:S&T V-2120
Asbaje y Ramírez de Santillana, Juana Inés. See
  Cruz, Sor Juana Inés de la
Asbury, Francis
  GE:Am I-420
Asclepas
  GE:A&M II-872
Asclepiades of Bithynia
  GL:A&M I-238
Asclepius
  GE:A&M I-302
Aserinsky, Eugene
  GE:S&T III-1424
Ash, Mary Kay
  GL:AmW I-98
Ash'ari, al-
  GL:A&M I-243
Ashburton, Baron (Alexander Baring)
  GE:Am II-801

Ashikaga Takauji
  GL:A&M I-249
Ashley, Bernard
  GE:A&C III-1562
Ashley, Laura Mountney
  GE:A&C III-1562
Ashton, Sir Frederick
  GE:A&C IV-1962
Ashurbanipal
  GE:A&M I-40
  GL:A&M I-254
Ashurnasirpal II
  GL:A&M I-259
Asimov, Isaac
  GE:A&C III-1094
Aske, Robert
  GE:ME I-110
Asner, Ed
  GE:A&C V-2218
Aśoka the Great
  GL:A&M I-264
Asplund, Erik Gunnar
  GE:A&C II-1067
Asprenas
  GE:A&M II-578
Asquith, H. H.
  GE:HR I-19
  GE:ME III-1214, 1223, 1233
  GL:B&C I-98
Assad, Hafez al-
  GE:HR IV-1967
  GE:W20 III-1182
Assad, Rifat al-
  GE:HR IV-1967
Assaf, Ronald
  GE:B&C IV-1421
Assis, Joaquim Maria Machado do. See Machado
  de Assis, Joaquim Maria
Assmann, Richard
  GE:S&T I-26
Assurbanipal. See Ashurbanipal
Assurnasirpal. See Ashurnasirpal II
Astaire, Fred
  GE:A&C II-984, III-1432
Astley, Philip
  GE:Am II-1066
Aston, Francis William
  GE:S&T II-471, 660
Astor, John J.
  GE:Am I-476, 539
  GL:Am I-97
Astor, Mary
  GE:A&C III-1223

Astor, Lady Nancy
  GE:HR I-442
  GL:B&C I-104
Astruc, Alexandre
  GE:A&C IV-1710
Asurbanipal. *See* Ashurbanipal
Asurnazirpal. *See* Ashurnasirpal II
Atanasoff, John Vincent
  GE:S&T III-1213
Atatürk, Kemal
  GL:20 I-65
Atchison, David Rice
  GE:Am II-871
Athanasius, Saint
  GE:A&M II-767, 779, 852, 862, 872, 888
  GL:A&M I-269
Athenagoras
  GE:A&M II-707
Atherton, Gertrude
  GL:AmW I-103
Atherton, Warren
  GE:B&C II-845
Atilus Regulus, Marcus. *See* Regulus, Marcus
  Atilus
Atkins, Chet
  GE:A&C V-2365
Atkinson, George
  GE:B&C V-1745
Attalus I (Soter)
  GE:A&M I-432, 486
Attalus II
  GE:A&M I-486
Attalus III
  GE:A&M I-486
Attenborough, Richard
  GE:A&C III-1551
Attila
  GE:A&M II-975
  GL:A&M I-275
Attlee, Clement
  GE:B&C II-857
  GE:HR II-731
  GE:ME III-1512, 1517
  GL:B&C I-109
Attwood, Thomas
  GE:ME II-704 741
Atwood, Luther
  GE:Am II-912
Atwood, Margaret
  GL:AmW I-108
Aubrac, Lucie
  GE:HR II-646
Aubrey, James
  GE:A&C IV-1835

Auchinleck, Sir Claude John Eyre
  GE:ME III-1467
Auden, W. H.
  GE:A&C II-857, III-1514
Audrieth, Ludwig Frederick
  GE:S&T V-2226
Audry, Colette
  GE:A&C III-1449
Audubon, John James
  GL:Am I-102
Auerbach, Arnold "Red"
  GE: B&C V-1939
August of Saxony
  GE:ME I-148
Augustine of Canterbury
  GE:A&M II-1029, 1058
Augustine, Saint
  GE:A&M II-757, 852, 935, 940, 946, III-1338
  GL:A&M I-281
Augustulus, Romulus. *See* Romulus Augustulus
Augustus
  GE:A&M I-546, 551, 556, 562, II-578, 584,
    621
  GL:A&M I-285
Augustus II of Wettin
  GE:ME I-376
Aulenti, Gae
  GE:A&C V-2588
Aulus Manlius. *See* Manlius, Aulus
Aurangzeb
  GL:Ren I-86
Aurelius, Marcus. *See* Marcus Aurelius
Aurelius Antoninus, Marcus. *See* Marcus Aurelius
Aurelius Commodus, Lucius Aelius. *See*
  Commodus, Lucius Aelius Aurelius
Aurelius Valerius Diocletianus, Gaius. *See*
  Diocletian
Aurelius Valerius Maxentius, Marcus. *See*
  Maxentius, Marcus Aurelius Valerius
Aurelius Valerius Maximianus, Marcus. *See*
  Maximian
Auric, Georges
  GE:A&C I-435
Aurness, James. *See* Arness, James
Aurobindo, Sri
  GL:20 I-70
Austen, Jane
  GL:B&C I-115
Austerlitz, Frederick. *See* Astaire, Fred
Austin, Nancy
  GE:B&C V-1815
Austin, Stephen Fuller
  GE:Am II-736
  GL:Am I-107

Avempace
  GE:A&M III-1395
Averbakh, Leopold
  GE:A&C II-908
Averroës
  GE:A&M III-1395
  GL:A&M I-290
Avery, Clarence
  GE:B&C I-234
Avery, Oswald
  GE:S&T III-1203
Avicebron. *See* Ibn Gabirol
Avicenna
  GE:A&M III-1226, 1391, 1395, 1478
  GL:A&M I-297
Awad, Muhamed
  GE:HR II-902
Ayala, Eusebio
  GE:W20 I-289
Aykroyd, Dan
  GE:A&C V-2355

Aylmer, Felix
  GE:A&C III-1378
Ayres, Richard
  GE:B&C V-2034
Azaña y Diaz, Manuel
  GE:ME III-1368, 1416
Azhari, Ismā'īl al-
  GE:HR II-941
Azikiwe, Nnamdi
  GE:HR IV-2180
  GL:20 I-75
Aziz, Fahd ibn Abdul
  GE:HR IV-2095
Aziz, Khalid ibn Abdul
  GE:HR IV-2095
Aziz, Sultan ibn Abdul
  GE:HR IV-2095
Aziz, Tariq Mikhayi
  GE:HR V-2397
Azócar, Patricio Aylwin
  GE:HR V-2540

B

Baade, Walter
  GE:S&T II-878, 884, III-1008, 1271, IV-1449
  GE:W20 II-1009
Baader, Andreas
  GE:W20 II-1028
Baᶜal Shem Tov
  GL:Ren I-91
Baba, Alhaji Ali
  GE:HR IV-2180
Babakin, G. N.
  GE:S&T IV-1797, 1819, V-1928, 1950
Babayan, Eduard
  GE:HR IV-1926
Babb, Eugene
  GE:HR IV-2130
Babbage, Charles
  GE:S&T II-846
  GL:B&C I-121
Babbit, Milton
  GE:A&C IV-1785
Babcock, Orville E.
  GE:Am II-1054
Babson, Roger W.
  GE:B&C II-574
Bābur
  GL:Ren I-96
Bacall, Lauren
  GL:AmW I-113
Bacchylides
  GE:A&M I-215
Bach, Johann Sebastian
  GE:A&C IV-1818
  GE:ME I-380
  GL:Ren I-101
Bachelet, Jean
  GE:A&C II-1073
Bacheller, Irving Addison
  GE:Am II-1255
Backus, Isaac
  GE:Am I-318
Backus, John
  GE:S&T IV-1475
Bacon, Francis
  GE:ME I-254
  GL:B&C I-126
Bacon, Lloyd
  GE:A&C II-925
Bacon, Nathaniel
  GE:Am I-151

Bacon, Roger
  GE:A&M III-1509, 1539, 1555
  GL:B&C I-130
Baden, Prince Maximilian von
  GE:HR I-241
Badoglio, Pietro
  GE:B&C II-723
  GE:ME III-1401, 1486
Baeck, Leo
  GL:20 I-81
Baekeland, Leo Hendrik
  GE:B&C II-527
  GE:S&T I-280
Baer, George F.
  GE:Am II-1329
  GE:B&C I-122
Baer, Karl Ernst von
  GL:Ren I-106
Baeyer, Adolf von
  GE:S&T I-280, V-1918
Baez, Joan
  GL:AmW I-118
Bagley, William T.
  GE:B&C IV-1567
Bagration, Prince Pëtr Ivanovich
  GE:ME II-585
Bahcall, John Norris
  GE:S&T IV-1830
Bahr, Egon
  GE:W20 III-1167
Bahram I
  GE:A&M II-807
Bailey, Frederick Augustus Washington. *See*
  Douglass, Frederick
Bailey, Gamaliel
  GE:Am II-859
Bailey, James A.
  GE:Am II-1066
Bailey, Joseph
  GE:Am III-1415
Bailly, Jean-Sylvain
  GE:ME I-510
Baird, John Logie
  GE:B&C II-758
Baird, Spencer Fullerton
  GE:Am II-831
Baker, Edward D.
  GE:Am II-946

Baker, Ella Jo
  GE:HR II-974
Baker, Eric
  GE:HR II-1119
Baker, Fred
  GE:B&C IV-1501
Baker, George F.
  GE:B&C I-134, 157
Baker, George Pierce
  GE:A&C I-343
Baker, Howard Henry
  GE:W20 III-1331
Baker, James A., III
  GE:B&C V-1953, 1986
Baker, Josephine
  GE:A&C II-665
  GL:AmW I-122
Baker, Mary. *See* Eddy, Mary Baker
Baker, Newton Diehl
  GE:Am III-1466
Baker, Ray Stannard
  GE:Am III-1353
Bakes, Philip, Jr.
  GE:B&C V-1865
Bakhmin, Vyacheslav
  GE:HR IV-1909
Bakhtiar, Shahpoor
  GE:HR IV-2013
Bakhtin, Mikhail
  GL:20 I-87
Bakke, Allan Paul
  GE:HR IV-1697
Bakker, Jim
  GE:B&C V-2001
Bakker, Tammy Faye
  GE:B&C V-2001
Bakr, Abu. *See* Abu Bakr
Bakr, Ahmad Hasan al-
  GE:HR II-1050
Bakst, Léon
  GE:A&C I-241, 263, 269, 332
Bakunin, Mikhail
  GE:ME II-897
  GL:Ren I-111
Balaban, Barney
  GE:A&C III-1307
  GE:B&C III-937
Balanchine, George
  GE:A&C II-974, III-1088, 1301, V-2459
  GL:Am I-112
Balanchivadze, Georgi Melitonovitch. *See*
  Balanchine, George
Balbo, Italo
  GE:ME III-1319

Balboa, Vasco Núñez de
  GL:Ren I-116
Balch, Emily Greene
  GL:Am I-118
  GL:AmW I-127
Balcon, Michael
  GE:A&C II-946, III-1427
Baldrige, Malcolm
  GE:B&C V-1948
Baldus de Ubaldis
  GE:A&M II-784, III-1344
Baldwin, Abraham
  GE:Am I-312
Baldwin, James
  GE:A&C IV-1929
  GL:Am I-123
Baldwin, John. *See* Jones, John Paul
Baldwin, Robert
  GL:B&C I-135
Baldwin, Roger Nash
  GE:HR I-327, II-590
Baldwin, Stanley
  GE:A&C II-712
  GE:B&C II-510, 591
  GE:HR I-321, 429, 442
  GE:ME III-1324, 1420
  GL:B&C I-141
Balenciaga, Cristobal
  GE:A&C IV-1824
Balewa, Abubakar Tafawa
  GE:HR III-1194
  GE:W20 II-1003
Balfour, Arthur
  GE:Am III-1531
  GE:B&C I-351
  GE:HR I-235, 287, 453, II-749, 761, 814
  GE:ME III-1214, 1372
  GE:W20 I-231, 411
  GL:B&C I-147
Balian de Adam. *See* Salimbene
Baliles, Gerald L.
  GE:HR V-2517
Baline, Israel. *See* Berlin, Irving
Balke, Hermann
  GE:A&M III-1472
Ball, George
  GE:Am III-1888
Ball, Hugo
  GE:A&C I-419
Ball, Lucille
  GE:A&C III-1525
  GL:AmW I-132
Balla, Giacomo
  GE:A&C I-235

Ballard, Robert D.
  GE:S&T V-2058
Ballinger, Richard Achilles
  GE:Am III-1390
Ballou, Adin
  GE:Am I-642
Ballou, Hosea
  GE:Am I-570
Balmain, Pierre
  GE:A&C III-1346
Baltimore, David
  GE:S&T I-459
Baltimore, First Lord. See Calvert, George
Baltimore, Second Lord. See Calvert, Cecilius
Balzac, Honoré de
  GL:Ren I-120
Bancroft, Aaron
  GE:Am II-730
Bancroft, Anne
  GL:AmW I-137
Bancroft, George
  GE:Am II-730
  GL:Am I-128
Bancroft, Richard
  GE:ME I-241
Band, the
  GE:A&C IV-2180
Bandaranaike, Sirimavo
  GE:HR II-1090, III-1590, IV-2068
Bandinelli, Roland. See Alexander III, Pope
Banerjea, Surendranath
  GL:20 I-92
Bankhead, Tallulah
  GL:AmW I-141
Banks, Dennis
  GE:HR IV-1709
  GE:W20 II-865
Banks, Sir Joseph
  GL:B&C I-151
Banks, Nathaniel Prentiss
  GE:Am II-1037
Banneker, Benjamin
  GL:Am I-136
Banting, Sir Frederick Grant
  GE:S&T I-179, II-720
  GL:B&C I-157
Banton, Travis
  GE:A&C II-845
Banzhaf, John F., III
  GE:B&C IV-1443
  GE:HR III-1527
Bao Dai
  GE:W20 II-696

Baptiste, Gaston Jean (Duke of Orléans)
  GE:ME I-278, 324
Barabbas
  GE:A&M II-601
Baraka, Amiri
  GE:A&C IV-2000, V-2370
Baranov, Aleksandr
  GE:W20 II-790
Baratieri, General Oreste
  GE:ME II-1094
Barbarizo, Augustino
  GE:ME I-180
Barbarossa, Frederick I. See Frederick I
  Barbarossa
Barber, Samuel
  GE:A&C III-1536
  GL:Am I-141
Barbera, Joseph
  GE:A&C IV-1840
Barberet, Joseph
  GE:ME II-1044
Barbie, Klaus
  GE:HR IV-2193
Barbot, Clement
  GE:HR II-1009
Barca, Hamilcar
  GE:A&M I-408
Barca, Hasdrubal
  GE:A&M I-437
Barca, Pedro Calderón de la
  GE:A&C III-1179
  GL:Ren I-335
Barcelo, Randy
  GE:A&C V-2254
Barclay, Sir Thomas
  GE:ME III-1152
Bardas Scleros. See Scleros
Bardeen, John
  GE:S&T III-1304, IV-1528, 1533
  GE:W20 II-612
Bardeen, William
  GE:S&T V-1966
Barden, Graham Arthur
  GE:B&C III-1122
Bardi, Donato di Niccolò di Betto. See Donatello
Bardon, L.
  GE:S&T I-428
Bare, Bobby
  GE:A&C V-2365
Barghoorn, Elso
  GE:S&T IV-1481, 1851
Bar Hiyya, Abraham
  GE:A&M III-1524
Baring, Alexander. See Ashburton, Baron

Baring, Sir Evelyn
GE:HR II-891
Barker, Frank A.
GE:HR III-1555
Barkla, Charles Glover
GE:S&T I-309, II-746
Barkley, Alben William
GE:Am III-1800
Bar Kokhba, Simon
GE:A&M II-702
Barlow, Joel
GE:Am I-194, 636
Barlowe, Arthur
GE:Am I-46
Barnard, Chester I.
GE:B&C II-770, III-890
Barnard, Christiaan
GE:S&T IV-1866
GE:W20 II-1016
GL:20 I-97
Barnard, Edward Emerson
GE:S&T I-213
Barnard, Henry
GE:Am I-576, II-1031
GL:Am I-147
Barnes, Djuna
GL:AmW I-145
Barnett, Ross R.
GE:HR III-1167
Barnum, P. T.
GE:Am II-1066
GL:Am I-152
Barone, Domenico
GE:ME III-1354
Barr, Alfred H., Jr.
GE:A&C II-782
Barrett, Aston "Family Man"
GE:A&C V-2344
Barrett, Carlton
GE:A&C V-2344
Barrett, Majel
GE:A&C V-2260
Barrio, Próspero Peñados del
GE:HR IV-1972
Barrios de Chamorro, Violeta. See Chamorro,
    Violeta Barrios de
Barron, Clarence W.
GE:B&C I-324
Barrow, Edward Grant
GE:B&C I-341
Barrows, Harlan H.
GE:Am II-1627
Barry, Sir Charles
GL:B&C I-163

Barry, John
GE:A&C IV-1913
Barry, Philip
GE:A&C I-343
Barrymore, Ethel
GL:AmW I-150
Barrymore, Lionel
GE:A&C III-1335
Bart, Ben
GE:A&C IV-2059
Bartels, Julius
GE:S&T III-1035
Barth, Karl
GE:Am III-1604
GL:20 I-101
Barthes, Roland
GL:20 I-106
Barthle, Robert C.
GE:S&T IV-1598
Bartók, Béla
GE:A&C I-102
GL:20 I-111
Bartolomé de las Casas. See Las Casas,
    Bartolomé de
Bartolus of Sassoferrato
GE:A&M II-784, III-1344
Barton, Clara
GL:Am I-158
GL:AmW I-156
Barton, Sir Derek H. R.
GE:S&T V-1918
Barton, Sir Edmund
GE:W20 I-14
GL:B&C I-169
Barton, James
GE:W20 I-107
Barton, Otis
GE:S&T III-1018
Baruch
GE:A&M I-149
Baruch, Bernard M.
GE:Am III-1460
GE:B&C I-246
GE:W20 II-564
Baryshnikov, Mikhail
GE:A&C IV-1962, V-2288, 2459, 2559, 2663
Barzani, Masoud
GE:HR V-2397
Barzani, Mulla Mustafa al-
GE:HR II-1050
Basch, Bert E.
GE:B&C IV-1647
Basedow, Johann Bernhard
GL:Ren I-125

Basehart, Richard
GE:A&C III-1596
Baselitz, Georg
GE:A&C V-2464
Basil II Bulgaroctonus
GE:A&M III-1215
Basil the Eunuch
GE:A&M III-1215
Basil the Great
GE:A&M II-893
Basil the Macedonian
GL:A&M I-302
Basil, Colonel Wassili de
GE:A&C III-1088
Basilevsky, Alexander
GE:S&T V-2042
Baskerville, John
GL:B&C I-174
Basov, Nikolay Gennadiyevich
GE:W20 II-881
GL:20 I-116
Bass, Saul
GE:A&C IV-1855
Bates, Alan
GE:A&C IV-1721, 1861
Bates, Daisy
GE:W20 II-770
Bates, Katharine Lee
GL:AmW I-161
Bates, Ruby
GE:Am II-1588
Bateson, William
GE:S&T I-61, 270, 314
Bathurst, Third Earl of (Henry Bathurst)
GE:Am I-533
Batista, Fulgencio
GE:HR II-1026
GE:W20 II-743
Batlle y Ordóñez, José
GE:HR IV-1715
Battani, al-
GE:A&M II-716
GL:A&M I-307
Batu
GE:A&M III-1462
Baucus, Max
GE:B&C V-2034
Baudelaire, Charles
GL:Ren I-130
Baudot, Jean Marie Emile
GE:W20 I-1
Bauer, Georg. See Agricola, Georgius
Bauer, Max
GE:B&C I-293

Baulieu, Étienne-Émile
GE:S&T V-2185
Baumfree, Isabella. See Truth, Sojourner
Baumgarner, James. See Garner, James
Bava-Beccaris, General Fiorenzo
GE:ME II-1109
Bavadra, Timoci
GE:HR V-2309
Bavaria, Duke of. See Maximilian of Wittelsbach
Bavolek, Cecelia
GE:S&T III-1024
Baxter, Richard
GE:W20 I-38
GL:B&C I-178
Baxter, Warner
GE:A&C II-925
Baxter, William F.
GE:B&C V-1821
Bayard, James A.
GE:Am I-426, 522
Bayard, Thomas Francis
GE:Am II-1190
Bayazid I
GE:A&M III-1660
Baybars I
GL:A&M I-311
Bayezid I. See Bayazid I
Bayezid II
GL:Ren I-135
Bayle, Pierre
GL:Ren I-140
Bayley, Elizabeth Ann. See Seton, Elizabeth Ann
(Saint)
Bayliss, Sir William Maddock
GE:S&T I-179
GL:B&C I-185
Baz, Abd al-Aziz ibn
GE:HR IV-2095
Bazaine, Marshal Achille François
GE:ME II-954
Bazelon, David L.
GE:HR III-1622
Bazin, André
GE:A&C IV-1710
Bazzaz, Abdul Rahman al-
GE:HR II-1050
Bea, Cardinal Augustin
GE:ME III-1633
Beach, Amy Marcy
GL:AmW I-165
Beach, Michael Edward Hicks
GE:B&C I-218

Beach, Sylvia
GE:A&C II-555
GE:Am III-1560
Beaconsfield, Earl of. *See* Disraeli, Benjamin
Beale, Dorothea
GL:B&C I-190
Beall, George Brooke
GE:W20 III-1188
Bean, Alan L.
GE:S&T IV-1913, V-1997
Beard, Charles A.
GE:Am III-1426
GL:Am I-164
Beard, Mary
GL:AmW I-170
Beardsley, Aubrey
GL:B&C I-195
Beatles, the. *See also* Harrison, George, Lennon,
John, McCartney, Paul, and Starr, Ringo
GL:B&C I-200
Beatty, Sir David
GE:ME III-1266
Beatty, Edward
GE:B&C II-597
Beatty, Talley
GE:A&C IV-1774, V-2521
Beauchamp, Lord
GE:ME I-224
Beaudette, Richard A.
GE:B&C IV-1647
Beaudouin, Eugène Elie
GE:A&C II-1021
Beaulieu, Edward, Third Baron Montagu of
GE:HR II-991
Beaumont, Francis, and John Fletcher
GL:B&C I-206
Beauregard, Pierre Gustave Toutant
GE:Am II-952
Beauvais, Vincent of. *See* Vincent of Beauvais
Beauvoir, Simone de
GE:A&C III-1262, 1449
GE:W20 I-252
GL:20 I-121
Beaux, Cecilia
GL:AmW I-175
Beaverbrook, Lord. *See also* Aitken, William
Maxwell
GL:B&C I-212
Bebel, August
GE:ME II-992, 1013, 1028
Beck, Józef
GE:ME III-1440
Becker, Gary S.
GE:B&C III-931

Beckers, Jacques
GE:S&T V-2291
Becket, Thomas
GE:A&M III-1375
GL:B&C I-218
Beckett, Samuel
GE:A&C III-1498, 1573, IV-1871, 1903
GL:B&C I-223
Beckley, John
GE:Am I-350
Beckmann, Max
GE:A&C II-631
Becknell, William
GE:Am I-588
Beckwith, E. G.
GE:Am II-865
Becquerel, Alexandre-Edmond. *See* Becquerel
family, The
Becquerel, Antoine-César. *See* Becquerel family,
The
Becquerel, Antoine-Henri. *See also* Becquerel
family, The
GE:ME II-1084
GE:S&T I-93, 199, 412, III-992
Becquerel family, The
GL:Ren I-145
Bedau, Hugo Adam
GE:HR III-1674
Beddoes, Thomas
GE:ME II-560
Bede the Venerable, Saint
GE:A&M II-877, 1091
GL:B&C I-230
Bedford, Duke of
GE:A&M III-1697
Bedford, Duke of (John Russell)
GE:ME I-451
Bednorz, J. Georg
GE:S&T V-2311
Beebe, William
GE:S&T III-1018
Beecher, Catharine
GL:AmW I-180
Beecher, Harriet. *See* Stowe, Harriet Beecher
Beecher, Henry Ward
GL:Am I-172
Beecher, Lyman
GE:Am I-570, II-859
Beecroft, John
GE:B&C I-196
Beekman, Isaac
GE:ME I-294
Beethoven, Ludwig van
GL:Ren I-150

Beetson, Fred
    GE:A&C II-799
Begin, Menachem
    GE:HR IV-1943, 2003, 2164
    GE:W20 I-145
    GL:20 I-127
Behan, Brendan
    GE:A&C IV-1757
Behem, Martin
    GE:A&M III-1503
Behn, Sosthenes
    GE:B&C II-827
Behrens, Peter
    GE:A&C I-181, 219
Behring, Emil Adolf von
    GE:S&T I-6, II-567
Behrman, S. N.
    GE:A&C I-343
Bekkers, William
    GE:ME III-1659
Bélanger, Alain
    GE:S&T V-2185
Belar, Herbert
    GE:A&C IV-1785
Belasco, David
    GE:A&C I-224
Bel Geddes, Barbara
    GE:A&C V-2418
Bel Geddes, Norman. *See* Geddes, Norman Bel
Belhaj, Ali
    GE:HR V-2583
Belknap, William
    GE:Am II-1054
Bell, Alexander Graham
    GE:Am II-1089
    GE:S&T II-595, V-2078
    GL:Am I-177
Bell, Garrett de
    GE:HR III-1386
Bell, Howard
    GE:B&C IV-1501
Bell, Jocelyn
    GE:S&T IV-1862
    GE:W20 II-1009
Bell, John
    GE:Am II-935
Bell, Vanessa
    GE:A&C II-637
Bella, Ahmed Ben
    GE:HR III-1155
Bellarmine, Cardinal Robert
    GE:ME I-285
Bellingham, Richard
    GE:Am I-103

Bellini, Giovanni
    GL:Ren I-155
Bellow, Saul
    GL:Am I-182
Belmondo, Jean-Paul
    GE:A&C IV-1845
Belmont, August
    GE:Am II-1135
Belshazzar
    GE:A&M I-179
Belushi, John
    GE:A&C V-2355
Belyayev, Pavel I.
    GE:S&T IV-1787
Belzel, George
    GE:S&T V-2169
Bencivieni di Pepo. *See* Cimabue
Benda, Władysław Theodore
    GE:A&C I-452
Ben David, Abraham
    GE:A&M III-1391
Bendetsen, Major Karl R.
    GE:HR II-595
Bendix, William
    GE:A&C III-1470
Benedetti, Count Vincente
    GE:ME II-949, 954
Benedict XII, Pope
    GE:A&M III-1620
Benedict XIII, Pope
    GE:A&M III-1680
Benedict of Aniane
    GE:A&M II-1029
Benedict of Nursia, Saint
    GE:A&M II-1029
    GL:A&M I-317
Benedict, Paul
    GE:A&C V-2339
Benedict, Ruth
    GL:AmW I-185
    GE:S&T III-997
Beneduce, Alberto
    GE:B&C II-645
Benenson, Peter
    GE:HR II-1119, IV-1955, 2204
Beněs, Edvard
    GE:ME III-1429
    GE:W20 II-626
    GL:20 I-133
Bénévente, Prince of. *See* Talleyrand
Ben-Gabirol. *See* Ibn Gabirol
Ben Giora, Simon
    GE:A&M II-648

Ben-Gurion, David
GE:HR II-749, 761, 814, 832, 963
GE:ME III-1589
GE:W20 II-634
GL:20 I-139
Benincasa, Caterina. *See* Catherine of Siena, Saint
Benioff, Hugo
GE:S&T I-51
Benjamin of Tudela
GL:A&M I-322
Benjamin, Walter
GL:20 I-145
Benjedid, Chadli
GE:HR V-2583
Ben Joseph. *See* Akiba ben Joseph
Ben Khedda, Youssef
GE:ME III-1628
Ben Maimon, Moses. *See* Maimonides, Moses
Benn, Tony
GE:B&C IV-1347
Bennett, Frederick
GE:B&C I-151
Bennett, Harry
GE:HR I-143
Bennett, Hugh Hammond
GE:Am III-1627
Bennett, James Gordon
GE:Am II-713
GL:Am I-187
Bennett, John C.
GE:Am III-1604
Bennett, Richard Bedford
GE:B&C II-591, 597, 624
Bennett, Wallace
GE:B&C IV-1443
Bennett, William
GE:HR V-2359
Bennett, William Ralph, Jr.
GE:W20 II-881
Bennett, W. R.
GE:B&C V-1848
Bennigsen, Count Levin August Theophil
GE:ME II-590
Benny, Jack
GE:A&C II-828
Benois, Alexandre
GE:A&C I-241, 247
Benson, Ezra Taft
GE:B&C III-1052
Bentham, Jeremy
GE:ME I-456
GL:B&C I-235
Bentinck, Lord George
GE:ME II-764

Bentinck, Lord William
GE:HR I-401
Benton, John Dalmer
GE:HR III-1474
Benton, Thomas Hart
GE:Am I-582, 660, II-696, 772, 865
GL:Am I-194
Benton, William
GE:B&C II-674
Benvenuti, Lodovico
GE:HR III-1137
Benz, Carl
GL:Ren I-161
Ben Zakkai, Johanan. *See* Johanan ben Zakkai
Ber, Israel. *See* Neumann, J. B.
Berenger, Henri
GE:B&C I-351
Berenquer III, Ramon
GE:A&M III-1514
Beresford, Lord Charles William de la Poer
GE:ME II-1057
Beresford, William Carr (Viscount Beresford)
GE:ME II-645
Berg, Alban
GE:A&C I-193, 367, 528, II-680, 1078
GL:20 I-151
Berg, Helene
GE:A&C II-1078
Berg, Paal
GE:HR II-985
Berg, Patty
GL:AmW I-189
Berg, Paul
GE:S&T V-1987, 2115
Berge, Wendell
GE:B&C III-1164
Bergengren, Roy F.
GE:B&C II-690
Berger, Hans
GE:S&T II-890
Bergeron, Tor
GE:S&T II-675
Bergius, Friedrich
GL:20 I-157
Bergman, Ingmar
GE:A&C IV-1742
GL:20 I-162
Bergman, Ingrid
GE:A&C III-1245
Bergson, Henri
GE:A&C I-161
GE:ME III-1183
GL:20 I-168

Bergstresser, Charles Milford
  GE:B&C I-1
Beria, Lavrentii
  GE:HR II-952
  GE:ME III-1566
  GE:W20 II-736
Berkeley, Busby
  GE:A&C II-925, III-1432
Berkeley, George
  GL:B&C I-241
Berkeley, Sir William
  GE:Am I-132, 151
Berkman, Alexander
  GE:HR I-258
Berkner, Lloyd Viel
  GE:W20 II-764
Berle, Adolf A., Jr.
  GE:B&C II-619
Berle, Milton
  GE:A&C III-1394
Berliawsky, Leah. See Nevelson, Louise
Berlichingen, Götz von
  GE:ME I-76
Berlin, Irving
  GE:A&C II-984
  GL:Am I-200
Berliner, Emile
  GE:S&T I-138
Berlinger, Milton. See Berle, Milton
Berlinguer, Enrico
  GE:HR IV-1988
Berlioz, Hector
  GL:Ren I-166
Berman, Pandro S.
  GE:A&C II-984
Bermejo, Juan José Arévalo
  GE:B&C III-1040
Bermont-Avalov, Prince P. R.
  GE:HR I-207
Bernadott, Count Folke
  GE:HR II-749, 814
  GE:W20 II-634
Bernadotte, Jean-Baptiste-Jules. See Charles XIV
  John
Bernal, Paul
  GE:HR III-1573
Bernanos, Georges
  GE:A&C II-1026
Bernard of Chartres
  GE:A&M III-1231
Bernard of Clairvaux, Saint
  GE:A&M III-1313, 1324
  GL:A&M I-327

Bernard of Cluny
  GE:A&M III-1349
Bernard of Pavia
  GE:A&M III-1491
Bernard of Quintavalle
  GE:A&M III-1447
Bernard, Claude
  GL:Ren I-174
Bernardina, Minerva
  GE:HR II-885
Bernardini, Micheline
  GE:A&C III-1324
Bernardone, Francesco di Pietro di. See Francis of
  Assisi, Saint
Bernhard, Karl
  GE:A&C I-219
Bernini, Gian Lorenzo
  GL:Ren I-180
Berno of Baume
  GE:A&M II-1029, 1184
Bernoulli, Daniel. See Bernoulli family, The
Bernoulli, Jakob I. See Bernoulli family, The
Bernoulli, Johann I. See Bernoulli family, The
Bernoulli family, The
  GL:Ren I-185
Bernstein, Eduard
  GL:20 I-173
Bernstein, Felix
  GE:S&T I-143
Bernstein, Leonard
  GE:A&C III-1274, IV-1731
  GL:Am I-206
Bernstein, Robert L.
  GE:HR V-2494
Berrill, Kevin
  GE:HR V-2364
Berry, Chuck
  GE:A&C IV-1635
Berry, Sir John
  GE:Am I-151
Bershad, Sheldon Leonard
  GE:A&C IV-2044
Bertelsen, Aage
  GE:HR II-641
Bertha
  GE:A&M II-1058
Berthelot, Philippe
  GE:B&C I-351
Berthold, Arnold
  GE:S&T I-179
Bertie, Sir Francis
  GE:B&C I-41

Besant, Annie
  GE:HR I-156, 401
  GL:B&C I-246
Bessel, Friedrich Wilhelm
  GL:Ren I-190
Bessemer, Sir Henry
  GL:B&C I-251
Besserer, Eugénie
  GE:A&C II-734
Bessus
  GE:A&M I-358
Best, Charles Herbert
  GE:S&T II-610, 720
Best, Werner
  GE:HR II-641
Bestuzhev-Ryumin, Mikhail
  GE:ME II-665
Betancourt, Rómulo
  GE:B&C I-385
  GE:HR II-755
Beteille, Roger
  GE:B&C III-1303
Bethe, Hans Albrecht
  GE:S&T II-815, III-1282
  GL:Am I-211
Bethlen, Stephen
  GE:W20 I-181
Bethmann Hollweg, Theobald von
  GE:Am III-1450
  GE:B&C I-293
  GE:ME III-1245, 1340
  GE:W20 I-46
Bethune, Mary McLeod
  GL:AmW I-193
Betto Bardi, Donato di Niccolò di. See Donatello
Beust, Friedrich von
  GE:ME II-939
  GL:Ren I-195
Beuys, Joseph
  GE:A&C V-2464
Bevan, Aneurin
  GE:B&C III-885
  GL:B&C I-257
Bevan, Edward John
  GE:S&T I-238
Beveridge, Lord
  GE:B&C III-885
  GL:B&C I-262
Beveridge, Albert J.
  GE:B&C I-63
  GE:HR I-64
Beveridge, William. See Beveridge, Lord
Beverley, Robert
  GE:Am I-151

Bevin, Ernest
  GE:Am III-1806
  GE:B&C II-510
  GE:HR I-429, II-706, 771
  GE:ME III-1512, 1532, 1555
  GE:W20 II-591
  GL:B&C I-269
Bevis, Douglas
  GE:S&T IV-1439
Beyle, Marie-Henri. See Stendhal
Bhindranwale, Jarnail Singh
  GE:HR IV-2215, 2232
Bhonsle, Śivajī. See Śivajī
Bhutto, Benazir
  GE:HR IV-1898, V-2403, 2426
Bhutto, Nusrat
  GE:HR IV-1898, V-2403
Bhutto, Zulfikar Ali
  GE:HR III-1611, IV-2018, V-2403
  GE:W20 II-1091
Bianchi, Manuel
  GE:HR II-1032
Bianchi, Michele
  GE:ME III-1319
Bidault, Georges
  GE:ME III-1532
  GE:W20 II-591
Biddle, Francis B.
  GE:HR II-595
Biddle, George
  GE:A&C II-995
Biddle, Nicholas
  GE:Am I-539, II-696
  GL:Am I-217
Biden, Joe
  GE:B&C IV-1595
Bieber, Irving
  GE:HR IV-1741
Bielecki, Jan Krzysztof
  GE:B&C V-2017
Biermann, Ludwig
  GE:S&T IV-1577
Bierstadt, Albert
  GE:Am I-613
  GL:Am I-223
Bigod, Hugh
  GE:A&M III-1528
Biko, Steven Bantu
  GE:HR IV-1887
Billings, John Shaw
  GE:A&C II-1031
Bing, Rudolf
  GE:A&C III-1126

Bing, Samuel
GE:A&C I-34
Bingham, George Caleb
GL:Am I-227
Bingham, Hiram
GE:S&T II-491
Bingham, John A.
GE:Am II-1049
Bini, Lucino
GE:S&T III-1086
Binnig, Gerd
GE:S&T V-2093
Birch, Thomas
GE:Am I-613
Birdseye, Clarence
GE:S&T II-635
Birnbaum, Morton
GE:HR III-1622
Birnbaum, Nathan. *See* Burns, George
Birney, James Gillespie
GE:Am I-642, II-719
Biruni, al-
GL:A&M I-332
Bish, Walter
GE:B&C V-1854
Bishop, Elizabeth
GL:AmW I-198
Bismarck, Otto von
GE:ME II-880, 912, 918, 923, 949, 954, 963,
    969, 988, 992, 1007, 1013, 1019, 1028,
    1048, 1070
GE:W20 I-54
GL:Ren I-200
Bissell, George Henry
GE:Am II-912
Bissell, Melville R.
GE:S&T I-88
Bissell, Richard Mervin
GE:W20 II-926
Bitzer, Billy
GE:A&C I-402
Bizet, Georges
GL:Ren I-205
Bjerknes, Jacob
GE:S&T II-675
Bjerknes, Vilhelm
GE:S&T I-21, II-675
GL:20 I-179
Bjorken, James
GE:S&T IV-1871
Björnson, Björnstjerne
GE:ME III-1164
Black Berthold. *See* Schwarz, Berthold

Black Hawk
GL:Am I-238
Black, Cathleen
GE:B&C V-1842
Black, Davidson
GE:S&T II-761, III-1096
Black, Eugene
GE:B&C II-717, III-1276
Black, Greene Vardiman
GE:S&T III-1260
Black, Hugo L.
GE:Am III-1893
GE:B&C III-997
GE:HR II-629, III-1167, 1182, 1521
GE:W20 I-507
GL:Am I-232
Black, Joseph
GE:ME I-460
Black, Shirley Temple. *See also* Temple, Shirley
GL:AmW I-202
Blackmun, Harry A.
GE:B&C IV-1437, V-1882
GE:HR IV-1703
GE:W20 III-1154
Blackmur, R. P.
GE:A&C III-1169
Blackstone, William
GL:B&C I-276
Blackwell, Chris
GE:A&C V-2344
Blackwell, Elizabeth
GL:Am I-243
GL:AmW I-207
Blackwell, Mr.
GE:B&C I-396
Blackwell, Mrs. Henry Brown. *See* Stone, Lucy
Blain, James G.
GE:Am II-1140, 1190
GE:HR II-879
GL:Am I-250
Blair, Eric Arthur. *See* Orwell, George
Blair, Ezell, Jr.
GE:HR II-1056
Blair, Montgomery
GE:Am II-900, 980
Blair, Sir Robert
GE:HR I-109
Blake, Amanda
GE:A&C IV-1668, 1768
Blake, Robert
GL:B&C I-281
Blake, William
GL:B&C I-287

Blakey, Art
    GE:A&C V-2454
Blakey, G. Robert
    GE:B&C IV-1449
Blalock, Alfred
    GE:S&T III-1250
Blamauer, Karoline. *See* Lenya, Lotte
Blanc, Louis
    GE:ME II-786
    GL:Ren I-210
Blanche of Castile
    GE:A&M III-1496
Blanck, Max
    GE:B&C I-191
Blanco, Luis Carrero
    GE:HR IV-2079
    GE:W20 II-1043
Blanqui, Louis Auguste
    GE:ME II-786, 897, 984
Blanton, Jimmy
    GE:A&C III-1617
Blasko, Béla. *See* Lugosi, Bela
Blatch, Harriot Stanton
    GE:Am III-1513
Blatchford, Joseph H.
    GE:Am III-1877
Blavatsky, Helena Petrovna
    GE:A&C I-286, 320
Blay, Andre
    GE:B&C V-1745
Blenkinsop, John
    GE:ME II-608
Blennerhassett, Harman
    GE:Am I-461
Blériot, Louis
    GE:S&T I-448
    GL:20 I-184
Bleuler, Eugen
    GL:20 I-189
Blewett, John Paul
    GE:S&T III-1336
Bleyl, Fritz
    GE:A&C I-134
Bloch, Robert
    GE:A&C IV-1855
Block, John
    GE:B&C V-1859
Blocker, Dan
    GE:A&C IV-1800
Blok, Aleksandr
    GL:20 I-194
Blomberg, Werner von
    GE:ME III-1391
    GE:W20 I-375

Blomquist, Clarence D. D.
    GE:HR IV-1926
Bloodworth-Thomason, Linda
    GL:AmW I-212
Bloody Mary. *See* Mary I
Bloom, Benjamin
    GE:HR III-1284
Bloomer, Amelia Jenks
    GL:AmW I-217
Bloomfield, Maurice
    GE:Am II-1077
Bloomfield, Meyer
    GE:B&C II-419
Bloomfield, Mike
    GE:A&C IV-2038
Bloomingdale, Alfred
    GE:B&C III-959
Blore, Eric
    GE:A&C II-984
Blossom, Virgil T.
    GE:W20 II-770
Blount, William
    GE:Am I-396
Blount, Winton M.
    GE:B&C IV-1506
Blücher, Gebhard Leberecht von
    GE:ME II-590, 618
    GL:Ren I-216
Blum, Léon
    GE:B&C II-735
    GE:ME III-1411
    GL:20 I-198
Blum, René
    GE:A&C III-1088
Blunschy-Steiner, Elisabeth
    GE:HR III-1605
Bly, Nellie
    GL:AmW I-222
Boabdil
    GE:A&M III-1747
Boas, Franz
    GE:S&T II-481, 869, III-997
    GL:Am I-255
Bobeck, Andrew H.
    GE:S&T IV-1886
Bobrikov, Nikolai
    GE:HR I-70, 212
Boccaccio, Giovanni
    GL:A&M I-337
Boccherini, Luigi
    GL:Ren I-221
Boccioni, Umberto
    GE:A&C I-235
    GL:20 I-204

Bochco, Stephen
  GE:A&C V-2470
Bock, Fedor von
  GE:W20 I-450
Böckler, Hans
  GE:B&C III-981
Bodin, Jean
  GE:ME I-202
Bodley, Sir Thomas
  GL:B&C I-294
Boesky, Ivan
  GE:B&C V-1921, 1958
Boethius
  GE:A&M II-834, 1000, 1018, III-1410
  GL:A&M I-343
Boethius of Dacia
  GE:A&M III-1564
Boffrand, Germain
  GL:Ren I-226
Bogan, Louise
  GL:AmW I-227
Bogart, Humphrey
  GE:A&C III-1223, 1245
Bogen, Joseph
  GE:S&T IV-1635
Boggs, Hale
  GE:HR III-1296
Boggs, Lindy
  GE:B&C IV-1595
Bogoliubov, Nikolai Nikolaevich
  GE:S&T III-1129
Bohemond I
  GL:A&M I-349
Bohlen, Charles Eustis
  GE:Am III-1736
Böhler, Peter
  GE:ME I-409
Böhme, Jakob
  GL:Ren I-231
Bohn, René
  GE:S&T I-98
Bohr, Niels
  GE:S&T I-83, II-507, 527, 590, 741, 800, 835,
    III-1265, IV-1533
  GE:W20 I-166, 246, II-881
  GL:20 I-209
Bojaxhiu, Agnes Gonxha. See Teresa, Mother
Bojaxhiu, Lazar
  GE:HR IV-2051
Bokassa, Jean-Bedel
  GE:HR IV-2136
Boleyn, Anne
  GE:ME I-103

Bolger, Ray
  GE:A&C III-1109
Bolin, Bert R.
  GE:S&T III-1118
Bolingbroke, First Viscount
  GE:ME I-400
  GL:B&C I-299
Bolívar, Simón
  GE:HR II-879
  GL:Ren I-236
Böll, Heinrich
  GE:A&C III-1357
  GL:20 I-214
Bolton, Elmer Keiser
  GE:B&C II-798
  GE:S&T III-1055
Boltwood, Bertram Borden
  GE:S&T I-93, 285
Bolzano, Bernhard
  GE:S&T IV-1751
Bonaparte, Joseph
  GE:ME II-581, 594
Bonaparte, Louis Napoleon. See Napoleon III
Bonaparte, Lucien
  GE:ME I-547
Bonaparte, Napoleon. See Napoleon I
Bonar Law. See Law, Bonar
Bonaventure, Saint
  GL:A&M I-354
Bond, Alan
  GE:A&C V-2603
Bond, Christopher S. "Kit"
  GE:HR IV-2118
Bond, Ward
  GE:A&C IV-1768
Bondfield, Margaret
  GL:B&C I-307
Bondi, Hermann
  GE:S&T III-1320
Bonesana, Cesare (Marchese di Beccaria)
  GE:ME I-456
Bonham, John
  GE:A&C V-2228
Bonhoeffer, Dietrich
  GL:20 I-219
Boniface VIII, Pope
  GE:A&M III-1491, 1592
  GL:A&M I-365
Boniface, Count
  GE:A&M II-958
Boniface of Montferrat
  GE:A&M III-1436

Boniface, Saint
GE:A&M II-1126
GL:A&M I-360
Bonnard, Pierre
GL:20 I-224
Bonner, Elena
GE:HR IV-1852
Bonnet, Georges
GE:Am III-1806
GE:ME III-1429, 1440
Bonnet, Henri
GE:HR II-590
Bonnier, Louis
GE:A&C II-654
Bonnot, Étienne. *See* Condillac, Étienne
Bonnot de
Bono, Sonny
GE:A&C V-2244
Boone, Daniel
GL:Am I-259
Boone, Mary
GE:A&C V-2438
Boone, Richard
GE:A&C IV-1768
Booth, Andrew D.
GE:S&T V-1923
Booth, Edwin
GL:Am I-264
Booth, George
GE:A&C II-610
Booth, Herbert Cecil
GE:S&T I-88
Booth, John Wilkes
GE:Am II-1014
Booth, William
GL:B&C I-312
Boothe, Clare. *See* Luce, Clare Boothe
Borah, William E.
GE:Am III-1484, 1649
GE:B&C II-662
GL:Am I-269
Bordaberry, Juan María
GE:HR IV-1715
Borden, Sir Robert Laird
GE:B&C I-174
GE:ME III-1372
GL:B&C I-316
Borel, Émile
GE:S&T I-36
Borg, Björn
GL:20 I-229
Borges, Jorge Luis
GE:A&C III-1268, IV-1689
GL:20 I-234

Borgia, Cesare
GE:ME I-26, 35
Borgia, Francis (Duke of Gandia)
GE:ME I-96
Borgia, Giovanni
GE:ME I-26
Borgia, Lucrezia
GE:ME I-26
Borgia, Roderigo. *See* Alexander VI, Pope
Boris I of Bulgaria
GL:A&M I-370
Boris III of Saxe-Coburg
GE:W20 I-444
Boris, Saint
GE:A&M III-1205
Borja y Doms, Rodrigo de. *See* Alexander VI, Pope
Bork, Robert H.
GE:B&C III-970
GE:HR IV-2124
Borlaug, Norman E.
GE:B&C III-1133
GE:HR III-1515
Borman, Frank
GE:S&T IV-1803
Bormann, Martin Ludwig
GE:ME III-1522
Born, Max
GE:S&T II-851
Borodin, Aleksandr
GL:Ren I-242
Borromini, Francesco
GL:Ren I-248
Borsini, Fred
GE:B&C IV-1721
Borton, Hugh
GE:HR II-725
Bosch, Carl
GE:S&T I-385
Bosch, Hieronymus
GL:Ren I-253
Bose, Subhas Chandra
GE:HR I-447
Bosley, Tom
GE:A&C V-2305
Boso
GE:A&M III-1291
Bossuet, Jacques-Bénigne
GL:Ren I-259
Boström, Erik Gustaf
GE:ME III-1164
Boswell, James
GL:B&C I-320

Botha, Louis
  GE:ME II-1128
  GE:W20 I-87
  GL:20 I-240
Botha, Pieter Willem
  GE:HR IV-1937, 2008, V-2244, 2304, 2559
Bothe, Walther
  GE:S&T III-973
  GL:20 I-245
Botterill, Joyce A. *See* Carne, Judy
Botticelli, Sandro
  GE:A&M III-1723, 1766
  GL:Ren I-264
Bottomley, Horatio W.
  GL:B&C I-326
Boubacar, Diallo Telli
  GE:HR III-1194
Boudin, Eugène
  GE:A&C II-718
Bougainville, Louis-Antoine de
  GL:Ren I-269
Boulanger, Georges Ernest Jean Marie
  GE:ME II-1053
Boulanger, Nadia
  GE:A&C I-508, II-561
Boule, Marcellin
  GE:S&T I-428
Boulez, Pierre
  GE:A&C IV-1656
  GL:20 I-250
Boult, Sir Adrian
  GE:A&C I-90
Boulton, Matthew
  GE:ME I-460
  GL:B&C I-332
Boumedienne, Houari
  GE:HR III-1155
Bourassa, Robert
  GE:HR III-1543
Bourbon, Duke of. *See* Charles, Duke of Bourbon
Bourbon, Antoine de
  GE:ME I-162
Bourbon, Henry I de. *See* Henry, Prince of Condé
Bourbon, Louis I de. *See* Louis, Prince of Condé
Bourbon, Louis-Antoine-Henri de. *See* Enghien, Duc d'
Bourgault, Pierre
  GE:W20 II-820
Bourgeois, Léon
  GE:HR I-270
Bourgeois, Léon Victor Auguste
  GE:ME II-1123, III-1289
Bourgeois, Louise
  GL:AmW I-232

Bourguiba, Habib
  GL:20 I-257
Bourke-White, Margaret
  GE:A&C II-1031
  GL:AmW I-237
Bouvin, J. A.
  GE:HR I-345
Bouyssonie, A.
  GE:S&T I-428
Bouyssonie, J.
  GE:S&T I-428
Boven, Theo C. van
  GE:HR IV-2146
Boveri, Theodor
  GE:S&T I-148, 153
Bowen, Ira Sprague
  GE:S&T II-694
Bowles, Chester
  GE:Am III-1759
  GE:B&C II-833
Bowron, Fletcher
  GE:HR II-624
Box, John
  GE:HR I-377
Boycott, Arthur Edwin
  GE:S&T I-365
Boyd, William Clouser
  GE:S&T III-1373
Boyer, Herbert
  GE:B&C IV-1616
  GE:S&T V-1987
Boyle, Robert
  GL:B&C I-337
Bracciolini, Giovanni Francesco Poggio. *See* Poggio
Bracewell, Ronald
  GE:S&T IV-1902
Bracton, Henry de
  GE:A&M II-784
  GL:B&C I-343
Brademas, John
  GE:HR IV-1731, 1780
Bradford, David
  GE:Am I-377
Bradford, Gamaliel
  GE:HR I-7
Bradford, William
  GE:Am I-74
  GL:Am I-275
Bradley, F. H.
  GL:B&C I-348
Bradley, Omar N.
  GE:Am III-1720, 1748, 1783
  GE:ME III-1496

GE:W20 II-577
GL:Am I-280
Bradley, Richard
  GE:Am I-188
Bradman, Donald G.
  GL:B&C I-354
Bradstreet, Anne
  GL:AmW I-242
Bradstreet, Simon
  GE:Am I-169
Bradwardine, Thomas
  GE:A&M III-1614
Brady, Mathew B.
  GL:Am I-285
Brady, Nicholas
  GE:B&C V-1953
Braga, Teófilo
  GE:ME III-1219
Braganza, Duke of. See John, Duke of Braganza
Bragg, Braxton
  GE:Am II-997
Bragg, Sir Lawrence
  GE:S&T II-517, III-1336
  GL:B&C I-358
Bragg, Sir William Henry
  GE:S&T I-118, II-517
Brahe, Tycho
  GE:ME I-236
  GE:S&T V-2351
  GL:Ren I-274
Brahic, André
  GE:S&T V-2211
Brahm, Otto
  GE:A&C I-145
Brahmagupta
  GL:A&M I-375
Brahms, Johannes
  GL:Ren I-279
Braille, Louis
  GL:Ren I-284
Brainard, Morgan Bulkeley
  GE:B&C III-964
Braine, John
  GE:A&C III-1454
Bramah, Joseph
  GE:ME I-524
Bramante, Donato
  GL:Ren I-289
Branch, Elmer
  GE:W20 III-1279
Brancusi, Constantin
  GL:20 I-263
Brand, Max. See Faust, Frederick

Brandeis, Louis D.
  GE:Am III-1369, 1405
  GE:B&C I-269, 275, 282, II-635
  GE:HR I-36, 172
  GL:Am I-292
Brandenberger, Jacques Edwin
  GE:S&T I-238
Brando, Marlon
  GE:A&C III-1164, 1487, V-2265
Brandt, Willy
  GE:B&C IV-1549
  GE:HR III-1125
  GE:ME III-1624, 1690
  GE:W20 III-1167
  GL:20 I-269
Branley, Édouard
  GE:ME II-1080
Brannan, Samuel
  GE:Am III-812
Brannum, Hugh
  GE:A&C IV-1678
Brant, Joseph
  GE:Am I-383
  GL:Am I-299
Branting, Karl Hjalmar
  GE:HR I-345
Braque, Georges
  GE:A&C I-204, 337
  GL:20 I-275
Brattain, Walter H.
  GE:S&T III-1304, IV-1528
  GE:W20 II-612
Brauchitsch, Heinrich Alfred Hermann
    Walther von
  GE:W20 I-375, 450
Braudel, Fernand
  GL:20 I-281
Brauer, Richard
  GE:S&T V-2130
Braun, Wernher von
  GE:Am III-1940
  GE:S&T III-1235, IV-1545, 1583, 1698
  GE:W20 II-741, 776, 934
  GL:Am I-305
Bravais, Auguste
  GE:S&T II-517
Bray, Count
  GE:ME II-963
Breakspear, Nicholas. See Adrian IV
Brecht, Bertolt
  GE:A&C II-724, III-1410, IV-2005
  GL:20 I-286
Breckinridge, John Cabell
  GE:Am II-935

Breech, Ernest Robert
  GE:B&C III-1087
Breeden, Richard C.
  GE:B&C V-1991
Breedlove, Sarah. *See* Walker, Madam C. J.
Breen, Robert
  GE:A&C II-1016
Brennan, William J., Jr.
  GE:B&C IV-1704, V-1915
  GE:HR III-1628, IV-1697, 2029, V-2320
  GE:W20 III-1279
Brent, Charles Henry
  GE:ME III-1550
Brentano, Lujo
  GE:ME II-1028
Breton, André
  GE:A&C II-604, 750
  GL:20 I-291
Breuer, Josef
  GE:ME III-1139
  GL:20 I-297
Breuer, Lee
  GE:A&C V-2571
Breuer, Marcel
  GE:A&C IV-2064
Breugel, Willem Johannes van. *See* Van Breugel,
  Willem Johannes
Breuil, Henri-Édouard-Prosper
  GE:S&T III-1176
  GL:20 I-303
Brewer, Dr. Francis Beattie
  GE:Am II-912
Brewster, William
  GE:Am I-74
Brezhnev, Leonid Ilich
  GE:B&C III-1287
  GE:HR III-1177, 1408, 1441, 1662, IV-1764,
    1806, 1852, 1909, 1915, 1949, 2062, 2152,
    V-2298
  GE:ME III-1666
  GE:W20 II-974, 988, 1050, 1054, III-1257
  GL:20 I-308
Briand, Aristide
  GE:Am III-1531
  GE:HR I-423
  GE:ME III-1143
  GE:W20 I-197
Brice, Fanny
  GL:AmW I-247
Bricklin, Daniel
  GE:B&C IV-1687
Bricklin, Malcolm N.
  GE:B&C V-1898
Brickman, Marshall
  GE:A&C V-2381

Brico, Antonia
  GL:AmW I-252
Bridge, Herbert
  GE:S&T IV-1708
Bridger, James
  GE:Am II-812
Bridges, Calvin Blackman
  GE:S&T I-407
  GE:W20 I-7
Bridges, Harry
  GE:HR I-486
Bridgman, Percy Williams
  GL:Am I-310
Briggs, Geoffrey Arthur
  GE:S&T V-1944
Bright, John
  GE:ME II-764, 929
  GL:B&C I-364
Brill, A. A.
  GE:A&C I-19
Brindley, James
  GL:B&C I-370
Brinkley, Parke C.
  GE:B&C IV-1460
Brinster, Ralph
  GE:S&T V-2154
Briscoe, Benjamin
  GE:B&C II-533
Britten, Benjamin
  GE:A&C III-1296
  GL:B&C I-374
Broca, Paul
  GE:ME II-822
Broccoli, Albert R. "Cubby"
  GE:A&C IV-1913
Brock, William
  GE:B&C IV-1595
Brod, Max
  GE:A&C I-396
Broda, Christian
  GE:HR V-2414
Broder, Samuel
  GE:S&T V-2382
Broderick, Joseph
  GE:B&C II-603
Broderick, Matthew
  GE:A&C V-2537
Brodribb, John Henry. *See* Irving, Henry
Broglie, Louis de
  GE:S&T II-590, 741, 851, III-958, 1293
  GE:W20 I-166
  GL:20 I-313
Bronson, Charles
  GE:A&C IV-1984

Bronstein, Leib Darydovich. *See* Trotsky, Leon
Bronstein, Lev Davidovich. *See* Trotsky, Leon
Brook, Peter
  GE:A&C IV-1888, 2005
Brooke, Alan Francis. *See* Alanbrooke, First
  Viscount
Brooks, Cleanth
  GE:A&C III-1169
Brooks, Gwendolyn
  GL:AmW I-256
Brooks, Henry Sands
  GE:A&C I-24
Brooks, James L.
  GE:A&C V-2218, 2652
Brooks, John E.
  GE:A&C I-24
Brooks, Richard
  GE:A&C IV-1650
Brooks, Romaine
  GL:AmW I-261
Brooks, Steven K.
  GE:HR III-1555
Broom, Robert
  GE:S&T II-780
  GE:W20 I-218
Broome, Earl of. *See* Kitchener, Lord
Broome, G. Calvin
  GE:S&T V-2052
Broonzy, "Big Bill"
  GE:A&C I-252
Brother Angelo. *See* Angelo, Brother
Brother Giles. *See* Giles, Brother
Brother Leo. *See* Leo, Brother
Brother Rufino. *See* Rufino, Brother
Brothers, Joyce
  GL:AmW I-266
Brotman, Jeffrey H.
  GE:B&C IV-1621
Brougham, Henry
  GE:ME II-654, 715, 799
  GL:B&C I-383
Broughton, Hugh
  GE:ME I-241
Brouwer, L. E. J.
  GE:S&T I-228
Brown, Charles L.
  GE:B&C V-1821
Brown, Edmund G. "Pat"
  GE:Am III-1912
  GE:HR III-1301
Brown, George
  GL:B&C I-389
Brown, George E., Jr.
  GE:B&C IV-1567

Brown, George H.
  GE:B&C IV-1374
Brown, Gilbert John
  GE:S&T V-2099
  GE:W20 III-1324
Brown, Gordon
  GE:B&C III-1128
Brown, Helen Gurley
  GL:AmW I-270
Brown, Helen Hayes. *See* Hayes, Helen
Brown, Henry Billings
  GE:Am II-1261, 1318
Brown, J. A.
  GE:Am II-766
Brown, James
  GE:A&C IV-2059
Brown, Jerry
  GE:HR III-1567
Brown, John
  GE:Am II-889, 918
  GL:Am I-315
Brown, John Mason
  GE:A&C I-343
Brown, Joyce
  GE:HR IV-2226
Brown, Lancelot
  GL:B&C I-394
Brown, Lesley
  GE:S&T V-2099
  GE:W20 III-1324
Brown, Louise Joy
  GE:W20 III-1324
Brown, Margaret Wise
  GL:AmW I-275
Brown, Moses
  GE:Am I-362
Brown, Prentiss M.
  GE:B&C II-833
Brown, Rachel Fuller
  GL:AmW I-280
Brown, Rita Mae
  GL:AmW I-285
Brown, Samuel
  GE:ME II-1033
Brown, Trisha
  GE:A&C V-2480
Brown, Vandiver
  GE:HR V-2274
Brown, William H., III
  GE:HR III-1650
Browne, Byron
  GE:A&C II-1001
Brownell, Frank A.
  GE:B&C I-11

Brownell, Herbert
  GE:HR II-997, 1003
Browning, Roy
  GE:S&T V-2245
Browning, Tod
  GE:A&C II-863
Brownlow, Kevin
  GE:A&C II-642
Brownson, Orestes Augustus
  GE:Am I-654
Broz, Josip. *See* Tito
Bruce, Edward
  GE:A&C II-995
Bruce, James
  GL:B&C I-400
Bruce, Nigel
  GE:A&C III-1131
Bruce, Robert
  GL:B&C I-404
Bruce, Victor Alexander (Ninth Earl of Elgin)
  GE:W20 I-14
Bruckner, Anton
  GL:Ren I-294
Bruegel, Pieter (the Elder)
  GL:Ren I-300
Brueys, F. P.
  GE:ME I-538
Brugha, Cathal
  GE:ME III-1314
Brundage, Avery
  GE:HR IV-1685
Brunel, Isambard Kingdom
  GL:B&C I-413
Brunel, Marc Isambard
  GE:ME I-524, II-834
  GL:B&C I-419
Brunelleschi, Filippo
  GE:A&M III-1665, 1691
  GL:Ren I-305
Bruni, Leonardo
  GL:Ren I-310
Brüning, Heinrich
  GE:W20 I-276
Brunner, Alois
  GE:HR V-2370
Brunner, Emil
  GE:Am III-1604
  GL:20 I-317
Bruno of Egisheim. *See* Leo IX, Pope
Bruno, Giordano
  GL:Ren I-314
Brunswick, Duke of. *See* Karl Wilhelm Ferdinand
Bryan, William Jennings
  GE:Am II-1268, 1273, III-1432, 1549

GE:W20 I-121
  GL:Am I-322
Bryant, Louise
  GL:AmW I-290
Bryant, William Cullen
  GE:Am I-481
  GL:Am I-328
Bryce, Viscount James
  GE:W20 I-107
Bryson, William C.
  GE:HR V-2443
Bryukhanov, Viktor
  GE:S&T V-2321
Brzezinski, Zbigniew
  GE:HR IV-1903, 1943
Buber, Martin
  GL:20 I-323
Bucer, Martin
  GE:ME I-116
  GL:Ren I-319
Buch, Gunther
  GE:A&C IV-2126
Buchanan, George
  GE:ME I-224
Buchanan, James
  GE:Am II-889, 906, 946, 962, 974
  GL:Am I-333
Buchanan, James M.
  GE:B&C III-931
Buchanan, Judd
  GE:HR IV-1876
Buchinsky, Charles. *See* Bronson, Charles
Büchner, Georg
  GE:A&C II-680
Buck, Pearl S.
  GL:AmW I-295
Buckingham, First Duke of
  GE:ME I-224, 259, 263
  GL:B&C I-424
Buckland, William
  GE:ME II-678
Buckley, William F., Jr.
  GE:A&C IV-1683
  GE:Am III-1861
Buddha
  GL:A&M I-380
Buergenthal, Thomas
  GE:HR III-1503
Buffalo Bill. *See* Cody, William Frederick
Buffington, Joseph
  GE:B&C I-346
Buffon, Comte de
  GL:Ren I-325

Bukharin, Nikolai Ivanovich
GE:A&C II-908
GE:B&C I-374, II-563
GE:ME III-1304, 1329
GE:W20 I-336
GL:20 I-328
Bukovsky, Vladimir
GE:HR IV-1926
Bulan
GE:A&M III-1334
Bulfinch, Charles
GL:Am I-338
Bulganin, Nikolai Aleksandrovich
GE:ME III-1589
GE:W20 II-715, 721
Bulkley, Robert J.
GE:B&C II-781
Bull, Francis A.
GE:S&T III-1260
Bull, William
GE:Am I-213
Bullock, Anna Mae. See Turner, Tina
Bülow, Bernhard von
GE:ME III-1202, 1207
GE:W20 I-46
GL:20 I-332
Bultmann, Rudolf
GL:20 I-337
Bulwer, Sir Henry
GE:ME II-818
Bunau-Varilla, Philippe Jean
GE:Am II-1339
GE:HR I-25
Bunche, Ralph
GE:HR II-814
GL:Am I-344
Bundmann, Emil Anton. See Mann, Anthony
Bundy, McGeorge
GE:Am III-1888
Bunn, C. W.
GE:S&T III-1240
Buñuel, Luis
GE:A&C II-750, III-1179, V-2310
GL:20 I-341
Bunyan, John
GL:B&C I-429
Buonarroti, Michelangelo. See Michelangelo
Buoninsegna, Duccio di. See Duccio di
Buoninsegna
Burali-Forti, Cesare
GE:S&T I-184
Burbage, Richard
GE:ME I-208

Burbank, Luther
GL:Am I-349
Burbidge, Margaret
GE:S&T IV-1757
Burch, Dean
GE:B&C IV-1658
Burchard, Samuel D.
GE:Am II-1140
Burchenal, John J.
GE:B&C I-330
Burckhardt, Jacob
GL:Ren I-330
Burdett, Sir Francis
GE:ME II-669
Burdett, Henry
GE:B&C III-885
Burel, Léonce-Henry
GE:A&C II-642
Burgee, John
GE:A&C V-2407
Burger, Warren E.
GE:B&C IV-1495, V-1778, 1915
GE:HR IV-1617, 1628, 1703, 2029, 2141
GE:W20 I-513, III-1154, 1174
Burgess, Ernest W.
GE:Am III-1357
Burgh, Hubert de
GL:B&C I-435
Burghley, Lord. See Cecil, William
Burghoff, Gary
GE:A&C V-2271
Burgoyne, John
GE:Am I-277
Burgoyne, Paul S.
GE:S&T V-2346
Burgundio of Pisa
GE:A&M II-1111
Buridan, Jean
GL:A&M I-384
GE:A&M III-1614
Burkan, Nathan
GE:A&C I-379
GE:B&C I-252
Burke, Bernard
GE:S&T IV-1492
Burke, Edmund
GE:Am I-241
GL:B&C I-441
Burke, James E.
GE:B&C V-1837
Burke, Thomas
GE:Am I-288
Burks, Arthur Walter
GE:S&T III-1213

Burleson, Albert S.
   GE:B&C I-357
Burlingame, Byers A.
   GE:B&C III-1190
Burliuk, David Davidovich
   GE:A&C I-320
Burliuk, Vladimir Davidovich
   GE:A&C I-320
Burnell, Enid. *See* Lyons, Dame Enid Muriel
Burnell, Jocelyn. *See* Bell, Jocelyn
Burnet, Sir Macfarlane
   GE:S&T IV-1517
   GL:B&C I-446
Burnett, Carol
   GL:AmW I-300
Burnett, Charles
   GE:A&C V-2565
Burney, Charles
   GL:B&C I-451
Burnham, Daniel Hudson
   GE:Am II-1231
   GL:Am I-355
Burnham, James
   GE:A&C IV-1683
Burns, Allan
   GE:A&C V-2218
Burns, Arthur
   GE:B&C IV-1483
   GE:W20 III-1097
Burns, E. L. M.
   GE:ME III-1589
Burns, George
   GE:A&C II-828
Burns, John
   GE:HR I-58
Burns, Ken
   GE:A&C V-2657
Burns, Ric
   GE:A&C V-2657
Burns, Robert
   GL:B&C I-456
Burr, Aaron
   GE:Am I-350, 426, 456, 461
   GL:Am I-360
Burrhus
   GE:A&M II-696
Burritt, Elihu
   GE:Am I-642
Burroughs, William S.
   GE:A&C III-1460
Burton, LeVar
   GE:A&C V-2397
Burton, Sir Richard Francis
   GL:B&C I-463

Burton, William Merriam
   GE:S&T II-573
Busch, Adolphus
   GE:ME II-1100
Busch, Hans
   GE:S&T III-958
Bush, Al
   GE:B&C III-925
Bush, George
   GE:B&C IV-1727, V-1991, 2028, 2034, 2072
   GE:HR V-2364, 2397, 2443, 2455, 2564,
      2595, 2600
Bush, Vannevar
   GE:Am III-1692
   GE:S&T II-846
   GE:W20 I-389
Bushnell, David
   GE:Am I-267
Busoni, Ferruccio
   GE:A&C I-166, 292, II-724, III-1629
Buster, John E.
   GE:S&T V-2235
Bustillo, Maria
   GE:S&T V-2235
Bute, Earl of. *See* Stuart, John
Buthelezi, Mangosuthu Gatsha
   GE:HR V-2606
   GE:W20 III-1272
Butler, Benjamin F.
   GE:Am II-1140
Butler, Harold B.
   GE:HR I-281, III-1509
Butler, Josephine
   GE:HR I-30
Butler, Michael
   GE:A&C IV-2121
Butler, Nicholas Murray
   GE:A&C I-407
   GL:Am I-366
Butler, Pierce
   GE:B&C II-431
Butler, R. A.
   GL:B&C I-468
Butor, Michel
   GE:A&C III-1481
Buxton, Charles Lee
   GE:HR III-1290
Buxton, Thomas Fowell
   GE:ME II-715
   GL:B&C I-475
Buzzi, Ruth
   GE:A&C IV-2115
Byers, William Newton
   GE:Am II-1104

Byrd, Harry F.
    GE:B&C III-1175
Byrd, Richard E.
    GL:Am I-373
Byrd, Robert C.
    GE:B&C V-2034
    GE:HR IV-1812
    GE:W20 III-1331
Byrd, William
    GL:B&C I-480

Byrne, Ethel
    GE:HR I-184
Byrne, Jane
    GL:AmW I-304
Byrnes, James F.
    GE:Am III-1680, 1753, 1776
    GE:B&C II-820, 833
    GE:ME III-1512, 1526
    GE:W20 II-591, 647
Byron, Lord
    GL:B&C I-487

C

Caballero, Bernardino
  GE:HR I-533
Caballero, Francisco Largo. *See* Largo Caballero,
  Francisco
Cabata, Giovanni. *See* Cabot, John
Cabeza de Vaca, Álvar Núñez
  GE:Am I-40
Cabot, George
  GE:Am I-517
Cabot, John
  GE:Am I-23
  GL:Am I-378
Cabot, Sebastian
  GE:Am I-23
Cabral, Amilcar
  GE:ME III-1673
Cabreira, Colonel Sebastian de Brito
  GE:ME II-645
Cabrel, Luiz
  GE:B&C IV-1589
Cabrillo, Juan Rodríguez
  GE:Am I-272
Cabrini, Frances Xavier
  GL:AmW I-309
Cachin, Françoise
  GE:A&C V-2588
Cadman, John
  GE:B&C I-351, II-551
Cadogan, Sir Alexander
  GE:HR II-584
Cadwallon
  GE:A&M II-1081
Cady, Elizabeth. *See* Stanton, Elizabeth Cady
Caecilian
  GE:A&M II-857
Caesar Augustus. *See* Augustus
Caesar, Julius
  GE: A&M I-516, 531, 536, 541, II-584, 616
  GL:A&M I-390
Caesar, Lucius Julius
  GE:A&M I-506
Caeso, Duillius. *See* Duillius, Caeso
Caetani, Benedict. *See* Boniface VIII, Pope
Caetano, Marcello Jose De Neves Alves
  GE:ME III-1673
Caffey, Francis G.
  GE:B&C III-869
Caffey, John
  GE:HR IV-1752

Cage, John
  GE:A&C III-1546, IV-1955, 1979, 2011
Cagney, James
  GE:A&C II-839
Cahill, Holger
  GE:A&C II-995
Caiaphas, Joseph
  GE:A&M II-601
Cajetan, Cardinal Thomas
  GE:ME I-54
Calderón de la Barca, Pedro. *See* Barca, Pedro
  Calderón de la
Calderwood, Stanford
  GE:A&C IV-2168
Caldwell, Sarah
  GL:AmW I-314
Calhoun, John
  GE:Am II-889
Calhoun, John C.
  GE:Am I-539, 546, 558, 607, 648, 660, II-690,
    702, 748, 854
  GL:Am I-383
Caliari, Paolo. *See* Veronese, Paolo
Calixtus II
  GE:A&M III-1257, 1318
Callaghan, James
  GE:HR III-1485
Callendar, G. S.
  GE:S&T III-1118
Calles, Plutarco Elías
  GE:W20 I-69
  GL:20 I-346
Calley, William L.
  GE:HR III-1555
Callicrates
  GE:A&M I-276
Callimachus
  GL:A&M I-396
Callistus (Freedman)
  GE:A&M II-621
Callistus (Pope)
  GE:A&M II-762
Calmette, Albert
  GE:S&T II-705
  GL:20 I-351
Calvert, Cecilius (Second Lord Baltimore)
  GE:Am I-115
Calvert, George (First Lord Baltimore)
  GE:Am I-115

Calvert, Leonard
  GE:Am I-115
Calvin, John
  GE:ME I-116
  GE:W20 I-38
  GL:Ren I-340
Calvin, Melvin
  GE:S&T IV-1703
Camargo, Alberto Lleras
  GE:HR II-755, 879
Cambacérès, Jean-Jacques-Régis de
  GL:Ren I-345
Cambio, Arnolfo di. See Arnolfo di Cambio
Cambó, Francisco
  GE:ME III-1259
Cambon, Jules
  GE:HR I-287
Cambon, Pierre Paul
  GE:ME III-1152
Cameron, George Harvey
  GE:S&T II-694
Camões, Luís de
  GL:Ren I-350
Campbell, Charles J.
  GE:S&T IV-1714
Campbell, Henry H.
  GE:ME III-1254
Campbell, John (Earl of Loudon)
  GE:Am I-200
Campbell, John W., Jr.
  GE:A&C III-1094, IV-1883
Campbell, Kim
  GL:AmW I-319
Campbell, Walter Gilbert
  GE:B&C II-787
Campbell, William Wallace
  GE:S&T II-785
Campbell-Bannerman, Sir Henry
  GE:ME III-1192
Camphausen, Ludolf
  GE:ME II-790
Campion, Edmund
  GE:ME I-174
Campochiaro, Duke of
  GE:ME II-638
Campos, Arsenio Martínez
  GE:ME II-1003
Camus, Albert
  GE:A&C III-1174, 1573, IV-1742, 1812
  GE:W20 I-252
  GL:20 I-356
Can Grande della Scala. See Della Scala, Can
  Grande
Canal, Giovanni Antonio. See Canaletto

Canaletto
  GL:Ren I-355
Canby, Henry Seidel
  GE:A&C II-686
  GE:B&C II-504
Candau, Marcolino Gomes
  GE:HR III-1644
Candela, Felix
  GL:20 I-361
Candy, John
  GE:A&C V-2527
Caneva, Carlo
  GE:ME III-1228
Canham, Erwin D.
  GE:A&C I-209
Canisius, Peter
  GE:ME I-96
Cann, J. R.
  GE:S&T IV-1718
Cannell, Stephen Joseph
  GE:A&C V-2330
Canning, George
  GE:Am I-505, 593
  GE:ME II-654, 715
  GL:B&C I-492
Canning, Stratford (Viscount de Redcliffe)
  GE:ME II-794, 813, 818
Cannon, Annie Jump
  GL:AmW I-324
Cannon, Bishop James
  GE:Am III-1566
Cannon, Joseph
  GE:Am III-1390
  GE:B&C I-168
Cannon, Walter Bradford
  GE:S&T III-1336
Cano, Melchor
  GE:ME I-96
Canova, Antonio
  GL:Ren I-361
Canrobert, François Certain
  GE:ME II-813
Cansino, Margarita Carmen. See Hayworth, Rita
Canterbury, Robert H.
  GE:HR III-1532
Cantor, Eddie
  GE:A&C II-828
Cantor, Georg
  GE:S&T I-143, 184, 233, IV-1751
Cantwell, Nigel
  GE:HR V-2529
Canudo, Ricciotto
  GE:A&C II-642

Canuleius, Gaius
    GE:A&M I-281
Canute the Great
    GL:B&C I-497
Canutt, Yakima
    GE:A&C III-1115
Cão, Diogo
    GE:ME I-11
Čapek, Karel
    GL:20 I-366
Capel, Arthur "Boy"
    GE:A&C I-474
Capella-Pavlovsky, Martine
    GE:S&T V-2205
Capet, Hugh
    GE:A&M III-1200
Capone, Alphonse "Al"
    GE:Am III-1507
Capper, Arthur
    GE:B&C II-690
Capra, Frank
    GE:A&C II-822, 833, 951, III-1335
Capron, Alexander Morgan
    GE:HR IV-2090
Caraway, Hattie W.
    GE:HR I-190
Carden, Sir Sackville Hamilton
    GE:W20 I-129
Cárdenas, Lázaro
    GL:20 I-371
Cardona, José Miró
    GE:W20 II-926
Cardozo, Benjamin Nathan
    GE:B&C II-608
    GL:Am I-389
Carey, Hugh L.
    GE:HR IV-1961
Carey, James Barron
    GE:W20 II-730
Caritat, Marie-Jean-Antoine-Nicolas. *See*
    Condorcet, Marquis de
Carl XVI Gustaf
    GE:A&C V-2423
Carleton, Guy
    GL:B&C I-504
Carlos I
    GE:ME III-1219
Carlos I, Don
    GE:ME II-726
Carlota (Marie Charlotte Ámelie Augustine
    Victoire Clémentine Léopoldine)
    GE:ME II-876
Carlson, Chester F.
    GE:W20 I-382

Carlstadt, Andreas
    GE:ME I-76
Carlyle, Thomas
    GL:B&C I-510
Carmichael, Stokely
    GE:Am III-1861
    GE:HR III-1348
Carnap, Rudolf
    GL:20 I-376
Carnarvon, George Edward Stanhope Molyneux
    Herbert, Fifth Earl of
    GE:S&T II-730
Carne, Judy
    GE:A&C IV-2115
Carné, Marcel
    GE:A&C IV-1742
Carneades
    GE:A&M I-471
Carnegie, Andrew
    GE:Am II-1167
    GE:B&C I-29
    GE:HR I-41
    GE:S&T III-1325
    GL:Am I-394
Carnegie, Dale
    GE:A&C II-1048
Carnes, Howard
    GE:B&C IV-1647
Carney, Art
    GE:A&C IV-1673
Carnot, Nicolas Léonard Sadi
    GE:ME II-1100
Carnovsky, Morris
    GE:A&C II-874
Carol II, of Hohenzollern-Sigmaringen
    GE:W20 I-444
Carothers, Wallace Hume
    GE:B&C II-798
    GE:S&T III-1055
Carpenter, M. Scott
    GE:S&T IV-1723, 1792
Carpentier, Alejo
    GE:A&C IV-2086
Carpini, Giovanni da Pian del
    GL:A&M I-400
Carr, Gerald P.
    GE:S&T V-1997
Carr, Michael
    GE:W20 III-1294
Carr, Robert
    GE:ME I-224
Carrà, Carlo
    GE:A&C I-235
Carracci, Agostino. *See* Carracci family, The

Carracci, Annibale. *See* Carracci family, The
Carracci, Ludovico. *See* Carracci family, The
Carracci family, The
  GL:Ren I-366
Carranza, Venustiano
  GE:Am III-1438
  GE:HR I-196
  GE:W20 I-69
Carrascaloã, Mário Viegas
  GE:HR IV-1835
Carrasco, Sergeant
  GE:S&T II-491
Carrel, Alexis
  GE:S&T I-134, 275, II-512
Carrero Blanco, Luis. *See* Blanco, Luis Carrero
Carrillo, Santiago
  GE:HR IV-1921
Carroll, Charles
  GE:Am I-288, 624
Carroll, James
  GE:S&T I-73
Carroll, Madeleine
  GE:A&C II-946
Carruth, Hayden
  GE:A&C III-1443
Carsey, Marcy
  GE:A&C V-2532
Carson, Anton Julius
  GE:B&C III-1097
Carson, Christopher "Kit"
  GE:Am II-795
  GL:Am I-401
Carson, Sir Edward
  GE:HR I-309
  GE:ME III-1233
Carson, Johnny
  GE:A&C III-1623
Carson, Rachel
  GE:B&C IV-1395, 1416
  GE:S&T IV-1740, V-1982
  GE:W20 I-425, II-542, 942, III-1069
  GL:Am I-408
  GL:AmW I-329
Carter, Howard
  GE:S&T II-730
Carter, James G.
  GE:Am I-576
Carter, Jimmy
  GE:B&C IV-1466, 1555, 1670, 1676, 1682,
    1693, 1699, V-1757, 1763, 1865, 1933
  GE:HR III-1503, IV-1769, 1806, 1903, 1937,
    1943, 1949, 1961, 2003, 2040, 2045, 2084,
    2090, 2106

  GE:W20 I-145, II-872, 988, 1050, 1054,
    III-1235, 1302, 1317, 1331, 1338
  GL:Am I-413
Carter, W. G.
  GE:W20 I-355
Cartier, Jacques
  GE:Am I-28
  GL:B&C I-515
Cartier-Bresson, Henri
  GL:20 I-381
Cartwright, Edmund
  GE:Am I-371
Carty, John J.
  GE:B&C II-470
  GE:S&T II-615
Caruso, Enrico
  GE:A&C I-69
Carver, George Washington
  GL:Am I-420
Carver, John
  GE:Am I-74
Cary, Frank
  GE:B&C V-1809
  GE:S&T V-2169
Cary, Joyce
  GE:A&C IV-1763
Casals, Pablo
  GL:20 I-387
Cascariolo, Vincenzo
  GE:S&T III-1080
Casement, Sir Roger
  GE:HR I-178
Casey, Edward Pearce
  GE:Am II-1279
Casey, Harry Wayne
  GE:A&C V-2386
Casey, Thomas Lincoln
  GE:Am II-1279
Cash, Johnny
  GE:A&C V-2365
Casimir IV Jagiello
  GE:A&M III-1650, 1742
Casimir the Great
  GL:A&M I-406
Caso Yrujo, Marquis of
  GE:Am I-461
Cassatt, Alexander J.
  GE:B&C I-122
Cassatt, Mary
  GL:Am I-425
  GL:AmW I-333
Cassin, René
  GE:HR II-789, 849, III-1353, 1462
  GL:20 I-393

Cassinelli, Joseph Patrick
  GE:S&T V-2164
Cassiodorus
  GE:A&M II-1000, 1046
  GL:A&M I-413
Cassirer, Ernst
  GL:20 I-399
Casson, Dollier de
  GE:S&T IV-1608
  GE:W20 II-783
Castaneda, Jorge
  GE:W20 III-1206
Castelfranco, Giorgio da. See Giorgione
Castelli, Francesco. See Borromini, Francesco
Castelli, Leo
  GE:A&C V-2191, 2438
Castelo Branco, Humberto de Alencar
  GE:HR III-1468
Casteñeda, Jorge Ubico
  GE:B&C III-1040
Castillo, Ramón S.
  GE:HR II-673
Castle, Irene
  GL:AmW I-338
Castle, Lewis Gould
  GE:S&T IV-1608
Castlereagh, Viscount
  GE:Am I-522, 593
  GE:ME II-612, 623, 638, 654
  GL:B&C I-520
Castro, Fidel
  GE:B&C III-1117, 1287
  GE:HR II-1026, 1044, V-2409
  GE:W20 II-743, 926, III-1251, 1317
  GL:20 I-404
Castro, José
  GE:Am II-818
Castro, Raúl
  GE:HR II-1026
Cather, Willa
  GE:A&C I-452
  GL:Am I-431
  GL:AmW I-343
Catherine II, the Great. See Catherine the Great
Catherine de Médicis
  GE:ME I-162, 184, 202
  GL:Ren I-371
Catherine of Aragon
  GE:ME I-103
Catherine of Siena, Saint
  GL:A&M I-417
Catherine the Great
  GE:ME I-414, 456, 464, 469, 475
  GL:Ren I-376

Catherwood, Frederick
  GE:S&T V-2145
Catlin, George
  GL:Am I-438
Cato the Censor
  GE:A&M I-448, 465, 531
  GL:A&M I-423
Cato, "Censorius" Marcus Porcius. See Cato the
  Censor
Caton, Richard
  GE:S&T II-890
Catron, John
  GE:Am II-900
Catt, Carrie Chapman
  GE:Am III-1513
  GE:HR I-190, 339
  GL:AmW I-347
Catullus
  GL:A&M I-429
Cauliaco, Guy de. See Guy de Chauliac
Caussidiére, Maro
  GE:ME II-786
Cavaignac, Louis Eugène
  GE:ME II-786
Cavalcanti, Guido
  GL:A&M I-434
Cavallini, Pietro
  GE:A&M III-1691
Cavanagh, Jerome Patrick
  GE:HR III-1376
Cavelier, René-Robert. See La Salle, Sieur de
Cavendish, Henry
  GL:B&C I-527
Cavendish, Spencer Compton. See Devonshire,
  Duke of
Cavendish, Thomas
  GL:B&C I-533
Cavendish, William (Marquis of Newcastle)
  GE:ME I-313
Cavour, Count
  GL:Ren I-381
Caxton, William
  GE:A&M III-1713
  GL:B&C II-537
Cayley, Sir George
  GL:B&C II-542
Ceausescu, Nicolae
  GE:HR V-2546
Cech, Thomas
  GE:S&T V-2190
Cecil, Lord Robert
  GE:HR I-270, 361
  GE:ME III-1289

Cecil, Robert, (1563-1612). *See* Salisbury, First
  Earl of
Cecil, Robert, (1830-1903). *See* Salisbury, Third
  Marquess of
Cecil, William
  GE:ME I-174
  GL:B&C II-547
Celan, Paul
  GE:A&C IV-2070
Celestine I
  GE:A&M II-914, 952, 969
Celestine V
  GE:A&M III-1592
Celestius
  GE:A&M II-946
Céline, Louis-Ferdinand
  GE:A&C II-890
Celler, Emanuel
  GE:B&C I-35, II-764, III-970, 1229, 1259,
    IV-1364, V-1882
  GE:HR III-1251, 1521
Cellini, Benvenuto
  GL:Ren I-386
Celsus
  GE:A&M II-731
Celsus, Aulus Cornelius
  GL:A&M I-438
Cendrars, Blaise
  GE:A&C I-435
Cerletti, Ugo
  GE:S&T III-1086
Černík, Oldrich
  GE:ME III-1666
Cerularius, Michael
  GE:A&M III-1237
Cervantes, Miguel de
  GE:A&C II-890
  GL:Ren I-392
Cervera y Topete, Admiral Pasqual
  GE:Am II-1284
Césaire, Aimé
  GL:20 I-409
Cesarini, Julian
  GE:A&M III-1708
Cézanne, Paul
  GE:A&C I-204
  GE:Am III-1411
  GL:Ren I-399
Chabrol, Claude
  GE:A&C IV-1710, 1845
Chadwick, Edwin
  GE:ME II-730
  GL:B&C II-552

Chadwick, James
  GE:S&T III-973
  GE:W20 I-246, 283
  GL:B&C II-560
Chafee, John H.
  GE:B&C V-2034
Chagall, Marc
  GE:A&C II-544
  GL:20 I-415
Chaikovsky, Nikolai Vasilievich
  GE:W20 I-152
Chain, Ernst Boris
  GE:ME III-1335
  GE:S&T II-873, III-1171
Chakrabarty, Ananda M.
  GE:B&C V-1778
Chalidze, Valery
  GE:HR III-1549
Challe, General
  GE:ME III-1628
Chamberlain, Austen
  GE:B&C I-218
  GE:HR I-423
Chamberlain, Sir Austen
  GE:W20 I-197
Chamberlain, Houston Stewart
  GE:HR I-389
  GE:ME III-1363
Chamberlain, Joseph
  GE:HR I-453
  GE:ME II-1038, 1128
  GE:W20 I-14, 87
  GL:B&C II-565
Chamberlain, Neville
  GE:HR I-321
  GE:ME III-1429, 1433, 1440
  GL:B&C II-571
Chambers, Julius LeVonne
  GE:HR III-1628
Chambers, Kenneth Carter
  GE:S&T V-2367
Chambers, Robert
  GE:S&T IV-1808
Chambers, Whittaker
  GE:A&C IV-1683
Chamorro, Pedro Joaquin
  GE:HR IV-2035
Chamorro, Violeta Barrios de
  GE:HR IV-2035, V-2564
Chamoun, Camille
  GE:W20 II-748, III-1235
Champlain, Samuel de
  GE:Am I-52
  GL:Am I-443

Chance, Ronald E.
GE:S&T V-2221
Chancellor, Sir John Robert
GE:W20 I-231
Chandler, A. B. "Happy"
GE:HR II-712
Chandler, Chas
GE:A&C IV-2092
Chandler, Otis
GE:B&C IV-1636
Chandler, Robert F., Jr.
GE:B&C III-1133
Chandra, Hareesh
GE:HR IV-2238
Chandrasekhar, Subrahmanyan
GE:S&T II-948, IV-1577
Chanel, Gabrielle "Coco"
GE:A&C I-474
GL:20 I-420
Chaney, James Earl
GE:HR III-1149, 1246
Chang, P. C.
GE:HR II-789
Chang Chih-tung
GE:HR I-1
GL:Ren I-404
Chang Ch'un-ch'iao
GE:W20 III-1264
Chang Hsüeh-liang
GE:W20 I-211
Channing, William Ellery
GE:Am I-570
GL:Am I-448
Chanute, Octave
GE:Am II-1346
GE:S&T I-203
Chapin, Daryl M.
GE:S&T IV-1487
Chaplin, Charles ("Charlie")
GE:A&C I-224, 230, II-659
GE:Am III-1501
GL:Am I-453
Chaplin, Lita Grey
GE:A&C II-659
Chapman, Graham
GE:A&C IV-2174
Chapman, Sydney
GE:S&T III-1035, IV-1577
GE:W20 II-764
Char, René
GE:A&C IV-1656, 2070
Chardin, Jean Siméon
GL:Ren I-409

Charlemagne
GE:A&M II-1136, 1142, 1146, III-1308
GL:A&M I-442
Charles. See Carlos I, Don
GE:ME II-726
Charles I (of Austria)
GE:W20 I-158
Charles I (of England)
GE:ME I-259, 263, 313, 329
GL:B&C II-578
Charles I (of Spain)
GE:ME, I-40, 54, 64, 68, 72, 76, 82, 87, 91,
103, 123, 129, 143, 148, 153, 158
Charles II (of England)
GE:Am I-121, 157
GE:ME I-337
GL:B&C II-583
Charles II (of Spain)
GE:ME I-372
Charles III (of Spain)
GE:ME I-442
GL:Ren I-415
Charles IV, Holy Roman Emperor
GL:A&M I-454
Charles IV of Anjou
GE:A&M III-1733
Charles IV (of Luxemburg)
GE:A&M III-1620, 1635
Charles IV (of Spain)
GE:ME II-581
Charles V, Holy Roman Emperor. See Charles I
(of Spain)
Charles V (of France)
GE:A&M III-1644
Charles V (of Spain)
GL:Ren I-419
Charles VI, Holy Roman Emperor
GE:ME I-400, 405
Charles VII, Holy Roman Emperor
GE:ME I-419
Charles VII of Valois
GE:A&M III-1703, 1733
Charles VIII, of France
GE:ME I-21, 26, 82
Charles VIII of Valois
GE:A&M III-1723
Charles IX, of France
GE:ME I-162, 184
Charles X, of France
GE:ME II-682
Charles XII, of Sweden
GE:ME I-376
GL:Ren I-425

Charles XIV John, of Sweden
GE:ME II-590
GL:Ren I-429
Charles, Archduke of Austria
GE:ME I-372
Charles, Count of Artois
GE:ME II-598
Charles d'Orléans
GL:A&M I-449
Charles, Duke of Bourbon
GE:ME I-82
Charles Martel
GE:A&M II-1117
GL:A&M I-464
Charles of Anjou
GE:A&M III-1496
Charles of Berry
GE:A&M III-1723
Charles of Lannoy
GE:ME I-82
Charles of Lorraine
GE:A&M III-1200
Charles of Luxemburg. *See* Charles IV (of Luxemburg)
Charles of Mayenne
GE:ME I-202
Charles the Bald
GE:A&M II-1158
GL:A&M I-460
Charles the Bold
GE:A&M III-1723
GL:Ren I-434
Charles, Lord Howard of Effingham
GE:ME I-193
Charles, Jacques
GE:A&C II-665
Charles, Jacques Alexandre César
GE:ME I-496
Charles Albert, of Sardinia
GE:ME II-697, 775
Charlone, Cesar
GE:HR II-985
Charren, Peggy
GE:B&C IV-1426, 1658
Chartier, Alain
GL:A&M I-468
Chase, Chevy
GE:A&C V-2355
Chase, Lucia
GE:A&C II-1036
Chase, Salmon P.
GE:Am II-871, 877, 980, 985, 1026
GL:Am I-458

Chase, Samuel
GE:Am I-288
Chase, Stuart
GE:HR I-527
Chashnik, Ilia
GE:A&C I-413
Chateaubriand
GL:Ren I-439
Chatelain, Leon J., Jr.
GE:HR III-1435
Chatfield-Taylor, Hobart C.
GE:A&C I-314
Chaucer, Geoffrey
GE:A&M III-1655
GL:B&C II-589
Chauchoin, Claudette Lily. *See* Colbert, Claudette
Chauhan, Jagmal Singh
GE:HR IV-2215
Chauliac, Guy de. *See* Guy de Chauliac
Chauncy, Charles (Pastor, First Church of Boston)
GE:Am I-176, 570
Chauncy, Charles (President of Harvard College)
GE:Am I-127
Chávez, César
GE:Am III-1866
GE:HR III-1161, 1567
GE:W20 II-842
Chavez, Linda
GL:AmW I-352
Chehab, Fuad. *See* Shehab, Fuad
Chekhov, Anton
GE:A&C I-1
GL:Ren I-445
Chelomei, Vladimir N.
GE:S&T V-1950
Chelvanayakam, S. J. V.
GE:HR II-1090
Ch'en Tu-hsiu
GE:HR I-276
GL:20 I-427
Ch'en Yi. *See* Hsüan-tsang
Chen Yun
GE:B&C III-1003
GE:HR II-1015
Cheney, Richard
GE:B&C IV-1727
Cheng. *See* Ch'in Shih Huang Ti
Cheng Ch'eng-kung
GL:Ren I-450
Cheng Heng
GE:W20 III-1212
Cheng Ho
GL:A&M I-473
Ch'eng-tsu. *See* Yung-lo

43

Cheops
GE:A&M I-25
Cher
GE:A&C V-2244
GL:AmW I-357
Cherenkov, Pavel Alekseyevich
GE:S&T III-1003
Cherwell, Frederick Alexander Lindemann,
Viscount
GE:S&T II-579
Chesnut, Mary Boykin
GL:AmW I-362
Chess, Leonard
GE:A&C IV-1635
Chester, George F.
GE:Am II-1116
Chetverikov, Sergei S.
GE:W20 I-7
Chevalier, Maurice
GE:A&C II-941
Chevalley, Claude
GE:S&T V-2130
Cheves, Langdon
GE:Am I-539
Chevrier, Lionel
GE:S&T IV-1608
GE:W20 II-783
Chiang Ch'ing
GE:W20 III-1264
Chiang Kai-shek
GE:Am III-1764
GE:HR I-474, 539
GE:ME III-1583
GE:W20 I-211, 361, II-654, 690, 709, III-1110
GL:20 I-432
Chia-ni-se-chia. See Kanishka
Ch'iao Kuan-hua
GE:W20 III-1110
Chiappe, Jean
GE:ME III-1386
Chicago, Judy
GL:AmW I-367
Chicheley, Sir Henry
GE:Am I-151
Chichester-Clark, James
GE:HR III-1485
Ch'ien-lung
GL:Ren I-454
Child, Lydia Maria
GE:Am II-719
GL:Am I-465
GL:AmW I-373
Childeric III
GE:A&M II-1121, 1131

Childs, Lucinda
GE:A&C V-2480
Chilowski, Constantin
GE:S&T II-620
Ch'in Shih Huang Ti
GL:A&M I-479
Ch'in Teh-ch'un
GE:W20 I-361
Chinda, Sutemi
GE:HR I-287
Chirac, Jacques
GE:A&C V-2619
GE:B&C IV-1353
Chisholm, G. Brock
GE:HR II-678
Chisholm, Jesse
GE:Am II-1020
Chisholm, Shirley
GE:HR III-1451, 1579
GL:AmW I-378
Chitepo, Herbert
GE:HR III-1224
Chiu, Hong-Lee
GE:W20 II-899
Chlodovech. See Clovis
Chlodwig. See Clovis
Chlopicki, Joséf
GE:ME II-691
Choate, Joseph Hodges
GE:ME II-1123, III-1192
Choh Hao Li
GE:S&T III-1358
Chopin, Frédéric
GL:Ren I-459
Chopin, Kate
GL:AmW II-383
Choquette, Jérôme
GE:HR III-1543
Chosroes. See Khosrow I
Chotzinoff, Samuel
GE:A&C III-1536
Chou En-lai
GE:Am III-1764
GE:ME III-1678
GE:W20 II-654, 709, III-1110, 1124, 1264
GL:20 I-438
Chou Shu-jên. See Lu Hsün
Chrétien de Troyes
GL:A&M II-485
Chrétien, Jean
GE:B&C V-2072
Christ, Jesus. See Jesus Christ
Christian
GE:A&M III-1472

Christian X
  GE:HR II-641
Christian, Charlie
  GE:A&C III-1617
  GE:B&C III-919
Christie, Agatha
  GE:A&C I-496, III-1551
  GL:B&C II-595
Christina
  GE:ME I-294
  GL:Ren I-465
Christine de Pisan
  GL:A&M II-490
Christo
  GE:A&C V-2548
Christopher, Warren
  GE:HR IV-1903
Chrysippus of Soloi
  GE:A&M I-388
Chrysler, Walter P.
  GE:B&C II-533
Chrysorrhoas. See John of Damascus
Chrysostom, Saint John
  GL:A&M II-498
Chu Hi. See Chu Hsi
Chu Hsi
  GL:A&M II-502
Chu Teh
  GE:W20 I-211, III-1264
  GL:20 I-444
Chu Ti. See Yung-lo
Ch'ü Yüan
  GL:A&M II-507
Chuang-tzu
  GL:A&M II-512
Chudakov, Aleksandr
  GE:S&T IV-1614
Chu-fu-tzu. See Chu Hsi
Ch'un, Prince
  GE:W20 I-92
Chung, Connie
  GL:AmW II-388
Church, Alonzo
  GE:S&T II-664, III-1045
Church, Frederick Stuart
  GE:Am I-613
Churchill, H.
  GE:S&T III-1260
Churchill, Harold E.
  GE:B&C III-1190
Churchill, John. See Marlborough, First Duke of
Churchill, Lord Randolph
  GE:ME II-1038

Churchill, Winston
  GE:Am III-1686, 1715, 1736, 1741, 1748,
    1776
  GE:HR I-321, 429, 442, II-567, 584, 612, 657,
    731, 849
  GE:ME III-1223, 1233, 1324, 1420, 1446,
    1451, 1456, 1461, 1467, 1477, 1486, 1491,
    1501, 1507, 1512, 1517, 1526
  GE:W20 I-129, 404, 457, II-577
  GL:B&C II-600
Chu-tzu. See Chu Hsi
Ciano Galeazzo (Ciano di Cortellazzo)
  GE:ME III-1440
Ciccone, Madonna Louise Veronica. See Madonna
Cicero
  GE:A&M I-541
  GL:A&M II-518
Cicero, Marcus Tullius (the Elder)
  GE:A&M I-521, 526, 531, 541, 546
Cicotte, Ed
  GE:Am III-1497
Cid, El
  GE:A&M III-1308
  GL:A&M II-524
Cimabue
  GE:A&M III-1587
  GL:A&M II-529
Cimon
  GE:A&M I-158, 242
  GL:A&M II-533
Cione, Andrea di. See Orcagna, Andrea
Cione, Andrea di Michele. See Verrocchio,
  Andrea del
Cipollone, Antonio
  GE:HR V-2381
Cipollone, Rose
  GE:HR V-2381
Cisneros, Francisco Jiménez de. See Jiménez de
  Cisneros, Francisco
Citrine, Walter
  GE:HR I-429
Citroën, André-Gustave
  GL:20 I-450
Claiborne, Liz
  GL:AmW II-393
Clare, Saint. See Saint Clare
Clarenbach, Kathryn
  GE:W20 II-998
Clarendon, First Earl of
  GE:Am I-121
  GE:ME I-337
  GL:B&C II-605
Claris, Pau
  GE:ME I-299

Clark, Barney
  GE:S&T V-2195
Clark, Carroll
  GE:A&C II-984
Clark, Dick
  GE:B&C III-1148
Clark, Donovan L.
  GE:S&T IV-1645
Clark, E. E.
  GE:Am II-1329
Clark, George Rogers
  GL:Am I-471
Clark, James Beauchamp "Champ"
  GE:Am III-1405
Clark, James G.
  GE:HR III-1278
Clark, Joe
  GE:HR IV-2158
Clark, Joel Bennett "Champ"
  GE:B&C II-845
Clark, Sir Kenneth
  GE:A&C III-1190
Clark, Les
  GE:A&C II-1053
Clark, Mark Wayne
  GE:ME III-1486
Clark, Ramsey
  GE:HR III-1376
Clark, Tom C.
  GE:B&C III-997
  GE:HR III-1262, 1343
  GE:W20 II-949
Clark, Victor S.
  GE:HR II-801
Clark, William, and Meriwether Lewis
  GE:Am I-450
  GL:Am III-1363
Clarke, Arthur C.
  GE:S&T IV-1545, 1728
  GE:W20 II-751
Clarke, Carter W.
  GE:B&C IV-1421
Clarke, Edward Young
  GE:HR I-258, 298
Clarke, John
  GE:Am I-97
Clarke, T. E. B.
  GE:A&C III-1427
Clarke, Thomas
  GE:HR I-178
Claude, Albert
  GE:W20 I-501
Claude, Georges
  GL:20 I-455

Claude Lorrain
  GL:Ren I-470
Claudius I
  GE:A&M II-616, 621
  GL:A&M II-540
Claudius, Appius
  GE:A&M I-253
Claudius Caudex, Appius
  GE:A&M I-408
Claudius Crassus, Appius "Caecus"
  GE:A&M I-373, II-636
Claudius Drusus Germanicus, Nero. See Nero
  Claudius Drusus Germanicus
Claudius Marcellus, Marcus. See Marcellus
Claudius Nero, Tiberius. See Tiberius
Claudius Ptolemaeus. See Ptolemy
Claus, Carl
  GE:S&T I-422
Clausewitz, Carl von
  GL:Ren I-475
Clay, Cassius. See Ali, Muhammad
Clay, Henry
  GE:Am I-505, 522, 582, 593, 607, II-690, 696,
    702, 748, 760, 772, 854
  GL:Am I-476
Clay, John
  GE:Am II-1020
Clay, Lucius D.
  GE:Am III-1794
  GE:HR II-771
  GE:ME III-1543
  GE:W20 II-647
Clay, William
  GE:B&C V-1803
Clayton, Henry D.
  GE:B&C I-275
Clayton, William L.
  GE:B&C III-902
Cleanthes of Assos
  GE:A&M I-388
Clearchus
  GE:A&M I-313
Cleese, John
  GE:A&C IV-2174
Cleisthenes of Athens
  GE:A&M I-205
  GL:A&M II-545
Clemenceau, Georges
  GE:A&C II-718
  GE:Am III-1484
  GE:B&C I-351
  GE:HR I-252, 287
  GE:ME II-984, 1053, III-1283
  GL:20 I-460

Clemens Romanus. *See* Clement I
Clemens, Samuel Langhorne. *See* Twain, Mark
Clemens, Titus Flavius. *See* Flavius Clemens,
   Titus
Clement I, Pope
   GL:A&M II-549
Clement VI, Pope
   GE:A&M III-1620
Clement VII, Pope
   GE:ME I-91, 103
Clement VII, the Avignon Pope
   GE:A&M III-1644
Clement VIII, Pope
   GE:ME I-214, 220, 224
Clement of Alexandria
   GE:A&M II-757, 773, 795, 801
Clement of Rome
   GE:A&M II-669, 681
Clément, Jacques
   GE:ME I-202
Clements, Earle C.
   GE:HR III-1338
Clements, William
   GE:HR V-2512
Clemons, Clarence
   GE:A&C V-2325
Cleomenes
   GE:A&M I-205
Cleopatra VII
   GE:A&M I-551
   GL:A&M II-554
Cleveland, Grover
   GE:Am II-1140, 1157, 1161, 1190, 1237,
      1268, 1273, 1307
   GE:HR I-231
   GL:Am I-483
Clewell, William H.
   GE:S&T V-2174
Clifford, Clark
   GE:Am III-1800
   GE:B&C III-880
   GE:W20 II-1036
Clifford, John M.
   GE:B&C IV-1379
Cline, Patsy
   GL:AmW II-397
Clinton, Bill
   GE:B&C V-2072
Clinton, DeWitt
   GE:Am I-546, 576
   GL:Am I-489
Clinton, Sir Henry
   GE:Am I-277, 294

Clinton, Hillary Rodham
   GL:AmW II-402
Clive, Robert
   GL:B&C II-611
Close, Glenn
   GL:AmW II-407
Clotilde
   GE:A&M II-995
Cloud, Henry Roe
   GE:HR I-121
Clouston, Sir Edward Seaborne
   GE:B&C I-174
Clovis
   GE:A&M II-995, 1005
   GL:A&M II-559
Clurman, Harold
   GE:A&C II-874
Cluseret, Gustave
   GE:ME II-984
Coad, Bert Raymond
   GE:S&T II-640
Coase, Ronald
   GE:B&C III-931
Coasta, Joaquín
   GE:ME II-1119
Cobb, Howell,
   GE:Am II-941
Cobb, Ty
   GL:Am I-497
Cobbett, William
   GE:ME I-424, II-704
   GL:B&C II-617
Cobbold, Baron Cameron Fromanteel
   GE:A&C IV-2131
Cobden, Richard
   GE:ME II-764
   GL:B&C II-622
Coburn, Alvin Langdon
   GE:A&C I-63
Cochran, Jacqueline
   GL:AmW II-412
Cochrane, Sir Alexander Forrester Inglis
   GE:Am I-533
Cockburn, Sir Alexander
   GE:Am II-1072
Cockcroft, Sir John Douglas
   GE:S&T III-978, 1336
Cocteau, Jean
   GE:A&C I-435, 474, 513, II-561, 979
   GL:20 I-468
Coddington, William
   GE:Am I-97

Cody, William Frederick (Buffalo Bill)
  GE:Am II-925
  GL:Am I-502
Coe, Sebastian
  GL:B&C II-627
Coelho, Tony
  GE:B&C V-2028
  GE:HR V-2595
Coffin, Charles A.
  GE:B&C I-17
Cogny, René
  GE:ME III-1577
Cohan, George M.
  GE:A&C I-108
Cohen, Felix
  GE:HR I-497
Cohen, Fritz A.
  GE:A&C II-920
Cohen, Gerson D.
  GE:HR V-2262
Cohen, Judith. *See* Chicago, Judy
Cohen, Paul J.
  GE:S&T IV-1751
Cohen, Stanley Norman
  GE:S&T V-1987
Cohen, Wilbur J.
  GE:HR I-520, III-1435
Cohn, Ferdinand Julius
  GE:ME III-1174
  GL:Ren I-480
Cohn-Bendit, Daniel
  GE:HR III-1425
Coke, Sir Edward
  GE:ME I-224, 263
  GL:B&C II-633
Colbert, Claudette
  GE:A&C II-822, 951
Colbert, Jean-Baptiste
  GE:Am I-52
  GE:ME I-345, 400
  GL:Ren I-484
Colden, Cadwallader
  GE:Am I-194
Cole, Henry
  GE:ME II-799
Cole, Sydney W.
  GE:S&T I-46
Cole, Thomas
  GE:Am I-613
Coleman, J. Marshall
  GE:HR V-2517
Coleman, James S.
  GE:HR IV-1786

Coleman, William T., Jr.
  GE:B&C IV-1606
Coleridge, Samuel Taylor
  GL:B&C II-643
Colet, John
  GL:B&C II-648
Colette
  GL:20 I-473
Colette, Sidonie-Gabrielle. *See* Colette
Coligny, Admiral
  GE:ME I-162
Colin, Paul
  GE:A&C II-665
Colleton, Sir John
  GE:Am I-132
Collier, John
  GE:HR I-497, II-897, III-1573
Collier, William
  GE:Am I-109
Collins, David
  GE:B&C V-1837
Collins, Joseph Lawton
  GE:W20 II-676
Collins, Marva
  GL:AmW II-417
Collins, Michael (Irish revolutionary)
  GE:Am III-1940
  GE:HR I-309
  GE:ME III-1314
Collins, Michael (American astronaut)
  GE:S&T V-1907
Collins, Norman
  GL:B&C II-652
Collins, Tom
  GE:A&C III-1138
Collins, Wayne
  GE:HR V-2392
Collip, James Bertram
  GE:S&T II-720
Colón, Cristóbal. *See* Columbus, Christopher
Colonna, Marco Antonio
  GE:ME I-180
Colt, LeBaron
  GE:HR I-350
Columban
  GE:A&M II-1052
Columbus, Chris
  GE:A&C V-2527
Columbus, Christopher
  GE:A&M III-1756
  GE:Am I-17
  GE:ME I-16
  GL:Ren I-490

Colwell, William Earle
  GE:HR III-1515
Combes, Justin Louis Émile
  GE:ME III-1143
Comden, Betty
  GL:AmW II-422
Commodus, Lucius Aelius Aurelius
  GE:A&M II-725
Commoner, Barry
  GE:W20 II-542
Commons, John Rogers
  GE:Am II-1077
  GE:B&C II-770
Compton, Arthur Holly
  GE:S&T II-694, 746, III-1198
  GL:Am II-507
Compton, Sir Edmund
  GE:HR IV-1720
Comrie, L. D.
  GE:S&T III-1240
Comstock, Anthony
  GE:HR I-184, III-1290
Comte, Auguste
  GE:ME II-803
  GL:Ren I-496
Conant, James Bryant
  GE:Am III-1692
  GE:W20 I-389
  GL:Am II-512
Condé, Prince of. See Henry, Prince of Condé
Condé, Prince of. See Louis, Prince of Condé
Condé, The Great (Louis II de Bourbon)
  GL:Ren I-502
Condell, Henry
  GE:ME I-208
Condillac, Étienne Bonnot de
  GL:Ren I-507
Condon, Edward Uhler
  GE:S&T II-851
Condorcet, Marquis de
  GE:ME I-533
  GL:Ren I-513
Confucius
  GL:A&M II-564
Conley, William Lee. See Broonzy, "Big Bill"
Connally, John
  GE:Am III-1899
  GE:B&C IV-1489
Connally, Tom
  GE:Am III-1741
Conneau, Doctor
  GE:ME II-838
Connery, Lawrence Joseph
  GE:HR I-508

Connery, Sean
  GE:A&C IV-1913
Connolly, James
  GE:HR I-178
Connolly, Maureen
  GL:AmW II-428
Connolly, Walter
  GE:A&C II-951
Connor, John Thomas
  GE:B&C III-1254
Connor, T. Eugene "Bull"
  GE:HR III-1188, 1419
Connors, Chuck
  GE:A&C IV-1768
Conon of Samos
  GE:A&M I-422
Conover, C. Todd
  GE:B&C V-1870
Conrad III
  GE:A&M III-1364
Conrad of Masovia
  GE:A&M III-1472
Conrad, Charles ("Pete")
  GE:S&T IV-1913, V-1997
Conrad, Frank
  GE:A&C I-469
  GE:Am III-1519
  GE:B&C I-363
Conrad, Joseph
  GE:A&C I-51, 96
  GL:B&C II-659
Constable, John
  GL:B&C II-666
Constans
  GE:A&M II-852
Constantine I. See Constantine the Great
Constantine II, King
  GE:HR III-1359, IV-1747
Constantine V
  GE:A&M II-1152
Constantine XI
  GE:A&M III-1718
Constantine, Baron
  GL:B&C II-672
Constantine, Flavius Valerius. See Constantine
  the Great
Constantine, Grand Duke (Nikolaevich)
  GE:ME II-886
Constantine, Grand Duke (Pavlovich)
  GE:ME II-691
Constantine the African
  GE:A&M III-1478

Constantine the Great
GE:A&M II-846, 852, 857, 862, 867, 884,
1121
GL:A&M II-569
Constantius
GE:A&M II-829
Constantius II
GE:A&M II-852
Constantius Chlorus, Flavius Valerius. *See*
Constantius
Contarini, Gaspar
GE:ME I-96
Conti, Prince Piero Ginori
GE:S&T II-547
Cook, A. J.
GE:HR I-429
Cook, Barbara
GE:A&C IV-1752
Cook, Captain James
GL:B&C II-677
Cook, Paul
GE:A&C V-2299, 2360
Cook, William. *See* Tudor, Antony
Cooke, Alistair
GE:A&C IV-2168
Cooke, Jay
GE:Am II-985
GL:Am II-519
Cooke, Juan I.
GE:HR II-918
Cooke, Morris L.
GE:Am II-1627
Cooke, Philip St. George
GE:Am II-818
Cooke, William Fothergill, and Charles
Wheatstone
GL:B&C II-683
Cooley, Charles H.
GE:Am III-1357
Cooley, Thomas M.
GE:Am II-1157
Coolidge, Calvin
GE:Am III-1472, 1525, 1542
GE:B&C II-464, 516
GE:HR I-383
GL:Am II-525
Coolidge, Martha
GE:A&C V-2443
GL:AmW II-432
Coolidge, William D.
GE:B&C I-17
Cooney, Joan Ganz
GE:A&C V-2185

Cooper, Anthony Ashley. *See* Shaftsbury, First
Earl of
Cooper, Francis D'Arcy
GE:B&C I-201
Cooper, Irving Ben
GE:B&C IV-1437
Cooper, James Fenimore
GE:Am I-481
GL:Am II-531
Cooper, Kent
GE:W20 I-1
Cooper, L. Gordon
GE:S&T IV-1723
Cooper, Leon N.
GE:S&T IV-1533
Cooper, Paula
GE:A&C V-2191
Coote, William Alexander
GE:HR I-30
Coowescoowe. *See* Ross, John
Cop, Nicholas
GE:ME I-116
Copeland, Melvin T.
GE:B&C I-157
Copeland, Royal S.
GE:B&C II-787
Copernicus, Nicolaus
GE:ME I-26, 138
GL:Ren I-518
Copland, Aaron
GE:A&C I-508, III-1234, 1284
GL:Am II-538
Copley, John Singleton
GE:ME II-737
GL:Am II-544
Coppola, Francis Ford
GE:A&C V-2265, 2428
Corbin, Abel Rathbone
GE:Am II-1054
Corbusier, Le
GE:A&C II-869, 1021, 1067, III-1503, 1629,
IV-1716, 1919, 2064
GL:20 III-1298
Corea, Chick
GE:A&C IV-2153
Corelli, Arcangelo
GL:Ren I-523
Cori, Gerty
GL:AmW II-437
Corliss, John B.
GE:S&T V-2058
Cormack, Allan M.
GE:S&T V-1961

Corman, James C.
  GE:HR III-1527
Corneille, Pierre
  GL:Ren I-528
Cornelius
  GE:A&M II-812
Cornelius Tacitus. *See* Tacitus, Cornelius
Cornelius, Henry
  GE:A&C III-1427
Cornelius Fronto, Marcus. *See* Fronto, Marcus
  Cornelius
Cornelius Maluginensis, Marcus
  GE:A&M I-253
Cornell, Julien
  GE:A&C III-1443
Cornwall, David John Moore. *See* Le Carré, John
Cornwallis, First Marquess
  GE:Am I-294
  GE:ME II-551
  GL:B&C II-690
Coronado, Francisco Vásquez de
  GL:Am II-550
Correggio
  GL:Ren I-533
Correll, Charles. *See also* "Amos 'n' Andy"
  GE:A&C II-755
Correns, Carl Erich
  GE:S&T I-61, 153, 270
Corrigan, Mairead
  GE:HR IV-1932
Corso, Gregory
  GE:A&C III-1460
Cortázar, Julio
  GE:A&C IV-1689, 2086
Cortelyou, George B.
  GE:B&C I-86
Cortés, Hernán
  GE:ME I-59, 129
  GL:Ren I-538
Corwin, Jonathan
  GE:Am I-169
Cosby, Bill
  GE:A&C IV-2044, V-2532
Cosby, William
  GE:Am I-188
Cosgrave, William T. ("Liam")
  GE:HR IV-1870, 1978
  GL:B&C II-695
Cosimo de Medici. *See* de Medici, Cosimo
Cosmas
  GE:A&M II-1111
Costa, Affonso da
  GE:HR I-287

Costa e Silva, Artur da
  GE:HR III-1468
Coster, Laurens Janszoon
  GE:A&M III-1713
Cotes, Peter
  GE:A&C III-1551
Cottam, Clarence
  GE:S&T IV-1740
Cotton, John
  GE:Am I-85
  GL:Am II-556
Cottrell, Frederick Gardner
  GE:S&T I-320
Coty, René Jules Gustave
  GE:ME III-1607
Coubertin, Pierre de
  GL:20 I-478
Coudert, Frederic René
  GE:Am II-1318
Coughlin, Charles Edward
  GE:Am III-1582
Country Joe and the Fish
  GE:A&C IV-2180
Coup, William C.
  GE:Am II-1066
Couperin, François
  GL:Ren I-544
Courbet, Gustave
  GL:Ren I-549
Couric, Katie
  GL:AmW II-442
Courrèges, André
  GE:A&C IV-1824
Cousins, Morison
  GE:B&C II-863
Cousteau, Jacques-Yves
  GE:S&T III-1219, IV-1792
  GE:W20 II-1069
  GL:20 I-484
Couthon, Georges
  GE:ME I-529
Couveing, John van. *See* Van Couveing, John
Couzens, James
  GE:Am III-1421
  GE:B&C I-234
Cover, Franklin
  GE:A&C V-2339
Coverdale, Miles
  GL:B&C II-700
Covici, Pascal
  GE:A&C III-1138
Covilhã, Pêro da
  GL:Ren I-554

Cowan, Thomas H.
  GE:A&C I-469
Coward, Noël
  GE:A&C II-936
  GL:B&C II-706
Cowell, Henry
  GE:A&C I-425
Cox, Allan V.
  GE:S&T IV-1777
Cox, Archibald
  GE:Am III-1883
  GE:HR III-1262
Cox, Harold
  GE:HR I-356
Cox, Harvey Gallagher, Jr.
  GE:W20 I-507
Cox, James M.
  GE:Am III-1472
Coy, Edwin A.
  GE:S&T V-2245
Craft, Edward B.
  GE:B&C II-470, 545
Craig, Sir James
  GE:HR I-309
Craig, Lyman C.
  GE:S&T IV-1459
Craig, Samuel
  GE:A&C II-686
  GE:B&C II-504
Craig, Thomas
  GE:Am II-1077
Craig, William
  GE:W20 III-1117
Cranach, Lucas (the Elder)
  GL:Ren II-559
Crandall, Prudence
  GL:AmW II-446
Crane, Frederick E.
  GE:HR I-184
Crane, Hart
  GE:A&C II-851
Crane, Stephen
  GE:Am II-1255
  GL:Am II-560
Cranmer, Thomas
  GE:ME I-103, 123, 168
  GL:B&C II-714
Cranston, Alan
  GE:B&C IV-1454
  GE:HR IV-1731
Crassus, Lucius Licinius
  GE:A&M I-521
Crassus, Marcus Licinius
  GE:A&M I-516

Crassus "Caecus," Appius Claudius. *See*
  Claudius, Appius Claudius "Caecus"
Crawford, Cheryl
  GE:A&C II-874
  GL:AmW II-451
Crawford, William H.
  GE:Am I-607
Crawford-Seeger, Ruth
  GL:AmW II-456
Crazy Horse
  GE:Am II-1094
  GL:Am II-565
Creedence Clearwater Revival
  GE:A&C IV-2180
Creel, George
  GE:Am III-1454
Creighton, Edward
  GE:Am II-930
Cret, Paul Philippe
  GE:A&C IV-1919
Crichton, Charles
  GE:A&C III-1427
Crick, Francis
  GE:ME III-1572
  GE:S&T III-1406, IV-1687
  GL:B&C II-719
Crile, George Washington
  GE:S&T I-275
Crippen, Robert L.
  GE:S&T V-2180
Cripps, Sir Richard Stafford
  GE:W20 II-605
Crispi, Francesco
  GE:ME II-860, 1094, 1109
Crispin, Gilbert
  GE:A&M III-1291
Crissinger, Daniel Richard
  GE:B&C II-539
Crist, Steven G.
  GE:B&C IV-1472
Critias
  GE:A&M I-318
Crito
  GE:A&M I-318
Croce, Benedetto
  GL:20 I-489
Crocker, Charles
  GE:Am II-969
Crocker, Chester
  GE:HR V-2409
Croesus
  GE:A&M I-144
Croly, Herbert
  GE:A&C I-385

Crompton, Samuel
  GE:Am I-371
Cromwell, Oliver
  GE:ME I-313, 329
  GL:B&C II-724
Cromwell, Richard
  GE:ME I-329
Cromwell, Thomas
  GE:ME I-6, 103, 110, 123
  GL:B&C II-729
Cromwell, William Nelson
  GE:Am II-1339
Cronenweth, Jordan
  GE:A&C V-2486
Crook, General George
  GE:Am II-1094
Crookes, Sir William
  GE:ME II-1084
  GE:S&T I-412
Crooks, Ramsey
  GE:Am I-476
Crosby, Bing
  GE:A&C II-828
Crosby, Stills, Nash, and Young
  GE:A&C IV-2180
Crosland, Edward B.
  GE:B&C IV-1325
Cross, Charles Frederick
  GE:S&T I-238
Cross, James
  GE:HR III-1543
Crothers, Rachel
  GL:AmW II-461
Crowe, Frank
  GE:S&T III-1075
Crown, Henry
  GE:B&C IV-1538
Croxatto, Horacio B.
  GE:S&T V-2235
Cruz, Sor Juana Inés de la
  GL:Ren II-565
Ctesibius of Alexandria
  GL:A&M II-576
Cuauhtémoc
  GE:ME I-59
Cuéllar, Javier Pérez de
  GE:HR IV-1841
Cuevas, Esmeralda Arboleda
  GE:HR IV-2057
Cullen, Countée
  GE:A&C I-480
Cullen, James G.
  GE:B&C V-2066

Cullen, Michael
  GE:B&C I-302
Culligan, Matthew J.
  GE:B&C IV-1379
Cullinan, Joseph S.
  GE:B&C I-24
Cullman, Joseph, III
  GE:B&C IV-1443
Cullom, Shelby M.
  GE:Am II-1157
Culp, Oveta. See Hobby, Oveta Culp
Culp, Robert
  GE:A&C IV-2044
Culpeper, John
  GE:Am I-132
Cummings, E. E.
  GE:A&C III-1443
Cummings, Homer Stillé
  GE:Am III-1667
Cummins, Albert
  GE:Am III-1415
Cunningham, Imogen
  GL:AmW II-466
Cunningham, Merce
  GE:A&C III-1284, IV-2011
Cuomo, Mario
  GE:HR IV-2220, V-2359
Curcio, Renato
  GE:W20 II-1028
Curiatius, Publius
  GE:A&M I-253
Curie, Irène Joliot-. See Joliot, Frederic, and
  Joliot-Curie, Irène
Curie, Marie, and Pierre Curie
  GE:S&T I-93, 199, III-987, IV-1562
  GL:20 I-494
Curley, John J.
  GE:B&C V-1842
Curran, James
  GE:S&T V-2149
Curtin, John
  GL:B&C II-734
Curtis, Benjamin Robbins
  GE:Am II-900
Curtis, Carl T.
  GE:B&C IV-1567
Curtis, Cyrus H. K.
  GE:B&C IV-1379
Curtis, George William
  GE:Am II-1128
Curtis, Heber Doust
  GE:S&T I-218, II-502, 655, 790
Curtis, Ken
  GE:A&C IV-1668

Curtiss, Glenn Hammond
    GE:Am II-1346
Curtiz, Michael
    GE:A&C III-1245
Curzon, Lord
    GL:B&C II-739
Cushing, Harvey Williams
    GL:Am II-573
Cushing, Peter
    GE:A&C III-1378
Custer, George A.
    GE:Am II-1094
    GL:Am II-579
Cutler, Manasseh
    GE:Am I-306, 312
Cuvier, Georges
    GL:Ren II-570

Cyprian
    GE:A&M II-762, 812, 818
Cyril, Bishop of Alexandria
    GE:A&M II-888, 952
Cyril, Saint, and Saint Methodius
    GE:A&M II-1173
    GL:A&M II-579
Cyrus II. *See* Cyrus the Great
Cyrus the Great
    GE:A&M I-179, 184, 189, 313
    GL:A&M II-585
Czartoryski, Prince Adam
    GE:ME II-691
Czolgosz, Leon
    GE:Am II-1325

D

Da Costa, Afonso Augusto
  GE:ME III-1219
Da Costa, Morton
  GE:A&C IV-1752
Daffos, Fernand
  GE:S&T V-2205
Dafora, Asalta
  GE:A&C V-2521
Daguerre, Jacques
  GE:ME II-747
  GL:Ren II-575
Daimler, Gottlieb
  GE:ME II-1033
  GL:Ren II-581
Daladier, Édouard
  GE:ME III-1359, 1386, 1411 1429, 1433, 1440
Dalai Lama, fourteenth. *See* Gyatso, Tenzin
Dalberg-Acton, Lord John Emerich Edward (First
  Baron Acton). *See* Acton, Lord
D'Albret, Jeanne
  GE:ME I-184
Dale, Sir Henry Hallett
  GE:S&T I-243, IV-1459
D'Alembert, Jean Le Rond. *See* Alembert, Jean
  Le Rond d'
Daley, Richard
  GE:HR III-1446
Dalhousie, First Marquess of
  GL:B&C II-745
Dalí, Gala
  GE:A&C V-2310
Dalí, Salvador
  GE:A&C II-604, 750, 979, III-1179, V-2310
  GL:20 I-499
Dalio, Marcel
  GE:A&C II-1073
Dallas, Alexander James
  GE:Am I-539
Dalrymple, Brent
  GE:S&T IV-1777
Dalton, John
  GL:B&C II-749
Dalton, John H.
  GE:B&C V-1788
Daly, John
  GE:A&C V-2576
Damant, G. C. C.
  GE:S&T I-365
Damascene, John. *See* John of Damascus

Damasus I
  GE:A&M II-893, 909, 914
D'Amboise, Cardinal Georges
  GE:ME I-31
Damian, Peter
  GE:A&M III-1269
Dampier, William
  GL:B&C II-754
Damrosch, Leopold
  GE:Am II-1135
Dandolo, Enrico
  GE:A&M III-1436
  GL:A&M II-589
Danielovitch, Issur. *See* Douglas, Kirk
Daniels, Josephus
  GE:B&C II-464
Daniels, Paul Clement
  GE:W20 II-798
Danilova, Alexandra
  GL:AmW II-471
Danjon, André-Louis
  GL:20 I-504
D'Annunzio, Gabriele
  GE:W20 I-138
Danquah, J. B.
  GE:HR II-980
Dante Alighieri
  GE:A&M III-1598
  GL:A&M II-593
Danton, Georges
  GE:ME I-529
  GL:Ren II-585
D'Antonio, Donato de Pascuccio. *See* Bramante,
  Donato
Daphtary, C. K.
  GE:HR III-1430
Da Polenta, Guido
  GE:A&M III-1598
Darby, Abraham
  GL:B&C II-759
D'Argenlieu, Georges Thierry
  GE:HR II-683
Darius III
  GE:A&M I-158
Darius the Great
  GL:A&M II-598
Darlan, Jean Louis
  GE:Am III-1714

D'Arlandes, Marquis
    GE:ME I-496
Darrow, Clarence
    GE:Am II-1237, III-1549
    GE:B&C II-662
    GL:Am II-584
Dart, Raymond Arthur
    GE:S&T II-780, IV-1808
    GE:W20 I-218
Dartmouth, Second Earl of. *See* Legge, William
D'Artois, Comte de Chambord, Henri Charles
        Ferdinand Marie Dieudonné, (Duc de
        Bordeaux)
    GE:ME II-974
Darvall, Denise
    GE:S&T IV-1866
    GE:W20 II-1016
Darvall, Edward
    GE:W20 II-1016
Darwin, Charles
    GE:A&C I-161
    GE:Am III-1167
    GE:ME II-678, 855, 908
    GE:S&T I-163, 390, IV-1808
    GL:B&C II-764
Darwin, Charles Galton
    GE:S&T II-507
Darwin, Erasmus
    GE:ME II-855
Das, Chittaranjan
    GE:HR I-315
Dauch, Martin
    GE:ME I-506
Daud, Mohammad
    GE:HR IV-2062, V-2449
Daudet, Léon
    GE:ME III-1386
Daugherty, Harry
    GE:Am III-1472, 1525
    GE:B&C I-282, II-516
Dauphin, The
    GE:A&M III-1697
Daven, André
    GE:A&C II-665
Davenport, John
    GE:Am I-91
David
    GE:A&M I-90, 101
    GL:A&M II-605
David I
    GL:B&C II-769
David II
    GL:B&C II-774
David, Abraham ben. *See* Ben David, Abraham

David, Jacques-Louis
    GL:Ren II-590
Davies, Arthur B.
    GE:A&C I-361
    GE:Am III-1411
Davies, Marion
    GE:B&C I-396
Davies, Samuel
    GE:Am I-176
Davies, Sanders W.
    GE:B&C I-308
Da Vinci, Leonardo. *See* Leonardo da Vinci
Davis, Adelle
    GE:B&C IV-1416
Davis, Arthur Powell
    GE:S&T III-1075
Davis, Bette
    GL:AmW II-476
Davis, Chester
    GE:Am III-1627
Davis, Chuck
    GE:A&C V-2521
Davis, Elmer H.
    GE:Am III-1703
Davis, Geena
    GL:AmW II-480
Davis, Hugh
    GE:HR V-2342
Davis, James J.
    GE:HR I-377
Davis, Jameson
    GE:ME II-1080
Davis, Jefferson
    GE:Am II-865, 871, 941
    GL:Am II-590
Davis, Jim
    GE:A&C V-2418
Davis, John
    GL:B&C II-780
Davis, John Marcell
    GE:S&T V-1976
Davis, John W.
    GE:HR II-913
Davis, Kingsley
    GE:HR III-1386
Davis, Marvin
    GE:B&C V-1928
Davis, Miles
    GE:A&C III-1318, 1438, 1617, IV-2153
Davis, Raymond, Jr.
    GE:S&T IV-1830
Davis, Rennie
    GE:HR III-1446

Davis, Richard Harding
GE:Am II-1243
Davis, Stuart
GE:A&C II-1001
Davout, Marshal Louis Nicholas
GE:ME II-568
Davy, Sir Humphry
GE:ME II-560, 649, 753
GL:B&C II-784
Dawes, Charles Gates
GE:Am III-1537, 1594
GE:B&C I-406
GE:HR I-423
Dawes, Henry Laurens
GE:Am II-1123
Dawidowicz, Lucy S.
GL:AmW II-484
Dawson, Geoffrey
GE:ME III-1420
Day, Benjamin Henry
GE:Am II-713
Day, Dorothy
GL:AmW II-489
Day, Sandra. See O'Connor, Sandra Day
Day, William Rufus
GE:B&C I-168
Dayan, Moshe
GE:HR IV-1943, 2003
GE:ME III-1589, 1654
GE:W20 III-1182
GL:20 II-507
Day Lewis, Cecil
GE:A&C II-857
Dayton, Bruce
GE:B&C III-1070
Dayton, Donald
GE:B&C III-1070
Deacon, Richard
GE:A&C IV-1908
De Acuña, Antonio
GE:ME I-72
Deák, Ferenc
GE:ME II-939
GL:Ren II-595
Deakin, Alfred
GE:W20 I-14
GL:B&C II-789
De Alcántara Borbon, Dom Antonio Pedro
GE:ME II-645
De Alhuemas, Marqués (Manual Garcia Prieto)
GE:ME III-1259
Dean, Dizzy
GE:A&C III-1362

Dean, H. Trendley
GE:S&T III-1260
Dean, James
GE:A&C IV-1640
Dean, John Wesley, III
GE:W20 III-1131
Deane, Silas
GE:Am I-282
De Anza, Juan Bautista
GE:Am I-272
De Aranda, Conde (Pedro Pablo Abarca y Bolea)
GE:Am I-300
Dearden, John F.
GE:ME III-1659
De Arriaga, Manuel José
GE:ME III-1219
De Austria, Mariana
GE:ME I-372
De Avilés, Pedro Menendez
GE:Am I-33
De Ayala, Juan Manuel
GE:Am I-272
De Ayllón, Lucas Vásquez
GE:Am I-33
De Barbé-Marbois, Marquis François
GE:Am I-445
De Barr, Edwin
GE:HR I-367
De Beaumarchais, Pierre Augustin Caron
GE:Am I-282
De Beaumont, Gustave
GE:Am II-673
De Bellegarde, Elisabeth-Sophie (Mme.
D'Houdetot)
GE:ME I-446
De Belle-Isle, Duc. See Fouquet, Marshall
Charles Louis Auguste
De Bellievre, Pompone
GE:ME I-220
De Benevant, Prince. See Talleyrand
De Berulle, Pierre
GE:ME I-294
De Béthune, Maximilien, Duc de Sully
GE:ME I-214, 353
De Bèze, Théodore
GE:ME I-241
De Boisdeffre, Le Mouton
GE:ME II-1070
De Bono, Emilio
GE:ME III-1319
De Borbón, Joaquina Carlota
GE:ME II-645, 675
De Bordeaux, Duc. See D'Artois, Comte de
Chambord

De Bosset, Vera
GE:A&C II-561
De Bourbon, Antoine. *See* Bourbon, Antoine de
De Bourbon, Charles. *See* Charles, Duke of
Bourbon
De Bourbon, Henry I. *See* Henry, Prince of Condé
De Bourbon, Louis I. *See* Louis, Prince of Condé
De Bourbon, Louis-Antoine-Henri de. *See*
Enghien, Duc d'
De Bourgmound, Etienne
GE:Am I-144
DeBow, J. D. B.
GE:Am I-371
De Bracton, Henry. *See* Bracton, Henry de
De Bragança, Dom Miguel Maria Evaristo
GE:ME II-645
Debrie, André
GE:A&C II-642
De Brion, Sieur. *See* De Chabot, Philippe
De Broglie, Duc. *See* Albert, Jacques Victor
De Broglie, Louis. *See* Broglie, Louis de
Debs, Eugene V.
GE:Am II-1237, III-1454, 1472
GL:Am II-599
De Buade, Louis (Comte de Frontenac)
GE:Am I-144
De Burgh, Hubert. *See* Burgh, Hubert de
Debussy, Claude
GE:A&C I-332
GL:20 II-513
De Butts, John Dulany
GE:A&C V-2407
De Calonne, Charles Alexandre
GE:ME I-502, 516
De Campomanes, Pedro Rodríquez (Count of
Campomanes)
GE:ME I-442
De Carondelet, Barón Francisco Luis Héctor
GE:Am I-396
De Casson, Dollier
GE:Am I-52
De Castelnau, General Nöel Marie Joseph
Édouard de Curières
GE:ME III-1262
De Cermeñon, Sebastian Rodrigues
GE:Am I-272
De Chabot, Philippe (Sieur de Brion)
GE:Am I-28
De Chambord, Comte. *See* D'Artois, Comte de
Chambord
De Champlain, Samuel. *See* Champlain,
Samuel de
De Chateaubriand, Duc
GE:ME II-654

De Chievres, Sieur. *See* De Croy, Guillaume
De Choiseul, Duc. *See* François Étienne
De Cisneros, Cardinal Jiménez
GE:A&M III-1728
GE:ME I-1, 40
Decius
GE:A&M II-812
Decker, Karl
GE:Am II-1243
De Clare, Richard. *See* Gloucester, Earl of
De Coëtquis, Philippe
GE:A&M III-1703
De Coligny, Gaspard
GE:Am I-33
GE:ME I-184
De Commines, Philippe
GE:ME I-21
De Córdoba, Gonsalo Fernández
GE:ME I-1
De Coronado, Francisco Vásquez
GE:Am I-40
De Cortellazzo, Ciano. *See* Ciano Galeazzo
De Cource, Geoffroy
GE:B&C IV-1606
De Courçon, Robert
GE:A&M III-1400
De Croy, Guillaume (Sieur de Chièvres)
GE:ME I-40, 72
Dedekind, Richard
GE:S&T II-716
GL:Ren II-602
De Dieu Soult, Marshal Nicholas Jean
GE:ME II-568
Dee, Ruby
GE:A&C IV-1795
Deere, John
GE:Am II-679
Deering, William
GE:B&C I-52
De Estrada José Maria Gutierrez
GE:ME II-876
De Figueroa y de Torres, Alvaro. *See* De
Romanones, Conde
De Flesselles, Jacques
GE:ME I-510
De Floridablanca, Conde (José Moñino y
Redondo)
GE:Am I-282
GE:ME I-442
De Forest, Lee
GE:A&C I-469
GE:Am III-1519
GE:B&C II-640
GE:S&T I-255, II-537, 615

GE:W20 II-612
GL:Am II-605
De Freycinet, Charles Louis de Saulces
GE:ME II-1053
De Frontenac, Comte. *See* De Buade, Louis
De Gálvez, José
GE:Am I-272
De Gardoqui, Don Diego
GE:Am I-396
Degas, Edgar
GL:Ren II-607
De Gasperi, Alcide
GE:ME III-1538, 1601
GL:20 II-519
De Gaulle, Charles. *See* Gaulle, Charles de
De Geer, Gerard Louis
GE:HR I-345
De Giers, Nikolai Karlovich
GE:ME II-1070
Degli Armati, Salvino
GE:A&M III-1555
De Godoy, Manuel (Manuel de Godoy y Alvarez
    de Faria)
GE:Am I-396
GE:ME II-581
De Graaf, Robert Jemison Van. *See* Van de Graaf,
    Robert Jemison
De Gramont, Antoine Alfred Agenor (Duc de
    Guiche)
GE:ME II-954
De Granvelle, Cardinal Antoine Perrenot
GE:ME I-189
De Grouchy, Marquis Emmanuel
GE:ME II-618
De Guiche, Duc. *See* De Gramont, Antoine
    Alfred Agenor
De Guzmán, Don Alonzo Pérez. *See*
    Medina-Sidonia, Duke of
De Guzmán, Eugénie Marie de Montijo
GE:ME II-849
De Guzmán, Gaspar (Count-Duke of Olivares)
GE:ME I-299, 304
De Guzman, Luisa
GE:ME I-304
De Harcourt, Marquis
GE:ME I-372
De Haro, Luís
GE:ME I-299, 341
De Havilland, Olivia
GE:A&C III-1154
Dehousse, Fernand
GE:HR II-843, III-1137
De Hulst, Hendrik Christoffel van. *See* Van de
    Hulst, Hendrik Christoffel

De Jaucourt, Louis Chevalier
GE:ME I-428
Dejoie, Louis
GE:HR II-1009
Dekker, Wisse
GE:B&C V-1848
De Klerk, Frederik Willem
GE:HR IV-1736, V-2409, 2559, 2606
De Kooning, William
GE:A&C III-1557
Delacroix, Eugène
GL:Ren II-612
De la Croix De Castries, Christian Marie
    Ferdinand
GE:ME III-1577
De Lafayette, Marquis
GE:ME I-510
De Lagarde, Paul Anton
GE:ME III-1363
De la Luzerne, Chevalier
GE:Am I-288
De Lamartine, Alphonse
GE:ME II-786
De Lancy, James,
GE:Am I-188
Delaney, James J.
GE:B&C II-787, III-1097
Delano, Frederic
GE:B&C II-845
Delaroque, Colonel
GE:ME III-1411
De la Roque, Jean-François (Sieur de Roberval)
GE:Am I-28
De la Rosa, Francisco Martinez
GE:ME II-634
De la Rue, Warren
GE:ME II-753
De la Salle, Sieur. *See* Cavelier, René Robert
De la Tour, Françoise-Marie, Baronne De Warens
GE:ME I-446
De las Casas, Bartolomé. *See* Las Casas,
    Bartolomé de
De Laudonnière, René Goulaine
GE:Am I-33
De Launay, Bernard-René
GE:ME I-510
Delaunay, Robert
GE:A&C I-337
GL:20 II-531
De Lavallade, Carmen
GE:A&C IV-1774
De la Vérendrye, Sieur (Pierre Gaultier
    De Varennes)
GE:Am I-144

De la Warr, Lord. *See* West, Thomas

Delbecque, Léon
GE:ME III-1607

Del Canno, Juan Sebastián
GE:ME I-68

Délcassé, Théophile
GE:ME II-1113, III-1152

Del Castillo, Antonio Cánavos
GE:ME II-1003, 1119

Del Corso, Sylvester
GE:HR III-1532

De Leon, Mosed. *See* Moses de León

Delescluze, Charles
GE:ME II-984

De Lesseps, Comte Charles Aimée Marie
GE:ME II-1066

De Lesseps, Ferdinand. *See* Lesseps, Ferdinand de

De Leyva, Antonio
GE:ME I-82

Delfim Neto, Antonio
GE:HR III-1468

Delfini, Gil
GE:A&M III-1728

De L'Hôpital, Michael
GE:ME I-162

Delibes, Léo
GL:Ren II-618

Delius, Frederick
GL:B&C II-794

Della Gondola, Andrea di Pietro. *See* Palladio, Andrea

Della Mirandola, Pico
GE:A&M III-1723, 1766

Della Rovere, Cardinal Giuliano. *See also* Julius II, Pope
GE:ME I-21

Della Scala, Can Grande
GE:A&M III-1598

Dellenbaugh, Frederick Samuel
GE:Am II-1104

Dellinger, David
GE:HR III-1446

Dellums, Ronald V.
GE:HR IV-2174

De Lome, Dupuy
GE:Am II-1243

De Longueville, Duc
GE:ME I-308

Deloria, Vine, Jr.
GE:Am III-1866
GE:W20 II-865

De Lorris, Guillaume
GE:A&M III-1467

Delors, Jacques
GE:B&C V-2051

De los Castillejos, Marqués. *See* Prim y Prats, Juan

De Louvois, Marquis. *See* Louvois, Marquis de

Del Riego, Major Rafael
GE:ME II-634

Delson, Eric
GE:S&T V-2279

De Luzarches, Robert
GE:A&M III-1416

Del Virgilio, Giovanni
GE:A&M III-1598

De Machaut, Guillaume
GE:A&M III-1410

De MacMahon, Marshal Marie Edme Patrice Maurice
GE:ME II-954, 974

DeMain, John
GE:A&C V-2599

De Malebranche, Nicholas
GE:ME I-294

De Malesherbes, Chrétien-Guillaume
GE:ME I-428

De Man, Paul
GE:A&C IV-2075

De Mare, Rolf
GE:A&C II-665

De Marillac, Louis
GE:ME I-278

De Marillac, Michel
GE:ME I-278

De Marsin, Marchal Comte Ferdinand
GE:ME I-390

De Medici, Cosimo
GE:A&M III-1723

De Medici, Lorenzo (the Magnificent). *See* Medici, Lorenzo de

De Medici, Piero
GE:ME I-21

De Médicis, Catherine. *See* Catherine de Médicis

De Médicis, Marie
GE:ME I-278

De Mendoza, Cardinal Pedro González
GE:A&M III-1728

De Menil, Dominique
GL:AmW II-494

Dement, William
GE:S&T III-1424

Demeter
GE:A&M I-158

Demetrius of Phaleron
GE:A&M II-924

De Meun, Jean
GE:A&M III-1467
De Mille, Agnes
GE:A&C II-1036, III-1234, 1256
GL:AmW II-498
DeMille, Cecil B.
GE:A&C II-567, 833
GL:Am II-611
DeMille, William C.
GE:A&C II-799
Deming, W. Edwards
GE:B&C V-1948
Demirchian, Karen
GE:HR V-2348
Demjanjuk, John
GE:HR V-2370
Democritus
GE:A&M I-264
GL:A&M II-610
De Montcalm De Saint-Véran (Marquis Louis
Joseph)
GE:Am I-200
De Montesquieu, Baron. See Montesquieu
De Montfort, Simon (Earl of Leicester). See
Montfort, Simon V de
De Montgomery, Gabriel
GE:ME I-162
De Montmorency, Duc
GE:ME II-654
De Morgan, M. J.
GE:S&T I-169
De Morny, Duc Charles Auguste Louis Joseph
GE:ME II-808
Demosthenes
GE:A&M I-308, 338
GL:A&M II-616
De Moura, Cristobal
GE:ME I-189
Dempsey, James Raymon
GE:S&T IV-1734
Dempsey, Jack
GL:Am II-617
De Murville, Maurice Couve
GE:ME III-1648
De Narváez, Panfilo
GE:Am I-33
GE:ME I-59
Deng Xiaoping
GE:B&C III-1003, 1281, V-1887, 2012
GE:HR II-826, III-1332, IV-1983, 2073,
V-2483, 2535
D'Enghien, Duc. See Enghien, Duc d'
Denham, Sergei
GE:A&C III-1088

De Niccolo Bardi, Donato. See Donatello
Denikin, Anton Evanovich
GE:W20 I-152
De Niro, Robert
GE:A&C V-2265
Denis, Maurice
GL:20 II-536
De Niza, Fray Marcos
GE:Am I-40
Denktash, Rauf
GE:HR III-1218
Denman, Lady Gertrude
GE:HR I-167
Dennis, David
GE:HR III-1149
Dennis, Ruth. See St. Denis, Ruth
Denoff, Sam
GE:A&C IV-1908
De Novaes, Bartholomeu Dias
GE:ME I-11
Densmore, Frances
GL:AmW II-503
Dent, Alan
GE:A&C III-1378
Dent, John H.
GE:B&C IV-1561
GE:HR III-1397
De Oñate, Juan
GE:Am I-40
De Onís, Luis
GE:Am I-558
De Padilla, Juan
GE:ME I-72
De Paris, Compte (Louis Philippe Albert
D'Orléans)
GE:ME II-974
De Peralta, Pedro
GE:Am I-40
De Pineda, Alonzo Alvarez
GE:Am I-33
De Poitiers, Guillaume
GE:A&M III-1296
De Polignac, Prince
GE:Am I-593
GE:ME II-682
De Portocarrero, Luis Cardinal
GE:ME I-372
De Portolá, Gaspar
GE:Am I-272
Depretis, Agostino
GE:ME II-1019
D'Equevilley-Montjustin, Raymond Lorenzo
GE:S&T I-350

Derain, André
  GE:A&C I-140, 156
De Rayneval, Gérard
  GE:Am I-300
Derby, Earl of (Edward Henry Smith Stanley)
  GE:ME II-998
Derby, Fourteenth Earl of
  GE:ME II-929
  GL:B&C II-800
De Redcliffe, Viscount. See Canning, Stratford
De Reinach, Baron Jacques
  GE:ME II-1066
Derian, Patricia
  GE:HR IV-1903
De Richelieu, Duc (Armand Emmanuel du
  Plessis)
  GE:ME II-623
De Rivera, General Fernando Primo
  GE:ME II-1003
De Rivera, José Antonio Primo
  GE:ME III-1416
Der Meer, Simon van. See Van der Meer, Simon
De Roberval, Sieur. See De la Roque,
  Jean-François
De Robespierre, Maximilien François Marie
  Isidore
  GE:ME I-520, 529
De Rochambeau, Comte (Jean Baptiste Donatien
  de Vimeur)
  GE:Am I-294
De Rochas, Alphonse Beau
  GE:ME II-1033
De Rohan, Benjamin (Seigneur de Soubise)
  GE:ME I-259
De Romanones, Conde (Álvaro de Figueroa y de
  Torres)
  GE:ME III-1259
De Rossi, Michele Stefano
  GE:S&T III-1050
Déroulède, Paul
  GE:ME II-1053
De Rouvroy, Claude Henri (Comte
  De Saint-Simon)
  GE:ME II-803
De Rozier, Jean François Pilâtre
  GE:ME I-496
Derrida, Jacques
  GE:A&C IV-2075
  GL:20 II-541
De Saint-Arnaud, General Le Roy
  GE:ME II-808, 813
De Saint-Just, Louis Antoine Léon
  GE:ME I-529

De Saint-Simon, Comte. See De Rouvroy, Claude
  Henri
De Santa Anna, Antonio López
  GE:Am II-736, 825
Descartes, René
  GE:ME I-294
  GE:S&T I-243
  GL:Ren II-623
De Sica, Vittorio
  GE:A&C III-1228
De Sitter, Willem. See Sitter, Willem de
Desjardins, Alphonse
  GE:B&C II-690
Deslandres, Henri-Alexandre
  GE:S&T I-213
Desnos, Robert
  GE:A&C I-513
De Sosa, Gaspar Castaño
  GE:Am I-40
De Soto, Hernando. See Soto, Hernando de
De Soubise, Seigneur. See De Rohan, Benjamin
De Sousa, Antonio José (Duke of Terceira)
  GE:ME II-722
De Sousa, Pedro (Duke of Palmela)
  GE:ME II-722
Dessalines, Jean Jacques
  GE:HR II-1009
Dessauer, John H.
  GE:S&T III-1013
  GE:W20 I-382
D'Estaing, Giscard. See Giscard d'Estaing, Valéry
De Stoeckl, Baron Edouard
  GE:Am II-1037
Destouches, Louis-Ferdinand. See Céline,
  Louis-Ferdinand
De Sully, duc. See De Béthune, Maximilien
De Talleyrand-Périgord, Charles Maurice. See
  Talleyrand
Deterding, Hendrik W. A.
  GE:B&C II-551
De Tocqueville, Alexis
  GE:Am II-673
De Tolly, Prince Mikhail Barclay
  GE:ME II-585
De Torcy, Marquis. See Colbert, Jean Baptiste
De Torquemada, Tomás
  GE:A&M III-1752
De Tousard Major Louis
  GE:Am I-432
De Triana, Rodrigo
  GE:ME I-16
De Turenne, Vicomte
  GE:ME I-345

De Unamuno y Jugo, Miguel
GE:ME II-1119
Deupree, Richard R.
GE:B&C I-330
De Valera, Eamon
GE:ME III-1314
GL:B&C II-806
De Varennes, Pierre Gaultier. *See* De la
Vérendrye, Sieur
De Vauban, Seigneur
GE:ME I-345
De Vaucouleurs, Gérard Henri
GE:S&T IV-1454, V-2306
De Vaux, Clotilde
GE:ME II-803
De Vaux, Roland
GE:W20 II-598
De Vecchi, Cesare Maria
GE:ME III-1319
Devereux, Robert (Earl of Essex)
GE:ME I-224
De Vergennes, Comte (Charles Gravier)
GE:Am I-282, 300
De Veygoux, Louis Charles Antoine Desaix
GE:ME II-556
De Vimeur, Jean Baptiste Donatien. *See*
De Rochambeau, Brigadier General Comte
Devlin, Bernadette
GE:W20 III-1117
Devonshire, Duke of (Spencer Compton
Cavendish, Marquis of Hartingdon)
GE:ME II-1038
De Vries, Hugo
GE:ME II-908
GE:S&T I-61, 270
DeVries, William Castle
GE:S&T V-2195
Dew, Thomas R.
GE:Am I-648
De Warens, Baronne. *See* De la Tour,
Francoise-Marie
De Wet, Christiaan Rudolph
GE:ME II-1128
Dewey, George
GE:Am II-1284, 1290
GL:Am II-623
Dewey, John
GE:Am II-1077, 1301, III-1363
GL:Am II-629
Dewey, Thomas Edmund
GE:Am III-1800
De Witt, John
GE:ME I-345

DeWitt, John L.
GE:Am III-1703
GE:HR II-595
D'Houdetot, Mme. *See* De Bellegarde,
Elisabeth-Sophie
Diaghilev, Sergei
GE:A&C I-113, 187, 241, 247, 269, 332, 373,
II-561
GL:20 II-547
Diamond, Sidney A.
GE:B&C V-1778
Dias, Bartolomeu
GL:Ren II-628
Díaz, Adolfo
GE:HR I-137
Diaz, Jose
GE:HR II-624
Díaz, Porfirio
GE:HR I-196
GE:W20 I-69
Díaz de Vivar, Rodrigo. *See* Cid, El
Di Banco, Nanni
GE:A&M III-1665
Di Beccaria, Marchese. *See* Bonesana, Cesare
D'Iberville, Pierre Lemoyne (Sieur D'Iberville)
GE:Am I-144
Di Betto Bardi, Donato di Niccolò. *See* Donatello
Di Bondone, Giotto. *See* Giotto
Di Buoninsegna, Duccio. *See* Duccio di
Buoninsegna
Di Cavour, Count Camillo Benso
GE:ME II-770, 838, 849, 860, 870
Dick, Philip
GE:A&C V-2486
Dicke, Robert H.
GE:S&T IV-1762
Dickens, Charles
GL:B&C II-810
Dickerson, Ernest
GE:A&C V-2641
Dickinson, Emily
GE:A&C IV-1662
GL:Am II-634
GL:AmW II-508
Dickinson, John
GE:Am I-225, 288
GL:Am II-642
Dickinson, Robert Latou
GE:HR III-1290
Dickson, William Kennedy Laurie
GE:S&T II-537
Dickstein, Samuel
GE:HR I-550

Diderot, Denis
GE:ME I-428
GL:Ren II-634
Didrikson, "Babe." *See* Zaharias, "Babe"
Didrikson
Didymus. *See* Thomas Didymus, Saint
Diebitsch-Zabalkanski, Ivan
GE:ME II-691
Diefenbaker, John
GE:HR II-1079
Diels, Otto Paul Hermann
GL:20 II-553
Diem, Ngo Dinh. *See* Ngo Dinh Diem
Diemand, John Anthony
GE:B&C III-964
Dienstbier, Jiri
GE:HR V-2570
Dies, Martin
GE:HR I-486, 550, II-701
Diesel, Rudolf
GE:ME II-1100
GL:Ren II-640
Dietrich. *See* Theodoric the Great
Dietrich, Marlene
GE:A&C II-845
GL:AmW II-513
Dietrich, General Sepp
GE:ME III-1496
Dietrich-Genscher, Hans
GE:HR IV-1685
Dietz, Robert S.
GE:S&T IV-1650
Dieudonné, Jean
GE:S&T III-1140
Diggs, Ira
GE:HR IV-2101
Dighenis, George Grivas
GE:HR II-1084, III-1218
Di la Marmora, Marchese (Alfonso Ferrero)
GE:ME II-923
Dilke, Sir Charles
GE:HR I-13
Diller, Barry
GE:A&C V-2652
GE:B&C V-1928
Dillingham, William P.
GE:B&C II-459
GE:HR I-350
Dillon, (Clarence) Douglas
GE:B&C III-1218, 1235
DiMaggio, Joe
GE:A&C III-1362, 1567
Dimitrov, Georgi
GE:HR I-480

GE:ME III-1377
GE:W20 II-640
Dimitry the Pretender ("false" tsar)
GE:ME I-231
Dimling, John
GE:B&C I-401
Di Neghelli, Marshall Rodolfo. *See* Graziani,
Marshal Rodolfo
Ding Ling
GE:HR II-958
Dingell, John David, Jr.
GE:B&C IV-1460, V-2034
GE:W20 II-872
Dingley, Nelson
GE:Am II-1273
Dinkelbach, Heinrich
GE:B&C III-981
Dinocrates of Macedonia
GE:A&M I-353
Dinsmore, William B.
GE:Am II-925
Diocles. *See* Diocletian
Diocles of Carystus
GL:A&M II-622
Diocletian
GE:A&M II-829
GL:A&M II-627
Diokno, Jose
GE:HR III-1680
Dionysius, Bishop of Alexandria
GE:A&M II-812, 818
Dionysius Exiguus
GE:A&M II-877, 914, 1091
Dionysius the Areopagite
GE:A&M II-1011
Diophantus
GL:A&M II-632
Dior, Christian
GE:A&C III-1346
Dioscorides, Pedanius
GL:A&M II-638
Dioscoros
GE:A&M II-952
Dioscurus
GE:A&M II-963
Diphilus
GE:A&M I-368
Dirac, Paul Adrien Maurice
GE:S&T III-983, 992, 1293
GE:W20 I-166
Dirksen, Everett
GE:B&C III-1175, 1229, 1235, 1259, V-1882
GE:HR III-1251, 1296, 1414
GE:W20 II-806, 965

Di Rudini, Antonio
GE:ME II-1094, 1109
Di Savoia, Amadeo Ferdinando Maria (Duke of
Aosta)
GE:ME II-945
Disney, Roy
GE:A&C III-1612
GE:B&C III-1058
Disney, Walt
GE:A&C II-1053, III-1195, 1368, 1612
GE:B&C III-1058, 1138
GL:Am II-648
Disraeli, Benjamin
GE:ME II-730, 764, 929, 998, 1007
GL:B&C II-815
Dix, Dorothea
GL:Am II-655
GL:AmW II-518
Dix, Otto
GE:A&C II-631, III-1083
Dixon, Alan J.
GE:B&C IV-1454
Dixon, Archibald
GE:Am II-871
Dixon, J. E.
GE:S&T IV-1718
Dixon, Joseph M.
GE:HR I-373
Dixon, Robert
GE:W20 II-827
Dixon, Thomas
GE:A&C I-402
Dixon, Walter F.
GE:B&C I-103
Dizdarevic, Raif
GE:HR V-2386
Djemal Pasha, Ahmed
GE:W20 I-107
Djevdet Bey
GE:W20 I-107
Djilas, Milovan
GE:HR IV-1949
GL:20 II-558
Djoser. See Zoser
Dobrynin, Anatoly F.
GE:Am III-1888
GE:W20 II-1054
Dobson, Gordon Miller Bourne
GE:S&T II-579
Dodd, Samuel C. T.
GE:Am II-1116
Dodge, Grenville M.
GE:Am II-969

Dodge, Joseph
GE:W20 II-584
Doell, Richard Rayman
GE:S&T IV-1777
Doenitz, Karl
GE:ME III-1522
Doerfer, John C.
GE:B&C III-1148
Doesburg, Theo van
GE:A&C I-429, 458
Doheny, Edward Laurence
GE:Am III-1525
GE:B&C II-464
Dohnal, Johenna
GE:HR IV-2057
Dole, Bob
GE:B&C V-1859
Dole, Elizabeth
GE:HR IV-2220
GL:AmW II-523
Dole, Sanford
GE:W20 II-790
Dollfuss, Engelbert
GE:ME III-1395, 1425
Domagk, Gerhard
GE:S&T III-968
GL:20 II-562
Domingo de Guzmán. See Dominic, Saint
Dominguez, Francisco Serrano y. See Serrano y
Dominguez, Francisco
Dominic, Saint
GE:A&M III-1441, 1457
GL:A&M II-643
Domitian
GE:A&M II-669
Domitius Ulpianus. See Ulpian
Doms, Rodrigo de Borja y. See Alexander VI,
Pope
Donald, Frank C.
GE:B&C I-47
Donald, Ian
GE:S&T IV-1562
Donaldson, Kenneth
GE:HR IV-2226
Donat, Robert
GE:A&C II-946
Donatello
GE:A&M III-1665
GL:Ren II-645
Donatus
GE:A&M II-857
Don Carlos I. See Carlos I, Don
Donen, Stanley
GE:A&C III-1432

Donham, Wallace B.
GE:B&C I-335
Doniphan, Colonel A. W.
GE:Am II-818
Dönitz, Karl
GE:W20 I-404
Donizetti, Gaetano
GL:Ren II-650
Donne, John
GL:B&C II-821
Donnelly, Ignatius
GE:Am II-1225
Donohue, Jerry
GE:S&T III-1406
Donoso, José
GE:A&C IV-1689
Doolittle, Hilda. See H. D.
Doorman, Karel W. F. M.
GE:W20 I-457
Döpfner, Cardinal Julius
GE:ME III-1659
D'Orbais, Jean
GE:A&M III-1416
Dorchester, Lord. See Carleton, Guy
Dorgon
GL:Ren II-654
Doria, Giovanni Andria
GE:ME I-180
D'Orléans, Louis Philippe Albert. See De Paris,
Comte
D'Orléans, Marie Louise. See Marie Louise
d'Orléans
Dornberger, Walter Robert
GE:S&T III-1235
Dornbush, Albert Carl
GE:S&T III-1255
Dorolle, Pierre Marie
GE:HR II-678
Dorr, Thomas Wilson
GE:Am II-766
Dorsey, Thomas A.
GE:A&C III-1329
Dorsey, Tommy
GE:A&C III-1250
Dortch, Richard
GE:B&C V-2001
Dos Passos, John
GE:A&C I-343
Dos Santos, Antonio Machado
GE:ME III-1219
Dostoevski, Fyodor
GE:A&C II-890
GL:Ren II-659

Dotter, Charles T.
GE:S&T V-2088
Doubleday, Frank Nelson
GE:A&C I-39
Doubleday, Nelson
GE:A&C II-686
GE:B&C II-504
Doughty, Thomas
GE:Am I-613
Douglas, Donald, Jr.
GE:B&C III-1314
Douglas, Donald, Sr.
GE:B&C II-752, III-1112, 1314
Douglas, Helen Gahagan
GL:AmW II-528
Douglas, Kirk
GE:A&C V-2320
Douglas, Michael
GE:A&C V-2320
Douglas, Paul
GE:B&C IV-1358
Douglas, Roy
GE:A&C I-90
Douglas, Stephen A.
GE:Am II-854, 871, 889, 906, 935
GL:Am II-659
Douglas, William O.
GE:Am III-1883, 1893
GE:B&C III-937, IV-1437
GE:HR II-629, III-1290
GE:W20 III-1154, 1279
Douglas-Home, Sir Alec
GE:W20 II-955
Douglass, Frederick
GE:Am II-719
GL:Am II-664
Doumergue, Gaston
GE:ME III-1411
Dow, Henry Charles
GE:B&C I-1
Dow, Neal
GE:Am I-642
Dowding, Sir Hugh Caswall
GE:W20 I-430
Downing, Sir George
GE:Am I-121
Downshire, Marquis of. See Hillsborough, Earl of
Doyle, Sir Arthur Conan
GE:A&C I-496
GL:B&C II-827
Dozier, Lamont
GE:A&C IV-1790
Draco
GE:A&M I-153

Drake, Charles Lum
    GE:S&T V-2120
Drake, "Colonel" Edwin Laurentine
    GE:Am II-912
Drake, Sir Francis
    GE:ME I-193
    GL:B&C II-832
Drake, Frank Donald
    GE:W20 II-827
Drapeau, Jean
    GE:A&C IV-2081
    GE:HR III-1543
Dreiser, Theodore
    GE:A&C I-39
    GL:Am II-670
Drew, Jane
    GE:A&C III-1503
Dreyer, Carl Theodor
    GL:20 II-567
Dreyfus, Captain Alfred
    GE:ME II-1075, 1089
Dreyfuss, Doris Marks
    GE:A&C II-1057
Dreyfuss, Henry
    GE:A&C II-777, 1057
Drinker, Philip
    GE:S&T II-895
Dronenburg, James L.
    GE:HR IV-2124
Drouilliard, George
    GE:Am I-450
Drucker, Peter F.
    GE:B&C III-1020
Drucki-Lubecki, Prince Ksawery
    GE:ME II-691
Drummond, Sir Eric
    GE:HR I-361
    GE:ME III-1289
Drummond, William
    GE:Am I-132
Drumont, Édouard
    GE:ME II-1066, 1075
Drusus, Marcus Livius
    GE:A&M I-506
Drusus, Nero Claudius
    GE:A&M II-584
Drusus Nero Germanicus, Tiberius Claudius. See
    Claudius I
Dryden, John
    GL:B&C II-836
Dryja, Thaddeus P.
    GE:S&T V-2331
Du Fu. See Tu Fu

Duane, William
    GE:Am I-414
Duane, William John
    GE:Am I-696
Duarte, José Napoleon
    GE:HR V-2336
Dubček, Alexander
    GE:A&C IV-1967
    GE:HR III-1408, 1441, IV-1852, V-2570
    GE:ME III-1666
    GL:20 II-573
Dubinsky, David
    GE:HR I-545
Dubois, Marie Eugène F. T.
    GE:ME II-822
Du Bois, W. E. B.
    GE:Am III-1384
    GE:HR I-41
    GL:Am II-677
Dubos, René
    GE:S&T III-1224
Dubrovin, Alexander
    GE:ME III-1169
Duccio di Buoninsegna
    GE:A&M III-1587, 1691
    GL:A&M II-649
Duchamp, Gaston. See Villon, Jacques
Duchamp, Marcel
    GE:A&C I-349, 361, 513, III-1239
    GE:Am III-1411
    GL:20 II-579
Duchamp-Villon, Raymond
    GE:A&C I-349
Duckwitz, Georg
    GE:HR II-641
Duckworth, George
    GE:A&C II-637
Duclos, Jacques
    GE:HR II-646
Dudevant, Amandine-Aurore-Lucille Dupin,
    Baronne. See Sand, George
Dudley, Caroline
    GE:A&C II-665
Dudley, Thomas
    GE:Am I-103, 109
Duer, William
    GE:Am I-306, 356
Duffy, Henry
    GE:B&C V-1865
Duffy, Marguerite Josephine. See Terry, Megan
Duffy, Patrick
    GE:A&C V-2418
Dufour, William Henry
    GE:ME II-794

Dufy, Raoul
    GE:A&C I-263
Dugas, Gaetan
    GE:S&T V-2149
Duggar, Benjamin Minge
    GE:S&T III-1255
Duillius, Caeso
    GE:A&M I-253
Duke, Bill
    GE:A&C V-2565
Duke, James Buchanan
    GE:B&C I-57, 212
    GL:Am II-684
Dulaney, R. G.
    GE:W20 II-1022
Dulany, Daniel
    GE:Am I-219
Dulbecco, Renato
    GE:S&T IV-1522
Dulles, Allen
    GE:B&C III-1040
    GE:W20 II-926
Dulles, John Foster
    GE:Am III-1906
    GE:B&C III-1040, 1052
    GE:HR II-963
    GE:ME III-1589
    GE:W20 I-260, 690, 703, 709
    GL:Am II-690
Dumas, Alexandre, *père*
    GL:Ren II-665
Dumbleton, John
    GE:A&M III-1614
Dunant, Jean Henri
    GE:HR II-808
    GL:Ren II-670
Duncan, Isadora
    GE:A&C I-113, 187
    GL:AmW II-533
Duncan, Robert Kennedy
    GE:B&C I-17
Dung, Van Tien
    GE:W20 III-1227, 1346
Dunham, Edward (Ted)
    GE:S&T V-2068
Dunham, Katherine
    GL:AmW II-538
Dunk, George Montagu. *See* Halifax, Earl of
Dunn, Douglas
    GE:A&C V-2480
Duns Scotus, Johannes. *See* Duns Scotus, John
Duns Scotus, John
    GE:A&M III-1564
    GL:B&C II-841

Dunstable, John
    GL:B&C II-850
Dunster, Henry
    GE:Am I-103
Dupanloup, Félix Antoine Philibert
    GE:ME II-902
Dupee, Paul R., Jr.
    GE:B&C V-1939
Dupin, Amandine-Aurore-Lucile. *See* Sand, George
Du Plessis, Armand Emmanuel. *See* De Richelieu, Duc
Du Plessis, Armand-Jean. *See* Richelieu, Cardinal de
Duplessis-Normay, Philippe
    GE:ME I-214
Du Pont, Alfred I.
    GE:B&C I-69
Du Pont, Eleuthère Irénée
    GL:Am II-696
Du Pont, Irénée
    GE:B&C I-368
Du Pont, Pierre S.
    GE:B&C I-368, III-1164
Durand of Huesca
    GE:A&M III-1381
Durand, Asher Brown
    GE:Am I-613
Durant, Ariel
    GL:AmW II-544
Durant, Thomas C.
    GE:Am II-969
Durant, William Crapo
    GE:B&C I-368, II-533
Duras, Marguerite
    GE:A&C III-1481
Dürer, Albrecht
    GE:A&C V-2464
    GL:Ren II-674
Durey, Louis
    GE:A&C I-435
Durham, First Earl of
    GL:B&C II-855
Durkheim, Émile
    GL:20 II-584
Durr, Clifford
    GE:HR II-947
Durrer, Robert
    GE:B&C III-991
Duryea, Charles E.
    GE:B&C II-533
Duryea, J. Frank
    GE:B&C II-533
Dušan, Stefan. *See* Stefan Dušan

Dushkin, Samuel
  GE:A&C II-561
Du Tisné, Charles Claude
  GE:Am I-144
Du Tremblay, François le Clerq. *See* Joseph,
  Father
Dutton, Clarence Edward
  GE:Am II-1104
Duvalier, François
  GE:HR II-1009
Duvall, Robert
  GE:A&C V-2265
Duve, Christian Rene de
  GE:W20 I-501
Du Vigneaud, Vincent
  GE:S&T IV-1459
Dvořák, Antonín
  GL:Ren II-680
Dwight, Theodore
  GE:Am I-552

Dwight, Timothy
  GE:Am I-420, 636
Dyatlov, Anatoly
  GE:S&T V-2321
Dye, Dale A.
  GE:A&C V-2576
Dyer, Reginald
  GE:HR I-156, 264
Dylan, Bob
  GE:A&C IV-2038, 2158
Dymling, Carl-Anders
  GE:A&C IV-1742
Dyson, Sir Frank
  GE:S&T II-684
Dzerzhinsky, Feliks
  GE:A&C V-2277
Dzhugashvili, Iosif Vissarionovich. *See* Stalin,
  Joseph
Dzhugashvili, Joseph Vissarionovich. *See* Stalin,
  Joseph

E

Eadmer
  GE:A&M III-1291
Eads, Gary W.
  GE:B&C V-1803
Eads, James Buchanan
  GL:Am II-701
Eakins, Thomas
  GL:Am II-706
Ealhwine. *See* Alcuin
Eames, Charles
  GE:A&C II-610, III-1290, IV-1716
Earhart, Amelia
  GL:Am II-710
  GL:AmW II-549
Earl of Gloucester. *See* Gloucester, Earl of
Earl of Northumberland. *See* Percy, Henry
Eastland, James
  GE:HR IV-1817
Eastman, Charles
  GE:HR I-121
Eastman, Crystal
  GE:HR I-327
Eastman, George
  GE:B&C I-11, II-527
  GE:S&T I-280, II-537
  GL:Am II-715
Eastwood, Clint
  GE:A&C IV-1984
Eaton, Dorman B.
  GE:Am II-1128
Eaton, Frederick
  GE:B&C II-453
Eaton, Nathaniel
  GE:Am I-103
Eaton, Theophilus
  GE:Am I-91, 109
Eban, Abba
  GL:20 II-590
Eberst, Jacob. *See* Offenbach, Jacques
Ebert, Friedrich
  GE:HR I-241
  GE:ME III-1295
Éboué, Félix
  GL:20 II-595
Eccles, Sir John Carew
  GL:B&C II-860
Eccles, Marriner
  GE:B&C II-717

Ecevit, Bülent
  GE:W20 III-1193
Echeandía, José Mariá
  GE:Am I-619
Echegary, Joaquin Gonzalez. *See* Gonzalez
  Echegary, Joaquin
Echeverría, Luís
  GE:B&C III-1241
  GE:HR IV-1796
  GE:W20 III-1206
Eck, John
  GE:ME I-54
Eckener, Hugo
  GL:20 II-602
Eckersley, Peter
  GE:A&C II-712
Eckert, Johanna. *See* Holm, Hanya
Eckert, John Presper
  GE:S&T III-1213, 1347, 1396
  GE:W20 II-535
Eckford, Elizabeth
  GE:W20 II-770
Eckhart, Meister Johannes
  GE:A&M III-1670
Eco, Umberto
  GE:A&C III-1268
Eddington, Sir Arthur Stanley
  GE:S&T I-213, II-684, 700, 785, 815, 948
Eddy, Mary Baker
  GE:A&C I-209
  GE:B&C I-224
  GL:Am II-720
  GL:AmW II-554
Ede, James Chuter
  GE:HR III-1316
Edell, Marc
  GE:HR V-2381
Edelman, Marian Wright
  GL:AmW II-561
Edelson, Ira
  GE:B&C V-1898
Eden, Anthony
  GE:Am III-1736
  GE:B&C II-723
  GE:HR II-657, 963
  GE:ME III-1456, 1501, 1512, 1589
  GE:W20 I-348, 494, II-721
  GL:B&C II-865

Ederle, Gertrude
  GL:AmW II-565
Edison, Thomas Alva
  GE:A&C I-74
  GE:Am II-1089, 1110, 1333
  GE:B&C I-117, II-527
  GE:ME II-753
  GE:S&T I-138, 255, II-537
  GE:W20 I-1
  GL:Am II-724
Edlefsen, Niels
  GE:S&T III-953
Edmond, John M.
  GE:S&T V-2058
Edward I
  GE:A&M III-1386, 1528, 1569, 1581
  GL:B&C II-883
Edward II
  GL:B&C II-889
Edward III
  GE:A&M III-1630
  GL:B&C II-893
Edward IV
  GL:B&C II-898
Edward VI
  GE:ME I-123, 168
  GL:B&C II-902
Edward VII (Albert Edward, the Peacemaker)
  GE:ME III-1152, 1197, 1214
  GL:B&C II-907
Edward VIII. See Windsor, Duke of
Edward, Prince of Portugal
  GE:A&M III-1686
Edward the Confessor
  GE:A&M III-1248
  GL:B&C II-873
Edward the Elder
  GL:B&C II-878
Edwardes, Michael
  GE:B&C IV-1347
Edwards, Benjamin
  GE:Am II-736
Edwards, Bernard
  GE:A&C V-2386
Edwards, Don
  GE:HR IV-1812, 1817
Edwards, Esther Gordy
  GE:B&C III-1143
Edwards, Haden
  GE:Am II-736
Edwards, Jonathan
  GE:Am I-176, II-730
  GL:Am II-730
Edwards, Ninian
  GE:Am I-582

Edwards, Robert Geoffrey
  GE:S&T V-2099
  GE:W20 III-1324
Edwin
  GE:A&M II-1081
Effingham, Lord Howard of. See Charles, Lord
  Howard of Effingham
Effiong, Philip
  GE:HR III-1365
Effler, Donald B.
  GE:S&T IV-1835
Egan, Sir John
  GE:B&C V-2007
Egan, Robert
  GE:S&T II-562
Egan, William Allen
  GE:W20 II-1022
Egas Moniz, António. See Moniz, António Egas
Egbert, Sherwood H.
  GE:B&C III-1190
Egisheim, Bruno of. See Leo IX, Pope
Egremont, Earl of (Charles Wyndham)
  GE:Am I-207
Egstrom, Norma Deloris. See Lee, Peggy
Ehrenfels, Christian von
  GL:20 II-613
Ehrenwiesen, Baroness Hildegard Rebay von. See
  Rebay, Hilla
Ehrlich, Eugen
  GL:20 II-618
Ehrlich, Paul
  GE:HR III-1386
  GE:S&T I-1, 6, 422, II-476, III-968
  GE:W20 II-542, 1069
  GL:20 II-623
Ehrlichman, John Daniel
  GE:W20 III-1131
Eichmann, Adolf
  GE:HR II-1108, V-2370
  GE:W20 I-303, 396
Eicke, Theodor
  GE:HR I-491
Eijkman, Christiaan
  GE:S&T I-103, 330, II-771
Eilberg, Amy
  GE:HR V-2262
  GL:AmW II-569
Einaudi, Luigi
  GE:ME III-1538
Einhard
  GE:A&M II-1136
Einstein, Albert
  GE:A&C V-2375
  GE:ME III-1160

GE:S&T I-83, 260, 297, II-625, 630, 650, 684,
    689, 835, III-1293, 1320, IV-1640, 1881,
    V-2020
GE:W20 I-295, II-835, 881
GL:Am II-736
Einthoven, Willem
    GE:S&T I-41
    GL:20 II-628
Eisenhower, Dwight D.
    GE:Am III-1715, 1720, 1748, 1806, 1823,
        1843, 1849
    GE:B&C II-499, III-975, 1030, 1117, 1122,
        1169, 1196
    GE:HR II-963, 997, 1003, 1044
    GE:ME III-1477, 1486, 1491, 1496, 1589,
        1624
    GE:S&T IV-1583
    GE:W20 I-260, II-564, 577, 690, 703, 709,
        721, 758, 770, 776, 783 790, 798, 906, 934
    GL:Am II-741
Eisenman, Peter D.
    GE:A&C V-2614
Eisenstaedt, Alfred
    GE:A&C II-1031
Eisenstein, Sergei
    GE:A&C II-615, 701
    GL:20 II-634
Eisner, Michael
    GE:A&C V-2646
    GE:B&C III-1058, V-2056
Ekerot, Bengt
    GE:A&C IV-1742
Ekholm, Nils
    GE:S&T I-21
Eki, Hioki
    GE:W20 I-121
Eldridge, Roy
    GE:A&C III-1617
Eleanor of Aquitaine
    GL:B&C II-912
Eleazar the Priest
    GE:A&M II-702
Elgar, Sir Edward
    GE:A&C I-214
    GL:B&C II-918
El Greco. See Greco, El
Eliachim (Alcimus)
    GE:A&M I-459
Eliade, Mircea
    GL:20 II-640
Eliécer Gaitán, Jorge. See Gaitán, Jorge Eliécer
Elijah ben Solomon
    GL:Ren II-686
Elion, Gertrude Belle
    GL:AmW II-573

Eliot, Charles William
    GE:Am II-1077
    GE:B&C I-157
    GE:HR I-172
    GL:Am II-747
Eliot, George
    GL:B&C II-924
Eliot, Sir John
    GE:ME I-263
Eliot, T. S.
    GE:A&C I-445, II-539, 851, 857, III-1169,
        1443
    GL:B&C II-929
Elizabeth I (of England)
    GE:Am I-46
    GE:ME I-158, 162, 168, 174, 184, 193, 202,
        224
    GL:B&C II-934
Elizabeth II (of Great Britain)
    GE:W20 III-1287
    GL:B&C II-940
Elizabeth of Hungary, Saint
    GL:A&M II-655
Elizabeth Petrovna
    GE:ME I-414, 432
El-Kader, Abd, Messali Hadj. See Kader, Abd el-,
    Messali Hadj
Ellenberger, Jules
    GE:HR I-304
Ellender, Allen J.
    GE:B&C II-840, III-1175
Ellerbee, Linda
    GL:AmW II-578
Ellet, Charles
    GE:Am II-1060
Ellington, Duke
    GE:A&C I-480, II-739
    GL:Am II-752
Elliot, Anne
    GE:B&C I-401
Elliot, James
    GE:S&T V-2068
Elliott, Mary Lou
    GE:HR V-2320
Elliott, Matthew
    GE:Am I-383
Ellis, Havelock
    GE:HR II-991
    GL:B&C II-945
Ellison, Ralph
    GE:A&C III-1541
Ellsworth, Oliver
    GE:Am I-345
Elohist, The
    GE:A&M I-96

El-Sadat, Anwar. *See* Sadat, Anwar el-
Elster, Julius
  GE:S&T I-93, 208
Elting, Victor, Jr.
  GE:B&C IV-1501
Éluard, Paul (Eugène Grindel)
  GL:20 II-645
Elwell, Herbert
  GE:A&C I-508
Emde, Carl
  GE:Am III-1421
Emerson, Ralph Waldo
  GE:Am I-613, 654, II-848
  GL:Am II-756
Emerson, William A., Jr.
  GE:B&C IV-1379
Emmons, Glenn L.
  GE:HR II-820, 897
Emory, Major William H.
  GE:Am II-818, 865
Empedocles
  GE:A&M I-270
  GL:A&M II-660
Enders, John Franklin
  GE:S&T II-921, IV-1522
Engel, Erich
  GE:A&C III-1410
Engels, Friedrich
  GE:ME II-781
  GL:Ren II-690
Engen, Hans
  GE:HR II-902
Enghien, Duc d' (Louis-Antoine-Henri de
    Bourbon)
  GE:ME II-564
Engle, Joe H.
  GE:S&T V-2180
Engler, Carl
  GE:S&T I-385
English, Diane
  GL:AmW II-583
Engman, Lewis
  GE:B&C IV-1631
En-lai, Chou. *See* Chou En-lai
Ennals, Martin
  GE:HR IV-1955, 2204
Ennis, Bruce
  GE:HR IV-2226
Ennius, Quintus
  GE:A&M I-378, 453
  GL:A&M II-665
Enos, William Berkeley. *See* Berkeley, Busby
Enrico, Roger
  GE:B&C V-1904

Enrile, Juan Ponce
  GE:HR III-1680, V-2286
Entenza, John
  GE:A&C III-1290
Enver Pasha
  GE:HR I-98, 150
  GE:W20 I-107, 129
  GL:20 II-651
Epaminondas
  GL:A&M II-670
Ephron, Nora
  GL:AmW II-588
Epicurus
  GE:A&M I-264, 511
  GL:A&M II-676
Epstein, Abraham
  GE:Am III-1643
  GE:HR I-373
Epstein, Sir Jacob
  GL:B&C II-950
Epstein, Jean
  GE:A&C II-642
Epstein, Julius
  GE:A&C III-1245
Epstein, Philip
  GE:A&C III-1245
Erasistratus
  GE:A&M II-737
  GL:A&M II-681
Erasmus, Desiderius
  GE:ME I-49
  GL:Ren II-695
Eratosthenes of Cyrene
  GE:A&M I-398
  GL:A&M II-688
Erdman, Constantine Jacob
  GE:B&C I-140
Erdrich, Louise
  GL:AmW II-593
Erhard, Ludwig
  GE:HR III-1457
  GE:ME III-1690
  GL:20 II-658
Eric the Red
  GE:Am I-11
Erickson, Charles J.
  GE:S&T I-11
Erickson, John
  GE:S&T I-11
Ericsson, John
  GE:Am II-957
Erigena, Johannes Scotus. *See* Johannes Erigena
    Scotus

Erikson, Thorvald
   GE:Am I-11
Eriksson, Leif. *See* Leif Eriksson
Erlach, Johann Fischer von. *See* Fischer von
   Erlach, Johann Bernhard
Erlanger, Abraham
   GE:A&C I-108
Erlenborn, John N.
   GE:HR III-1650
Erlich, Henry
   GE:S&T V-2362
Ermolaeva, Vera
   GE:A&C I-413
Ernst, Friedrich Wilhelm Viktor August. *See*
   William, Crown Prince of Germany
Ernst, Hans
   GE:HR II-1020
Ernst, Max
   GE:A&C I-349, II-604, III-1239
   GL:20 II-664
Errazuriz, Hernan Felipe
   GE:B&C V-1986
Erskine, First Baron
   GL:B&C II-956
Erskine, George
   GE:Am I-505
Erskine, John
   GE:A&C III-1351
Erté
   GE:A&C I-263
Ervin, Sam J., Jr.
   GE:B&C III-1122, 1259
   GE:HR IV-1650
   GE:W20 III-1131
Erzberger, Matthias
   GL:20 II-670
Esaki, Leo
   GE:S&T IV-1551
Eschenbach, Wolfram von. *See* Wolfram von
   Eschenbach
Escher, Maurits Cornelius
   GE:A&C III-1268
Escobar, Pablo
   GE:HR V-2465
Escudero, Gonzalo
   GE:HR II-1032
Eshelman, Von Russel
   GE:S&T IV-1598
Esher, Lord Oliver Sylvain Baliol
   GE:A&C IV-1924
Eshkòl, Levi
   GE:B&C IV-1336
   GE:ME III-1654

Espartero, Baldomero
   GE:ME II-726
Espejo, Antonio
   GE:Am I-40
Espinosa, Chris
   GE:S&T V-2073
Esquirol, Jean-Étienne-Dominique
   GE:A&C IV-1877
Essex, Earl of. *See* Devereux, Robert
Esslin, Martin
   GE:A&C IV-1812, 1871
Estebanico (Stephen)
   GE:Am I-40
Estefan, Gloria
   GL:AmW II-597
Esterhazy, Major Marie Charles Ferdinand Walsin
   GE:ME II-1075
Estigarribia, José Félix
   GE:HR I-533
   GE:W20 I-289
Estimé, Dumarsais
   GE:HR II-1009
Estrada, Emilio
   GE:S&T IV-1624
Estrada, Juan J.
   GE:HR I-137
Estridge, Philip D.
   GE:B&C V-1809
   GE:S&T V-2240
Ethelbert
   GE:A&M II-1058
Ethelburga
   GE:A&M II-1081
Ethelred II, the Unready
   GL:B&C II-962
Etheria
   GE:A&M II-877, 1091
Étienne Tempier. *See* Tempier, Étienne
Eucken, Rudolf Christoph
   GL:20 II-676
Euclid
   GE:A&M I-383, 422
   GL:A&M II-694
Eudes
   GE:A&M II-1117
Eudoxus of Cnidus
   GE:A&M I-383, II-712
   GL:A&M II-698
Eugene III
   GE:A&M III-1329
Eugène, Prince of Savoy
   GE:ME I-368, 390
Eugene, Frank
   GE:A&C I-63

Eugenius IV
    GE:A&M III-1338, 1703
Euhemerus
    GE:A&M I-378, 403
Euler, Leonhard
    GL:Ren II-701
Eumenes II
    GE:A&M I-486
Eunomius
    GE:A&M II-893
Eupalinus of Megara
    GL:A&M II-704
Euric
    GE:A&M II-1005
Euripides
    GL:A&M II-709
Eurybiades
    GE:A&M I-237
Eusebius of Caesarea
    GE:A&M II-767, 779, 840, 867
    GL:A&M II-715
Eusebius of Nicomedia
    GE:A&M II-867
Eustachio, Bartolommeo
    GE:ME I-133
Eutyches
    GE:A&M II-952, 963
Evans, Sir Arthur
    GE:S&T I-67
Evans, Clifford
    GE:S&T IV-1624, 1645
Evans, George
    GE:A&C III-1250
Evans, George Henry
    GE:Am II-962
Evans, Herbert
    GE:HR IV-2101
Evans, Herbert McLean
    GE:S&T III-1358
Evans, Hiram Wesley
    GE:HR I-298
Evans, Mary Ann. See Eliot, George

Evans, Mike
    GE:A&C V-2339
Evans, Oliver
    GE:Am I-471, 546
    GE:S&T II-542
Evarts, Jeremiah
    GE:Am I-666
Evatt, Herbert Vere
    GL:B&C II-967
Eve, Arthur O.
    GE:HR III-1633
Eveleth, J. G.
    GE:Am II-912
Everett, Edward
    GE:Am I-576
Everett, Robert R.
    GE:W20 II-535
Evert, Chris
    GL:AmW II-601
Evrard of Béthune
    GE:A&M II-1023
Ewen, Harold Irving
    GE:S&T IV-1496
Ewen, William
    GE:B&C IV-1501
Ewing, Maurice
    GE:S&T IV-1508, 1876
Exner, Franz
    GE:S&T II-532
Eyadéma, Gnassingbe
    GE:B&C IV-1589
Eyck, Jan van, and Hubert van Eyck
    GL:Ren II-706
Eythin, Lord
    GE:ME I-313
Ezekiel
    GL:A&M II-721
Ezoe, Hiromasa
    GE:B&C V-1964
Ezra
    GE:A&M I-189, II-664
    GL:A&M II-726
Ezra, Abraham ibn-. See Ibn-Ezra

F

Fabian
GE:A&M II-812
Fabius, Laurent
GE:B&C V-1793
GE:HR V-2268
Fabius Vibulanus, Quintus
GE:A&M I-253
Fabrikant, V. A.
GE:W20 II-881
Fabry, Charles
GE:S&T II-579
Fackenthal, Frank Diehl
GE:A&C I-407
Facta, Luigi
GE:ME III-1319
Fagan, Eleanora. See Holiday, Billie
Fagan, Garth
GE:A&C V-2521
Fages, Pedro
GE:Am I-272
Fagley, Richard M.
GE:HR II-1096
Fahlberg, Constantin
GE:S&T V-2226
Fahmy, Ismail
GE:HR IV-1943
Faidherbe, Louis
GL:Ren II-712
Fairbanks, Douglas, Sr.
GE:A&C I-224, II-799
Fairchild, George
GE:B&C II-447
Fairfax, Third Baron
GL:B&C II-972
Fairfax, Sir Thomas
GE:ME I-313
Fairweather, D. V. I.
GE:S&T V-2205
Faisal
GE:B&C IV-1533, 1544
GL:20 II-680
Faisal I
GL:20 II-687
Fakhr al-Din al-Razi
GL:A&M II-732
Falck, August
GE:A&C I-199
Falier, Ordelafo
GE:A&M III-1354

Faliero I Vitale. See Vitale, Faliero
Falk, Adalbert
GE:ME II-969
Falkenhayn, Erich von
GE:B&C I-293
GE:HR I-161
Fall, Albert Bacon
GE:Am III-1525
GE:B&C II-464
Falla, Manuel de
GL:20 II-694
Falloux, Vicomte Frédéric Pierre
GE:ME II-786
Falwell, Jerry
GE:B&C V-2001
Fama, Eugene F.
GE:B&C III-931
Fancher, Hampton
GE:A&C V-2486
Fang Lizhi
GE:HR V-2483
Fanning, Edmund
GE:Am I-213
Farabi, Al-. See Al-Farabi
Faraday, Michael
GE:ME II-560, 649
GL:B&C II-978
Farel, William
GE:ME I-116
Fargo, William George
GE:Am II-925
Faris, Ellsworth
GE:Am III-1357
Farley, Eliot
GE:B&C III-948
Farley, James Aloysius
GE:Am III-1609
Farley, James T.
GE:Am II-1123
Farman, Joseph C.
GE:S&T V-2285
Farmer, Fannie Merritt
GL:AmW II-605
Farmer, James
GE:HR II-601, 618, III-1451
Farmer, Moses G.
GE:Am II-1110
Farmer, Sarah Jane
GL:AmW II-609

76

Farnese, Alessandro (1468-1549). *See* Paul III, Pope

Farnese, Alessandro (1545-1592)
GL:Ren II-717

Farnsworth, Philo T.
GE:A&C III-1143
GE:Am III-1674
GE:B&C II-803

Farooq, Mohammad
GE:HR V-2426

Farragut, David G.
GL:Am II-763

Farrand, Beatrix Jones
GL:AmW II-614

Farrell, Suzanne
GL:AmW II-619

Farrelly, P. A.
GE:HR IV-1829

Farris, Paul
GE:B&C IV-1410

Farrow, Mia
GE:A&C IV-2017

Fathalla, Ahmed
GE:HR V-2529

Faubus, Orval
GE:HR II-1003
GE:W20 II-770

Faulkner, Brian
GE:W20 III-1117

Faulkner, William
GE:A&C II-805
GE:Am III-1571
GL:Am II-768

Faure, Edgar
GE:W20 II-721

Faure, Élie
GE:A&C II-642

Faust, Frederick
GE:A&C I-304

Favaloro, Rene
GE:S&T IV-1835

Favre, Peter
GE:ME I-96

Fawcett, Henry
GE:B&C I-218

Fawcett, Dame Millicent Garrett
GE:B&C III-1185
GE:HR I-19, 75, 247
GL:B&C II-984

Fawkes, Guy
GE:ME I-224

Fawwaz
GE:HR IV-2095

Fay, Frank J.
GE:A&C I-119

Fay, Sidney Bradshaw
GE:ME III-1340

Fay, William George
GE:A&C I-119, 176

Fayol, Henri
GE:B&C I-287

Fechner, Gustav Theodor
GL:Ren II-722

Feigen, Richard L.
GE:A&C V-2191

Feighton, Michael
GE:B&C III-1259

Feininger, Lyonel
GE:A&C I-463, II-583

Feinstein, Dianne
GL:AmW II-623

Feldman, Paul D.
GE:S&T V-1992

Feldman, William Hugh
GE:S&T III-1224

Felici, Archbishop Pericle
GE:ME III-1633

Felix II
GE:A&M II-989

Fellini, Federico
GE:A&C III-1228, 1596
GL:20 II-699

Fels, Baron Colona
GE:ME I-250

Felsch, Oscar "Happy"
GE:Am III-1497

Felton, John
GE:ME I-174

Fender, Leo
GE:B&C III-919

Fenner, Charles E.
GE:Am II-1261

Fenwick, George
GE:Am I-109

Ferber, Edna
GE:A&C II-745

Ferdinand
GE:A&M III-1728, 1747, 1752, 1756

Ferdinand I, of Aragon, Holy Roman Emperor
GE:ME I-40, 64, 76, 87, 91, 148, 153, 174

Ferdinand I, of the Two Sicilies
GE:ME II-638

Ferdinand II and Isabella I
GL:Ren II-732

Ferdinand II, of Aragon (Ferdinand V of Castile)
GE:ME I-1, 16, 31, 40

Ferdinand II, of Austria, Holy Roman Emperor
  GE:ME I-250, 270, 274, 290, 357
  GL:Ren II-727
Ferdinand II, of the Two Sicilies
  GE:ME II-775
Ferdinand III, Holy Roman Emperor
  GE:ME I-308
Ferdinand V (of Castile). See Ferdinand II, of
  Aragon
Ferdinand VII (of Spain)
  GE:Am I-558
  GE:ME II-581, 594, 634, 726
Ferdinand of Saxe-Coburg
  GE:ME III-1240
Ferdowsi. See Firdusi
Ferguson, Adam
  GL:B&C II-990
Ferguson, Charles Wesley
  GE:S&T III-1160
Ferguson, Judge John H.
  GE:Am II-1261
Ferlinghetti, Lawrence
  GE:A&C III-1460
Fermat, Pierre de
  GL:Ren II-738
Fermi, Enrico
  GE:B&C III-1046
  GE:S&T III-992, 1101, 1135, 1198, 1230,
    1265, IV-1557
  GE:W20 I-246
  GL:Am II-774
Fernando, S. Saman Piyasiri (Keerthi
    Wiyayabahu)
  GE:HR V-2315
Ferrar, Nicholas
  GL:B&C II-996
Ferrari, Enzo
  GL:20 II-704
Ferraro, Geraldine
  GE:HR IV-2209
  GL:AmW II-628
Ferrell, Robert H.
  GE:W20 II-663
Ferretti, Giovanni Maria Mastai. See Pius IX
Ferris, James Peter
  GE:S&T IV-1662
Ferry, Jules François Camille
  GE:ME II-1048
Fessenden, Reginald Aubrey
  GE:Am III-1519
  GE:B&C I-363
  GE:S&T I-361, II-615, IV-1508
Fessenden, William Pitt
  GE:Am II-1049

Fetter, Frank A.
  GE:B&C I-35
Feuchtwanger, Lion
  GE:W20 I-241
Feuchtwanger, Walter. See Wanger, Walter
Fey, Emil
  GE:ME III-1395
Feynman, Richard P.
  GE:S&T III-1293, IV-1533
Fibonacci, Leonardo. See Leonardo of Pisa
Fichte, Johann Gottlieb
  GL:Ren II-743
Ficker, Roberta Sue. See Farrell, Suzanne
Ficino, Marsilio
  GE:A&M III-1723, 1766
Fidanza, Giovanni di. See Bonaventure, Saint
Fiedler, Arthur
  GE:W20 III-1287
Field, Cyrus West
  GE:Am II-895, 1135
  GE:ME II-834
  GE:S&T IV-1502
Field, James G.
  GE:Am II-1225
Field, Marshall
  GL:Am II-780
Field, Matthew D.
  GE:Am II-895
Field, Stephen J.
  GE:Am II-1167
  GL:Am II-785
Field, Winston
  GE:ME III-1642
Fielden, John
  GE:ME II-730
Fielding, Henry
  GL:B&C II-1001
Fields, Dorothy
  GL:AmW II-633
Fierstein, Harvey
  GE:A&C V-2502
Fieschi, Sinibaldo. See Innocent IV
Fiesole, Giovanni da. See Angelico, Fra
Fignolé, Daniel
  GE:HR II-1009
Filaret, Metropolitan Patriarch of Moscow
  GE:ME II-866
Filaret, Patriarch of Russian Church
  GE:ME I-247
Filartiga, Dolly
  GE:HR IV-2106
Filartiga, Joel
  GE:HR IV-2106

Filartiga Speratti, Joelito
    GE:HR IV-2106
Filene, Edward A.
    GE:B&C II-690
Filipepi, Alessandro di Mariano. *See* Botticelli,
    Sandro
Fillmore, Millard
    GE:Am II-854, 884
    GL:Am II-792
Filotheus
    GE:A&M III-1738
Filov, Bogdan
    GE:W20 I-444
Fimmel, Richard O.
    GE:S&T V-1956
Finch, Robert
    GE:B&C IV-1390
Finestra, Carmen
    GE:A&C V-2532
Finetti, Bruno de
    GE:S&T II-664
Fini, Leonor
    GE:A&C II-979
Fink, Morton
    GE:B&C V-1745
Fink, Uwe
    GE:S&T V-2141
Finlay, Carlos Juan
    GE:Am II-1313
Finney, Charles Grandison
    GE:Am I-420, 642, II-708
Fino, Paul
    GE:B&C IV-1472
Fiorelli, Giuseppe
    GE:A&M II-659
Firdusi
    GL:A&M II-737
Firmilian
    GE:A&M II-818
Firuz
    GE:A&M II-985
Fischer, Fritz
    GE:W20 II-918
Fischer von Erlach, Johann Bernhard
    GL:Ren II-749
Fish, Hamilton
    GE:Am II-1072
Fisher, Alva J.
    GE:S&T I-453
Fisher, Ames
    GE:Am I-356
Fisher, Irving
    GE:Am III-1577
    GE:B&C II-574

Fisher, J. Richard
    GE:S&T V-2306
Fisher, John
    GE:ME I-103
Fisher, Ronald A.
    GE:W20 I-7
Fisher, Saint John
    GL:B&C II-1006
Fisher, Sir John Arbuthnot
    GE:ME III-1187
    GE:W20 I-129
Fitch, John
    GE:Am I-471
Fitzgerald, Ella
    GL:AmW II-637
Fitzgerald, Ernest
    GE:B&C IV-1384
Fitzgerald, F. Scott
    GE:A&C II-626, 696
    GL:Am II-797
Fitzgerald, Robert
    GE:A&C IV-1645
Fitzgerald, Zelda
    GE:A&C II-626
Fitzhugh, George
    GE:Am I-648
Fitzpatrick, John
    GE:HR I-293
Fitzpatrick, Robert John
    GE:B&C V-2056
Fitzpatrick, Thomas
    GE:Am II-795
Fitzsimmons, Frank E.
    GE:B&C III-1213
Flaccus. *See* Alcuin
Flaccus, Marcus Verrius. *See* Verrius Flaccus,
    Marcus
Flaccus, Quintus Horatius. *See* Horace
Flagler, Henry M.
    GE:Am II-1116
Flanagan, Hallie
    GE:A&C II-989
    GE:Am III-1632
Flandin, Pierre Étienne
    GE:W20 I-348
Flatt, Lester
    GE:A&C III-1121
Flaubert, Gustave
    GE:A&C I-396
    GE:ME II-827
    GL:Ren II-754
Flavian
    GE:A&M II-963

Flavius Clemens, Titus
  GE:A&M II-669
Flavius Sabinus Vespasianus, Titus. *See*
  Vespasian
Flavius Stilicho. *See* Stilicho, Flavius
Flavius Valerius Constantine. *See* Constantine
Flavius Valerius Constantius Chlorus. *See*
  Constantius
Fleming, Sir Alexander
  GE:ME III-1335
  GE:S&T II-873
  GL:B&C II-1010
Fleming, Ian
  GE:A&C IV-1913
Fleming, Sir John Ambrose
  GE:S&T I-255
Fleming, Sir Sandford
  GE:B&C I-174
Fleming, Victor
  GE:A&C III-1109, 1154
Fleming, Williamina Paton Stevens
  GL:AmW II-641
Flemming, Arthur S.
  GE:HR IV-1786
Fletcher, Duncan
  GE:B&C II-679
Fletcher, Frank J.
  GE:Am III-1709
  GE:W20 I-472
Fletcher, Harvey
  GE:S&T I-443
Fletcher, John, and Francis Beaumont
  GL:B&C I-206
Fletcher, Robert
  GE:Am I-485
Fleury, Cardinal André Hercule
  GE:ME I-419
Flexner, Abraham
  GL:Am II-804
Flick, J. B.
  GE:S&T III-1024
Flint, Charles Ranlett
  GE:B&C II-447
Flohr, Albert
  GE:B&C I-103
Flood, Curt
  GE:B&C IV-1437
Florensky, Kiril
  GE:S&T V-2042
Florey, Baron. *See* Florey, Sir Howard Walter
Florey, Sir Howard Walter
  GE:ME III-1335
  GE:S&T II-873, III-1171
  GL:B&C II-1014

Floridablanca, Count of. *See* De Floridablanca,
  Conde
Florio, James J.
  GE:B&C IV-1426
  GE:HR IV-2084
Florus, Gessius
  GE:A&M II-648
Flower, Fordham
  GE:A&C IV-1888
Flowers, John
  GE:B&C V-1826
Flowers, Thomas H.
  GE:S&T III-1155
Fly, James
  GE:B&C II-827
Flynn, Elizabeth Gurley
  GL:AmW II-645
Foch, Ferdinand
  GE:Am III-1466
Fokine, Michel
  GE:A&C I-113, 187, 241, 247, 269, 332,
    III-1088
Fokker, Anthony Herman Gerard
  GE:S&T II-600
Folger, Abiah
  GE:Am I-236
Foliot, Gilbert
  GE:A&M III-1375
Follett, Mary Parker
  GE:B&C II-770
Follett, Wilson
  GE:A&C IV-1898
Folsom, Frank
  GE:A&C III-1362
Fomin, Alexandr S.
  GE:Am III-1888
Fomin, Nikolai
  GE:S&T V-2321
Fonda, Henry
  GE:A&C IV-1984
Fonda, Jane
  GE:HR IV-1691
  GL:AmW II-650
Fonda, Peter
  GE:A&C IV-2158
Fontanne, Lynn
  GE:A&C II-936
Fonteyn, Dame Margot
  GE:A&C IV-1962
  GL:B&C II-1019
Foot, Samuel Augustus
  GE:Am I-582, 660
Foote, Shelby
  GE:A&C V-2657

Forbes, Bertie Charles (B. C.)
  GE:B&C I-314
Forbes, Bruce
  GE:B&C I-314
Forbes, Sir Charles
  GE:ME III-1446
Forbes, Charles R.
  GE:Am III-1525
Forbes, Malcolm
  GE:B&C I-314
Forbes, Malcolm Stevenson, Jr.
  GE:B&C I-314
Force, Juliana Rieser
  GE:A&C II-885, 1001
Ford, Edsel Bryant
  GE:B&C III-1087
Ford, Eileen
  GL:AmW II-654
Ford, Ford Madox
  GE:A&C I-445
Ford, Gerald R.
  GE:B&C IV-1555, 1561, 1584
  GE:HR III-1595, IV-1769, 1806, 1812, 1823
  GE:W20 I-513, II-1054, III-1200, 1227, 1257,
    1287, 1302, 1331
  GL:Am II-809
Ford, Glenn
  GE:A&C IV-1650
Ford, Harrison
  GE:A&C V-2391
Ford, Henry
  GE:Am III-1421, 1501
  GE:B&C I-151, 234, 287, II-476, 533, III-1020
  GE:HR I-143
  GE:S&T II-542
  GL:Am II-814
Ford, Henry, II
  GE:A&C III-1579
  GE:B&C III-1087, 1224, V-1751
Ford, John (film director)
  GE:A&C III-1115, 1313
Ford, John (theologian)
  GE:ME III-1659
Forel, François-Alphonse
  GE:S&T III-1050
Foreman, Carl
  GE:A&C III-1340
Forest, Lee de. See De Forest, Lee
Forestier, François
  GE:S&T V-2205
Forman, Miloš
  GE:A&C IV-1967, V-2320
Forrest, Edwin
  GL:Am II-820

Forrestal, James Vincent
  GE:Am III-1783
Forrester, Jay W.
  GE:W20 II-535
Forster, E. M.
  GL:B&C II-1025
Forster, William Edward
  GL:B&C II-1031
Fortas, Abe
  GE:Am III-1893
  GE:HR III-1182
Forten, Charlotte
  GL:AmW II-659
Fortescue, Sir John
  GL:B&C II-1036
Fortune, Thomas R.
  GE:HR III-1451
Fosdick, Raymond
  GE:S&T III-1325
Foss, Eugene N.
  GE:HR I-126
Fossey, Dian
  GL:AmW II-663
Foster, David
  GE:B&C III-1202
Foster, Jodie
  GL:AmW II-668
Foster, Sir Michael
  GE:S&T I-243
Foster, Stephen Collins
  GL:Am II-825
Foster, W. H.
  GE:Am II-1152
Foster, William Zebulon
  GE:Am III-1609
  GE:HR I-293
Foucault, Jean-Bernard-Léon
  GE:S&T I-303
Foucault, Michel
  GE:A&C IV-1877
Fouler, Henry H.
  GE:B&C IV-1341
Fouquet, Marshal Charles Louis Auguste (Duc de
    Belle-Isle)
  GE:ME I-419
Fourier, Charles
  GL:Ren II-759
Fourier, Joseph
  GE:S&T V-2200
  GL:Ren II-765
Fowler, Jacob
  GE:Am I-588
Fowler, Lydia Folger
  GL:AmW II-672

Fowler, Ralph Howard
  GE:S&T II-815, 948, III-1070
Fox, Charles James
  GL:B&C II-1041
Fox, Mrs. Cyril
  GE:B&C III-1254
Fox, George
  GL:B&C II-1047
Fox, Ruth
  GE:S&T III-1314
Fox, William
  GE:A&C II-761
  GE:B&C I-117
Fracastoro, Girolamo
  GL:Ren II-770
Frachon, Benoît
  GE:HR II-873
Fraenkel, Abraham Adolf
  GE:S&T I-233
Fraenkel, Michael
  GE:A&C II-963
Fragonard, Jean-Honoré
  GL:Ren II-775
Frahm, Herbert. *See* Brandt, Willy
Franchet D'Esperey, Louis Felix Marie François
  GE:ME III-1249
Francia, José Gaspar Rodríguez de. *See*
  Rodríguez de Francia, José Gaspar.
Francis I, Holy Roman Emperor
  GE:ME I-419
Francis I (of France)
  GE:ME I-44, 64, 82, 87, 91, 116, 123, 143
  GL:Ren II-780
Francis II, Holy Roman Emperor
  GE:ME II-568
Francis II (of France)
  GE:ME I-162
Francis Joseph I (of Austria)
  GE:ME II-849, 912, 939, 988
  GE:W20 I-158
  GL:Ren II-785
Francis, Duke of Anjou (Duke of Alençon)
  GE:ME I-184, 202
Francis Ferdinand, Archduke of Austria
  GE:ME III-1245, 1340
  GE:W20 I-158
Francis of Assisi, Saint
  GE:A&M III-1447, 1457
  GL:A&M II-743
Francis, Clarence
  GE:B&C III-1052
Francis, Lydia Maria. *See* Child, Lydia Maria
Francis, Thomas, Jr.
  GE:S&T IV-1444

Francis, Thomas F., Jr.
  GE:Am III-1835
Franck, César
  GL:Ren II-790
Franck, Jean-Michel
  GE:A&C II-979
Franco, Francisco
  GE:A&C II-1062, V-2203
  GE:Am III-1661
  GE:HR II-695, IV-1921, 2079
  GE:ME III-1416
  GE:W20 II-1043
  GL:20 II-709
Franco, Rafael
  GE:HR I-533
François I (of France)
  GE:Am I-28
François, Étienne, Duc de Choiseul
  GE:ME I-451
Franjieh, Suleiman
  GE:W20 III-1235
Frank, Hans
  GE:HR II-667
Frank, Ilya Mikhailovich
  GE:S&T III-1003
Frank, Jerome D.
  GE:HR III-1497
Franken, Al
  GE:A&C V-2355
Frankenthaler, Helen
  GL:AmW II-676
Frankfurter, Felix
  GE:Am III-1883
  GE:B&C II-426
  GE:HR II-629
  GL:Am II-830
Franklin, Aretha
  GL:AmW II-681
Franklin, Benjamin
  GE:Am I-194, 200, 219, 236, 256, 261, 282,
    300
  GE:B&C II-499
  GL:Am II-836
Franklin, Deborah Read
  GE:Am I-236
Franklin, James
  GE:Am I-236
Franklin, Josiah
  GE:Am I-236
Franklin, Kenneth
  GE:S&T IV-1492
Franklin, Rosalind
  GE:ME III-1572
  GE:S&T III-1406

Franklin, R. W.
  GE:A&C IV-1662
Franklin, William
  GE:Am I-236
Franklin, William Temple
  GE:Am I-236
Frankston, Robert
  GE:B&C IV-1687
Fraser, Douglas A.
  GE:B&C V-1763
Frawley, William
  GE:A&C III-1525
Frazer, George E.
  GE:B&C II-481
Frazer, Sir James George
  GL:B&C II-1052
Fréchet, Maurice-René
  GE:S&T I-325
Frederick I Barbarossa
  GE:A&M III-1364
  GL:A&M II-748
Frederick I (of Prussia)
  GE:ME I-396
  GL:Ren II-796
Frederick II, Holy Roman Emperor
  GE:A&M III-1457, 1472, 1478, 1484
Frederick II (of Prussia)
  GE:ME I-396, 414, 419, 437, 469, 475
  GL:A&M II-755
  GL:Ren II-806
Frederick II, The Wise of Five Electors of the
  Palatinate
  GE:ME I-54
Frederick III, Emperor of Germany
  GE:ME II-1013
Frederick III of Hapsburg
  GE:A&M III-1603, 1620
Frederick III, The Pious of Five Electors of the
  Palatinate
  GE:ME I-148
Frederick IV of Denmark and Norway
  GE:ME I-376
Frederick V of Five Electors of the Palatinate
  GE: ME I-250, 290
Frederick, Crown Prince of Prussia
  GE:ME II-912
Frederick Henry
  GL:Ren II-800
Frederick the Great. *See* Frederick II (of Prussia)
Frederick the Handsome of Hapsburg. *See*
  Frederick III of Hapsburg
Frederick, John
  GE:ME I-91

Frederick Charles, Prince
  GE:ME II-912
Frederick William I (of Prussia)
  GE:ME I-396, 414
Frederick William II (of Prussia)
  GE:ME I-469
Frederick William III (of Prussia)
  GE:ME II-572, 711
Frederick William IV (of Prussia)
  GE:ME II-790
  GE:W20 I-54
Frederick William, Crown Prince
  GE:ME II-963
Frederick William, The Great Elector
  GL:Ren II-811
Fredericks, Carlton
  GE:B&C IV-1416
Freed, Alan
  GE:A&C IV-1635
Freed, Arthur
  GE:A&C III-1109, 1432
Freeman, Derek
  GE:S&T II-869
Freeman, Harry Lawrence
  GE:A&C V-2350
Freeman, Leslie G.
  GE:S&T V-2110
Freeman, Morgan
  GE:A&C V-2565
Freeman, Orville L.
  GE:B&C IV-1369
Freeman, Walter Jackson
  GE:S&T III-1060
Frege, Gottlob
  GE:A&C I-518
  GE:S&T I-184, 465
  GL:Ren II-816
Frei, Eduardo
  GE:B&C III-1207
  GE:HR IV-1725
Frelinghuysen, Theodore
  GE:Am I-666
Frémont, Jessie Benton
  GL:AmW II-686
Frémont, John C.
  GE:Am II-795, 818, 877
  GL:Am II-843
French, Sir John Denton Pinkstone
  GE:ME III-1249
Frerichs, Friedrich von
  GE:S&T II-476
Fresnay, Pierre
  GE:A&C II-1073

Freud, Sigmund
    GE:A&C I-19, 309
    GE:ME III-1139, 1310
    GL:20 II-714
Freund, Karl
    GE:A&C II-707, III-1525
Frey, Emile
    GE:HR I-75
Frey, Roger
    GE:ME III-1683
Freyssinet, Eugène
    GL:20 II-719
Frick, Henry Clay
    GE:Am II-1167
    GE:B&C I-29
Friedan, Betty
    GE:HR III-1327, 1656
    GE:W20 II-893, 998
    GL:AmW II-691
Friedland, Duke of. See Wallenstein, Albrecht
    von Wenzel
Friedman, Herbert
    GE:S&T IV-1708
Friedman, Irving
    GE:S&T IV-1645
Friedman, Jerome I.
    GE:S&T IV-1871
Friedman, Milton
    GE:B&C II-740, III-931
Friendly, Edward
    GE:A&C IV-2115
Friendly, Fred W.
    GE:W20 II-669
Frings, Cardinal Josef
    GE:ME III-1633
Frisch, John G.
    GE:S&T III-1260
Frisch, Karl von
    GE:S&T II-679
    GL:20 II-724
Frisch, Max
    GL:20 II-729
Frisch, Otto Robert
    GE:S&T III-1135, 1265
Fritigern
    GE:A&M II-898
Fritsch, Werner von
    GE:W20 I-375
Fritzsch, Harald
    GE:S&T V-1966
Frobenius, Leo
    GL:20 II-735
Froebel, Friedrich
    GL:Ren II-821

Froissart, Jean
    GL:A&M II-760
Fromm, Erich
    GL:20 II-741
Frontinus, Sextus Julius
    GE:A&M II-626
Fronto, Marcus Cornelius
    GE:A&M II-725
Frost, Edwin Brant
    GE:S&T I-213
Frost, Mark
    GE:A&C V-2470
Fry, James B.
    GE:Am II-991
Fry, Maxwell
    GE:A&C III-1503
Fry, Roger
    GL:B&C II-1059
Frye, Jack
    GE:B&C II-752
Fu Ssu-nien
    GE:HR I-276
Fu Yuehua
    GE:HR IV-1983
Fuchs, Klaus
    GE:Am III-1817
Fuentes, Carlos
    GE:A&C III-1268, IV-1689, 2086
Fugard, Athol
    GE:A&C V-2496
    GL:20 II-746
Fuhlrott, Johann Carl
    GE:ME II-822
Fujiwara Michinaga
    GL:A&M II-766
Fulbert of Chartres, Saint
    GE:A&M III-1231
    GL:A&M II-771
Fulbright, William
    GE:B&C III-1014
Fuld, Stanley H.
    GE:B&C IV-1626
Fuller, Alfred Carl
    GE:B&C I-224
Fuller, Anne Hewlett
    GE:A&C III-1579
Fuller, Avard E.
    GE:B&C I-224
Fuller, Calvin S.
    GE:S&T IV-1487
Fuller, Howard
    GE:B&C I-224
Fuller, Loie
    GL:AmW II-695

Fuller, Margaret
  GE:Am I-654
  GL:Am II-850
  GL:AmW II-700
Fuller, Melville Weston
  GE:Am II-1318
  GE:B&C I-63, 146
Fuller, Meta Vaux Warrick
  GL:AmW II-705
Fuller, R. Buckminster
  GE:A&C III-1579, IV-2081, V-2208
  GL:Am II-856
Fuller, Walter D.
  GE:B&C IV-1379
Fulton, Robert
  GE:Am I-471, 600
  GL:Am II-862
Fumimaro, Prince Konoye
  GE:W20 I-361
Funk, Casimir
  GE:S&T I-330

Funston, Frederick
  GE:Am II-1290, III-1438
Furman, William Henry
  GE:HR III-1674
  GE:W20 III-1279
Furrer, Jonas
  GE:ME II-794
Furse, Roger K.
  GE:A&C III-1378
Furth, George
  GE:A&C V-2213
Furtwängler, Wilhelm
  GE:A&C II-816
Fust, Johann
  GE:A&M III-1713
Futrell, Mary Hatwood
  GL:AmW II-710
Fyfe, Sir David Maxwell
  GE:HR II-843
Fylstra, Daniel
  GE:B&C IV-1687

G

Gabirol, Solomon ibn. *See* Ibn Gabirol
Gable, Clark
  GE:A&C II-951, III-1154
Gabor, Dennis
  GE:S&T III-1288
Gabrieli, Andrea
  GL:Ren II-826
Gabrieli, Giovanni
  GL:Ren II-831
Gacha, Gonzalo Rodríguez
  GE:HR V-2465
Gaetani, Benedict. *See* Boniface VIII, Pope
Gagarin, Yuri Alekseyevich
  GE:ME III-1618
  GE:S&T IV-1693
Gage, Matilda Joslyn
  GL:AmW II-715
Gage, Thomas
  GE:Am I-225, 231, 251
  GL:B&C II-1065
Gagnan, Émile
  GE:S&T III-1219
Gahagan, Helen. *See* Douglas, Helen Gahagan
Gaherin, John
  GE:B&C IV-1512
Gaines, LaDonna. *See* Summer, Donna
Gainsborough, Thomas
  GL:B&C III-1071
Gaisberg, Frederick William
  GE:A&C I-69
Gaiseric
  GE:A&M II-958, 975
Gaismaier, Michael
  GE:ME I-76
Gaitán, Jorge Eliécer
  GE:Am III-1789
  GE:HR II-737, V-2465
Gaius
  GE:A&M II-721
Gaius Aurelius Valerius Diocletianus. *See* Diocletian
Gaius Canuleius. *See* Canuleius, Gaius
Gaius Galerius Valerius Maximianus. *See* Maximian
Gaius Julius. *See* Julius, Gaius
Gaius Julius Caesar. *See* Caesar, Julius
Gaius Julius Caesar Octavianus. *See* Augustus
Gaius Laelius. *See* Laelius, Gaius

Gaius Licinius. *See* Licinius, Gaius
Gaius Maecenas. *See* Maecenas, Gaius
Gaius Marius. *See* Marius, Gaius
Gaius Memmius. *See* Memmius, Gaius
Galán, Luis Carlos
  GE:HR V-2465
Galarza, Ernesto
  GE:HR III-1161
Gale, Benjamin
  GE:Am I-267
Gale, Leonard
  GE:Am II-742
Galen
  GE:A&M II-737
  GE:ME I-133
  GL:A&M II-776
Galerius Valerius Maximianus, Gaius. *See* Maximian
Galey, John H.
  GE:B&C I-24
Galileo
  GE:ME I-236, 285
  GL:Ren II-836
Gall (c. 560-c. 615)
  GE:A&M II-1052
Gall (1840?-1894)
  GE:Am II-1094
Galla Placidia
  GE:A&M II-958, 975
Gallagher, Paul B.
  GE:S&T IV-1598
Gallant, Mavis
  GL:AmW II-720
Gallatin, Albert
  GE:Am I-350, 377, 414, 491, 522, 539, 546, 582, II-673
  GL:Am II-868
Gallieni, Joseph Simon
  GE:ME III-1249
Galloway, John Debo
  GE:S&T II-547
Galloway, Joseph
  GE:Am I-246
Galois, Évariste
  GL:Ren II-841
Galtieri, Leopoldo Fortunato
  GE:HR V-2280

Galton, Francis
  GE:ME III-1310
  GL:B&C III-1077
Galvani, Luigi
  GL:Ren II-846
Gama, Vasco da
  GL:Ren II-851
Gamanayake, Upatissa
  GE:HR V-2315
Gambetta, Léon
  GE:ME II-954, 974
  GL:Ren II-856
Gamble, Clarence James
  GE:HR III-1290
Gamble, James
  GE:Am II-930
Gamelin, Maurice Gustave
  GE:ME III-1451
Gamow, George
  GE:S&T II-851, III-1309, 1320, IV-1687
Gance, Abel
  GE:A&C II-642
  GL:20 II-752
Gandhi, Indira
  GE:HR II-924, III-1611, IV-1858, 2215, 2232
  GE:W20 II-1091
  GL:20 II-757
Gandhi, Mohandas Karamchand
  GE:HR I-156, 315, 401, 447, 459, 469, II-601,
    731, 743, 924
  GE:W20 I-175, II-605
  GL:20 II-762
Gandhi, Rajiv
  GE:B&C V-1893
  GE:HR IV-2068, 2215, 2238, V-2426
Gandhi, Sanjay
  GE:HR IV-1858
Gandia, Duke of. See Borgia, Francis
Gandil, Charles Arnold "Chick"
  GE:Am III-1497
Ganelon
  GE:A&M III-1308
Gapon, Father Georgi Appollonovich
  GE:ME III-1156
Garbo, Greta
  GE:A&C II-822
  GL:AmW II-724
Garcia, Celso-Ramon
  GE:S&T IV-1512
García, José Miguel Gallardo
  GE:HR II-801
Garcia, Robert
  GE:B&C V-1933

García, Romeo Lucas
  GE:HR IV-1972
García Lorca, Federico
  GE:A&C III-1179
  GL:20 II-767
García Márquez, Gabriel
  GE:A&C IV-1689, 2086
  GL:20 II-772
Gardener, Cornelius
  GE:HR I-7
Gardiner, Stephen
  GE:ME I-123
  GL:B&C III-1083
Gardner, Erle Stanley
  GE:A&C I-496
Gardner, Isabella Stewart
  GL:AmW II-729
Gardner, John W.
  GE:HR I-520
Garfield, James A.
  GE:Am II-1031, 1128
  GL:Am II-872
Garfield, James Rudolf
  GE:Am III-1390
  GE:B&C I-86
Garibaldi, Giuseppe
  GE:ME II-860, 870, 923, 958
  GL:Ren II-861
Garland, Hamlin
  GE:Am II-1255
Garland, Judy
  GE:A&C III-1109
  GL:AmW II-734
Garmes, Lee
  GE:A&C II-845
Garn, Jake
  GE:B&C IV-1595, V-1757
Garner, James
  GE:A&C IV-1768
Garner, John Nance
  GE:Am III-1594, 1609, 1667
Garnier, Tony
  GE:A&C II-1021
  GL:20 II-778
Garrett, David C.
  GE:B&C IV-1676
Garrett, Millicent. See Fawcett, Dame Millicent
  Garrett
Garrick, David
  GL:B&C III-1088
Garriott, Owen K.
  GE:S&T V-1997, 2256
Garrison, Lloyd K.
  GE:Am III-1637

Garrison, William Lloyd
    GE:Am I-642, II-719
    GL:Am II-878
Garrod, Dorothy Annie Elizabeth
    GE:S&T V-2341
Garros, Roland
    GE:S&T II-600
Garth, Charles
    GE:Am I-213
Garvey, Marcus
    GE:A&C IV-2022
    GE:Am III-1444
    GL:Am II-885
Gary, Elbert Henry
    GE:B&C I-29, 52, 346
    GE:HR I-293
Gascoyne-Cecil, Robert Arthur Talbot. *See*
    Salisbury, Third Marquis of
Gasparri, Cardinal Pietro
    GE:ME III-1354
Gassett, José Ortega y. *See* Ortega y Gassett, José
Gaston, Don F.
    GE:B&C V-1939
Gates, Curtis. *See* Curtis, Ken
Gates, Major Horatio
    GE:Am I-277
Gates, Robert M.
    GE:HR V-2426
Gates, William H.
    GE:S&T IV-1772
Gathing, Ezekial
    GE:A&C III-1465
Gattaz, Yvon
    GE:B&C V-1793
Gattinara, Mercurino
    GE:ME I-64
Gaud, William S.
    GE:B&C III-1133
Gaudí, Antonio
    GE:A&C I-257
    GL:20 II-783
Gaudier-Brzeska, Henri
    GE:A&C I-445
Gauguin, Paul
    GL:Ren II-866
Gaulle, Charles de
    GE:B&C II-735, III-875, 1081, 1169, 1320,
        IV-1353
    GE:HR II-646, 651, III-1155, 1425, 1462
    GE:ME III-1477, 1512, 1607, 1628, 1648,
        1654, 1683
    GE:W20 II-1003, III-1146
    GL:20 II-526

Gaultier, Jean-Paul
    GE:A&C V-2449
Gauss, Carl Friedrich
    GL:Ren II-872
Gautama. *See* Buddha
Gavin, John
    GE:A&C IV-1855
Gaviria Trujillo, César
    GE:HR V-2465
Gay, Edwin F.
    GE:B&C I-157, 335
Gay, Frank William
    GE:B&C II-442
Gaye, Marvin
    GE:A&C IV-1790
Gay-Lussac, Joseph-Louis
    GL:Ren II-877
Gazzaniga, Michael S.
    GE:S&T IV-1635
Geary, John White
    GE:Am II-889
Geber. *See* Jabir ibn Hayyan
Gebhard, Paul H.
    GE:HR III-1497
    GE:W20 II-619
Geddes, Auckland C.
    GE:Am III-1531
Geddes, Norman Bel
    GE:A&C II-777, 1057
Gedymin
    GE:A&M III-1650
Geer, Will
    GE:A&C II-810
Gehrig, Lou
    GL:Am II-890
Gehry, Frank
    GE:A&C V-2614, 2646
Geiger, Johannes Hans Wilhelm
    GE:S&T I-93, 412, II-527, 590, 851
Geiger, Rudolf Oskar Robert Williams
    GL:20 II-789
Geismar, Alain
    GE:HR III-1425
Geissler, Heinrich
    GE:S&T I-108, 118, III-1080
Geitel, Hans Friedrich
    GE:S&T I-93, 208
Gelasius
    GE:A&M II-989
Gelbart, Larry
    GE:A&C V-2271
Geldof, Bob
    GE:A&C V-2543
Gellée, Claude. *See* Claude Lorrain

Gell-Mann, Murray
  GE:S&T IV-1767, 1871, V-1966
Gemayel, Bashir
  GE:HR IV-2164
Gemayel, Pierre
  GE:W20 III-1235
Geneen, Harold
  GE:B&C IV-1527
Genêt, Citizen Edmond
  GE:Am I-403
Genet, Jean
  GE:A&C IV-1871
  GL:20 II-793
Genghis Khan
  GE:A&M III-1462
  GL:A&M II-781
Genne, William H.
  GE:HR II-1096
Genscher, Hans-Dietrich
  GE:HR V-2589
Gensfleisch zur Laden, Johannes. See Gutenberg,
  Johann
Gentile, Giovanni
  GE:ME III-1299
  GL:20 II-798
Gentili, Alberico
  GL:Ren II-884
Genucius, Titus
  GE:A&M I-253
Geoffroi de Villehardouin. See Villehardouin,
  Geoffroi de
George I (of Great Britain)
  GE:ME I-385
  GL:B&C III-1094
George II (of Great Britain)
  GE:ME I-419, 437
  GL:B&C III-1099
George III (of Great Britain)
  GE:Am I-251
  GE:ME I-451, II-551
  GL:B&C III-1105
George IV (of Great Britain)
  GE:Am I-593
  GE:ME II-669
  GL:B&C III-1112
George V (of Great Britain)
  GE:ME III-1214
  GL:B&C III-1118
George VI (of Great Britain)
  GE:ME III-1517
  GL:B&C III-1123
George, David Lloyd. See Lloyd George, David
George, Henry
  GL:Am II-895

George, John
  GE:ME I-270, 274, 290
George, Walter F.
  GE:W20 II-709
Georgi, Howard
  GE:S&T V-2014
Gerard of Cremona
  GE:A&M III-1524
Gerard, James Watson
  GE:Am III-1450
Gerbert of Aurillac. See Sylvester II
Geremek, Bronisław
  GE:HR IV-2112, V-2477, 2500
Gerento
  GE:A&M III-1276
Géricault, Théodore
  GL:Ren II-889
Germain, Lord George (George Sackville
  Germain, Viscount Sackville)
  GE:Am I-277
Germanicus, Tiberius Claudius Drusus Nero. See
  Claudius I
Gerö, Erno
  GE:ME III-1595
Geronimo
  GL:Am II-900
Gerry, Elbridge
  GE:Am I-367, 408
Gershon-Cohen, Jacob
  GE:S&T II-562
Gershvin, Jacob. See Gershwin, George
Gershwin, George
  GE:A&C II-598, 1016
  GL:Am II-905
Gershwin, Ira
  GE:A&C II-1016
Gesell, Arnold
  GL:Am II-911
Gesner, Conrad
  GL:Ren II-895
Gessius Florus. See Florus, Gessius
Gestetner, Sigmund
  GE:A&C II-777
Getty, Estelle
  GE:A&C V-2502
Getty, Gordon
  GE:B&C V-1876
Geyer, Florian
  GE:ME I-76
Geza
  GE:A&M III-1210
Ghazan, Mahmud
  GL:A&M II-786

Ghazzali, al-
  GE:A&M III-1395
  GL:A&M II-792
Gheorghiu-Dej, Gheorghe
  GE:HR V-2546
Ghiberti, Lorenzo
  GE:A&M III-1665
  GL:Ren II-900
Ghislieri, Antonio. *See* Pius V
Ghormley, Robert L.
  GE:Am III-1709
Ghose, Sri Aurobindo. *See* Aurobindo, Sri
Gia Long (Nguyen Phuc Anh)
  GE:W20 III-1243
Giacconi, Riccardo
  GE:S&T IV-1708
Giacometti, Alberto
  GL:20 II-803
Giacosa, Giuseppe
  GE:A&C I-29
Giannini, Amadeo P.
  GE:B&C II-603, IV-1739
Giap, Vo Nguyen. *See* Vo Nguyen Giap
Giaver, Ivar
  GE:S&T IV-1551
Gibb, Barry
  GE:A&C V-2386
Gibb, Maurice
  GE:A&C V-2386
Gibb, Robin
  GE:A&C V-2386
Gibbon, Edward
  GE:Am II-1184
  GL:B&C III-1129
Gibbon, Colonel John
  GE:Am II-1094
Gibbon, John H., Jr.
  GE:S&T III-1024
Gibbon, Mary Hopkinson
  GE:S&T III-1024
Gibbons, James
  GL:Am II-916
Gibbons, Thomas
  GE:Am I-600
Gibbs, Erna
  GL:AmW II-739
Gibbs, Josiah Willard
  GL:Am II-921
Gibbs, Lois Marie
  GE:HR IV-1961
Gibbs, Marla
  GE:A&C V-2339
Giberson, Walker E. (Gene)
  GE:S&T V-2003

Gibson, Althea
  GL:AmW II-744
Gibson, Edward G.
  GE:S&T V-1997
Gibson, Henry
  GE:A&C IV-2115
Gibson, Mark
  GE:HR V-2437
Giddings, Franklin H.
  GE:Am III-1357
Gide, André
  GE:A&C II-561, 620, 890
  GL:20 II-809
Gideon, Clarence Earl
  GE:Am III-1893
  GE:HR III-1182
Gierek, Edward
  GE:HR IV-2112
Giese, Tiedemann
  GE:ME I-138
Gifford, Walter Sherman
  GE:Am III-1582
  GE:B&C II-770
Gil, David G.
  GE:HR IV-1752
Gilbert, Grove Karl
  GE:Am II-1104
Gilbert, Sir Humphrey
  GE:Am I-46
Gilbert, Ruth
  GE:A&C III-1394
Gilbert, Walter
  GE:S&T V-2115
Gilbert, W. S., and Sir Arthur Sullivan
  GL:B&C III-1134
Gilbreth, Frank (Bunker)
  GE:B&C I-258
Gilbreth, Lillian (Evelyn)
  GE:B&C I-258
Gilder, George
  GE:B&C V-1782
Giles, Brother
  GE:A&M III-1447
Gilhool, Thomas
  GE:HR IV-1780
Gillespie, Archibald H.
  GE:Am II-818
Gillespie, Carl
  GE:S&T V-2068
Gillespie, John Birks "Dizzy"
  GE:A&C III-1318, 1617
Gillette, George
  GE:B&C I-75

Gillette, King Camp
GE:B&C I-75
Gilliam, Terry
GE:A&C IV-2174
Gilman, Charlotte Perkins
GL:AmW II-748
Gilman, Daniel Coit
GE:Am II-1077
Gilman, Howard
GE:A&C V-2663
Gilpin, Laura
GL:AmW II-753
Gilruth, Robert R.
GE:S&T IV-1698
GE:W20 II-934
Gilson, Étienne
GL:20 II-814
Ginsberg, Allen
GE:A&C III-1460
GE:HR III-1479
Ginzberg, Asher. *See* Haam, Achad
Ginzburg, Aleksandr
GE:HR IV-1915
Ginzton, Edward Leonard
GE:S&T III-1384
Gioberti, Vincenzo
GL:Ren II-905
Giolitti, Giovanni
GE:ME II-1094, 1109, III-1228
GE:W20 I-138
Gionfriddo, Al
GE:A&C III-1362
Giora, Simon ben. *See* Ben Giora
Giorgione
GL:Ren II-910
Giotto
GE:A&M III-1587, 1691
GL:A&M II-797
Giovanni da Fiesole. *See* Angelico, Fra
Girard, Gertrude
GE:HR III-1605
Girard, Stephen
GE:Am I-539
Girardin, Lise
GE:HR III-1605
Giraud, Henri Honoré
GE:ME III-1477
Giraudoux, Jean
GL:20 II-822
Girey, Mengli
GE:A&M III-1742
Girodmaine, Joseph A.
GE:S&T V-2025

Girouard, Sir E. P.
GE:B&C I-196
Giroux, Robert
GE:A&C IV-1645
Giscard d'Estaing, Valéry
GE:A&C V-2588
GE:B&C IV-1353, V-1793
GE:ME III-1683
GE:W20 III-1104, 1257
Gish, Lillian
GE:A&C I-402
GL:AmW II-758
Giuliani, Rudolph
GE:B&C IV-1449, V-1958
Giustiniani, John
GE:A&M III-1718
Gizenga, Antoine
GE:ME III-1613
Gizzi, Cardinal
GE:ME II-770
Gladstone, William Ewart
GE:ME II-929, 1038, 1048
GL:B&C III-1141
Glaser, Donald A.
GE:S&T IV-1470
Glashow, Sheldon L.
GE:S&T V-2014
Glass, Carter
GE:Am III-1432
GE:B&C I-240, II-539, 656, 717
Glass, Fridolin
GE:ME III-1395
Glass, Philip
GE:A&C IV-1979, V-2375, 2571
Gleason, Jackie
GE:A&C III-1470, IV-1673
Gleb
GE:A&M III-1205
Gleissner, Franz
GE:ME I-542
Gleizes, Albert
GE:A&C I-337
Glenn, Hugh
GE:Am I-588
Glenn, John H.
GE:S&T IV-1723
Glines, John
GE:A&C V-2502
Gloucester, Earl of (Richard de Clare)
GE:A&M III-1528
Glover, Danny
GE:A&C V-2496
Glover, William Irving
GE:B&C II-493

Gluck, Christoph
   GL:Ren II-915
Glushko, Valentin P.
   GE:S&T IV-1819, V-1928, 1950
Gnaeus Pompeius Magnus. *See* Pompey
Gnaeus Pompeius Strabo. *See* Strabo
Gneisenau, August von
   GE:ME II-572
   GL:Ren II-920
Godard, Jean-Luc
   GE:A&C IV-1710, IV-1845
   GL:20 II-828
Goddard, James L.
   GE:B&C IV-1369
Goddard, Morrill
   GE:Am II-1243
Goddard, Robert H.
   GE:Am III-1555
   GE:S&T II-810, IV-1545
   GE:W20 II-751
   GL:Am II-927
Gödel, Kurt
   GE:S&T I-233, II-900, III-1045, IV-1751
Godey, Alexis
   GE:Am II-795
Godfrey, Arthur
   GE:A&C III-1383
Godke, R. A.
   GE:S&T V-2273
Godkin, Edwin Lawrence
   GL:Am II-932
Godolphin, First Earl of
   GL:B&C III-1147
Godron, Ishabel M., Countess of Aberdeen
   GE:HR I-75
Godunov, Boris Fyodorovich
   GE:ME I-198, 231
   GL:Ren II-926
Godwin, William
   GE:ME I-533
   GL:B&C III-1151
Godwinson, Harold
   GE:A&M III-1248
Goebbels, Joseph
   GE:A&C II-767, III-1083, 1217
   GE:HR I-480, II-567
   GE:ME III-1377, 1382, 1391
   GE:W20 I-311
   GL:20 II-834
Goemans, Camille
   GE:A&C V-2310
Goerdeler, Carl
   GE:W20 I-375

Goethals, George Washington
   GE:B&C I-264
   GE:S&T I-249
   GL:Am II-937
Goethe, Johann Wolfgang von
   GE:A&C I-396
   GL:Ren II-931
Gogh, Vincent van
   GE:A&C V-2603
   GE:Am III-1411
   GL:Ren II-936
Gogol, Nikolai
   GL:Ren II-943
Goizueta, Roberto C.
   GE:B&C V-1904
Gökalp, Ziya
   GE:HR I-98
Gold, Ronald
   GE:HR IV-1741
Gold, Thomas
   GE:S&T III-1320
   GE:W20 II-1009
Goldberg, Arthur Joseph
   GE:B&C IV-1437
   GE:HR III-1674
   GE:W20 II-730
Goldberg, Leonard
   GE:B&C IV-1578
Goldberg, Whoopi
   GE:A&C V-2565
   GL:AmW II-762
Goldenson, Leonard Harry
   GE:A&C III-1211, 1368, 1383, 1612
   GE:B&C IV-1578
Goldie, Sir George
   GL:B&C III-1158
Golding, William
   GE:A&C III-1585
Goldman, Emma
   GE:HR I-258
   GL:AmW II-767
Goldmann, Max. *See* Reinhardt, Max
Goldmark, Josephine
   GE:Am III-1363
Goldmark, Peter Carl
   GE:A&C III-1211
   GE:S&T III-1166
Goldsborough, T. Alan
   GE:B&C II-781
Goldsmith, Harvey
   GE:A&C V-2543
Goldsmith, Oliver
   GL:B&C III-1163
Goldstein, Eugen
   GE:S&T III-1070

Goldstein, Jonah J.
    GE:HR I-184
Goldstine, Herman Heine
    GE:S&T III-1213, IV-1475
Goldwater, Barry Morris
    GE:Am III-1918
    GE:B&C III-1122
Goldwyn, Samuel
    GE:A&C II-567
    GL:Am II-941
Golenor, Jack. See Gavin, John
Golgi, Camillo
    GE:S&T I-1, 243
Golitsyn, Boris
    GE:S&T I-51
Golovin, Alexander
    GE:A&C I-269
Goltz, Rüdiger von der
    GE:HR I-207
Gomer, Robert
    GE:S&T III-1070
Gomes Candau, Marcolino. See Candau,
    Marcolino Gomes
Gomez, Diego
    GE:A&M III-1686
Gomez, Juan Vincente
    GE:B&C I-385
Gómez, Laureano
    GE:HR II-737
Gompers, Samuel
    GE:Am II-1152
    GE:B&C I-146, II-459
    GE:HR I-126, 281, 293
    GL:Am II-946
Goncz, Arpad
    GE:HR V-2421
Gondola, Andrea di Pietro della. See Palladio,
    Andrea
Gongylus
    GE:A&M I-308
Gonne, Maud. See MacBride, Maud Gonne
Gonsaluez, Anton
    GE:A&M III-1686
Gonsaluez, John
    GE:A&M III-1686
González, Felipe
    GE:HR IV-1921
    GE:W20 II-1043
González, José Victoriano. See Gris, Juan
Gonzalez Echegaray, Joaquin
    GE:S&T V-2110
Gooch, Sir Daniel
    GE:ME II-834

Goodman, Alice
    GE:A&C V-2599
Goodman, Andrew
    GE:HR III-1149, 1246
Goodman, Benny
    GE:A&C II-930, 968
Goodwin, Hannibal W.
    GE:B&C II-527
Goodyear, Charles
    GL:Am II-951
Goodyear, Conger
    GE:A&C II-782
Goonetilleke, T. P. B.
    GE:HR II-985
Goosen, Pieter
    GE:HR IV-1887
Goossens, Eugene
    GE:A&C I-425
Gorbachev, Mikhail
    GE:B&C V-2022
    GE:HR III-1408, IV-1852, 2062, V-2249,
        2298, 2348, 2421, 2449, 2471, 2477, 2500,
        2523, 2570, 2577, 2589, 2618
    GL:20 II-840
Gorchakov, Aleksandr Mikhailovich
    GE:Am II-1037
    GE:ME II-988, 1007
Gordillo, Luis
    GE:A&C V-2203
Gordimer, Nadine
    GE:A&C V-2668
    GL:20 II-845
Gordon, General Charles George ("Chinese")
    GE:A&C I-214
    GL:B&C III-1170
Gordon, David
    GE:A&C V-2480
Gordon, George. See Byron, Lord
Gordon, George Hamilton. See Aberdeen, Earl of
Gordon, Mary
    GE:A&C III-1131
Gordon, Max
    GE:A&C II-936
Gordon, Patrick
    GE:ME I-364
Gordon, Richard F.
    GE:S&T IV-1913
Gordon, Ruth
    GL:AmW III-773
Gordon, Walter Lockhart
    GE:HR III-1321
Gordy, Berry, Jr.
    GE:A&C IV-1790, V-2294, 2512
    GE:B&C III-1143

Goremykin, Ivan Longinovich
  GE:ME III-1179
Gorenstein, Daniel
  GE:S&T V-2130
Gorgas, William Crawford
  GE:Am II-1313
  GE:S&T I-73, 223, 249
  GL:Am II-956
Gorges, Sir Ferdinando
  GE:Am I-59
Gorgias of Leontini
  GE:A&M I-286
Goring, George
  GE:ME I-313
Göring, Hermann
  GE:HR I-480, 491, II-667
  GE:ME III-1377, 1391, 1456, 1472, 1522
  GE:W20 I-303, 311, 375, 396, 430
  GL:20 II-850
Gorky, Arshile
  GE:A&C II-1001
Gorky, Maxim
  GE:A&C II-908
  GL:20 II-856
Gorst, Sir John
  GE:HR I-109
Gort, Lord John Standish Surtees Prendergast
    Vereker
  GE:ME III-1456
Gorton, Samuel
  GE:Am I-97
Gosden, Freeman Fisher. See also "Amos 'n'
    Andy"
  GE:A&C II-755
Gossage, Howard Luck
  GE:A&C IV-1973
Gosslau, Ing Fritz
  GE:S&T III-1235
Gothardt, Matthias. See Grünewald, Matthias
Goto, Shimpei
  GE:HR I-417
Gottfried von Strassburg
  GL:A&M II-802
Gottwald, Klement
  GE:W20 II-626
Götz, Friedrich Wilhelm Paul
  GE:S&T II-579
Gouge, William M.
  GE:Am II-748
Gould, Elgin R. L.
  GE:B&C I-180
Gould, Gordon
  GE:W20 II-881

Gould, Harold
  GE:A&C V-2239
Gould, Jay
  GE:Am II-1135
Goulden, Emmeline. See Pankhurst, Emmeline
Goulian, Mehran
  GE:S&T IV-1857
Gounod, Charles
  GL:Ren II-948
Gove, Philip B.
  GE:A&C IV-1898
Gowers, Sir Ernest
  GE:HR III-1316
Gowland, Gibson
  GE:A&C II-593
Gowon, Yakubu
  GE:B&C IV-1589
  GE:HR III-1365
  GE:W20 II-1003
Goya, Francisco de
  GL:Ren II-953
Goyathlay. See Geronimo
Graaf, Robert Hemison Van de. See Van de
    Graaf, Robert Jemison
Graber, Vincent J.
  GE:HR IV-2220
Gracchi, The
  GE:A&M I-481, 486
  GL:A&M II-806
Gracchus, Gaius Sempronius. See Gracchi, The
Gracchus, Tiberius Sempronius. See Gracchi, The
Grace, William Gilbert
  GL:B&C III-1175
Graham, Bill
  GE:A&C V-2543
Graham, Florence Nightingale. See Arden,
    Elizabeth
Graham, Katharine
  GL:AmW III-778
Graham, Martha
  GE:A&C I-390, III-1284
  GL:Am II-962
  GL:AmW III-782
Grahn, Judy
  GE:A&C V-2370
Gramsci, Antonio
  GL:20 II-862
Grandes, Muñoz
  GE:W20 II-1043
Granger, Gideon
  GE:Am I-485
Granger, Walter Willis
  GE:S&T II-735

Grant, Cary
GE:A&C II-951
Grant, Jane
GE:A&C II-648
Grant, Madison
GE:HR I-350
Grant, Ulysses S.
GE:Am II-997, 1026, 1054, 1072
GE:B&C I-264
GL:Am II-968
Granville-Barker, Harley
GE:A&C I-85
Gras, N. S. B.
GE:B&C I-335
Grass, Günter
GE:A&C III-1357, IV-1780
GL:20 II-868
Grateful Dead, the
GE:A&C IV-2180
Gratian
GE:A&M II-852, 898, 904, III-1491
Grattan, Henry
GE:ME II-551
Grau San Martín, Ramón
GE:W20 II-743
Graves, Michael
GE:A&C V-2646
Gravier, Charles. See De Vergennes, Comte
Gray, Asa
GL:Am II-975
Gray, Donald M.
GE:S&T V-2082
Gray, Linda
GE:A&C V-2418
Graziani, Marshal Rodolfo (di Neghelli)
GE:ME III-1467
Greco, El
GL:Ren II-959
Greeley, Horace
GE:Am II-877, 962, 980
GL:Am II-979
Green, Bernard R.
GE:Am II-1279
Green, Edith
GE:HR III-1172
Green, Lawrence E.
GE:B&C III-948
Green, Nicholas St. John
GE:Am III-1363
Green, Paul
GE:A&C II-874
Green, Thomas Hill
GL:B&C III-1180

Green, William
GE:Am III-1655
GE:B&C II-706, 729, 792
GE:HR I-377
Greenberg, Clement
GE:A&C III-1557
Greenberg, Jack
GE:HR III-1617
Greene, Alexander Plunkett
GE:A&C IV-1824
Greene, Graham
GL:B&C III-1185
Greene, Harold H.
GE:B&C V-1821
Greene, Hugh Carleton
GE:B&C II-758
Greene, Lorne
GE:A&C IV-1800
Greene, Nathanael
GE:Am I-294
GL:Am II-986
Greenspan, Alan
GE:B&C V-1953
Greenstein, Jesse Leonard
GE:S&T IV-1640
GE:W20 II-899
Greenstreet, Sydney
GE:A&C III-1223
Greenway, Francis
GL:B&C III-1191
Gregg, Josiah
GE:Am I-588
Gregg, Troy Leon
GE:W20 III-1279
Gregorius Florentius. See Gregory of Tours
Gregory I, Pope. See Gregory the Great
Gregory II, Pope
GE:A&M II-1126
Gregory IV, Pope
GE:A&M II-1158
Gregory VII, Pope (Hildebrand)
GE:A&M III-1257, 1263, 1269, 1318
GL:A&M II-812
Gregory IX, Pope
GE:A&M III-1400, 1441, 1472, 1491
GL:A&M II-817
Gregory X, Pope
GE:A&M III-1550
Gregory XI, Pope
GE:A&M III-1644, 1680
Gregory XIII, Pope
GE:A&M II-1091
GE:ME I-174

Gregory of Nazianzus
  GE:A&M II-893
  GL:A&M II-822
Gregory of Nyssa
  GE:A&M II-893
  GL:A&M II-826
Gregory of Tours
  GE:A&M II-995
  GL:A&M II-832
Gregory the Great (Gregory I)
  GE:A&M II-1058, 1063, 1069, III-1243, 1257
  GL:A&M II-838
Gregory, Lady Augusta
  GE:A&C I-119, 176, 440
Gregory, Robert
  GE:A&C I-440
Gregson, Thomas
  GE:Am I-109
Grenville, Baron. See Grenville, William
  Wyndham
Grenville, George
  GE:Am I-219
Grenville, Sir John
  GE:ME I-337
Grenville, Sir Richard
  GE:Am I-46
  GL:B&C III-1197
Grenville, William Wyndham (Baron Grenville)
  GE:Am I-389
Grey, Second Earl
  GE:ME II-704, 715
  GL:B&C III-1202
Grey, Sir Edward
  GE:Am III-1450
  GE:HR I-103
  GE:ME III-1192, 1197, 1202, 1240, 1245,
    1340
  GE:W20 I-121
  GL:B&C III-1208
Grey, Sir George Edward
  GL:B&C III-1213
Grey, Zane
  GE:A&C I-304
Grieg, Edvard
  GL:Ren II-965
Griess, Robert Louis, Jr.
  GE:S&T V-2130
Griffin, Jocelyn Crane
  GE:S&T III-1018
Griffin, Merv
  GE:B&C IV-1600
Griffin, Robert P.
  GE:B&C III-1122
Griffith, Arthur
  GE:ME III-1314

Griffith, D. W.
  GE:A&C I-57, 224, 402
  GE:Am III-1501
  GL:Am II-993
Griffith, Frederick
  GE:S&T III-1203
Griffiths, John Willis
  GE:Am II-807
Griffiths, Martha
  GE:HR III-1327
Griggs, Willie S.
  GE:B&C IV-1495
  GE:HR III-1617
Grijns, Gerrit
  GE:S&T I-103
Grimaldi, Marquis of
  GE:ME I-442
Grimké, Angelina, and Sarah Grimké
  GL:AmW III-787
Grindel, Eugène. See Éluard, Paul
Gringauz, K. I.
  GE:S&T IV-1567
Gripenberg, Baroness Alexandra
  GE:HR I-70
Gris, Juan
  GE:A&C I-337
  GL:20 II-873
Grissom, Virgil I. (Gus)
  GE:S&T IV-1723
Griswold, Estelle T.
  GE:HR III-1290
Griswold, J. N. A.
  GE:Am II-1135
Groener, Wilhelm
  GE:B&C I-293
Groening, Matt
  GE:A&C V-2652
Grofé, Ferde
  GE:A&C II-598
Gromyko, Andrei A.
  GE:HR IV-1806
  GE:W20 II-564, 955, 1054
Gröner, Wilhelm
  GE:HR I-241
Groot, Huigh de. See Grotius, Hugo
Groote, Gerhard
  GE:A&M III-1670
Gropius, Walter
  GE:A&C I-79, 181, 463, II-583, 1021, 1067,
    III-1503, IV-1919, 2064
  GE:W20 I-295
  GL:20 II-878
Grosseteste, Robert
  GE:A&M III-1539, 1555

Grossman, Arthur. *See* Freed, Arthur
Grossman, Daniel Williams
  GE:A&C III-1602
Grossman, Jan
  GE:A&C IV-1967
Grossman, Marcel
  GE:S&T II-625
Grosvenor, Hugh "Bend'or"
  GE:A&C I-474
Grosz, George
  GE:A&C II-631, III-1083
Grosz, Karoly
  GE:HR V-2421
Grotefend, Georg Friedrich
  GE:S&T I-169
Grotius, Hugo
  GL:Ren II-971
Grove, Sir William Robert
  GE:ME II-753
  GL:B&C III-1219
Groves, Leslie Richard
  GE:Am III-1692
  GE:S&T III-1265
Grozier, Richard
  GE:B&C I-324
Gruen, David. *See* Ben-Gurion, David
Gruen, Victor
  GE:B&C III-1070
Gruening, Ernest Henry
  GE:HR III-1579
  GE:W20 II-790
Gruentzig, Andreas
  GE:S&T V-2088
Grumbach, Antoine
  GE:A&C V-2646
Grunberg-Manago, Marianne
  GE:S&T III-1363, IV-1687
Grundy, Gordon E.
  GE:B&C III-1190
Grünewald, Matthias
  GE:A&C II-816
  GL:Ren II-976
Guare, John
  GE:A&C V-2239
Guarini, Guarino
  GL:Ren II-980
Guber, Peter
  GE:B&C V-1996
Guchkov, Aleksandr Ivanovich
  GE:ME III-1179
Guderian, Heinz
  GE:W20 I-479
  GL:20 II-883

Güell, Eusebio
  GE:A&C I-257
Guericke, Otto von
  GL:Ren II-985
Guérin, Camille
  GE:S&T II-705
Guerrero, Manuel Amador
  GE:HR I-25
Guesde, Jules (Mathieu Bastile)
  GE:ME II-1044
Guevara, Che
  GE:HR II-1026
  GL:20 II-888
Guffey, James M.
  GE:B&C I-24
Guggenheim, Daniel
  GL:Am II-999
Guggenheim, Peggy
  GE:A&C III-1239
Guggenheim, Simon
  GE:Am II-1307
Guggenheim, Solomon R.
  GE:A&C IV-1806
Guicciardini, Francesco
  GE:ME I-35
  GL:Ren II-990
Guidi, Tommaso di Giovanni di Simone. *See* Masaccio
Guido D'Arezzo
  GL:A&M II-843
Guido de Cauliaco. *See* Guy de Chauliac
Guido di Pietro. *See* Angelico, Fra
Guilbert, Ann Morgan
  GE:A&C IV-1908
Guilford, Earl of. *See* North, Lord
Guillaume de Lorris. *See* De Lorris, Guillaume
Guillaume de Machaut. *See* Machaut, Guillaume de
Guillaume de Paris. *See* William of Auvergne
Guillaume de Poitiers. *See* De Poitiers, Guillaume
Guillaume, Charles-Édouard
  GL:20 II-893
Guimarães Rosa, João
  GE:A&C IV-1689
Guinan, E. F.
  GE:S&T V-2211
Guinness, Alec
  GE:A&C III-1427, V-2391
Guinzburg, Harold K.
  GE:A&C II-686
  GE:B&C II-504
Guise, Duke of
  GE:ME I-162

Guisewite, Cathy
    GL:AmW III-792
Guiteau, Charles J.
    GE:Am II-1128
Guiton, Jean
    GE:ME I-259
Gulbenkian, Calouste Sarkis
    GE:B&C II-551
Gulick, Luther
    GE:B&C III-890
Gullion, Allen W.
    GE:HR II-595
Gumm, Frances. *See* Garland, Judy
Gun, Hashimoto
    GE:W20 I-361
Gundebad
    GE:A&M II-995
Gunnison, John W.
    GE:Am II-865
Gupta, J. C.
    GE:S&T III-1353
Gurdin, Natasha. *See* Wood, Natalie
Gurney, Ronald Wilfred
    GE:S&T II-851
Gursky, Herbert
    GE:S&T IV-1708
Gusmão, José Alexandro
    GE:HR IV-1835
Gustafsson, Greta Louisa. *See* Garbo, Greta
Gustavus II Adolphus
    GE:ME I-270, 274
    GL:Ren II-995

Gutenberg, Beno
    GE:S&T I-340, II-552, III-1050, 1065
Gutenberg, Johann
    GE:A&M III-1713
    GL:A&M II-848
Guth, Alan
    GE:S&T V-2125
Guðjónsson, Halldór Kiljan. *See* Laxness, Halldór
Guthrie, Charles Claude
    GE:S&T I-134
Guthrie, Marjorie
    GE:A&C II-810
Guthrie, Woody
    GE:A&C II-810
Guy de Chauliac
    GL:A&M II-853
Guzmán, Domingo de. *See* Dominic, Saint
Guzmán, Jacobo Arbenz
    GE:B&C III-1040
Gvishiani, Jermen M.
    GE:B&C III-1293
Gwiazda, Andrzej
    GE:HR IV-2112, 2152, V-2477
Gwin, William McKendree
    GE:Am II-925
Gyatso, Tenzin
    GE:HR II-826, 837, V-2535
Gylippus
    GE:A&M I-308

H

Haagen-Smit, A. J.
  GE:B&C III-1265
Haakon VII
  GE:ME III-1164
Haam, Achad (Asher Ginzberg)
  GE:ME II-1089
Ha-Ari. *See* Luria, Isaac ben Solomon
Haas, Robert K.
  GE:B&C II-504
Habash, George
  GE:HR III-1241
  GE:W20 II-1028
Haber, Fritz
  GE:HR I-161
  GE:S&T I-385, II-805
  GL:20 II-898
Habib, Philip
  GE:HR IV-2164
Habicht, Theo
  GE:ME III-1395
Habré, Hissen
  GE:HR III-1273
Hacen, Muley
  GE:A&M III-1747
Hácha, Emil
  GE:ME III-1429
Hadamard, Jacques-Salomon
  GE:S&T I-325
Hadden, Briton
  GE:A&C II-577
  GE:B&C I-412
Haddon, William, Jr.
  GE:B&C III-1270
  GE:HR III-1267
Hadfield, Sir Robert Abbott
  GL:B&C III-1226
Hadrian
  GE:A&M II-616, 621, 702
  GL:A&M II-858
Haeckel, Ernst
  GL:Ren II-1000
Hafiz
  GL:A&M II-863
Haggai
  GE:A&M I-189
Hagman, Larry
  GE:A&C V-2418
Hahn, Kenneth
  GE:B&C III-1265

Hahn, Otto
  GE:S&T III-1135, IV-1557
  GE:W20 I-246
  GL:20 II-903
Haig, Alexander Maigs, Jr.
  GE:W20 III-1200
Haig, Sir Douglas
  GE:Am III-1466
Haigh, Kenneth
  GE:A&C IV-1721
Haile Selassie I Tafari Makonnen
  GE:B&C II-723
  GE:HR II-607, III-1194, 1491, IV-1758
  GE:ME III-1401
  GL:20 II-909
Hailsham, Lord
  GE:W20 II-955
Haines, Randa
  GE:A&C V-2443
Haitham, Ibn al-. *See* Alhazen
Hai-yüeh. *See* Mi Fei
Hakim, Tawfiq al-
  GE:A&C IV-1893
Hakim II, Al-. *See* Al-Hakim II
Hakluyt, Richard
  GE:Am I-46
Halaby, Najeeb E.
  GE:S&T IV-1897
Halas, George
  GE:B&C III-1298
Hald, Jens
  GE:S&T III-1314
Haldane, John Burdon Sanderson
  GE:S&T IV-1465
  GE:W20 I-7
Haldane, John Scott
  GE:S&T I-365
Haldeman, Harry R. "Bob"
  GE:W20 III-1131
Hale, George Ellery
  GE:S&T I-194, 417, II-645, 700, III-1325
Hale, Georgia
  GE:A&C II-659
Hale, Matthew
  GL:B&C III-1230
Hale, Sarah Josepha
  GL:AmW III-797
Halevi, Judah. *See* Judah ha-Levi

Haley, Alex
  GE:A&C IV-2022, V-2397
Haley, Bill
  GE:A&C IV-1635
Haley, Jack
  GE:A&C III-1109
Halide Edib Advar
  GL:20 II-915
Halifax, Earl of (George Montagu Dunk)
  GE:Am I-207
Halifax, Earl of (Edward Frederick Lindley
  Wood). See Irwin, Lord
Hall, Anthony Michael
  GE:A&C V-2527
Hall, Arthur
  GE:A&C V-2521
Hall, Caroline A.
  GE:Am II-1043
Hall, Charles F.
  GE:S&T V-1956
Hall, Charles Martin
  GE:B&C II-431
Hall, Diane. See Keaton, Diane
Hall, Edwin Herbert
  GE:S&T V-2136
Hall, Marshall
  GE:S&T I-243
Hall, Peter
  GE:A&C IV-1888
Hall, Radclyffe
  GE:HR II-991
Hall, William Hammond
  GE:B&C V-1773
Hallaj, al-
  GL:A&M II-869
Halleck, Fitz-Greene
  GE:Am I-481
Halley, Edmond
  GL:B&C III-1235
Halliday, Don
  GE:B&C IV-1721
Hallwachs, Wilhelm
  GE:S&T I-208
Halm, Jacob Karl Ernst
  GE:S&T II-785
Halmos, Charles
  GE:W20 I-181
Halpert, Edith
  GE:A&C II-1001
Hals, Frans
  GL:Ren II-1005
Halsey, William F.
  GE:Am III-1709, 1731

Halstead, L. Lindsey
  GE:B&C V-2007
Hamer, Fannie Lou
  GE:HR III-1149
Hamer, Robert
  GE:A&C III-1427
Hamid II, Abdul. See Abdul-Hamid II
Hamilcar Barca. See Barca, Hamilcar
Hamill, Mark
  GE:A&C V-2391
Hamilton, Alexander
  GE:Am I-330, 335, 350, 356, 377, 389, 403,
    408, 426, 432, 582, III-1394
  GL:Am II-1005
Hamilton, Alice
  GL:AmW III-801
Hamilton, Andrew
  GE:Am I-188
Hamilton, Lord George Francis
  GE:ME II-1057
Hamilton, Gordon
  GL:AmW III-805
Hamilton, Sir Ian Standish Monteith
  GE:W20 I-129
Hamilton, John. See Hayden, Sterling
Hamilton, Sir William Rowan
  GL:B&C III-1240
Hamlin, Hannibal
  GE:Am II-946
Hammarberg, Thomas
  GE:HR IV-1955, V-2414
Hammarskjöld, Dag
  GE:HR II-902, 918, 935, 985, 1038, 1068,
    1074
  GE:ME III-1589, 1613
  GL:20 II-920
Hammer, Robert
  GE:S&T V-2154
Hammerstein, Oscar, II
  GE:A&C II-745, III-1256
  GL:Am II-1012
Hammett, Dashiell
  GE:A&C II-793, III-1223
Hammond, George
  GE:Am I-389
Hammond, James Henry
  GE:Am I-648
Hammond, John
  GE:A&C II-930, 968, III-1329, V-2325
Hammurabi
  GE:A&M I-45
  GE:HR IV-2169
  GL:A&M II-876

Hampshire, Susan
  GE:A&C IV-2168
Hampton, Lionel
  GE:A&C II-968
Hamsun, Knut
  GL:20 II-925
Ha Nasi, Judah
  GE:A&M II-985
Hancock, John
  GE:Am I-231, 241, 256
  GL:Am III-1017
Hand, Augustus N.
  GE:B&C III-937
Hand, Learned
  GE:B&C I-163, III-869
  GL:Am III-1025
Handel, George Frideric
  GL:B&C III-1245
Handke, Peter
  GE:A&C IV-2126
Handy, W. C.
  GE:A&C I-252
Hanibal
  GE:A&M I-437
  GL:A&M II-882
Hanks, Nancy
  GE:A&C IV-2048
Hanlon, William
  GE:HR IV-2101
Hanna, Marcus Alonzo
  GE:Am II-1268, 1325, 1329, 1339
  GE:B&C II-476
  GL:Am III-1030
Hanna, William
  GE:A&C IV-1840
Hanno
  GL:A&M II-888
Hanratty, Patrick
  GE:B&C IV-1721
Hansberry, Lorraine
  GE:A&C IV-1795, 2000
  GL:AmW III-811
Hansen, Alvin
  GE:B&C II-740
Hansen, Emil. See Nolde, Emil
Hansen, Peder
  GE:HR II-641
Hansen, William Webster
  GE:S&T III-1384
Hara, Kei
  GE:HR I-417
Harbau, Thea von
  GE:A&C II-707

Hardenberg, Karl von
  GE:ME II-572
  GL:Ren II-1010
Hardie, James Keir
  GE:HR I-58
  GL:B&C III-1251
Hardin, Lil. See Armstrong, Lillian Hardin
Harding, G. Lankester
  GE:W20 II-598
Harding, Warren G.
  GE:Am III-1472, 1525, 1531, 1542, 1560
  GE:B&C I-357, II-516
  GE:HR I-350
  GL:Am III-1036
Hardinge, Sir Charles
  GE:ME III-1197
Hardouin-Mansart, Jules. See Mansart, Jules
  Hardouin-
Hardrada, Harold
  GE:A&M III-1248
Hardy, Godfrey Harold
  GE:S&T I-390
Hardy, Thomas
  GL:B&C III-1256
Harel, Isser
  GE:HR II-1108
Hargis, Reverend Billy James
  GE:Am III-1861
Hargreaves, James
  GE:Am I-371
  GL:B&C III-1261
Häring, Bernard
  GE:ME III-1659
Harkin, Tom
  GE:B&C V-2028
  GE:HR V-2595
Harkness, Rebekah
  GE:A&C IV-1694
Harlan, John M. (Associate Justice of the United
    States 1955-1971)
  GE:Am III-1883
Harlan, John Marshall (Associate Justice of the
    United States 1877-1911)
  GE:Am II-1261, 1318
  GE:B&C I-63, 112, 140, IV-1364
  GE:HR I-36, III-1343, 1474
Harmar, Josiah
  GE:Am I-383
Harmon, Norman
  GE:S&T IV-1708
Harmsworth, Alfred, First Viscount Northcliffe
  GE:S&T I-448
  GL:B&C III-1265
Harmsworth, Harold, First Viscount Rothermere
  GL:B&C III-1265

Harnack, Adolf von
  GL:20 II-930
Harper, Ken
  GE:A&C V-2334
Harper, Valerie
  GE:A&C V-2218
Harper, William Rainey
  GL:Am III-1042
Harrah, Bill
  GE:B&C IV-1600
Harrar, Jacob George
  GE:HR III-1515
Harriman, Edward H.
  GE:B&C I-91
Harriman, George
  GE:B&C IV-1347
Harriman, Leslie O.
  GE:HR IV-1937
Harriman, Pamela Digby Churchill
  GL:AmW III-817
Harriman, William Averell
  GE:Am III-1736, 1753, 1806
  GE:W20 II-955
  GL:Am III-1049
Harrington, Michael
  GE:Am III-1866
  GE:HR III-1284
Harris, Sir Arthur Travers
  GE:ME III-1461
Harris, Issac
  GE:B&C I-191
Harris, Jed
  GE:A&C III-1099
Harris, Julie
  GL:AmW III-822
Harris, La Donna
  GE:W20 II-865
Harris, Mary, "Mother" Jones. See Jones, Mary
  Harris "Mother"
Harris, Oren
  GE:B&C III-1148
  GE:HR III-1310
Harris, Samuel
  GE:A&C I-108
Harrison, Benjamin
  GE:Am II-1206
  GL:Am III-1057
Harrison, Frederic
  GL:B&C III-1270
Harrison, George. See also Beatles, the
  GE:A&C IV-1944, 2098
Harrison, Michael R.
  GE:S&T V-2174

Harrison, Ross Granville
  GE:S&T I-380
Harrison, William Henry
  GE:Am I-498, 582, II-690, 760
  GL:Am III-1063
Harrod, Roy
  GE:B&C II-740
Harsha
  GL:A&M II-893
Hart, Emma. See Willard, Emma
Hart, Lorenz
  GL:Am III-1068
Hart, Philip
  GE:B&C III-1259
  GE:HR IV-1817
Hartford, John A.
  GE:B&C I-302
Hartingdon, Marquis of. See Devonshire, Duke of
Hartley, Fred L.
  GE:B&C IV-1374
Hartley, Vivian Mary. See Leigh, Vivien
Hartmann von Aue
  GL:A&M II-898
Hartmann, Johannes Franz
  GE:S&T I-213
Hartmann, Nicolai
  GL:20 II-935
Harun al-Rashid
  GE:A&M II-1142
  GL:A&M II-904
Harvard, John
  GE:Am I-103
Harvey, Bernard "Touter"
  GE:A&C V-2344
Harvey, Daniel
  GE:ME II-741
Harvey, William
  GE:ME I-254
  GL:B&C III-1276
Hasan al-Basri, al-
  GL:A&M II-909
Hasdai ibn-Shaprut. See Ibn-Shaprut
Hasdrubal Barca. See Barca, Hasdrubal
Hasegawa, Takashi
  GE:B&C V-1964
Hašek, Jaroslav
  GE:A&C I-523
Hashimoto, Kingoro
  GE:HR I-539
Hashimoto, Masujiro
  GE:B&C I-185
Haslam, "Pony Bob"
  GE:Am II-925

Hassel, Odd
  GE:S&T V-1918
Hassenfeld, Merrill
  GE:B&C III-986
Hastings, Warren
  GL:B&C III-1282
Hata, Sahachiro
  GE:S&T II-476
Hatasu. *See* Hatshepsut
Hatch, Carl A.
  GE:B&C II-476
Hathaway, Henry
  GE:A&C III-1567
Hathaway, William
  GE:HR IV-1823
Hathorne, John
  GE:Am I-169
Hatoyama Ichirō
  GL:20 II-940
Hatshepsut
  GL:A&M II-914
Hatshopsitu. *See* Hatshepsut
Hatta, Mohammad
  GL:20 II-945
Haugen, Gilbert
  GE:B&C II-569
Hauksbee, Francis
  GE:S&T III-1080
Hauser, Benjamin Gayelord
  GE:B&C IV-1416
Hausner, Gideon
  GE:HR II-1108
Haussmann, Jacques. *See* Houseman, John
Haüy, René-Just
  GE:S&T II-517
Havel, Václav
  GE:A&C IV-1967
  GE:HR V-2570
Hawking, Stephen William
  GE:W20 II-835
Hawkins, Erick
  GE:A&C III-1284
Hawks, Howard
  GE:A&C II-839, 951, III-1313, 1567
Hawksmoor, Nicholas
  GL:B&C III-1287
Hawley, Joseph R.
  GE:Am II-1123
Hawley, Willis
  GE:B&C II-591
Hawn, Goldie
  GE:A&C IV-2115
Haworth, Sir Walter Norman
  GE:S&T II-857

Hawthorne, Nathaniel
  GE:Am II-848
  GL:Am III-1075
Hawtrey, Ralph
  GE:B&C II-740
Hay, George D.
  GE:A&C II-675
Hay, Harry
  GE:HR IV-1801
Hay, John Milton
  GE:Am II-1296, 1339
  GE:HR I-25
  GL:Am III-1080
Haya de la Torre, Víctor Raúl
  GL:20 II-950
Hayashi Tadasu
  GE:B&C I-41
Hayden, Sterling
  GE:A&C IV-1989
Hayden, Tom
  GE:Am III-1861
  GE:HR III-1446
Hayden, William
  GE:B&C V-2007
Haydn, Franz Joseph
  GL:Ren II-1015
Hayes, Arthur H., Jr.
  GE:S&T V-2226
Hayes, Helen
  GL:AmW III-828
Hayes, Patrick H.
  GE:HR I-356
Hayes, Rutherford B.
  GE:Am II-1099
  GL:Am III-1085
Hayne, Robert Young
  GE:Am I-593, 660, II-702
Haynes, Daniel L.
  GE:A&C II-772
Haynes, John
  GE:Am I-109
Hays, Arthur Garfield
  GE:HR I-327
Hays, Brooks
  GE:W20 II-770
Hays, Will
  GE:B&C I-357
Hayslip, Le Ly
  GL:AmW III-833
Haywood, William Dudley "Big Bill"
  GE:Am III-1454
  GE:HR I-258
Hayworth, Rita
  GL:AmW III-838

Hazard, Cyril
  GE:S&T IV-1757
  GE:W20 II-899
Hazen, Allen
  GE:S&T I-401
H. D.
  GE:A&C I-326, 686
  GL:AmW III-844
Heacock, Raymond L.
  GE:S&T V-2082, 2104
Head, Edith
  GL:AmW III-849
Headlam, Stewart
  GE:HR I-109
Hearst, Phoebe Apperson
  GL:AmW III-853
Hearst, William Randolph
  GE:A&C III-1200
  GE:Am II-1243, 1284
  GL:Am III-1091
Heath, Edward
  GE:HR IV-1720, 1978, 2024
  GE:W20 III-1117, 1146
  GL:B&C III-1294
Heathcoate, Thomas W.
  GE:Am II-1237, 1284
Heaviside, Oliver
  GE:S&T I-174
Hebrang, Andreya
  GE:W20 II-640
Hecataeus of Miletus
  GE:A&M I-259
Hecataeus of Teos
  GE:A&M I-378
Heckel, Erich
  GE:A&C I-134
Heckerling, Amy
  GE:A&C V-2443
Heckroth, Hein
  GE:A&C II-920
Hedwig. See Władysław II Jagiełło and Jadwiga
Heeger, Alan J.
  GE:S&T V-2063
Heezen, Bruce Charles
  GE:S&T IV-1508, 1876
Hegel, Georg Wilhelm Friedrich
  GE:W20 I-54
  GL:Ren II-1020
Hegesippus
  GE:A&M II-742
Heidegger, Martin
  GE:W20 I-252
  GL:20 II-956

Heilborn, Jacob
  GE:B&C I-75
Heim, Jacques
  GE:A&C III-1324
Heimann, John G.
  GE:B&C V-1788
Hein, Piet
  GL:Ren II-1026
Heine, Heinrich
  GL:Ren II-1030
Heineman, Ben Walter
  GE:W20 I-520
Heinemann, Mitch
  GE:A&C I-491
Heinkel, Ernst Heinrich
  GE:W20 I-355
  GL:20 II-962
Heinlein, Robert A.
  GE:A&C III-1094, IV-1883
Heinmot Tooyalakekt. See Joseph, Chief
Heinze, F. Augustus
  GE:B&C I-134
Heisenberg, Werner
  GE:S&T II-741, 835, 851, III-1030
  GE:W20 I-166
  GL:20 II-967
Heitler, Walter Heinrich
  GE:S&T II-926
Heizer, Michael
  GE:A&C IV-1949
Helberg, Robert J.
  GE:S&T IV-1825
Helen, Grand Duchess
  GE:ME II-866
Helfgott, Dr.
  GE:B&C III-986
Heller, Adam
  GE:S&T V-2159
Heller, E. S.
  GE:S&T I-320
Heller, Joseph
  GE:A&C IV-1866
Heller, Walter W.
  GE:B&C III-1218, 1235
Hellman, Lillian
  GE:A&C II-793
  GL:AmW III-858
Helm, Sir Alexander Knox
  GE:HR II-941
Helmholtz, Hermann von
  GE:Am II-1089
  GL:Ren II-1035
Helmond, Katherine
  GE:A&C V-2239

Helms, Jesse
GE:A&C V-2636
GE:HR V-2364
Helms, Richard
GE:HR III-1595
Helton, Arthur C.
GE:HR V-2494
Heminge, John
GE:ME I-208
Hemingway, Ernest
GE:A&C II-626, 696
GE:Am III-1560
GE:W20 I-241
GL:Am III-1097
Hemsley, Sherman
GE:A&C V-2339
Henderson, Charles B.
GE:B&C II-630
Henderson, Fletcher
GE:A&C I-480, II-670, 968
Henderson, Leon
GE:B&C II-820, 833
Henderson, Paul
GE:B&C I-357, II-493
Hendrie, Joseph M.
GE:B&C IV-1693
Hendrix, Jimi
GE:A&C IV-2092, 2104, 2180
Heng Samrin
GE:HR V-2459
GE:W20 III-1346
Henie, Sonja
GL:20 II-972
Henking, Hermann
GE:S&T I-148
Henle, Friedrich Gustav Jacob
GE:ME III-1174
Henley, Beth
GL:AmW III-862
Henne, Albert
GE:S&T II-916
Henning, Paul
GE:A&C IV-1835
Hennings, Emmy
GE:A&C I-419
Henreid, Paul
GE:A&C III-1245
Henri, Robert
GE:A&C II-885
Henríquez, Raúl Cardinal Silva
GE:HR IV-2186
Henry I
GE:A&M III-1195, 1291, 1386
GL:B&C III-1299

Henry II (of Cyprus and Jerusalem)
GE:A&M III-1574
Henry II (of England)
GE:A&M III-1375, 1386
GL:B&C III-1303
Henry II (of France)
GE:ME I-153, 158, 162
Henry II the Saint
GL:A&M II-919
Henry III (of England)
GE:A&M III-1452, 1528
GL:B&C III-1308
Henry III (of France)
GE:ME I-202
Henry IV, Holy Roman Emperor. See Henry IV
(of Germany)
Henry IV (of England)
GL:B&C III-1313
Henry IV (of France)
GE:Am I-52
GE:ME I-202, 214, 220, 353
GL:Ren II-1040
Henry IV (of Germany)
GE:A&M III-1263, 1269, 1318
GL:A&M II-924
Henry V, Holy Roman Emperor
GE:A&M III-1318
Henry V (of England)
GL:B&C III-1319
Henry VI, Holy Roman Emperor
GE:A&M III-1436
Henry VI (of England and France)
GE:A&M III-1697
GL:B&C III-1325
Henry VII (of England)
GE:Am I-23
GE:ME I-6
GL:B&C III-1331
Henry VII of Luxemburg
GE:A&M III-1603
Henry VIII (of England)
GE:ME I-6, 49, 64, 103, 110, 123
GL:B&C III-1336
Henry, Cardinal (of Portugal)
GE:ME I-189
Henry de Bracton. See Bracton, Henry de
Henry Jasomirgott of Babenberg
GE:A&M III-1364
Henry of Anjou
GE:ME I-184
Henry of Guise
GE:ME I-184, 202
Henry of Lausanne
GE:A&M III-1329

Henry of Navarre
  GE:ME I-184
Henry, Prince of Condé
  GE:ME I-184
Henry the Lion
  GE:A&M III-1364
  GL:A&M II-930
Henry the Navigator (Prince of Portugal)
  GE:A&M III-1503, 1686
  GE:ME I-11
  GL:A&M II-936
Henry the Proud
  GE:A&M III-1364
Henry, Aaron
  GE:HR III-1149
Henry, E. William
  GE:W20 II-669
Henry, Major Hubert Joseph
  GE:ME II-1075
Henry, Joseph
  GE:Am II-742, 831
  GE:ME II-649
  GE:S&T I-128
  GL:Am III-1103
Henry, Patrick (1736-1799)
  GE:Am I-219, 318
  GL:Am III-1108
Henry, Patrick (1879-1916). See Pearse, Padhraic
Hensel, Kurt
  GE:S&T I-438
Hensen, Victor
  GE:S&T I-380
Henshaw, David
  GE:Am II-696
Henze, Hans Werner
  GL:20 II-977
Hepburn, Katharine
  GE:A&C II-951
  GL:AmW III-867
Heracles
  GE:A&M II-795
Heraclitus of Ephesus
  GE:A&M I-210
  GL:A&M II-941
Heraclius
  GL:A&M II-948
Herbert, George Edward Stanhope Molyneux,
  Fifth Earl of Carnarvon. See Carnarvon,
  George Edward Stanhope Molyneux, Fifth
  Earl of
Herbert, Victor
  GE:A&C I-379
  GE:B&C I-252
Herder, Johann Gottfried
  GL:Ren II-1045

Herjolfson, Bjarni
  GE:Am I-11
Herlie, Eileen
  GE:A&C III-1378
Herman, Robert C.
  GE:S&T III-1309
Hermas
  GE:A&M II-762
Hermerken, Thomas. See Thomas à Kempis
Hermocrates
  GE:A&M I-308
Hernandez, Aileen Clarke
  GL:AmW III-872
Herndon, William Henry
  GE:Am II-906
Hernu, Charles
  GE:HR V-2268
Hero of Alexandria
  GL:A&M II-954
Herod Agrippa II
  GE:A&M II-648
Herod the Great
  GL:A&M II-958
Herodotus
  GE:A&M I-259
  GL:A&M II-964
Herophilus
  GE:A&M II-737
  GL:A&M II-969
Herr, Michael
  GE:A&C V-2428
Herrera, José Joaquín
  GE:Am II-825
Herrick, Hiram H.
  GE:S&T I-88
Herriot, Édouard
  GE:HR II-849
  GE:W20 I-276
  GL:20 III-983
Herriott, Donald
  GE:W20 II-1881
Herrmann, Bernard
  GE:A&C III-1200, IV-1855
Herschel, Sir William
  GE:S&T III-1193
Hersholt, Jean
  GE:A&C II-593
Herter, Christian Archibald
  GE:HR I-555
Hertz, Gustav
  GL:20 III-988
Hertz, Heinrich
  GE:Am III-1519
  GE:ME II-1080

GE:S&T I-128, 174, 199, 260, II-471, 669,
  751, III-1113
GE:W20 I-324
Hertzog, James Barry Munnik
  GE:ME III-1372
Hertzsprung, Ejnar
  GE:S&T I-265, 370, II-496, 557, 585, 785
Herz, Cornelius
  GE:ME II-1066
Herzen, Aleksandr
  GL:Ren II-1050
Herzl, Theodor
  GE:HR II-761, 832
  GE:ME II-1089
  GE:W20 I-411, II-634
  GL:Ren II-1055
Hesburgh, Theodore
  GE:B&C V-1933
Hesiod
  GE:A&M I-139
  GL:A&M III-975
Hess, Harry Hammond
  GE:S&T II-522, IV-1508, 1650
Hess, Rudolf
  GE:HR I-389
  GE:ME III-1522
  GE:W20 I-188
Hess, Victor Franz
  GE:S&T II-532, 694
Hesse, Hermann
  GE:A&C IV-1829
  GL:20 III-992
Heth, Joice
  GE:Am II-1066
Heumann, Karl
  GE:S&T I-98
Heuss, Theodor
  GE:W20 II-647
Hevesy, Georg von
  GL:20 III-998
Hewish, Antony
  GE:S&T IV-1862
  GE:W20 II-1009
Hewitt, Don
  GE:A&C IV-2136
Hewitt, Peter Cooper
  GE:S&T I-108, III-1080
Hey, G. B.
  GE:S&T III-1240
Heydrich, Reinhard
  GE:W20 I-303,396
Heyerdahl, Thor
  GL:20 III-1004

Heytesbury, William
  GE:A&M III-1614
Heyward, DuBose
  GE:A&C II-1016
Hibbs, Ben
  GE:B&C IV-1379
Hickel, Walter
  GE:B&C IV-1374
  GE:W20 II-1022
Hickenlooper, Bourke B.
  GE:B&C III-1117, 1175
Hickok, James Butler "Wild Bill"
  GE:Am II-1020
Hickok, Lorena
  GL:AmW III-876
Hicks, Clarence J.
  GE:B&C II-419
Hiero I of Syracuse
  GE:A&M I-408
Hiero II of Syracuse
  GE:A&M I-422
Hieronymus, Eusebius. See Jerome, Saint
Higgins, Margaret. See Sanger, Margaret
Higgins, Marguerite
  GL:AmW III-881
Higgins, Patillo
  GE:B&C I-24
Hilary
  GE:A&M II-852
Hilbert, David
  GE:S&T I-31, 233, II-650, III-1045, IV-1751
Hildebrand. See Gregory VII, Pope
Hildebrandt, Johann Lucas von
  GL:Ren II-1061
Hildegard von Bingen
  GL:A&M III-982
Hilduin of Saint-Denis
  GE:A&M II-1011
Hill, Bertha "Chippie"
  GE:A&C I-252
Hill, James Jerome
  GE:B&C I-91
  GL:Am III-1113
Hill, Octavia
  GL:B&C III-1341
Hill, William S.
  GE:B&C III-1052
Hillary, Sir Edmund
  GL:B&C III-1347
Hillel
  GE:A&M I-477
Hilleman, Maurice R.
  GE:S&T IV-1655, V-2326

Hillis, Margaret
  GL:AmW III-886
Hillman, Sidney
  GE:B&C II-729, 820, III-1064
  GE:HR I-545
Hills, William
  GE:W20 II-942
Hillsborough, Earl of (Wills Hill, Marquis of
    Downshire)
  GE:Am I-207, 231
Himmler, Heinrich
  GE:HR I-491
  GE:ME III-1391
  GE:W20 I-303, 375, 396
  GL:20 III-1009
Hindemith, Paul
  GE:A&C II-724, 816
  GL:20 III-1014
Hindenburg, Paul von
  GE:B&C I-293
  GE:HR I-241, 491
  GE:ME III-1382
  GE:W20 I-101, 311
  GL:20 III-1020
Hine, Lewis W.
  GE:S&T II-906
Hines, Earl
  GE:A&C II-670
Hinkle, Beatrice Moses
  GE:A&C I-309
Hinshaw, H. Corwin
  GE:S&T III-1224
Hipparchus
  GE:A&M I-398, II-712, 716
  GL:A&M III-988
Hippias of Elis
  GE:A&M I-286
Hippisley, Alfred E.
  GE:Am II-1296
Hippocrates
  GE:A&M I-302
  GE:HR V-2169
  GL:A&M III-993
Hippocrates of Chios
  GE:A&M I-383
Hippolytus of Rome
  GE:A&M II-742, 752, 757, 762, 1069
  GL:A&M III-999
Hiram
  GE:A&M I-101
Hiraoka, Kimitake. See Mishima, Yukio
Hirohito
  GE:HR II-725
  GL:20 III-1025

Hiroshige
  GL:Ren II-1067
Hirsch, Étienne
  GE:B&C III-875
Hirsch, Karl
  GE:S&T V-2357
His, Wilhelm
  GE:S&T I-380
Hiss, Alger
  GE:Am III-1817
Hitchcock, Alfred
  GE:A&C II-946, IV-1855
Hitler, Adolf
  GE:A&C III-1083, 1217
  GE:Am III-1686, 1720, 1748
  GE:HR I-389, 480, 491, 561, II-695
  GE:ME III-1363, 1377, 1382, 1391, 1395,
    1416, 1425, 1429, 1433, 1440, 1446, 1451,
    1456, 1467, 1472, 1486, 1491, 1496
  GE:W20 I-188, 276, 295, 303, 311, 342, 348,
    375, 396, 444, 450, 465, 479, II-577
  GL:20 III-1030
Hiyya, Abraham bar. See Bar Hiyya, Abraham
Ho Chi Minh
  GE:Am III-1906
  GE:HR II-573, 683
  GE:ME III-1577
  GE:W20 II-696, 703, III-1243
  GL:20 III-1037
Hoar, George
  GE:Am II-1206
Hoare, Sir Samuel John Gurney
  GE:B&C II-723
  GE:ME III-1401
Hobart, Garret Augustus
  GE:Am II-1268
Hobbes, Thomas
  GL:B&C III-1353
Hobby, Oveta Culp
  GE:Am III-1835
  GL:Am III-1118
  GL:AmW III-891
Hobhouse, Leonard T.
  GL:B&C III-1360
Hobson, John Atkinson
  GE:W20 I-31
Hobson, Richmond Pearson
  GE:Am III-1507
Hockney, David
  GL:B&C III-1367
Hodel, Max
  GE:ME II-1013
Hodges, Courtney Hicks
  GE:ME III-1496

Hodges, Johnny
    GE:A&C II-739
Hodges, Wetmore
    GE:S&T II-635
Hodgins, Eric
    GE:B&C II-585
Hodgkin, Dorothy Crowfoot
    GE:S&T III-1240
Hoey, Jane M.
    GE:HR I-520
Hoff, Marcian Edward, Jr.
    GE:S&T V-1938
Hoffa, Jimmy
    GE:B&C III-1064, 1092, 1213
Hoffman, Abbie
    GE:Am III-1861
    GE:HR III-1446
Hoffman, Malvina
    GL:AmW III-896
Hoffman, Paul G.
    GE:B&C III-902, 1190
Hoffman, Walter Edward
    GE:W20 III-1188
Hoffmann, Josef
    GE:A&C I-79, 124
Hofmann, Albert
    GE:S&T III-1123
Hofmann, August Wilhelm von
    GE:S&T I-98
Hofstadter, Robert
    GE:S&T III-1384
Hogarth, William
    GL:B&C III-1372
Hohenheim, Philippus Aureolus Theophrastus
    Bombast von. See Paracelsus
Hohmann, Walter
    GE:S&T V-2003
Hokinson, Helen
    GL:AmW III-901
Hokusai
    GL:Ren II-1072
Holbein, Hans (the Younger)
    GL:Ren II-1076
Holbrooke, Richard
    GE:HR IV-2198
Holden, Roberto
    GE:W20 III-1219
Holder, Geoffrey
    GE:A&C V-2334
Holder, Wesley McDonald
    GE:HR III-1451
Holiday, Billie
    GE:A&C II-930
    GL:AmW III-906

Holifield, Chester
    GE:B&C III-1196
Holladay, Wilhelmina (Billy) Cole
    GE:A&C V-2608
Holland, Brian
    GE:A&C IV-1790
Holland, Eddie
    GE:A&C IV-1790
Holland, Spessard L.
    GE:HR III-1231
Hollerith, Herman
    GE:B&C II-447
Hollweg, Theobald von Bethmann. See Bethmann
    Hollweg, Theobald von
Holm, Hanya
    GL:AmW III-911
Holmes, Arthur
    GE:S&T II-522
Holmes, John Haynes
    GE:HR I-327
Holmes, Llowell D.
    GE:S&T II-869
Holmes, Oliver Wendell
    GE:Am III-1363
    GE:B&C I-107, 112, 140, 163, II-426
    GE:HR I-36
    GL:Am III-1123
Holst, Gustav
    GE:A&C I-90
Holstein, Friedrich von
    GE:W20 II-46
    GL:Ren II-1081
Holsti, Eino Rudolf
    GE:HR I-212
Holt, Frederick Rodney
    GE:S&T V-2073
Holt, John C.
    GE:B&C I-401
Homer
    GL:A&M III-1005
Homer, Winslow
    GL:Am III-1128
Honda, Soichiro
    GL:20 III-1044
Honecker, Erich
    GE:HR V-2523
Honegger, Arthur
    GE:A&C I-435
Honorius
    GE:A&M II-935, 940
Honorius III
    GE:A&M III-1441
Hood, John Bell
    GE:Am II-1010

Hood, Raymond
  GE:A&C III-1149
Hoodless, Adelaide Hunter
  GE:HR I-167
Hooker, Evelyn
  GE:HR III-1497
Hooker, John Daggett
  GE:S&T II-645
Hooker, Thomas
  GE:Am I-91, 109
Hookham, Margaret Evelyn. *See* Fonteyn, Dame
  Margot
Hoover, Herbert
  GE:Am III-1507, 1542, 1566, 1577, 1582,
    1594, 1599, 1609
  GE:B&C I-396, II-493, 516, 539, 569, 574,
    591, 597, 630, 668, 851
  GE:S&T III-1075
  GE:W20 I-260
  GL:Am III-1135
Hoover, J. Edgar
  GE:Am III-1491
  GE:HR I-258, 550, III-1246, 1595
  GL:Am III-1141
Hoover, William H.
  GE:S&T I-88
Hope, Bob
  GE:A&C II-828
Hope, Victor Alexander John. *See* Linlithgow,
  Lord
Hopkins, Edward
  GE:Am I-109
Hopkins, Sir Frederick Gowland
  GE:S&T I-46, 330, II-771
Hopkins, Harry L.
  GE:A&C II-995
  GE:Am III-1632, 1686
  GE:ME III-1477, 1501, 1512
  GL:Am III-1146
Hopkins, John P.
  GE:Am II-1237
Hopkins, Johns
  GE:Am II-1077
Hopper, Dennis
  GE:A&C IV-2158
Hopper, Grace Murray
  GE:S&T IV-1593
  GL:AmW III-915
Horace
  GL:A&M III-1010
Horne, Jeremiah
  GE:Am II-785
Horne, Lena
  GE:A&C III-1159

Horne, Marilyn
  GL:AmW III-920
Horney, Karen
  GL:AmW III-925
Horniman, Annie
  GE:A&C I-119
Horowitz, Jacob. *See* Harris, Jed
Horrigan, Edward A., Jr.
  GE:B&C V-1976
Horsfall, Frank L., Jr.
  GE:S&T IV-1682
Horst, Louis
  GE:A&C I-390, III-1284
Hortensius, Quintus
  GE:A&M I-393
Horthy, Miklós von Nagybánya
  GE:W20 I-181
Horton, Edward Everett
  GE:A&C II-941, 984
Horton, James E.
  GE:Am III-1588
Horton, Lester
  GE:A&C IV-1774
Hosius of Cordova
  GE:A&M II-867, 872, III-1257
Hosmer, Harriet
  GL:AmW III-929
Höss, Rudolf
  GE:HR I-491
Hossbach, Friedrich
  GE:W20 I-375
Hostiensis
  GE:A&M II-784
Hotman, François
  GL:Ren II-1086
Houdry, Eugene
  GE:S&T II-573
Houghton, Harry E.
  GE:B&C II-674
Hounsfield, Godfrey Newbold
  GE:S&T V-1961
Houphouët-Boigny, Félix
  GE:B&C IV-1589
  GL:20 III-1049
House, Edward M.
  GE:Am III-1450
  GE:HR I-252, 270
  GE:ME III-1289
Houseman, John
  GE:A&C II-989, III-1103, 1200
Houser, George M.
  GE:HR II-618, 718
Houshofer, Karl
  GE:W20 I-188

Houssay, Bernardo Alberto
  GL:20 III-1056
Houston, Gilbert "Cisco"
  GE:A&C II-810
Houston, Sam
  GE:Am II-736, 941
  GL:Am III-1153
Hovick, Rose Louise. *See* Lee, Gypsy Rose
Howard, Catherine
  GE:ME I-123
Howard, Sir Ebenezer
  GE:Am III-1811
Howard, John Eager
  GE:Am I-624
Howard, John
  GE:ME I-424
Howard, Leland Ossian
  GE:S&T II-640
Howard, Leslie
  GE:A&C III-1154
Howard, Oliver Otis
  GE:Am II-1010
Howard, Ron
  GE:A&C V-2305
Howard, Sidney
  GE:A&C I-343
Howard, Thomas
  GE:ME I-123
Howe, Elias
  GE:Am II-837
  GL:Am III-1158
Howe, Geoffrey
  GE:B&C V-1887
  GE:HR IV-2073
Howe, George
  GE:A&C IV-1919
Howe, Irving
  GE:A&C IV-2163
Howe, Julia Ward
  GL:Am III-1164
  GL:AmW III-933
Howe, Louis McHenry
  GE:Am III-1609
Howe, Richard
  GL:B&C III-1378
Howe, Samuel Gridley
  GL:Am III-1169
Howe, Tina
  GL:AmW III-937
Howe, William
  GE:Am I-277
  GL:B&C III-1383
Howell, William H.
  GE:S&T II-610, IV-1459

Howells, William Dean
  GE:A&C I-96
  GE:Am II-1255
Howland, John
  GE:S&T II-725
Hoxha, Enver
  GE:HR V-2553
  GE:W20 II-640
Hoyer, Steny H.
  GE:HR V-2595
Hoyle, Sir Fred
  GE:S&T III-1309, 1320
Hoyt, John
  GE:B&C V-1970
Hrabanus Maurus. *See* Rabanus Maurus
Hsia Kuei
  GL:A&M III-1016
Hsiang-yang. *See* Mi Fei
Hsieh Ling-yün
  GL:A&M III-1021
Hsüan T'ung. *See* P'u-yi, Henry
Hsüan-tsang
  GL:A&M III-1026
Hsün-tzu
  GL:A&M III-1034
Hu Shih
  GE:HR I-276
Hu Yaobang
  GE:HR II-826, V-2483
Hua Guofeng
  GE:B&C III-1281
  GE:W20 III-1264
Hua Kuo-feng. *See* Hua Guofeng
Huang Hsing
  GE:HR I-116
  GE:W20 I-92
Huang Hua
  GE:W20 III-1110
Hubbard, William B.
  GE:S&T V-2211
Hubbell, Raymond
  GE:B&C I-252
Hubble, Edwin Powell
  GE:S&T II-496, 502, 689, 700, 766, 790, 878,
    III-1193, 1320, IV-1449
Hudson, Henry
  GE:Am I-80
  GL:B&C III-1389
Hudspeth, Claude
  GE:HR I-377
Hueffer, Ford Madox. *See* Ford, Ford Madox
Huelsenbeck, Richard
  GE:A&C I-419

Huerta, Adolfo de la
    GE:W20 I-69
Huerta, Dolores
    GE:HR III-1161
    GE:W20 II-842
    GL:AmW III-942
Huerta, Victoriano de la
    GE:W20 I-69
Hugh of Cluny
    GE:A&M III-1269
Hugh of St. Victor
    GE:A&M III-1338
Hughes, Charles Evans
    GE:Am III-1531, 1537 1667
    GE:B&C I-97, II-459, 701, 706
    GE:HR I-377, 383, 545
    GL:Am III-1174
Hughes, Helena
    GE:A&C IV-1721
Hughes, Howard, Jr.
    GE:A&C III-1307
    GE:B&C II-442
Hughes, Howard, Sr.
    GE:B&C II-442
    GE:S&T I-396
Hughes, John
    GE:A&C V-2527
Hughes, Langston
    GE:A&C I-480, IV-2000
Hughes, Ted
    GE:A&C IV-1850
Hughes, William Morris
    GE:ME III-1372
    GL:B&C III-1394
Hugo, Victor
    GL:Ren II-1093
Huizenga, H. Wayne
    GE:B&C V-1745
Hull, Cordell
    GE:Am III-1649, 1661, 1686, 1741
    GE:B&C III-914
    GE:ME III-1507
    GE:W20 I-260, 438, 465
    GL:Am III-1181
Hulme, Thomas Ernest
    GE:A&C I-161, 326, 445
Hulst, Hendrik Christoffel van de. See Van de
    Hulst, Hendrik Christoffel
Humason, Milton L.
    GE:S&T II-689
Humbert I (of Italy)
    GE:ME II-1019, 1094
Humbert, Cardinal
    GE:A&M III-1237

Humbert of Silva Candida
    GE:A&M III-1269
Humboldt, Alexander von
    GL:Ren II-1100
Humboldt, Wilhelm von
    GE:ME II-572
Hume, David
    GE:ME I-485
    GL:B&C III-1399
Humphrey, Doris
    GE:A&C I-390
Humphrey, George Magoffin
    GE:B&C III-1030
Humphrey, Hubert H.
    GE:Am III-1918, 1933
    GE:B&C II-442, III-1229, IV-1495
    GE:HR II-1102, III-1251, 1446, 1537
    GE:W20 II-806, 893, 965
    GL:Am III-1186
Humphrey, John
    GE:HR II-789
Humphreys, Robert E.
    GE:S&T II-573
Hun Sen
    GE:HR V-2459
Hung Hsiu-ch'üan
    GL:Ren II-1105
Hung Taiji. See Abahai
Hung-li. See Ch'ien-lung
Hunt, Alfred
    GE:B&C II-431
Hunt, Lamar
    GE:B&C III-1298
Hunt, Richard Morris
    GE:Am II-1231
Hunt, Walter
    GE:Am II-837
Hunt, William Holman
    GL:B&C III-1404
Hunt, Wilson Price
    GE:Am I-476
Hunte, Otto
    GE:A&C II-707
Hunter-Gault, Charlayne
    GL:AmW III-947
Hunyadi, János
    GL:A&M III-1039
Hunyadi, Mátyás. See Matthias I Corvinus
Huong, Tran Van
    GE:W20 III-1227
Hurd, Douglas
    GE:HR IV-2073
Hurok, Solomon
    GE:A&C I-187, III-1126

Hurston, Zora Neale
  GL:AmW III-952
Hus, Jan
  GL:A&M III-1043
Husak, Gustáv
  GE:A&C IV-1967
  GE:HR V-2570
  GE:ME III-1666
Husayn ibn 'Alī
  GE:B&C I-351
Husayn, Taha
  GE:A&C V-2625
Husayni, Hajj Amin al-
  GE:W20 I-231
Husbands, Hermon
  GE:Am I-213
Huss, John
  GE:A&M III-1675, 1680
Hussami, Nazar al-Derweish al-
  GE:HR IV-1967
Hussein I
  GE:ME III-1654
  GL:20 III-1060
Hussein, Ibn Talal
  GE:HR III-1241
Hussein, Saddam
  GE:HR II-1050, V-2397, 2600
Husseini, Haj Amin al-
  GE:HR II-749
Husserl, Edmund
  GL:20 III-1067
Hussey, Obed
  GE:Am II-679
Huston, John
  GE:A&C III-1223
Hutcheson, Francis
  GE:ME I-485
Hutchins, Robert Maynard
  GE:A&C III-1351
  GL:Am III-1192
Hutchins, Thomas
  GE:Am I-306
Hutchinson, Anne
  GE:Am I-85, 97

GL:Am III-1198
GL:AmW III-957
Hutchinson, Elisha
  GE:Am I-241
Hutchinson, Roy Coryton
  GE:W20 I-241
Hutchinson, Thomas
  GE:Am I-241
  GL:Am III-1203
Hutchinson, Thomas, Jr.
  GE:Am I-241
Hutchison, Miller Reese
  GE:S&T II-537
Hutton, James
  GE:ME II-678
Huxley, Aldous
  GE:A&C II-896, III-1514
  GE:W20 I-241
Huxley, Thomas Henry
  GE:ME II-822, 855
  GL:B&C III-1410
Huygens, Christiaan
  GE:S&T III-1245
  GL:Ren II-1110
Hyde, Arthur M.
  GE:B&C II-569
Hyde, Edward. See Clarendon, First Earl of
Hyde, Edward (Governor of North Carolina)
  GE:Am I-132
Hyde, James F.
  GE:S&T I-123
Hyde, James Hazen
  GE:B&C I-97
Hyde, Orson
  GE:Am II-812
Hyde, Rosel H.
  GE:B&C IV-1325
Hymans, Paul
  GE:HR I-287, 436
Hyndman, Henry Mayers
  GE:HR I-58
Hypatia
  GE:A&M II-924
Hyrcanus, John
  GE:A&M I-477

I

Iacocca, Lee
GE:B&C II-533, III-1224, V-1751, 1763
Iamblichus
GE:A&M II-888
Ibn al-'Arabi
GL:A&M III-1049
Ibn al-Haitham. *See* Alhazen
Ibn-Bajjah. *See* Avempace
Ibn Battutah
GL:A&M III-1055
Ibn-Ezra, Abraham
GE:A&M III-1334
Ibn Gabirol
GE:A&M III-1334, 1559
GL:A&M III-1060
Ibn Hanbal. *See* Ahmad ibn Hanbal
Ibn Khaldun
GL:A&M III-1066
Ibn Nusair, Musa
GE:A&M II-1105
Ibn Rushd. *See* Averroës
Ibn-Rushid. *See* Averröes
Ibn-Shaprut, Hasdai
GE:A&M III-1334
Ibn Sina. *See* Avicenna
Ibn Talal. *See* Hussein I
Ibn-Tibbon, Samuel
GE:A&M III-1391
Ibn-Zakariyā' al-Rāzi, abū-Bakr Muhammad. *See*
Razi, al-
Ibn Ziyad, Tarik
GE:A&M II-1105
Ibsen, Henrik
GL:Ren III-1115
Ibuka, Masaru
GE:B&C III-1009, IV-1710
GE:S&T IV-1528
Icahn, Carl
GE:B&C IV-1449
Ickes, Harold
GE:Am III-1632
GE:HR I-497
Ictinus
GE:A&M I-276
Ide, William B.
GE:Am II-818
Idle, Eric
GE:A&C IV-2174

Idrisi, al-
GL:A&M III-1072
Ignatiev, Nikolai Pavlovich
GE:ME II-1007
Ignatius of Antioch
GE:A&M II-681, 696
GL:A&M III-1076
Ignatius of Loyola, Saint. *See* Loyola, Saint
Ignatius of
Ii Naosuke
GL:Ren III-1120
Iida, Shojiro
GE:W20 I-457
Ikeda, Hayato
GL:20 III-1071
Ikhnaton. *See* Akhenaton
Iliescu, Ion
GE:HR V-2546
Illica, Luigi
GE:A&C I-29
Imada, Shintarō
GE:W20 I-269
Imanyara, Gitobu
GE:HR V-2431
Imhotep
GL:A&M III-1081
Immelmann, Max
GE:S&T II-600
Imoudu, Michael
GE:B&C I-196
Imouthes. *See* Imhotep
Inge, William
GE:A&C III-1164
Ingersoll, Ralph
GE:B&C II-585
Ingram, Joseph
GE:Am I-151
Ingres, Jean-Auguste-Dominique
GL:Ren III-1125
Innocent I
GE:A&M II-914
Innocent II
GE:A&M III-1329
Innocent III
GE:A&M III-1381, 1436, 1441, 1447, 1457,
1484, 1491
GL:A&M III-1086

Innocent IV
GE:A&M III-1484
GL:A&M III-1092
Innocent VI
GE:A&M III-1630
Innocent XI
GE:ME I-368
Inönü, Ismet
GE:W20 I-225
Inoue, Tan
GE:S&T V-2190
Intendant, The Great. See Talon, Jean Baptiste
Inukai, Tsuyoshi
GE:HR I-417, 474
Ioannides, Dimitrios
GE:W20 III-1193
Ionesco, Eugène
GE:A&C III-1573, IV-1812, 1871, 1903
GL:20 III-1076
Ippen, Erich Peter
GE:S&T V-2020
Iqbāl, Muammad
GE:HR II-731
Iradier, Eduardo Dato
GE:ME III-1259
Ireland, William M.
GE:Am II-1043
Irenaeus, Saint
GE:A&M II-742, 747, 757 767, 779
GL:A&M III-1098
Irene
GE:A&M II-1146, 1152
Iribarne, Manuel Fraga
GE:HR IV-1921
Irnerius
GE:A&M III-1344
Ironsi, Johnson Aguiyi-
GE:W20 II-1003
Irving, Henry
GL:B&C III-1415
Irving, Washington
GE:Am I-481
GL:Am III-1209
Irwin, Lord (Edward Frederick Lindley Wood,
Earl of Halifax)
GE:HR I-447, 459
GE:ME III-1440
GE:W20 I-175
Isaac II
GE:A&M III-1436
Isaac, William Michael
GE:B&C V-1870
Isaacs, Alick
GE:S&T IV-1517

Isaacs, Godfrey
GE:A&C II-712
Isabella I (of Spain and Queen of Castile). See
also Ferdinand II and Isabella I
GE:A&M III-1728, 1747, 1752, 1756
GE:Am I-17
GE:ME I-1, 16, 40
Isabella II (of Spain)
GE:ME II-726, 945
Isagoras
GE:A&M I-205
Isaiah
GE:A&M I-184
GL:A&M III-1105
Isayev, A. M.
GE:S&T IV-1797, 1819, V-1928, 1950
Ishbaal
GE:A&M I-90
Isherwood, Christopher
GE:A&C II-857
Ishihara, Kanji
GE:W20 I-269
Isidor, Metropolitan of Russian Orthodox Church
GE:ME I-198
Isidore of Seville, Saint
GE:A&M II-1086
GL:A&M III-1110
Isidorus of Miletus
GE:A&M II-1040
Iskowitz, Edward Israel. See Cantor, Eddie
Ismail, Ahmed
GE:W20 III-1182
Ismail I, Khedive of Egypt
GE:ME II-998
Isocrates
GE:A&M I-338
Isozaki, Arata
GE:A&C V-2646
Israel ben Eliezer. See Baʿal Shem Tov
Israels, Belle Lindner. See Moskowitz, Belle
Itagaki, Seishirō
GE:W20 I-269
Italiano, Anna Maria Louisa. See Bancroft, Anne
Itliong, Larry
GE:W20 II-842
Itten, Johannes
GE:A&C I-463
Itzcóatl
GL:A&M III-1115
Ivan III Vasilyevich (of Russia). See Ivan the
Great
Ivan IV (of Russia). See Ivan the Terrible

Ivan the Great
    GE:A&M III-1738, 1742
    GL:Ren III-1131
Ivan the Terrible
    GE:ME I-198
    GL:Ren III-1138
Ivanek, Željko
    GE:A&C V-2496
Ivanov, Ilya Ivanovich
    GE:S&T I-113
Ivanovich, Dimitry
    GE:ME I-231

Ivanovich, Feodor
    GE:ME I-231
Ivanowsky, Dmitry Iosifovich
    GE:S&T I-459
Ives, Charles
    GE:A&C I-425
    GL:Am III-1214
Ivo of Chartres
    GE:A&M III-1231
Ixtocóatl. See Itzcóatl
Izcohuatl. See Itzcóatl
Izvolski, Aleksandr Petrovich
    GE:ME III-1192, 1197, 1202

J

Jabir ibn Hayyan
  GL:A&M III-1121
Jablonski, Wanda
  GE:B&C III-1154
Jabotinsky, Vladimir
  GE:W20 I-231
Jackson, Andrew
  GE:Am I-533, 558, 607, 631, 660, 666, II-673,
    690, 696, 702, 730, 760
  GL:Am III-1219
Jackson, Charles Thomas
  GE:Am II-742, 791
Jackson, Helen Hunt
  GL:AmW III-962
Jackson, Henry "Scoop"
  GE:B&C IV-1699
  GE:HR III-1177
  GE:W20 II-872
Jackson, Jackie
  GE:A&C V-2512
Jackson, James
  GE:Am I-356
Jackson, Jermaine
  GE:A&C V-2512
Jackson, Jesse
  GE:B&C IV-1495
  GE:HR III-1257, IV-2209
Jackson, Joseph Jefferson "Shoeless Joe"
  GE:Am III-1497
  GE:B&C I-341
Jackson, Lucious, Jr.
  GE:W20 III-1279
Jackson, Mahalia
  GE:A&C III-1329
  GL:AmW III-966
Jackson, Marlon
  GE:A&C V-2512
Jackson, Michael
  GE:A&C IV-1790, V-2475, 2512
  GE:B&C III-1143
Jackson, Robert H.
  GE:B&C III-997
  GE:HR II-629, 667
Jackson, Stonewall
  GL:Am III-1225
Jackson, Tito
  GE:A&C V-2512
Jacob, François
  GL:20 III-1082

Jacob, Max
  GE:A&C I-337
Jacobs, Amos. See Thomas, Danny
Jacobs, Irwin
  GE:B&C V-1909
Jacobsen, Eric
  GE:S&T III-1314
Jacopo della Quercia
  GL:Ren III-1144
Jadwiga and Władysław II Jagiełło
  GL:A&M V-2344
Jadwiga of Anjou. See also Jadwiga and
    Władysław II Jagiełło
  GE:A&M III-1650
Jaganmohan
  GE:HR V-2426
Jagger, Mick
  GE:A&C IV-2027
Jagiello, Anne
  GE:ME I-87
Jagiello, Casimir IV. See Casimir IV
Jagiello, Louis II
  GE:ME I-87
Jagiello, Vladislav II. See Jadwiga and
    Władysław II Jagiełło
Jagielski, Mieczysław
  GE:HR IV-2112
Jahiz, al-
  GL:A&M III-1127
Jahn, Gunnar
  GE:HR II-873, 907, 1020, III-1143
Jain, Davaki
  GE:HR IV-2057
Jakes, Milos
  GE:HR V-2570
Jakobson, Roman
  GL:20 III-1087
Jamāl al-Dīn al-Afghānī
  GL:Ren III-1149
James I (of Great Britain, James VI of Scotland)
  GE:ME I-224, 241, 254, 329
  GL:B&C III-1421
James I the Conqueror
  GE:A&M III-1514
  GL:A&M III-1131
James II (of England)
  GE:Am I-140, 163
  GE:ME I-357, 385
  GL:B&C III-1426

James VI (of Scotland). *See* James I (of Great Britain, James VI of Scotland)

James, Duke of York. *See* James II

James, Alice
GL:AmW III-971

James, Henry
GE:A&C I-96, III-1250
GL:Am III-1230

James, Jack N.
GE:S&T IV-1734

James, Thomas
GE:Am I-588

James, William
GE:A&C I-161, 171
GE:Am II-1301, III-1363
GE:B&C I-80
GE:HR III-1102
GL:Am III-1237

Jamison, Judith
GE:A&C IV-1774

Janáček, Leoš
GL:20 III-1092

Janco, Marcel
GE:A&C I-419

Janet, Pierre
GL:20 III-1098

Janis, Jay
GE:B&C V-1788

Janowitz, Hans
GE:A&C I-486

Janowsky, David Steffan
GE:S&T V-1976

Jansen, Cornelius Otto
GL:Ren III-1155

Jansky, Karl
GE:S&T II-934, III-1113, 1193, IV-1496, 1539

Jantzen, Carl
GE:A&C I-491

Jarman, John
GE:HR III-1561

Jaroslav the Wise
GE:A&M III-1205

Jarres, Karl
GE:B&C III-981

Jarry, Alfred
GE:A&C III-1410, IV-1812

Jaruzelski, Wojciech
GE:HR IV-2112, 2152, V-2477, 2500

Jarvik, Robert
GE:S&T V-2195

Jasomirgott of Babenberg, Henry. *See* Henry Jasomirgott of Babenberg

Jaspers, Karl
GL:20 III-1103

Jaurès, Jean Léon
GE:ME II-1044, III-1143

Javabu, J. T.
GE:W20 I-87

Javacheff, Christo. *See* Christo

Javin, Ali
GE:W20 II-881

Javits, Benjamin
GE:B&C IV-1325

Javits, Jacob
GE:B&C III-1235, IV-1561
GE:HR II-997, III-1650

Jawlensky, Alexey von
GE:A&C II-583

Jaworski, Leon
GE:W20 III-1131, 1200

Jay, John
GE:Am I-300, 335, 345, 389, 403
GL:Am III-1243

Jayawardene, Junius Richard
GE:HR II-1090, IV-2068

Jazdegerd II
GE:A&M II-985

Jean de Venette. *See* Venette, Jean de

Jeanneret, Charles-Édouard. *See* Corbusier, Le

Jeanneret, Pierre
GE:A&C II-869, III-1503

Jebb, Eglantyne
GE:HR II-1038

Jeffers, William Martin
GE:Am III-1680

Jefferson, "Blind Lemon"
GE:A&C I-252

Jefferson, Sir George
GE:B&C V-1831

Jefferson, Thomas
GE:Am I-194, 256, 261, 288, 306, 312, 318,
350, 356, 389, 403, 414, 426, 432, 437,
443, 450, 456, 461, 491, 505, II-1184
GL:Am III-1248

Jefferson Airplane, the
GE:A&C IV-2180

Jeffrey, Lord
GL:B&C III-1431

Jeffreys, Alec
GE:S&T V-2296, 2362

Jeffreys, Herbert
GE:Am I-151

Jeffries, Edward J., Jr.
GE:HR II-635

Jehoiakim
GE:A&M I-149

Jellicoe, Sir John Rushworth
GE:ME III-1266

Jelliffe, Derrick B.
  GE:B&C V-1798
  GE:HR IV-2130
Jenckes, Thomas Allen
  GE:Am II-1128
Jenkin, Patrick
  GE:B&C V-1831
Jenkins, Charles F.
  GE:S&T II-751
Jenkins, Roy
  GE:HR IV-1870
Jenkinson, Robert Banks. *See* Liverpool, Second
  Earl of
Jenner, Edward
  GE:S&T I-6
  GL:B&C III-1436
Jennings, Herbert Spencer
  GE:S&T I-433
Jennings, Waylon
  GE:A&C V-2365
Jensen, Arthur Robert
  GE:Am III-1866
Jensen, Michael C.
  GE:B&C II-619
Jeremiah
  GE:A&M I-149
  GE:ME I-198
  GL:A&M III-1137
Jeroboam I
  GE:A&M I-106
Jeroboam II
  GE:A&M I-125
Jerome of Prague
  GE:A&M II-1675
Jerome, Saint
  GE:A&M II-779, 909, 929, 935
  GL:A&M III-1142
Jessel, George
  GE:A&C II-734
Jesus (Jason)
  GE:A&M I-459
Jesus (son of Sirach)
  GE:A&M I-443
Jesus Christ
  GE:A&M I-477, 567, 589, II-595, 601
  GL:A&M III-1146
Jewett, Frank B.
  GE:B&C II-470
Jewett, John P.
  GE:Am II-859
Jewett, N. Clay
  GE:HR I-367
Jewett, Sarah Orne
  GL:AmW III-976

Jhabvala, Ruth Prawer
  GL:AmW III-981
Jiang Qing
  GE:HR III-1332
Jiang Zemin
  GE:HR V-2483
Jiménez de Cisneros, Francisco
  GL:Ren III-1160
Jinnah, Mohammed Ali
  GE:HR II-731, III-1611
  GE:W20 I-175, II-605
  GL:20 III-1108
Joab
  GE:A&M I-90
Joachim of Brandenburg
  GE:ME I-148
Joachim of Fiore
  GL:A&M III-1152
Joan of Arc
  GE:A&M III-1697
  GL:A&M III-1157
Joan of Navarre
  GE:A&M III-1421
Joanna
  GE:ME I-40
Job
  GE:ME I-198
Jobs, Steven
  GE:B&C III-1138, IV-1611, V-1809
  GE:S&T V-2073
Jochanan ben Zakkai. *See* Johanan ben Zakkai
Jōchō
  GL:A&M III-1163
Joffe, Charles
  GE:A&C V-2381
Joffre, Joseph-Jacques-Césaire
  GE:ME III-1249, 1262, 1359
  GL:20 III-1114
Joffrey, Robert
  GE:A&C IV-1694, V-2288
Johanan ben Zakkai
  GE:A&M II-664
  GL:A&M III-1168
Johannes Duns Scotus. *See* Duns Scotus, John
Johannes Eckhart. *See* Eckhart, Meister Johannes
Johannes Scotus Erigena
  GE:A&M II-1011
Johannsen, Wilhelm Ludwig
  GE:S&T I-433
Johanson, Donald C.
  GE:S&T V-2037
John I of Avis
  GE:A&M III-1686

John II (of Portugal)
GE:ME I-11
John III (of Portugal)
GE:ME I-189
John III Sobieski
GE:ME I-368
GL:Ren III-1166
John IV (of Ethiopia, Yohannis IV)
GE:ME II-1094
John VI (of Portugal)
GE:ME II-645, 675
John XII, Pope
GE:A&M III-1195
John XXI, Pope
GE:A&M III-1564
John XXII, Pope
GE:A&M III-1410, 1564, 1608, 1620
John XXIII, Pisan Pope
GE:A&M III-1680
John XXIII, Pope
GE:HR II-1113
GE:ME III-1633, 1659
GE:W20 I-507
GL:20 III-1119
John Paul II, Pope
GE:HR IV-1972
GL:20 III-1124
John, Disciple of Jesus. See John the Apostle
John, Duke of Braganza
GE:ME I-304
John, Elector of Saxony
GE:ME I-91
John Hyrcanus. See Hyrcanus, John
John, King
GL:B&C III-1442
John Lackland
GE:A&M III-1452, 1457
John of Damascus
GE:A&M II-1011, 1111, 1152
GL:A&M III-1174
John of Ephesus
GE:A&M II-681
John of Gishala
GE:A&M II-648
John of Salisbury
GE:A&M III-1231, 1370
John of the Cross, Saint
GL:Ren III-1171
John of Villiers
GE:A&M III-1574
John, Patriarch of Jerusalem
GE:A&M II-1111

John the Apostle
GE:A&M II-607
GL:A&M III-1180
John the Baptist
GE:A&M I-477, II-589
GL:A&M III-1184
John the Evangelist
GE:A&M I-210
John, Augustus
GL:B&C III-1447
Johns, Jasper, Jr.
GE:A&C III-1590
Johns, Ralph
GE:HR II-1056
Johnson, Albert
GE:B&C II-459
GE:HR I-350, 383
Johnson, Andrew
GE:Am II-962, 1003, 1026, 1031, 1049
GL:Am III-1255
Johnson, Arte
GE:A&C IV-2115
Johnson, Caryn. See Goldberg, Whoopi
Johnson, Claudia Alta Taylor. See Johnson, Lady
Bird
Johnson, Eldridge R.
GE:S&T I-138
Johnson, F. Ross
GE:B&C V-1976
Johnson, Frank M., Jr.
GE:HR III-1622
Johnson, Colonel Herbert
GE:A&C I-209
Johnson, Hiram Warren
GE:Am III-1484, 1649
GE:B&C II-476
Johnson, Hugh Samuel
GE:Am III-1637
GE:B&C II-662, 701
Johnson, Irving Stanley
GE:S&T V-2221
Johnson, Lady Bird
GE:Am III-1899
GE:B&C III-1254
Johnson, Louis A.
GE:Am III-1783
GE:B&C II-820
Johnson, Lyndon B.
GE:A&C IV-2048
GE:Am III-1866, 1871, 1899, 1906, 1918
GE:B&C III-1185, 1218, 1229, 1235, 1254,
1259, 1270, IV-1341, 1364, 1369, 1495,
V-1882

GE:HR II-997, III-1206, 1231, 1251, 1262,
  1278, 1284, 1296, 1310, 1338, 1370, 1376,
  1381, 1397, 1402, 1414, 1435, 1446, 1537,
  1595
GE:ME III-1648
GE:W20 II-806, 856, 965, 1036, III-1287
GL:Am III-1264
Johnson, Marguerite. *See* Angelou, Maya
Johnson, Marshall S.
  GE:S&T IV-1734
Johnson, Philip
  GE:A&C III-1590, V-2402, 2407, 2614
Johnson, Reynold B.
  GE:S&T V-1923
Johnson, Richard Mentor
  GE:Am II-760
Johnson, Samuel
  GE:Am I-636
  GL:B&C III-1452
Johnson, Thomas
  GE:Am I-288
Johnson, Thomas Frank
  GE:HR I-361
Johnson, Thomas Herbert
  GE:A&C IV-1662
Johnson, William (Associate Justice of the United
    States)
  GE:Am I-600
Johnson, Sir William (Superintendent of Indian
    Affairs)
  GE:Am I-207
Johnson, William Arthur
  GE:S&T III-1107
Johnson, Wyatt Thomas "Tom," Jr.
  GE:B&C V-1768
Johnson, Zack
  GE:HR II-929
Johnston, Alvanley
  GE:Am III-1759
  GE:B&C III-880
Johnston, Frances Benjamin
  GL:AmW III-986
Johnston, Joseph Eggleston
  GE:Am II-952, 997, 1010
Johnston, Samuel
  GE:Am I-213
Joliot, Frederic, and Irène Joliot-Curie
  GE:S&T III-973, 987, 1135
  GL:20 III-1129
Jolliet, Louis
  GE:Am I-52, 144
Jolson, Al
  GE:A&C II-734
  GE:Am III-1501
  GE:B&C II-545

Jonas
  GE:A&M II-1052
Jonathan
  GE:A&M I-459
Jones, Albert
  GE:S&T V-2351
Jones, Bobby
  GL:Am III-1270
Jones, Brian
  GE:A&C IV-2027
Jones, Edward Davis
  GE:B&C I-1
Jones, Grace
  GE:A&C V-2386
Jones, Inigo
  GL:B&C III-1457
Jones, James
  GE:A&C III-1373
Jones, Jesse H.
  GE:B&C II-630, 668, III-1014
Jones, John Paul (b. 1946)
  GE:A&C V-2228
Jones, John Paul (1747-1792)
  GL:Am III-1276
Jones, LeRoi. *See* Baraka, Amiri
Jones, Mary Harris "Mother"
  GE:HR I-293
  GL:AmW III-990
Jones, Quincy
  GE:A&C V-2512
Jones, Steve
  GE:A&C V-2299, 2360
Jones, Terry
  GE:A&C IV-2174
Jones, Thomas R.
  GE:HR III-1451
Jones, William
  GE:Am I-539
Jong, Bettie de
  GE:A&C III-1602
Jonson, Ben
  GE:ME I-208
  GL:B&C III-1461
Jooss, Kurt
  GE:A&C II-920
Joplin, Janis
  GE:A&C IV-2104, 2180
  GL:AmW III-995
Joplin, Lottie
  GE:A&C V-2350
Joplin, Scott
  GE:A&C I-13, V-2350
Jordan, Barbara
  GL:AmW III-1000

Jordan, John Newell
  GE:W20 I-121
Jordan, Paul
  GE:A&C I-219
Joseph I, Holy Roman Emperor
  GE:ME I-400
Joseph II, Holy Roman Emperor
  GE:ME I-414, 469, 480
  GL:Ren III-1177
Joseph, Chief
  GL:Am III-1284
Joseph, Father (François Le Clerq Du Tremblay)
  GE:ME I-278
Joseph Ferdinand, of Bavaria
  GE:ME I-372
Joseph, Akiba ben. See Akiba ben Joseph
Joseph, Frederick
  GE:B&C V-1958
Joseph, Sir Keith
  GE:HR IV-2024
Joseph, Sister Mary
  GE:Am II-1178
Joseph, Stephen C.
  GE:HR IV-2130
Joseph ben Matthias. See Josephus, Flavius
Josephson, Brian D.
  GE:S&T IV-1551
Josephus, Flavius
  GE:A&M II-648
  GL:A&M III-1189
Joshua
  GE:A&M I-84
Josiah
  GE:A&M I-149, II-664
Jouhaux, Léon
  GE:HR II-873
Jovius. See Diocletian
Joxe, Louis
  GE:ME III-1628
Joyce, James
  GE:A&C I-445, II-555, 851, III-1573
  GL:B&C III-1470
Joyce, John
  GE:B&C I-75
Joynson-Hicks, Sir William
  GE:ME III-1324
Juan Carlos I
  GE:HR IV-1921, 2079
  GE:W20 II-1043
Juan, Don
  GE:W20 II-1043
Juan, Don, of Austria
  GE:ME I-180

Juárez, Benito
  GE:ME II-876
  GL:Ren III-1182
Juchi
  GE:A&M III-1462
Judah Ha Nasi. See Ha Nasi, Judah
Judah ha-Levi
  GE:A&M III-1334, 1391
  GL:A&M III-1196
Judah, Theodore D.
  GE:Am II-969
Judas Maccabaeus. See Maccabaeus, Indas
Judas of Kerioth
  GE:A&M II-601
Judd, Donald
  GE:A&C IV-1949
Judkins, Steveland. See Wonder, Stevie
Judson, Walter E.
  GE:S&T III-1353, IV-1429
Jugurtha
  GE:A&M I-496
Julian, Count
  GE:A&M II-1105
Julian of Eclanum
  GE:A&M II-946
Julian the Apostate
  GE:A&M II-731, 888
Julius II, Pope
  GE:ME I-21, 26, 31, 44, 143
  GL:Ren III-1188
Julius Africanus, Sextus. See Africanus, Sextus
  Julius
Julius Caesar. See Caesar, Julius
Julius Frontinus, Sextus. See Frontinus, Sextus
  Julius
Julius, Pope
  GE:A&M II-872
Julius Severus, Sextus. See Severus, Sextus Julius
Julius, Gaius
  GE:A&M I-253
Julius, Nepos
  GE:A&M II-980
Jumblatt, Kamal
  GE:W20 III-1235
Jumelle, Clément
  GE:HR II-1009
Jung, Carl
  GE:A&C I-19, 309, IV-1829
  GE:ME III-1310
  GL:20 III-1134
Jung-lu
  GE:HR I-1
Junius Rusticus. See Rusticus, Junius

K

K., Jolly
GE:HR III-1639, IV-1752
Kaas, Ludwig
GE:ME III-1382
Kadar, Janos
GE:HR II-969, V-2421
GE:ME III-1595
Kadare, Ismail
GE:HR V-2553
Kader, Abd el-, Messali Hadj
GE:HR II-651
Kades, Charles Louis
GE:HR II-725
Kafka, Franz
GE:A&C I-396
GL:20 III-1139
Kaggia, Bildad Mwanganu
GE:HR II-891
Kagi, John H.
GE:Am II-918
Kahane, Jack
GE:A&C II-963
Kahl, Milt
GE:A&C II-1053
Kahler, John H.
GE:Am II-1178
Kahlo, Frida
GE:A&C II-957
Kahn, Alfred
GE:B&C IV-1676
Kahn, Louis I.
GE:A&C IV-1919
Kahn, Reuben Leon
GE:S&T II-756
Kahn, R. F.
GE:ME III-1406
Kahn, Richard
GE:B&C II-740
Kahnweiler, Daniel-Henry
GE:A&C I-204
Kai-shek, Chiang. See Chiang Kai-shek
Kajanus, Robert
GE:A&C I-292
Kakhovsky, Peter
GE:ME II-665
Kaku, Mori
GE:W20 I-269
Kalavun
GE:A&M III-1574

Kālidāsa
GL:A&M III-1217
Kallet, Arthur
GE:HR I-527, II-1062
Kallman, Chester
GE:A&C III-1514
Kalmus, Herbert
GE:A&C III-1307
Kálnoky, Count Gustav Siegmund
GE:ME II-1019
Kaltenbrunner, Ernst
GE:HR II-667
Kamau. See Kenyatta, Jomo
Kamehameha I (of Hawaii)
GE:W20 I-790
Kamehameha II (of Hawaii)
GE:W20 II-790
Kamenev, Lev
GE:B&C II-563
GE:HR I-503
GE:ME III-1347
Kameny, Frank
GE:HR IV-1741, 1801
Kamm, Oliver
GE:S&T IV-1459
Kämpfer, Engelbert
GL:Ren III-1194
Kanamori, Hiroo
GE:S&T III-1050
Kandinsky, Wassily
GE:A&C I-275, 320, 463, II-544, 583, 718,
III-1083
GL:20 III-1144
Kanellopoulos, Panayiotis
GE:HR III-1359
K'ang Yu-wei
GE:HR I-116
K'ang-hsi
GL:Ren III-1199
Kania, Stanisaw
GE:HR IV-2152
Kanishka
GL:A&M III-1222
Kanoldt, Alexander
GE:A&C II-631
Kant, Immanuel
GE:ME I-491
GL:Ren III-1205

Kao, Charles K.
  GE:S&T V-2078
Kapany, Narinder S.
  GE:S&T V-2078
Kapitsa, Pyotr Leonidovich
  GE:S&T III-1129
  GL:20 III-1149
Kappel, Frederick R.
  GE:B&C IV-1325, 1506
Kapteyn, Jacobus Cornelis
  GE:S&T I-218, II-655
Karageorgevich. See Paul, Prince
Karageorgevich. See Peter II of Yugoslavia
Karajan, Herbert von
  GE:A&C I-292
  GL:20 III-1155
Karamanlis, Konstantinos
  GE:HR II-1084
  GE:W20 III-1193
Karami, Rashid
  GE:W20 III-1235
Karan, Donna
  GL:AmW III-1005
Kariuki, Josiah M.
  GE:HR V-2431
Karl Wilhelm Ferdinand (Duke of Brunswick)
  GE:ME I-520
Karloff, Boris
  GE:A&C II-863
Karlsefni, Thorfinn
  GE:Am I-11
Karmal, Babrak
  GE:HR IV-2062, V-2449
Karsavina, Tamara
  GE:A&C I-241, 247, 269
Kasavubu, Joseph
  GE:HR II-1068, 1074
  GE:ME III-1613
Käsebier, Gertrude
  GE:A&C I-63
  GL:AmW III-1010
Kassem, Abdul Karim
  GE:HR II-1050
Kastenmeier, Robert W.
  GE:B&C IV-1626
Kato, Komei
  GE:HR I-417
Kato, Baron Takaakira
  GE:W20 I-121
Kato, Baron Tomosaburo
  GE:Am III-1531
Katsura Taro
  GE:B&C I-41
Katsushika Hokusai. See Hokusai

Katz, Robert L.
  GE:HR III-1497
Katzenbach, Nicholas
  GE:HR III-1296
Kauffmann, Angelica
  GL:Ren III-1210
Kaufman, Denis. See Vertov, Dziga
Kaufman, Irving
  GE:HR IV-2106
Kaufmann, Edgar, Jr.
  GE:A&C II-902
Kaunda, Kenneth D.
  GE:HR III-1224, IV-1736
Kawabata, Yasunari
  GE:A&C IV-2147
  GL:20 III-1160
Kawaguchi, Kiyotake
  GE:Am III-1709
Kawamata, Katsuji
  GE:B&C I-185
Kay, John
  GE:ME I-405
  GL:B&C III-1476
Kay, Robert
  GE:ME I-405
Kaye, Nora
  GE:A&C II-1036
Kay-Shuttleworth, First Baronet
  GL:B&C III-1480
Kazan, Elia
  GE:A&C II-874, III-1164, 1340, 1487
Kazanjoglou, Elia. See Kazan, Elia
Kazantzakis, Nikos
  GL:20 III-1165
Kean, Edmund
  GL:B&C III-1484
Keane, John
  GE:Am I-533
Kearney, A. T.
  GE:B&C II-481
Kearney, Denis
  GE:Am II-1123
Kearny, Stephen Watts
  GE:Am II-818
Keating, Kenneth B.
  GE:Am III-1888
Keaton, Buster
  GE:A&C II-691
Keaton, Diane
  GE:A&C V-2381
Keats, John
  GL:B&C III-1492
Keeler, Leonarde
  GE:S&T II-711

Keeler, Ruby
  GE:A&C II-925
Keeling, Charles D.
  GE:S&T III-1118
Keeshan, Bob
  GE:A&C IV-1678
Kefauver, Estes
  GE:B&C I-35, III-970, 1180
  GE:W20 II-856
Keitel, Wilhelm
  GE:HR II-667
Keith, A. E.
  GE:S&T I-11
Keith, Sir Arthur
  GE:S&T V-2341
Keith, Myron R.
  GE:Am II-1116
Keller, Helen
  GL:Am III-1289
  GL:AmW III-1015
Kelley, Florence
  GE:Am III-1369
  GE:HR I-75, 131
  GL:AmW III-1019
Kelley, Oliver Hudson
  GE:Am II-1043
Kelly, Gene
  GE:A&C III-1432
Kelly, Harry F.
  GE:HR II-635
Kelly, John
  GE:Am II-1140
Kelly, M. Clyde
  GE:B&C II-493
Kelly, Mervin
  GE:W20 II-612
Kelly, Thomas E.
  GE:W20 II-1022
Kelsey, Frances
  GE:B&C III-1180
Kelso, Louis
  GE:B&C V-1854
Kelvin, Sir William Thomson, Lord
  GE:ME II-834
  GE:S&T I-285, II-846
  GL:B&C III-1498
Kemal Atatürk, Mustafa. See Atatürk, Kemal
  GE:W20 I-107, 129, 225
Kemble, Fanny
  GL:AmW III-1024
Kemeny, John G.
  GE:S&T IV-1772
Kemp, Jack
  GE:B&C V-1782

Kempe, C. Henry
  GE:HR IV-1752
Kempis, Thomas à. See Thomas à Kempis
Kendall, Willmoore
  GE:A&C IV-1683
Kendell, Henry W.
  GE:S&T IV-1871
Kennan, George F.
  GE:Am III-1776
  GE:B&C III-902
  GE:HR II-706
  GE:ME III-1532
Kennedy, Adrienne
  GE:A&C V-2370
Kennedy, Edward M.
  GE:B&C III-1259, V-1798, 1933
Kennedy, Jacqueline Bouvier. See Onassis, Jacqueline Kennedy
Kennedy, John F.
  GE:Am III-1871, 1877, 1888, 1899, 1906, 1940
  GE:B&C III-975, 1117, 1122, 1175, 1185, 1218, 1235, 1259
  GE:HR I-406, II-1044, 1102, III-1125, 1167, 1172, 1188, 1200, 1206, 1231, 1251, 1262, 1284
  GE:ME III-1618, 1624
  GE:W20 I-260, 507, II-806, 856, 926, 934, 955, 965
  GL:Am III-1295
Kennedy, Kathleen
  GE:A&C V-2491
Kennedy, Robert F.
  GE:A&C IV-1929
  GE:Am III-1927
  GE:B&C III-1092, 1213, 1229
  GE:HR III-1167, 1246, 1262, 1267, 1567
  GL:Am III-1300
Kennedy, William
  GE:B&C IV-1636
Kennelly, Arthur Edwin
  GE:S&T I-174
Kennerley, Michael
  GE:Am III-1399
Kent, James
  GE:Am I-600, II-673
  GL:Am III-1306
Kenyatta, Jomo
  GE:HR II-891, III-1194
  GL:20 III-1171
Kenyon, William Squire
  GE:B&C II-476
Keough, Donald
  GE:B&C V-1904

Kepler, Johannes
  GE:ME I-236
  GE:S&T V-2351
  GL:Ren III-1215
Kerensky, Prince Aleksandr F.
  GE:HR I-225
  GE:ME III-1271
  GL:20 III-1177
Kerkorian, Kirk
  GE:B&C V-1768
Kern, Jerome
  GE:A&C II-745
Kerner, Otto
  GE:HR III-1370
Kerouac, Jack
  GE:A&C III-1460
Kerr, Clark
  GE:Am III-1912
Kerr, Robert
  GE:B&C III-1248
Kerr, Roy P.
  GE:W20 II-835
Kershaw, Andrew
  GE:B&C IV-1410
Kershner, Irvin
  GE:A&C V-2391
Kertész, Mihaly. See Curtiz, Michael
Kerwin, Joseph P.
  GE:S&T V-1997
Kesey, Ken
  GE:A&C V-2320
Kesselring, Albert
  GE:ME III-1486
  GE:W20 I-430
  GL:20 III-1183
Kessinger, Paul
  GE:B&C V-1842
Kettering, Charles F.
  GE:S&T II-916
Keynes, John Maynard
  GE:Am III-1770
  GE:B&C II-740, 851, III-914, 1218
  GE:ME III-1406
  GL:B&C III-1503
Keyserling, Leon H.
  GE:Am III-1770
Khachaturian, Aram Ilich
  GE:A&C III-1388
Khadija
  GE:A&M II-1075
Khairuddin, Khwaja
  GE:HR IV-1898
Khairzuran
  GE:A&M II-1142

Khaled, Leila
  GE:W20 II-1028
Khalifa Abdullah et Taaisha, The
  GE:ME II-1113
Khalil, Al-ashraf al-. See Al-ashraf al-Khalil
Khama III
  GE:HR I-304
Khama, Tshekedi
  GE:HR I-304
Khamenei, Hojatoleslam Ali Hoseini
  GE:A&C V-2630
Khammurabi. See Hammurabi
Khan, Abdullah Jaffa Anver Bey. See Joffrey,
  Robert
Khan, Agha Mohammad Yahya
  GE:HR III-1611, IV-2018
Khan Akhmad
  GE:A&M III-1742
Khan, Ghulam Ishaq
  GE:HR V-2403
Khan, Mirza Malkam
  GE:HR I-52
Khan, Mohammad Ayub
  GE:A&C IV-1919
Khan, Yahya
  GE:W20 II-1091
Khartoum, Earl of. See Kitchener, Lord
Khayyám, Omar. See Omar Khayyám
Khieu Samphan
  GE:HR V-2459
Khlebnikov, Velemir
  GE:A&C I-413
Khomeini, Ayatollah Ruhollah
  GE:A&C V-2630
  GE:HR IV-2013, 2045, 2062
  GE:W20 III-1338
  GL:20 III-1187
Khosrow I
  GL:A&M III-1228
Khowarizmi, Al-. See Khowarizmi, al-
Khrennikov, Tikhon
  GE:A&C III-1388
Khrunov, Yevgeni V.
  GE:S&T IV-1891
Khrushchev, Nikita S.
  GE:A&C IV-1747
  GE:Am III-1888
  GE:HR II-952, 963, 969, III-1125, 1177, 1408,
    IV-1764, 1852, V-2249, 2298
  GE:ME III-1566, 1595, 1618, 1624
  GE:S&T IV-1619
  GE:W20 II-715, 721, 736, 776, 906, 955, 974,
    988
  GL:20 III-1193

Khusrau. *See* Khosrow I
Khwarizmi, al-
  GE:A&M III-1282
  GL:A&M III-1233
Kibble, Thomas
  GE:S&T V-2047
Kiderlen-Wäechter, Alfred von
  GE:ME III-1228
  GE:W20 I-46
Kiefer, Anselm
  GE:A&C V-2464
Kieffer, Hugh H.
  GE:W20 III-1294
Kieft, William
  GE:Am I-80
Kienzle, Raymond Nicholas. *See* Ray, Nicholas
Kier, Samuel M.
  GE:Am II-912
Kierkegaard, Søren
  GE:W20 I-252
  GL:Ren III-1222
Kijūrō, Baron Shidehara
  GE:HR II-725
Kilburn, Patrick E.
  GE:A&C IV-1898
Kilby, Jack St. Clair
  GE:B&C IV-1721
  GE:S&T V-1938, 1971
Kildal, Otto
  GE:HR II-1020
Killy, Jean-Claude
  GL:20 III-1199
Kilwardby, Robert
  GE:A&M III-1564
Kim Il Sung
  GE:Am III-1823
Kimathi, Dedan
  GE:HR II-891
Kimball, Aubrey Pierce
  GE:S&T IV-1662
Kimball, Heber C.
  GE:Am II-812
Kimball, Justin Ford
  GE:B&C II-557
Kimball, Ward
  GE:A&C II-1053
Kimbangu, Simon
  GE:B&C I-201
Kimmel, Husband Edward
  GE:Am III-1697
Kimura, Doreen
  GE:S&T IV-1635
Kindi, al-. *See* Al-Kindi

King, Billie Jean
  GL:AmW III-1028
King, Cecil R.
  GE:B&C III-1248
King, Charles Glen
  GE:S&T II-857
King, Coretta Scott
  GE:HR II-974, III-1257, IV-2209
King, Edwin
  GE:HR III-1149
King, Ernest Joseph
  GE:Am III-1709
  GE:ME III-1477
  GE:W20 I-404
King, Martin Luther, Jr.
  GE:A&C III-1329, V-2294
  GE:Am III-1855, 1927
  GE:B&C III-1229, IV-1364, 1495
  GE:HR II-947, 974, III-1188, 1200, 1231,
    1257, 1278, 1296, 1301, 1414, 1419,
    IV-1691, 2209
  GE:W20 I-507, II-806, 893, 965
  GL:Am III-1312
King, Richard
  GE:Am II-1020
King, Rufus
  GE:Am I-552
King, Samuel W.
  GE:Am II-766
King, William Lyon Mackenzie
  GE:B&C I-174, II-591, 597, 624
  GE:HR III-1321
  GL:B&C III-1509
Kingsley, John Donald
  GE:HR II-855
Kingston, Maxine Hong
  GL:AmW III-1032
Kinney, Sharon
  GE:A&C III-1602
Kinsey, Alfred
  GE:HR II-991
  GE:W20 II-619
  GL:Am III-1319
Kinski, Klaus
  GE:A&C IV-1984
Kintner, Earl W.
  GE:B&C III-1148
Kintner, Robert E.
  GE:A&C III-1368
Kipfer, Paul
  GE:S&T III-963
Kipling, Rudyard
  GL:B&C III-1516
Kipping, Frederic Stanley
  GE:S&T I-123

Kirchner, Ernst Ludwig
    GE:A&C I-134, V-2464
    GL:20 III-1204
Kirkland, Gelsey
    GE:A&C V-2459
Kirkland, Joseph Lane
    GE:HR III-1585
Kirkland, Moses
    GE:Am I-213
Kirkpatrick, Jeane
    GL:AmW III-1037
Kirov, Sergei
    GE:B&C II-563
    GE:HR I-503
    GE:W20 I-336
Kirstein, Lincoln
    GE:A&C II-974, III-1301
Kisselgoff, Anna
    GE:A&C V-2480
Kissinger, Henry A.
    GE:B&C IV-1477, 1527, 1544
    GE:HR IV-1691, 1791, 1806
    GE:W20 I-145, 260, II-1050, 1054, 1083,
        III-1110, 1124, 1161, 1182, 1193, 1212,
        1227, 1251, 1257, 1331
    GL:Am III-1326
Kiszczak, Czesław
    GE:HR V-2477, 2500
Kitagawa, Sōtatsu. See Sōtatsu
Kitasato, Shibasaburo
    GE:S&T I-6
Kitchener, Lord
    GE:ME II-1113, 1128
    GE:W20 I-87, 129
    GL:B&C III-1523
Kitchlew, Saif-ud-Din
    GE:HR I-264
Kitzhaber, John
    GE:HR V-2437
Kiyomori. See Taira Kiyomori
Kizim, Leonid
    GE:S&T V-2316
Klann, William C.
    GE:Am III-1421
Klarsfeld, Serge
    GE:HR IV-2193
Klebs, Edwin
    GE:S&T I-6, II-567
Klee, Paul
    GE:A&C I-463, II-583
    GL:20 III-1209
Klehment, Reinhold
    GE:ME III-1207

Klein, Calvin
    GE:B&C IV-1400
Klein, Felix
    GE:S&T I-31, II-650
Klein, Harold P.
    GE:W20 III-1294
Kleist, Heinrich von
    GL:Ren III-1227
Kleitman, Nathaniel
    GE:S&T III-1424
Klimt, Gustav
    GE:A&C I-79, 124
Kline, Nathan S.
    GE:S&T III-1353
Kliun, Ivan
    GE:A&C I-413
Klusak, Milan
    GE:HR III-1391
Knerr, Richard
    GE:B&C III-1102
Knight, Frank H.
    GE:B&C III-931
Knight, John S.
    GE:A&C V-2507
Knight, Jonathan
    GE:Am I-624
Knight, Thomas E.
    GE:Am III-1588
Knipper, Olga
    GE:A&C I-1
Knoll, Max
    GE:S&T III-958
Knoop, Franz
    GE:S&T III-1107
Knopf, Blanche Wolf
    GL:AmW III-1042
Knowland, William F.
    GE:W20 II-709
Knowlton, Charles
    GE:HR III-1290
Knox, Henry
    GE:Am I-383, 432
Knox, John
    GL:B&C III-1528
Knox, John C.
    GE:B&C III-869
Knox, John Jay
    GE:Am II-1083
Knox, Philander Chase
    GE:Am II-1318, III-1379, 1415
    GE:B&C I-91, 107
Knudsen, William S.
    GE:Am III-1680
    GE:B&C I-234, II-820, 833

Knudson, Alfred G., Jr.
    GE:S&T V-2331
Kober, Theodor
    GE:S&T I-78
Koberger, Anthony
    GE:A&M III-1713
Koch, Howard
    GE:A&C III-1103, 1245
Koch, Robert
    GE:ME III-1174
    GE:S&T I-103, II-705
    GL:Ren III-1232
Kodály, Zoltán
    GE:A&C I-102
Koenig, Kurt
    GE:B&C V-2040
Koenig, Pierre
    GE:A&C III-1290
Koestler, Arthur
    GE:W20 I-241
Kofi, Francis Kwia. See Nkrumah, Kwame
Kogelnik, Herwig G.
    GE:S&T V-2025
Kohl, Helmut
    GE:B&C V-2051
    GE:HR V-2523, 2589
Kohl, Michael
    GE:W20 III-1167
Kohlberg, Jerome, Jr.
    GE:B&C IV-1641
Kohler, Eric L.
    GE:B&C I-308
Kohlhase, Charles E.
    GE:S&T V-2082
Kohoutek, Lubos
    GE:S&T V-1992
Kokhba, Simon bar. See Bar Kokhba, Simon
Kokoschka, Oskar
    GL:20 III-1215
Kolbin, Gennadii V.
    GE:HR V-2298
Kolchak, Aleksandr Vasilievich
    GE:W20 I-152
Kole, Marcel J.
    GE:B&C V-1898
Kolff, Willem Johan
    GE:S&T II-512
Kolhörster, Werner
    GE:S&T II-694
Kolko, Gabriel
    GE:W20 II-663
Kölliker, Rudolf Albert von
    GE:S&T I-1

Kollwitz, Käthe
    GL:20 III-1221
Kolmogorov, A. N.
    GE:S&T II-664
Komei
    GE:Am II-884
Komura Jutaro
    GE:B&C I-41
Konev, Ivan Stepanovich
    GE:W20 II-577, 715
König, Karin
    GE:HR V-2494
Konigsberg, Allen Stewart. See Allen, Woody
Konitz, Lee
    GE:A&C III-1438
Konopatov, Aleksandr
    GE:S&T V-1950
Koop, Charles Everett
    GE:HR V-2455
Kooper, Al
    GE:A&C IV-2038
Kopp, Elisabeth
    GE:B&C V-2045
Koreff, Nora. See Kaye, Nora
Korematsu, Fred
    GE:HR V-2392
Korff, Serge Alexander
    GE:S&T III-1160
Kornberg, Arthur
    GE:S&T IV-1857
Kornberg, Hans Leo
    GE:S&T III-1107
Kornei, Otto
    GE:S&T III-1013
    GE:W20 I-382
Kornilov, Lavr Georgievich
    GE:ME III-1271
    GE:W20 I-152
Korolev, Sergei P.
    GE:S&T IV-1545, 1619, 1797, 1819, V-1928
    GE:W20 II-776
    GL:20 III-1226
Koryagin, Anatoly
    GE:HR IV-1909
Korzeniowski, Józef Teodor Konrad Nałecz. See
    Conrad, Joseph
Kosciuszko, Thaddeus
    GE:ME I-469
Koster, Samuel W.
    GE:HR III-1555
Kostrowitzky, Guillaume Albert Wladimir
    Alexandre Apollinaire de. See Apollinaire,
    Guillaume

Kosygin, Aleksei Nikolaevich
    GE:ME III-1666, 1678
    GE:W20 II-974
Kott, Gary
    GE:A&C V-2532
Koussevitzky, Serge
    GE:A&C I-508, II-561
Kozbari, Muwaffaq al-Din al-
    GE:HR IV-1967
Kozoll, Michael
    GE:A&C V-2470
Kracht, Felix
    GE:B&C III-1303
Kramers, Hendrik Anthony
    GE:S&T II-815
Krampe, Hugh J. See O'Brian, Hugh
Krasner, Lee
    GL:AmW III-1046
Krassner, Lenore. See Krasner, Lee
Krauss, Werner
    GE:A&C I-486
Kravchuk, Leonid
    GE:HR V-2618
Kravis, Henry R.
    GE:B&C IV-1641
Krebs, Sir Hans Adolf
    GE:S&T III-1107, 1390
Krebs, Nicholas. See Nicholas of Cusa
Kremer, Alexander
    GE:ME II-1105
Kremer, Gerhard. See Mercator, Gerardus
Krenz, Egon
    GE:HR V-2523
Kreps, Juanita
    GL:AmW III-1052
Kretschmer, Ernst
    GE:ME III-1310
Krishnan, Tatparanandam Ananda
    GE:A&C V-2543
Krishnaswami, Arcot
    GE:HR IV-2146
Kristofferson, Kris
    GE:A&C V-2365
Kroc, Ray
    GE:B&C III-1025, 1138, IV-1406
Krogh, August
    GL:20 III-1232
Kronecker, Leopold
    GE:S&T I-438
Kruger, James T.
    GE:HR IV-1882, 1887
Kruger, Stephanus Johannes
    GE:ME II-1128

Krum, Charles
    GE:W20 I-1
Krum, Howard
    GE:W20 I-1
Krupa, Gene
    GE:A&C II-968
Krupp, Alfred
    GL:Ren III-1237
Krupp, Gustav
    GE:S&T I-350
Kryfts, Nicholas. See Nicholas of Cusa
Krylenko, Nikolay
    GE:A&C V-2277
Kuang-hsü
    GE:HR I-1
Kubai, Fred
    GE:HR II-891
Kubelsky, Benjamin. See Benny, Jack
Kubin, Alfred
    GE:A&C I-275
Kublai Khan
    GE:A&M III-1550
    GL:A&M III-1239
Kübler-Ross, Elisabeth
    GL:AmW III-1057
Kubrick, Stanley
    GE:A&C IV-1989
Kudriashev, Ivan
    GE:A&C I-413
Kuhn, Bowie
    GE:B&C IV-1437, 1512
Kuhn, Walt
    GE:A&C I-361
    GE:Am III-1411
Kuiper, Gerard Peter
    GE:S&T III-1245
Kuleshov, Lev Vladimirovich
    GE:A&C II-615, 701
Kumpe, David A.
    GE:S&T V-2088
Kunayev, Dinmukhamed
    GE:HR V-2298
Kundera, Milan
    GE:A&C IV-1967
Kundt, August
    GE:ME II-1084
Kundt, Hans
    GE:W20 I-289
Küng, Hans
    GE:ME III-1633
K'ung Ch'iu. See Confucius
Kungu, Waruhiu
    GE:HR II-891

Kunitsky, R. W.
  GE:S&T I-113
Kunstler, William
  GE:W20 II-865
Kuo Mo-jo
  GL:20 III-1237
Kupka, František
  GL:20 III-1242
Küpper, Christian Emil Marie. *See* Doesburg,
  Theo van
Kurbatov, Alexis
  GE:ME I-364
Kurchatov, Igor Vasilyevich
  GE:B&C III-1046
  GE:ME III-1561
  GL:20 III-1247
Kuria, Gibson
  GE:HR V-2431
Kurita, Takeo
  GE:Am III-1731
Kuroń, Jacek
  GE:HR V-2500

Kuropatkin, Aleksei Nikolaevich
  GE:ME III-1148
Kurosawa, Akira
  GE:A&C III-1476
  GL:20 III-1252
Kurtz, Thomas E.
  GE:S&T IV-1772
Kusevitsky, Sergey. *See* Koussevitzky, Serge
Kutchuk, Fazil
  GE:HR II-1084, III-1218, 1236
Kutuzov, Mikhail Ilarionovich
  GE:ME II-568, 585
Kuusinen, Hertta
  GE:HR IV-1796, 2057
Kuwatli, Shukri al-
  GE:W20 I-494
Kuznetsov, Vasili
  GE:W20 II-798
Kvenvolden, Keith
  GE:S&T IV-1851

L

Laban, Rudolf
  GL:20 III-1259
LaBuy, Walter J.
  GE:B&C III-1164
Lacan, Jacques
  GL:20 III-1264
Lack, John
  GE:A&C V-2475
Lacoste, Pierre
  GE:HR V-2268
Ladislas I. *See* László I, Saint
Ladislas II Jagello. *See* Władysław II Jagiełło and
  Jadwiga
Laelius, Gaius
  GE:A&M I-437
Laemmle, Carl
  GE:A&C I-224, II-833
  GE:B&C I-117
Laevinius, Marcus Valerius
  GE:A&M I-432
La Farge, John
  GE:A&C I-34
La Farge, Oliver
  GE:HR III-1573
LaFayette, Marquis de. *See* De La Fayette,
  Marquis
LaFeber, Walter
  GE:W20 II-663
Laffer, Arthur
  GE:B&C V-1782
La Flesche, Susan. *See* Picotte, Susan La Flesche
La Follette, Robert Marion, Jr.
  GE:Am II-1307, III-1390, 1484
  GE:B&C II-464
  GE:HR I-172, 555
  GL:Am III-1332
La Fontaine, Henri-Marie
  GL:20 III-1270
La Fontaine, Jean de
  GL:Ren III-1241
Lagerfeld, Karl
  GE:A&C I-474
Lagerkvist, Pär
  GE:A&C IV-1742
Lagerlöf, Selma
  GL:20 III-1275
Lagrange, Joseph-Louis
  GL:Ren III-1246

La Guardia, Fiorello Henry
  GE:B&C II-635
  GE:HR II-578, 635, 689
Lahr, Bert
  GE:A&C III-1109
Lahrheim, Irving. *See* Lahr, Bert
Laidoner, Johan
  GE:HR I-207
Laing, Hugh
  GE:A&C II-1036
Laird, Macgregor
  GE:B&C I-196
Laird, Melvin
  GE:HR IV-1691
Laloux, Victor
  GE:A&C V-2588
LaMarch, Judy
  GE:HR III-1321
Lamb, H. Richard
  GE:HR IV-2226
Lamb, William. *See* Melbourne, Viscount
  (William Lamb)
Lamb, William F.
  GE:A&C II-880
  GE:S&T II-906
Lamb, Willis Eugene, Jr.
  GE:S&T III-1293
Lambert, John
  GL:B&C III-1534
Lambruschini, Cardinal Luigi
  GE:ME I-770
Lambton, John George, Lord Durham
  GE:HR I-453
Lambton, John George. *See* Durham, First Earl of
Lamont, Thomas William
  GE:Am III-1577
  GE:B&C II-574
Lamormaini, William
  GE:ME I-270
L'Amour, Louis
  GE:A&C I-304
Lampland, Carl O.
  GE:S&T I-291
Lampton, Michael L.
  GE:S&T V-2256
La Muniere, Charles
  GE:HR V-2354
Lancaster, Joseph
  GL:B&C III-1540

Lanchester, Frederick William
    GL:B&C III-1545
Land, Edwin Herbert
    GE:B&C III-896
    GE:S&T III-1331
Land, Emory Scott
    GE:Am III-1680
Landa, Diego de
    GE:S&T V-2145
Landau, Jon
    GE:A&C V-2325
Landau, Lev Davidovich
    GE:S&T III-1008, 1129, 1150
    GL:20 III-1280
Landau, Moshe
    GE:HR II-1108
Landé, Alfred
    GE:S&T II-800
Landini, Francesco
    GL:A&M III-1244
Landis, Kenesaw Mountain
    GE:Am III-1497
    GE:B&C I-341
Landon, Michael
    GE:A&C IV-1800
Landrum, Philip M.
    GE:B&C III-1122
Landsbergis, Vytautas
    GE:HR V-2577
Landsteiner, Karl
    GE:S&T I-56
Lane, Sir Allen
    GE:B&C II-696
Lane, James Henry
    GE:Am II-889
Lane, Sir Ralph
    GE:Am I-46
Lane, Richard
    GE:B&C II-696
Lanfield, Sidney
    GE:A&C III-1131
Lanfranc
    GE:A&M III-1291
Lang, Cosmo Gordon
    GE:ME III-1420
Lang, Fritz
    GE:A&C II-707
    GL:20 III-1285
Lang, K. D.
    GL:AmW III-1061
Langdon, Harry
    GE:A&C I-230
Lange, David
    GE:HR V-2268

Lange, Dorothea
    GL:AmW III-1066
Langer, Susanne K.
    GL:AmW III-1071
Langevin, Paul
    GE:S&T II-620, IV-1562
Langhanke, Lucille Vasconcellos. See Astor, Mary
Langhorne, Nancy Witcher. See Astor, Nancy
Langiewicz, Marjan
    GE:ME II-886
Langley, Samuel P.
    GE:Am II-1346
Langlois, Henri
    GE:A&C IV-1710
Langmuir, Irving
    GE:B&C I-17
    GE:S&T III-1276
Lankard, J. R.
    GE:S&T V-2025
Lankester, Sir Edwin Ray
    GL:B&C III-1551
Lanman, Charles Rockwell
    GE:Am II-1077
Lannes, Gustave Louis (Marquis de Montebello)
    GE:ME II-1070
Lannes, Jean
    GE:ME II-556
Lansbury, Angela
    GL:AmW III-1076
Lansdowne, Fifth Marquess of
    GE:B&C I-41
    GE:ME III-1152, 1214
    GL:B&C III-1555
Lansdowne, Marquess of
    GE:Am I-207, 300
Lansing, Robert
    GE:Am II-1450
    GE:HR I-252
    GE:W20 I-121
Lanza, Giovanni
    GE:ME II-958, 978
Lao-tzu
    GL:A&M III-1248
LaPiere, Cherilyn. See Cher
Laplace, Pierre-Simon
    GE:S&T III-1035
    GL:Ren III-1252
Laporte, Pierre
    GE:HR III-1543
Lardner, Ring, Jr.
    GE:A&C III-1340
Largo Caballero, Francisco
    GE:ME III-1368, 1416

Larkin, Thomas O.
  GE:Am II-843
Larrick, George P.
  GE:B&C III-1097
L'Arronge, Adolphe
  GE:A&C I-145
Larsen, Knud
  GE:HR II-867, 918
Larsen, Roy E.
  GE:A&C II-577
  GE:B&C I-412
Larson, Eric
  GE:A&C II-1053
Larson, Henrietta M.
  GE:B&C I-335
Larson, John A.
  GE:S&T II-711
La Salle, Sieur de
  GE:Am I-52, 144, 443
  GL:Am III-1337
Las Casas, Bartolomé de
  GE:A&M III-1756
  GE:ME I-129
  GL:Ren III-1258
Lasche, Oskar
  GE:A&C I-219
Lasker, Eduard
  GE:ME II-1013
Laski, Harold J.
  GL:B&C III-1559
Lasky, Jesse L.
  GE:A&C II-567
Lasley, R. E.
  GE:W20 I-355
Lassalle, Ferdinand
  GE:ME II-992
  GL:Ren III-1263
László I, Saint
  GE:A&M III-1210
  GL:A&M III-1253
Latham, Hubert
  GE:S&T I-448
Lathrop, Julia C.
  GE:HR I-131
  GL:AmW III-1081
Latimer, Hugh
  GL:B&C III-1563
Latrobe, Benjamin Henry
  GL:Am III-1342
Lattimore, Owen
  GE:Am III-1817
Lau, H. E.
  GE:S&T I-370

Laub, Johann Jakob
  GE:S&T I-297
Laubeuf, Maxime
  GE:S&T I-350
Laud, William
  GL:B&C III-1567
Laue, Max von
  GE:S&T I-118, II-517
Lauer, Robert B.
  GE:B&C IV-1647
Laughlin, James
  GE:A&C III-1443
Laughlin, Robert Betts
  GE:S&T V-2136
Laugier, Henri
  GE:HR II-590
Lauren, Jerry
  GE:A&C IV-2141
Lauren, Ralph
  GE:A&C IV-2141
Laurents, Arthur
  GE:A&C IV-1731
Laurier, Sir Wilfrid
  GE:B&C I-174
  GE:HR I-453
  GL:B&C III-1572
Laval, François
  GL:B&C III-1579
Laval, Pierre
  GE:B&C II-723
  GE:ME III-1401
  GE:W20 I-342
Laveikin, Alexander
  GE:S&T V-2316
Laver, Rod
  GL:B&C III-1585
Lavoisier, Antoine-Laurent
  GL:Ren III-1268
Law, Bonar
  GE:HR I-309
  GE:ME III-1233
  GL:B&C III-1590
Lawrence, First Baron
  GL:B&C III-1595
Lawrence, D. H.
  GE:A&C I-502, II-896
  GL:B&C III-1600
Lawrence, Ernest Orlando
  GE:S&T III-953, 1101, 1282, 1336
  GE:W20 II-683
  GL:Am III-1347
Lawrence, Geoffrey
  GE:HR II-667

Lawrence, Harding L.
    GE:B&C IV-1676, V-1826
Lawrence, T. E.
    GL:B&C III-1608
Lawrence, Sir Thomas
    GL:B&C III-1616
Lawrence, Vera Brodsky
    GE:A&C V-2350
Laws, S. S.
    GE:Am II-1110
Laxness, Halldór
    GL:20 III-1290
Laynez, James
    GE:ME I-96, 143
Layton, Richard
    GE:ME I-110
Lazar I of Hrebelyanovich
    GE:A&M III-1660
Lazarevich, Stephen
    GE:A&M III-1660
Lazarus, Emma
    GL:AmW III-1086
Lazear, Jesse William
    GE:S&T I-73
Le Duan
    GE:W20 III-1227, 1243
Le Duc Tho
    GE:HR IV-1691
Le Hong Phong
    GE:HR II-573
Lea, Clarence Frederick
    GE:B&C II-775, 815
Leach, Archibald. See Grant, Cary
Leach, Edmund
    GE:A&C IV-1995
Leadbelly
    GE:A&C II-810
Leahy, William Daniel
    GE:Am II-1736
Leakey, L. S. B.
    GE:S&T IV-1603, V-2037
    GE:W20 I-218
    GL:B&C IV-1623
Leakey, Mary
    GE:S&T IV-1603, V-2037
Leakey, Richard E.
    GE:S&T V-2037
Leander of Seville
    GE:A&M II-1063, 1086
Lear, Norman
    GE:A&C V-2197, 2234, 2339
Leathes, Stanley
    GE:W20 I-24

Leavitt, Henrietta Swan
    GE:S&T II-496, 557, 655, 700, 766, 878
Lebedinsky, A. I.
    GE:S&T IV-1819
Lebesgue, Henri-Léon
    GE:S&T I-36
Leblanc, Nicolas
    GL:Ren III-1273
Le Bon, Gustave
    GL:20 III-1293
LeBoulaire, Jean
    GE:A&C III-1206
Le Breton, André-François
    GE:ME I-428
Le Carré, John
    GE:A&C IV-1934
Leck, Bart van der
    GE:A&C I-429
Leclerc, Georges-Louis. See Buffon, Comte de
Le Corbusier. See Corbusier, Le
Ledbetter, Huddie. See Leadbelly
Leder, Philip
    GE:B&C V-1970
Ledru-Rollin, Alexandre
    GE:ME II-786
Lee, Ann
    GL:AmW III-1090
Lee, Arthur
    GE:Am I-282
Lee, Ezra
    GE:Am I-267
Lee, Gypsy Rose
    GL:AmW III-1095
Lee, Ivy Ledbetter
    GE:B&C I-122
Lee, Martin
    GE:HR IV-2073
Lee, Peggy
    GL:AmW III-1100
Lee, Richard Henry
    GE:Am I-261, 367
Lee, Robert E.
    GE:Am II-918, 997
    GL:Am III-1352
Lee, Spike
    GE:A&C V-2565, 2641
Lee Kuan Yew
    GL:20 III-1303
Leeb, Wilhelm Joseph Franz von
    GE:W20 I-450
Leeds, First Duke of
    GL:B&C IV-1630
Leeuwenhoek, Antoni van. See Van
    Leeuwenhoek, Antoni

Lefever, Ernest W.
  GE:HR IV-2130
Lefferts, Marshall
  GE:Am II-1110
Le Gallienne, Eva
  GL:AmW III-1105
Legasov, Valery A.
  GE:S&T V-2321
Legator, Marvin S.
  GE:B&C IV-1390
Léger, Fernand
  GE:A&C I-337
  GL:20 III-1308
Legge, Alexander
  GE:B&C II-569
Legge, William
  GE:Am I-251
Legh, Thomas
  GE:ME I-110
Lehman, Ernest
  GE:A&C IV-2033
Lehman, Richard H.
  GE:B&C IV-1454
Lehmann, Inge
  GE:S&T I-340, III-1065
Leibniz, Gottfried Wilhelm
  GE:S&T IV-1751
  GL:Ren III-1285
Leibovitz, Annie
  GL:AmW III-1111
Leibowitz, Samuel
  GE:Am III-1588
Leicester, Earl of. See Montfort, Simon V de
Leiding, Rudolph
  GE:B&C IV-1664
Leif Eriksson
  GL:A&M III-1258
Leif the Lucky
  GE:Am I-11
Leigh, Denis
  GE:HR IV-1926
Leigh, Janet
  GE:A&C IV-1855
Leigh, Vivien
  GE:A&C III-1154, 1487
Leith, Emmett
  GE:S&T III-1288
Leitsch, Dick
  GE:HR III-1479
Leland, George Thomas (Mickey)
  GE:HR V-2354
Leland, Henry M.
  GE:B&C I-151

Lelewel, Joachim
  GE:ME II-691
Lelong, Lucien
  GE:A&C III-1346
Lemaître, Georges
  GE:S&T II-766, 825, 878, III-1309, 1320
  GL:20 III-1313
LeMay, Curtis E.
  GE:Am III-1933
  GE:ME III-1543
Lemkin, Raphael
  GE:HR II-783
Lenard, Philipp
  GE:ME II-1084
  GE:S&T I-118, 356, II-590
Lengyel, Peter
  GE:S&T III-1363
Lenin, Vladimir Ilich
  GE:A&C II-544, 615, 701
  GE:B&C I-374, II-563
  GE:HR I-202, 218, 225
  GE:ME II-1105, III-1271, 1304, 1347
  GE:W20 I-152, II-736
  GL:20 III-1318
Lennon, John. See also Beatles, the
  GE:A&C IV-1944, 2098
Leno, Jay
  GE:A&C III-1623
Lenoir, Étienne
  GE:ME II-1033
  GL:Ren III-1292
Le Nôtre, André
  GL:Ren III-1298
Lenya, Lotte
  GE:A&C II-724
Leo I, Pope. See Leo the Great
Leo III, Pope
  GE:A&M II-1111, 1146, 1152
Leo V, Pope
  GE:A&M II-1152
Leo IX, Pope
  GE:A&M III-1237, 1243, 1257
  GL:A&M III-1263
Leo X, Pope
  GE:ME I-44, 54, 64
  GL:Ren III-1304
Leo XIII, Pope
  GL:Ren III-1309
  GE:ME II-969, III-1143
  GE:HR II-1113
Leo, Brother
  GE:A&M III-1447
Leo the Great (Leo I)
  GE:A&M II-952, 963, III-1257

Leonard, Sheldon
  GE:A&C IV-1908, 2044
Leonardo da Vinci
  GE:A&M III-1761, 1766
  GL:Ren III-1315
Leonardo of Pisa
  GE:A&M III-1282
  GL:A&M III-1269
Leone, Sergio
  GE:A&C IV-1984
Leongómez, Carlos Pizarro
  GE:HR V-2465
Leonidas
  GE:A&M I-237
Leonin
  GE:A&M III-1410
Leonov, Alexei
  GE:S&T IV-1787
Leopold I
  GE:ME I-368, 372
  GL:Ren III-1321
Leopold II (of Belgium)
  GE:HR I-103
  GE:ME II-1048
Leopold of Anhalt-Dessau, Prince
  GE:ME I-396
Leopold of Hapsburg
  GE:A&M III-1603
Leopold of Hohenzollern-Sigmaringen, Prince
  GE:ME II-949, 954
Leopold of Saxe-Coburg, Prince
  GE:ME II-686
Leovy, Conway B.
  GE:S&T V-1944
Lepidus, Marcus Aemilius
  GE:A&M I-546
Lépoldine, Marie Charlotte. See Carlota
Lepsius, Johannes
  GE:W20 I-107
Lermontov, Mikhail
  GL:Ren III-1327
Le Roy, Édouard
  GE:A&C I-161
Leroy, Mervyn
  GE:A&C III-1109
Lerroux, Alejandro
  GE:ME III-1259, 1368
Lesage, Jean
  GE:HR II-1079
Lescot, Pierre
  GL:Ren III-1333
Lesher, William
  GE:B&C V-1859

Leskov, Nikolai
  GE:A&C II-1042
Leslie, Alexander (Earl of Leven)
  GE:ME I-313
Lesseps, Ferdinand de
  GE:B&C I-264
  GE:ME II-818, 998, 1066
  GE:S&T I-249
  GL:Ren III-1338
Lesser, Gerald S.
  GE:A&C V-2185
Lessing, Gotthold Ephraim
  GL:Ren III-1343
Lestrange, Gisèle
  GE:A&C IV-2070
Letelier, Orlando
  GE:HR IV-1725
Le Tellier, François-Michel. See Louvois,
  Marquis de
Le Tellier, Michel. See Louvois, Marquis de
Leucippus of Miletus
  GE:A&M I-264
Levchenko, Anatoli
  GE:S&T V-2316
Leven, Earl of. See Leslie, Alexander
Lever, William Hesketh
  GE:B&C I-201
Leverone, Louis E.
  GE:B&C II-579
Leverone, Nathaniel
  GE:B&C II-579
Lévesque, René
  GE:HR IV-2158
  GE:W20 II-820
Levi, Beppo
  GE:S&T I-143
Levi, Connie
  GE:HR V-2256
Levine, Dennis
  GE:B&C V-1921, 1958
Levine, Philip
  GE:S&T I-56
Levinthal, Elliott Charles
  GE:S&T V-1944
Levison, Stanley David
  GE:HR II-974
Lévi-Strauss, Claude
  GE:A&C IV-1995
  GL:20 III-1323
Levy, Herbert
  GE:B&C II-764
Levy, Jerre
  GE:S&T IV-1635

Levy, Norman J.
  GE:HR IV-2220
Levy, Sanford Edgar (Leeds)
  GE:S&T III-1250
Lewis, Andrew
  GE:B&C V-1803
Lewis, Cecil Day. *See* Day Lewis, Cecil
Lewis, Clive Staples
  GE:A&C III-1607
Lewis, David S., Jr.
  GE:B&C III-1314
Lewis, Edmonia
  GL:AmW III-1116
Lewis, Gibson
  GE:HR V-2512
Lewis, Gilbert Newton
  GE:S&T II-926
Lewis, Hobart L.
  GE:B&C I-390
Lewis, John (civil rights leader)
  GE:HR III-1200, 1278
Lewis, John (musician)
  GE:A&C III-1438
Lewis, John L.
  GE:Am III-1655, 1759
  GE:B&C II-635, 706, 729, III-908, 1064
  GE:HR I-508, II-545
  GE:W20 II-572
  GL:Am III-1357
Lewis, Meriwether
  GE:Am I-450
  GL:Am III-1363
Lewis, Oscar
  GE:Am III-1866
Lewis, Ralph
  GE:A&C I-402
Lewis, Robert
  GE:B&C V-1837
Lewis, Roger
  GE:B&C IV-1431
Lewis, Sinclair
  GL:Am III-1369
Lewis, Sir Thomas
  GE:S&T I-41
Lewis, Wyndham
  GE:A&C I-445
Lewisohn, Sam A.
  GE:B&C II-419
Ley, Herbert, Jr.
  GE:B&C IV-1390
Lezgin, Serbest
  GE:HR V-2397
Li Ch'ing-chao
  GL:A&M III-1273

Li Hung-chang
  GE:HR I-1
  GL:Ren III-1348
Li Peng
  GE:HR IV-2073
Li Po
  GL:A&M III-1278
Li Shih-min. *See* T'ai Tsung
Li Ta-chao
  GE:HR I-276
Liang Chi-chao
  GE:HR I-116
  GE:W20 I-92
Libby, Willard Frank
  GE:S&T III-1160
Liberius
  GE:A&M II-914
Lichtenberg, Byron K.
  GE:S&T V-2256
Licinius, Gaius
  GE:A&M I-221
Licinius, Valerius
  GE:A&M II-846
Lie, Trygve
  GE:HR II-678, 689, 855, 867, 885, 985
Lieber, Francis
  GE:Am II-673
Lieber, Leonard
  GE:HR III-1639
Liebig, Justus von
  GL:Ren III-1353
Liebknecht, Karl
  GE:HR I-241
Liebknecht, Wilhelm
  GE:ME II-992, 1013
  GL:Ren III-1357
Liedtke, John Hugh
  GE:B&C V-1876
Liénart, Achilles Cardinal
  GE:ME III-1633
Lifar, Serge
  GL:20 III-1328
Ligachev, Yegor
  GE:HR V-2249
Lilburne, John
  GE:ME I-317
Lilienthal, David Eli
  GE:Am III-1621
  GE:B&C II-650
  GE:W20 II-564
Lilienthal, Otto
  GE:Am II-1346

Liliuokalani
  GL:AmW III-1121
  GE:W20 II-790
Lima, Pedro Almeida
  GE:S&T III-1060
Liman von Sanders, Otto
  GE:W20 I-107, 129
Lin, Maya Ying
  GL:AmW III-1125
Lin Biao
  GE:B&C III-1281
  GE:HR III-1332
  GL:20 III-1333
Lin Piao. See Lin Biao
Lin Tse-hsü
  GL:Ren III-1362
Lincoln, Abraham
  GE:Am II-906, 935, 946, 974, 980, 991, 1003
  GL:Am III-1375
Lincoln, Benjamin
  GE:Am I-294
Lind, Jenny
  GE:Am II-1066
Lindbergh, Charles A.
  GE:B&C II-752
  GE:S&T II-841
  GL:Am III-1381
Lindblad, Bertil
  GE:S&T II-830
Linde, A. D.
  GE:S&T V-2125
Lindemann, Frederick Alexander, Viscount
  Cherwell. See Cherwell, Frederick Alexander
  Lindemann, Viscount
Lindenmann, Jean
  GE:S&T IV-1517
Linderman, Henry Richard
  GE:Am II-1083
Lindhagen, Carl Albert
  GE:HR I-345
Lindon, Jérôme
  GE:A&C III-1498
Lindsay, John
  GE:S&T IV-1708
Lindsay, John V.
  GE:HR III-1370, 1567
Lindsay, Vachel
  GE:Am III-1399
Lindsey, Benjamin Barr
  GE:HR I-131
Ling-yün. See Hsieh Ling-yün
Link, Edwin Albert
  GE:S&T IV-1792

Linkletter, Art
  GE:B&C III-1102
Linlithgow, Lord (Victor Alexander John Hope)
  GE:W20 II-605
Linnaeus
  GL:Ren III-1369
Linné, Carl von. See Linnaeus
Lionæs, Aase
  GE:HR III-1462
Lipchitz, Jacques
  GL:20 III-1339
Lipmann, Fritz Albert
  GE:S&T III-1390
Lippershey, Hans
  GL:Ren III-1374
Lippes, Jack
  GE:S&T IV-1629
Lippincott, Joseph Barlow
  GE:B&C II-453
Lippitt, Francis
  GE:Am II-673
Lippmann, Walter
  GE:A&C I-385
  GL:Am III-1388
Lipton, Martin
  GE:B&C V-1876
Lishman, Robert W.
  GE:B&C III-1148
Lispector, Clarice
  GE:A&C IV-1689
Lissitzky, El
  GE:A&C I-413
List, Friedrich
  GE:ME II-711
Lister, Joseph
  GE:ME II-935
  GL:B&C IV-1635
Liszt, Franz
  GL:Ren III-1379
Little, Dennis
  GE:B&C III-1303
Little, Malcolm. See Malcolm X
Little, Royal
  GE:B&C III-948
Littlejohn, Larry
  GE:HR IV-1741
Littleton, Jesse T.
  GE:S&T II-605
Littleton, Oliver. See Lord Chandos
Littleton, Sir Thomas
  GL:B&C IV-1640
Littlewood, Joan
  GE:A&C IV-1757

Litvinov, Maksim Maksimovich
    GE:ME III-1433, 1440
    GE:W20 I-219
    GL:20 III-1344
Liu Binyan
    GE:HR V-2483
Liu Shao-ch'i. *See* Liu Shaoqi
Liu Shaoqi
    GE:B&C III-1003, 1281
    GE:HR II-958, 1015
    GL:20 III-1350
Liverpool, Lord. *See* Jenkinson, Robert Banks
Liverpool, Second Earl of
    GE:ME II-654
    GL:B&C IV-1645
Livingston, Edward
    GE:Am III-1394
Livingston, M. Stanley
    GE:S&T III-953
Livingston, Neville "Bunny"
    GE:A&C V-2344
Livingston, Robert R.
    GE:Am I-341, 443, 471, 600
Livingstone, David
    GL:B&C IV-1650
Livius, Titus. *See* Livy
Livy
    GE:A&M I-531
    GL:A&M III-1283
Lleras Camargo, Alberto. *See* Camargo, Alberto
    Lleras
Llorenz, Juan
    GE:ME I-72
Llosa, Mario Vargas. *See* Vargas Llosa, Mario
Lloyd, David
    GE:Am I-157
Lloyd, Ralph Waldo
    GE:HR II-929
Lloyd, Thomas
    GE:Am I-157
Lloyd George, David
    GE:Am III-1484, 1537
    GE:B&C I-218, 351, III-885
    GE:HR I-19, 247, 252, 309, 321
    GE:ME III-1214, 1223, 1283, 1289, 1314,
        1372
    GL:B&C IV-1654
Llull, Ramon. *See* Lull, Raymond
Lo Chia-lun
    GE:HR I-276
Lobachevsky, Nikolay Ivanovich
    GL:Ren III-1384
Lobato, Nicolau
    GE:HR IV-1835

Locke, John
    GE:Am I-132
    GL:B&C IV-1660
Locker, Corrine
    GE:HR III-1573
Lockwood, Belva A.
    GL:AmW III-1130
Lockyer, Sir Joseph Norman
    GE:S&T II-585
    GL:B&C IV-1669
Lodge, Henry Cabot
    GE:Am II-1201, III-1472, 1484, 1531
    GE:B&C II-459, III-1040
    GE:HR I-7, 172, 231, 350, 383
    GL:Am III-1395
Lodge, Henry Cabot, II
    GE:Am III-1871
Lodge, Sir Oliver Joseph
    GE:S&T II-669
Lods, Marcel
    GE:A&C II-1021
Loewy, Raymond Fernand
    GE:A&C II-777, 1057, V-2208
Löffler, Friedrich August Johannes
    GE:S&T I-6, 459, 567
Logan, James
    GE:Am I-157
Logan, Marvel Mills
    GE:B&C II-746
Loleya, Renaldo
    GE:HR II-941
Lomax, Alan
    GE:A&C II-810
Lombard, Carole
    GE:A&C II-951
Lombard, Peter. *See* Peter the Lombard
Lombroso, Cesare
    GE:S&T II-711
Lomonosov, Mikhail Vasilyevich
    GE:ME I-432
    GL:Ren III-1388
Lon Nol
    GE:HR IV-1791
    GE:W20 II-1083, III-212
London, Fritz Wolfgang
    GE:S&T II-926, IV-1533
London, Heinz
    GE:S&T IV-1533
London, John
    GE:ME I-110
Long, Crawford Williamson
    GE:Am II-791

Long, Huey
    GE:Am III-1582
    GL:Am III-1401
Long, Russell B.
    GE:B&C IV-1561
Long, Stephen H.
    GE:Am I-624
Long, Walter
    GE:A&C I-402
Longgood, William
    GE:B&C IV-1395
Longowal, Harchand Singh
    GE:HR IV-2215, 2232
Longwell, Daniel
    GE:A&C II-1031
Longworth, Alice Roosevelt
    GL:AmW III-1135
Lönnrot, Elias
    GE:A&C I-292
    GE:HR I-212
Loos, Anita
    GL:AmW III-1140
Loosley, F. A.
    GE:B&C III-991
Łopatka, Adam
    GE:HR V-2529
Lope de Vega Carpio. See Vega Carpio, Lope de
López, Carlos Antonio
    GE:HR I-533
López, Francisco Solano
    GE:HR I-533
Lopez, Nancy
    GL:AmW III-1144
López Pumarejo, Alfonso
    GE:HR II-737
Lorca, Federico García. See García Lorca,
    Federico
Lord Chandos
    GE:A&C IV-1924
Lord, Miles
    GE:HR V-2342
Lorentz, Hendrik Antoon
    GE:ME III-1160
    GE:S&T I-297
    GL:20 III-1355
Lorenz, Konrad
    GE:S&T IV-1808
    GL:20 III-1360
Lorenzetti, Ambrogio
    GE:A&M III-1691
    GL:A&M III-1287
Lorenzetti, Pietro
    GL:A&M III-1287
Lorenzo de Medici. See Medici, Lorenzo de'

Lorenzo, Frank
    GE:B&C V-1865
Lorenzo, Nicola di. See Rienzo, Cola di
Lorimer, George Horace
    GE:B&C IV-1379
Loritz, Dan
    GE:HR V-2256
Lorraine, Cardinal of
    GE:ME I-162
Lorre, Peter
    GE:A&C II-946, III-1223
Lothair
    GE:A&M II-1158
Lothair of Segni. See Innocent III
Lothario of Segni. See Innocent III
Loubet, Émile
    GE:ME III-1152
Loudon, Earl of. See Campbell, John
Loughhead, Robert
    GE:B&C V-1854
Louis II. See Jagiello, Louis II
Louis II de Bourbon. See Condé, The Great
Louis II the German
    GE:A&M II-1158
    GL:A&M III-1293
Louis IV (of Bavaria)
    GE:A&M III-1603, 1608, 1620
Louis IV (of France)
    GE:ME I-324, 341, 345, 346, 349, 353, 357,
        368, 372, 400
Louis VI (of France)
    GE:A&M III-1323
Louis VII (of France)
    GE:A&M III-1323, 1375
Louis IX (of France)
    GE:A&M III-1496, 1533
    GL:A&M III-1299
Louis XI (of France)
    GE:A&M III-1733
    GE:ME I-31, 44, 82
    GL:Ren III-1392
Louis XIII (of France)
    GE:ME I-259, 278
    GL:Ren III-1397
Louis XIV (of France)
    GE:ME I-437
    GL:Ren III-1402
Louis XVI (of France)
    GE:Am I-282
    GE:ME I-496, 502, 506, 510, 516, 520
Louis XVIII (of France)
    GE:ME II-598, 634, 682
Louis Alexander, Prince of Battenburg
    GE:ME III-1187, 1254

Louis Napoleon. *See* Napoleon III
Louis Philippe
    GE:ME II-682, 686, 722
Louis, Prince of Condé (Louis I de Bourbon)
    GE:ME I-162, 184
Louis the German. *See* Louis II the German
Louis the Pious
    GE:A&M II-1158
Louis, Joe
    GL:Am III-1407
Lousma, Jack R.
    GE:S&T V-1997
L'Ouverture, Toussaint. *See* Toussaint-Louverture
Louvois, Marquis de
    GE:ME I-345, 353
    GL:Ren III-1408
Lovell, Sir Bernard
    GE:S&T III-1113, IV-1539, 1614
Lovell, James A.
    GE:S&T IV-1803
    GE:W20 II-1069
Lovelock, James
    GE:S&T V-2009
Lovett, Robert Abercrombie
    GE:ME III-1555
Lovett, William
    GE:ME II-741
Low, Barbara Wharton
    GE:S&T III-1240
Low, Juliette Gordon
    GL:AmW III-1149
Lowell, A. Lawrence
    GE:B&C I-157
    GE:HR I-172
    GE:S&T I-291
Lowell, Amy
    GE:A&C I-326
    GL:AmW III-1153
Lowell, Francis Cabot
    GE:Am III-1811
Lowell, John (Jack)
    GE:Am I-517
Lowell, Percival
    GE:S&T I-291, II-502, 689, 944
Lowell, Robert
    GE:A&C IV-1645
Lowenstein, Allard
    GE:HR III-1149
Löwenstein, Laszlo. *See* Lorre, Peter
Lowery, Grosvenor
    GE:Am II-1110
Lowry, W. McNeil
    GE:A&C IV-1736

Loyola, Saint Ignatius of
    GE:ME I-96
    GL:Ren III-1415
Lu Hsün
    GL:20 III-1365
Lubin, Charles
    GE:B&C III-1202
Lubitsch, Ernst
    GE:A&C II-941
Lucas, Anthony F.
    GE:B&C I-24
Lucas, George
    GE:A&C V-2391
Lucas, Robert E.
    GE:B&C III-931
Luce, Clare Boothe
    GE:A&C II-1031
    GE:B&C I-412
    GL:AmW III-1157
Luce, Henry R.
    GE:A&C II-577, 1031
    GE:B&C I-412, II-585
    GL:Am III-1413
Lucius Aelius Aurelius Commodus. *See*
    Commodus
Lucius Albinus. *See* Albinus, Lucius
Lucius Annaeus Seneca. *See* Seneca the Younger
Lucius Julius Caesar. *See* Caesar, Lucius Julius
Lucius Licinius Crassus. *See* Crassus, Lucius
    Licinius
Lucius Minucius. *See* Minucius, Lucius
Lucius Veturius. *See* Veturius, Lucius
Lucius Villius. *See* Villius, Lucius
Lucretius
    GE:A&M I-264, 511
    GL:A&M III-1305
Ludendorff, Erich
    GE:B&C I-293
    GE:HR I-241
    GL:20 III-1370
Ludlow, Roger
    GE:Am I-91
Ludwell, Philip
    GE:Am I-132, 151
Ludwig II
    GE:ME II-963
Ludwig, Carl Friedrich Wilhelm
    GE:S&T I-16
Ludwig, Daniel Keith
    GE:B&C IV-1336
Ludwig, Nikolaus. *See* Zinzendorf, Graf von
Lueger, Karl
    GE:ME II-1089

Luening, Otto
  GE:A&C IV-1785
Lugard, Sir Frederick J.
  GE:B&C I-196
  GE:HR I-436, II-902
  GL:B&C IV-1675
Lugosi, Bela
  GE:A&C II-863
Lukács, György
  GL:20 III-1375
Lull, Raymond
  GE:A&M III-1503
  GL:A&M III-1310
Lumière, Auguste, and Louis Lumière
  GE:A&C I-57
  GE:Am II-1333
  GE:S&T I-375
  GL:20 III-1380
Lumpkin, Wilson
  GE:Am I-666
Lumumba, Patrice
  GE:B&C I-201
  GE:HR II-1068, 1074
  GE:ME III-1613
Lunacharsky, Anatoly
  GE:A&C I-320, II-544
Lundy, Benjamin
  GE:Am II-719
Lunt, Alfred
  GE:A&C II-936
Lupicinus
  GE:A&M II-898
Lupino, Ida
  GL:AmW III-1162
Luria, Isaac ben Solomon
  GE:A&M III-1559
  GL:Ren III-1420
Lusser, Marcus
  GE:B&C V-2045
Luther, Hans
  GE:B&C I-406
Luther, Martin
  GE:ME I-54, 76, 91, 116
  GL:Ren III-1425
Luther, Seth
  GE:Am II-766
Lutuli, Albert
  GE:HR II-861, III-1143

Luening, Otto
  GE:W20 III-1272
  GL:20 III-1387
Luxemburg, Rosa
  GE:HR I-241
  GL:20 III-1392
Luzzato, Hayim
  GE:A&M III-1559
Lvov, Georgy Y.
  GE:HR I-202
  GE:ME III-1271
Lvov, Prince Georgi Evgenievich. See Lvov,
  Georgy Y.
Lydon, John. See Rotten, Johnny
Lyell, Sir Charles
  GE:ME II-678, 855
  GL:B&C IV-1680
Lynch, Edmund
  GE:B&C II-809
Lynch, Jack
  GE:HR III-1485, IV-1978
Lynd, Helen Merrell
  GL:AmW IV-1167
Lynd, Staughton
  GE:Am III-1861
Lynde, Frederick C.
  GE:B&C II-579
Lyndhurst, Baron. See Copley, John Singleton
Lynn, Loretta
  GL:AmW IV-1171
Lynn, Mitchell G.
  GE:B&C IV-1621
Lyon, Mary
  GL:Am III-1419
  GL:AmW IV-1175
Lyon, Matthew
  GE:Am I-414
Lyons, Dame Enid Muriel
  GL:B&C IV-1688
Lyons, Joseph Aloysius
  GL:B&C IV-1693
Lyot, Bernard
  GE:S&T II-911
Lysippus
  GL:A&M III-1315
Lytton, Earl of
  GE:HR I-474

M

Ma San-po. *See* Cheng Ho

Ma Vien. *See* Ma Yüan

Ma Yüan
GL:A&M III-1320

Maanen, Adriaan van. *See* Van Maanen, Adriaan

Mabini, Apolinario
GE:Am II-1290

McAdoo, William Gibbs
GE:Am III-1432

McAllister, Robert Wallace
GE:S&T III-1384

MacArthur, Douglas
GE:Am I-432, III-1731, 1823, 1829
GE:HR II-662, 725, III-1515
GE:W20 II-584, 676
GL:Am III-1425

Macarthur, Mary
GE:HR I-75

Macaulay, Thomas Babington
GL:B&C IV-1698

McAvoy, May
GE:A&C II-734

MacBride, Maud Gonne
GE:A&C I-440

MacBride, Seán
GE:HR II-1119, IV-1955

Maccabaeus, Judas
GE:A&M I-459

McCain, Franklin
GE:HR II-1056

McCain, William Ross
GE:B&C III-964

McCarran, Pat
GE:B&C II-815

McCarthy, Eugene
GE:Am III-1933
GE:HR III-1446

McCarthy, Joseph
GE:A&C III-1164
GE:Am III-1817, 1843
GL:Am III-1432

McCarthy, Mary
GL:AmW IV-1179

McCartney, Paul. *See also* Beatles, the
GE:A&C IV-1944, 2098

McCarty, Maclyn
GE:S&T III-1203, IV-1682

McCauley, John Francis
GE:S&T V-1944

McClellan, Captain George Brinton
GE:Am II-865

McClellan, John L.
GE:B&C III-1092, 1122, 1213, IV-1626

McClenahan, Jim
GE:S&T V-2068

McClintock, Barbara
GL:AmW IV-1183

McClintock, Robert
GE:W20 II-758

McCloy, John J.
GE:B&C III-981
GE:HR II-595

McClung, Clarence Erwin
GE:S&T I-148

McClure, Samuel S.
GE:Am III-1353

McCollum, Elmer Verner
GE:S&T II-725, 771

McConnell, David
GE:B&C V-2012

McCorkindale, Douglas
GE:A&C V-2507

McCormick, Cyrus H.
GE:B&C I-52

McCormick, Cyrus Hall
GE:Am II-679
GE:B&C I-52, III-1020
GL:Am III-1437

McCormick, Mrs. Cyrus Hall
GE:Am II-1173

McCormick, Katherine Dexter
GE:S&T IV-1512

McCormick, Nettie (Nancy) Fowler
GE:B&C I-52

McCorvey, Norma
GE:HR V-2489

McCown, F. Scott
GE:HR V-2512

McCown, Theodore Doney
GE:S&T V-2341

McCoy, Joseph Geating
GE:Am II-1020

McCullers, Carson
GL:AmW IV-1188

McCulloch, Hugh
GE:Am I-564, II-985

McCulloch, William
GE:B&C III-1229

McCullough, David
  GE:A&C V-2657
McCullough, Father Thomas
  GE:W20 II-842
McCune, William J., Jr.
  GE:B&C III-896
  GE:S&T III-1331
McDaniel, Hattie
  GE:A&C III-1154, 1159
McDaniels, Darryl
  GE:A&C V-2582
MacDermot, Galt
  GE:A&C IV-2121
MacDermott, Sean
  GE:HR I-178
MacDiarmid, Alan G.
  GE:S&T V-2063
McDonald, David John
  GE:W20 II-730
Macdonald, Dwight
  GE:A&C IV-1898
  GE:B&C II-585
McDonald, Frank Bethune
  GE:S&T IV-1708
McDonald, George E.
  GE:B&C IV-1636
MacDonald, Jeanette
  GE:A&C II-941
McDonald, John
  GE:Am II-1054
Macdonald, Sir John Alexander
  GL:B&C IV-1704
McDonald, Maurice
  GE:B&C III-1025, IV-1406
MacDonald, Ramsay
  GE:B&C II-591, 624
  GE:HR I-58, 321, 469
  GE:ME III-1372
  GL:B&C IV-1711
McDonald, Richard
  GE:B&C III-1025, IV-1406
McDonnell, Father Donald
  GE:W20 II-842
McDonnell, James S.
  GE:B&C III-1314
McDougall, Alexander
  GE:Am I-246
McDowell, Irvin
  GE:Am II-952
McDowell, Malcolm
  GE:A&C IV-1989
McDuffie, Arthur
  GE:HR IV-2101

McDuffie, George
  GE:Am II-702
McFadden, Louis Thomas
  GE:B&C II-539
McGillicuddy, John F.
  GE:B&C V-1763
McGillivray, Alexander
  GL:Am III-1442
McGowan, Sean
  GE:B&C III-986
McGowen, William J.
  GE:B&C V-1821
McGready, James
  GE:Am I-420
McGuffey, William Holmes
  GL:Am III-1448
Mach, Ernst
  GE:S&T II-625
Machado de Assis, Joaquim Maria
  GL:Ren III-1431
Machado y Morales, Gerardo
  GE:W20 II-743
Machaut, Guillaume de
  GE:A&M III-1410
  GL:A&M III-1325
Machel, Samora Moisès
  GL:20 III-1398
McHenry, James
  GE:Am I-432
Machet, Gérard
  GE:A&M III-1703
Machiavelli, Niccolò
  GE:ME I-35
  GL:Ren III-1436
McIntosh, Winston Hubert. *See* Tosh, Peter
Maciunas, George
  GE:A&C IV-1955
McKay, Claude
  GE:A&C I-480
McKay, Dean
  GE:S&T V-2169
McKay, Donald
  GE:Am II-807
McKay, Frederick S.
  GE:S&T III-1260
Macke, August
  GE:A&C I-275
McKean, Thomas
  GE:Am I-377
McKee, Alexander
  GE:Am I-383
McKee, Elizabeth
  GE:A&C IV-1645

Mackendrick, Alexander
  GE:A&C III-1427
McKenna, Joseph
  GE:B&C I-140, 346
McKenna, Reginald
  GE:HR I-19
McKenna, Regis
  GE:S&T V-2073
McKenney, Thomas L.
  GE:Am I-666
Mackenzie, Sir Alexander
  GL:B&C IV-1718
Mackenzie, Duncan
  GE:S&T I-67
McKenzie, Fayette A.
  GE:HR I-121
Mackenzie, William Lyon
  GL:B&C IV-1723
McKeown, Ciaran
  GE:HR IV-1932
McKhann, Charles F., III
  GE:S&T II-895
McKim, Charles Follen
  GE:Am II-1231
Mackinder, Sir Halford John
  GL:B&C IV-1732
McKinley, John
  GE:B&C V-1876
McKinley, William
  GE:Am II-1243, 1268, 1273, 1284, 1290,
    1296, 1325
  GE:HR I-7
  GE:ME II-1119
  GL:Am III-1454
McKinney, John A.
  GE:HR V-2274
McKinney, Nina Mae
  GE:A&C II-772
McKinney, Stewart B.
  GE:HR V-2326
MacKinnon, Catharine A.
  GL:AmW IV-1193
McKinsey, James Oscar
  GE:B&C II-481
McLane, Louis
  GE:Am II-696
McLaren, Malcolm
  GE:A&C V-2299, 2360
McLaughlin, John
  GE:A&C IV-2153
Maclaurin, Colin
  GL:B&C IV-1738
McLean, Jay
  GE:S&T II-610

McLean, John
  GE:Am II-877, 900
MacLeish, Archibald
  GE:A&C III-1443
  GE:B&C II-585
McLeod, Alexander
  GE:Am II-801
MacLeod, Colin Munro
  GE:S&T III-1203
Macleod, John James Rickard
  GE:S&T II-720
McLernon, James
  GE:B&C IV-1664
McLoughlin, John
  GE:Am I-619
McLuhan, Marshall
  GE:A&C IV-1973
  GE:W20 II-1069
  GL:B&C IV-1744
Maclure, William
  GE:Am I-511
McMahon, Brien
  GE:W20 II-683
McMahon, Ed
  GE:A&C III-1623
McMahon, Sir Henry
  GE:B&C I-351
McManamy, Frank
  GE:B&C II-685
McMath, Virginia Katherine. *See* Rogers, Ginger
Macmillan, Daniel, and Alexander Macmillan
  GL:B&C IV-1749
McMillan, Edwin Mattison
  GE:S&T III-1181, 1282
  GL:Am III-1460
Macmillan, Harold
  GE:B&C III-1169
  GE:HR II-980, 1084
  GE:W20 II-955, III-1146
  GL:B&C IV-1754
McMillan, James B.
  GE:HR III-1628
McMullin, Fred
  GE:Am III-1497
McNair, Archie
  GE:A&C IV-1824
McNamara, Francis X.
  GE:B&C III-959
McNamara, Robert S.
  GE:Am III-1888
  GE:B&C III-1224, IV-1384
  GE:HR IV-1998
McNamee, Graham
  GE:A&C I-469

McNary, Charles
  GE:B&C II-569
MacNeice, Louis
  GE:A&C II-857
McNeil, Joseph
  GE:HR II-1056
McNeill, Claudia
  GE:A&C IV-1795
MacNeill, Eoin
  GE:HR I-178
  GE:ME III-1233
McNutt, Paul V.
  GE:HR II-578
Macon, Nathaniel
  GE:Am I-552
Macon, Uncle Dave
  GE:A&C II-675
Macpherson, Jeanie
  GE:A&C II-567
McQuire, P. J.
  GE:Am II-1152
Macready, William Charles
  GL:B&C IV-1761
Macune, Charles W.
  GE:B&C II-668
McWhinnie, Donald
  GE:A&C IV-1861
McWilliams, Carey
  GE:HR II-624
Macy, Anne Sullivan
  GL:AmW IV-1198
Madani, Abassi
  GE:HR V-2583
Madero, Francisco Indalecio
  GE:W20 I-69
Madison, James
  GE:Am I-194, 318, 330, 335, 350, 356, 367,
    389, 403, 414, 437, 443, 456, 505, 517,
    522, 539, 546, II-1184
  GL:Am III-1467
Madonna
  GE:A&C V-2449, 2475
Madsen, James, H., Jr.
  GE:S&T V-2357
Maecenas, Gaius
  GE:A&M I-556
  GL:A&M III-1331
Maffeo, Polo. See Polo, Maffeo
Magellan, Ferdinand
  GE:ME I-68
  GL:Ren III-1442
Maginot, André
  GE:ME III-1359

Magnani, Anna
  GE:A&C III-1228
Magness, Bob John
  GE:B&C V-2066
Magnuson, Warren Grant
  GE:B&C III-1270, IV-1522, 1584
  GE:HR III-1338
Magoffin, James
  GE:Am II-818
Magowan, Peter
  GE:B&C V-1943
Magritte, René
  GE:A&C II-604
  GL:20 III-1404
Mahan, Alfred Thayer
  GE:Am II-1201
  GE:ME II-1123
Mahāvīra. See Vardhamāna
Mahdi, Sadiq al-
  GE:HR V-2354
Maheu, Robert Aime
  GE:B&C II-442
Mahfouz, Naquib
  GE:A&C V-2625
  GL:20 III-1411
Mahler, Alma Maria
  GE:A&C I-7, 298
Mahler, Gustav
  GE:A&C I-7, 193, 298, 367
  GL:20 III-1417
Mahler, Halfdan Theodor
  GE:HR IV-1893, 1998
Maibaum, Richard
  GE:A&C IV-1913
Mailer, Norman
  GE:A&C III-1373
Maillard, William Somers
  GE:W20 III-1251
Maiman, Theodore Harold
  GE:S&T IV-1672, 1714, V-2020, 2078
  GE:W20 II-881
Maimonides, Moses
  GE:A&M III-1391, 1478
  GL:A&M III-1336
Mair, Lucille
  GE:HR IV-2057
Maizière, Lothar de
  GE:HR V-2589
Major, John
  GE:B&C V-2051
  GE:HR IV-2073
Majors, Alexander
  GE:Am II-925

Makarios III, Archbishop
  GE:HR II-1084, III-1218, 1236
  GE:W20 III-1193
Makarova, Natalia
  GE:A&C V-2559
Ma-ka-tai-me-she-kia-kiak. *See* Black Hawk
Makhno
  GE:W20 I-152
Makhpíya-Lúta. *See* Red Cloud
Makonnen, Tafari. *See* Haile Selassie I
Malakoff, Duke of. *See* Pelissier, Jean-Jacques
Malan, Daniel François
  GE:HR II-861
Malchus. *See* Porphyry
Malcolm X
  GE:A&C IV-1929, 2022
  GE:HR III-1348
Malcomson, Alexander
  GE:HR I-143
Maleczech, Ruth
  GE:A&C V-2571
Malenkov, Georgi M.
  GE:ME III-1566
  GL:20 III-1425
Maléter, Colonel Pal
  GE:ME III-1595
Malevich, Kazimir Severinovich
  GE:A&C I-320, 413, II-544
Malik, Adam
  GE:HR IV-1835
Malik, Charles Habib
  GE:HR II-590, 783, 789, III-1353
Malik al-Zahir Rukn al-Din Baybars, al-. *See*
  Baybars I
Malina, Frank J.
  GE:S&T III-1342
Mallet, Paul and Peter Mallet
  GE:Am I-144
Mallory, Stephen Russell
  GE:Am II-957
Malloum, Félix
  GE:HR III-1273
Mallowan, Agatha. *See* Christie, Agatha
Malone, Dorothy
  GE:A&C IV-2017
Malone, John C.
  GE:B&C V-2066
Maloney, Dorothy. *See* Malone, Dorothy
Malory, Sir Thomas
  GL:B&C IV-1766
Malpighi, Marcello
  GL:Ren III-1448

Malraux, André
  GE:W20 I-241
  GL:20 III-1430
Malthus, Daniel
  GE:ME I-533
Malthus, Thomas Robert
  GE:HR III-1515
  GE:ME I-424, 533, II-629
  GL:B&C IV-1771
Maluginensis, Marcus Cornelius. *See* Cornelius
  Maluginensis, Marcus
Mamet, David
  GE:A&C V-2413
Mammenga, Gene
  GE:HR V-2256
Manabe, Syukuro
  GE:S&T III-1118, IV-1840
Manarov, Musa
  GE:S&T V-2316
Manchester, Earl of. *See* Montagu, Edward
Mancini, Pasquale Stanislao
  GE:ME II-1019
Mandela, Nelson
  GE:HR III-1143, IV-1847, V-2304, 2559, 2606
  GL:20 III-1436
Mandelbrot, Benoit B.
  GE:S&T IV-1845
Mandelstam, Osip
  GE:A&C IV-2070
Manet, Édouard
  GL:Ren III-1453
Manetti, Antonio
  GE:A&M III-1691
Manguin, Henri Charles
  GE:A&C I-140
Mani (Manichaeus)
  GE:A&M II-807
Manius Rabuleus. *See* Rabuleus, Manius
Manius Valerius. *See* Valerius, Manius
Mankiewicz, Herman J.
  GE:A&C III-1200
Mankiller, Wilma P.
  GL:AmW IV-1203
Manlius Aquillius. *See* Aquillius, Manlius
Manlius Torquatus, Titus. *See* Torquatus, Titus
  Manlius
Manlius, Aulus
  GE:A&M I-253
Mann, Anthony
  GE:A&C III-1313
Mann, Horace
  GE:Am I-576
  GL:Am III-1473

Mann, James Robert
  GE:B&C I-229
Mann, Thomas
  GE:A&C I-396, II-588
  GE:W20 I-295
  GL:20 III-1442
Mann, Woodrow Wilson
  GE:HR II-1003
Mannerheim, Carl Gustaf
  GE:HR I-212
  GL:20 III-1447
Manning, Henry Edward
  GL:B&C IV-1776
Mannix, Daniel
  GL:B&C IV-1781
Manny, John H.
  GE:Am II-679
Mansa Mūsā
  GL:A&M III-1341
Mansart, François
  GL:Ren III-1460
Mansart, Jules Hardouin-
  GL:Ren III-1465
Mansfield, First Earl of
  GL:B&C IV-1786
Mansfield, Michael H.
  GE:HR III-1231, 1521, IV-1812
Mansfield, Michael Joseph
  GE:W20 II-703
Mansfield, William Murray
  GE:B&C I-163
Mansholt, Sicco
  GE:B&C III-1320
Manson, Charles
  GE:A&C IV-1883
Manstein, Eric von
  GE:W20 I-479
Mansur, Al-. See Al-Mansur
Mantegna, Andrea
  GL:Ren III-1470
Mantua, Margaret of
  GE:ME I-304
Manuel I
  GL:Ren III-1476
Manuel II (of Portugal)
  GE:ME III-1219
Manutius, Aldus
  GE:A&M III-1713
Manzoni, Alessandro
  GL:Ren III-1481
Mao Tse-tung
  GE:Am II-1764
  GE:B&C III-1003, 1281

GE:HR II-826, 837, 958, 1015, III-1332,
  V-2535
GE:ME III-1583, 1678
GE:W20 I-211, 361, II-654, 1050, III-1124,
  1264
GL:20 III-1453
Mao Zedong. See Mao Tse-tung
Mapplethorpe, Robert
  GE:A&C V-2636
Mar 'Ammo
  GE:A&M II-807
Maran, Stephen P.
  GE:S&T V-1992
Marble, Alice
  GL:AmW IV-1208
Marbury, Anne. See Hutchinson, Anne
Marbury, William
  GE:Am I-437
Marc, Franz
  GE:A&C I-275, 320
  GL:20 III-1459
Marcel, Claude
  GE:ME I-184
Marcel, Gabriel
  GL:20 III-1464
Marcellinus, Bishop of Ancyra
  GE:A&M II-940
Marcellus
  GE:A&M II-752, 872
Marcellus, Marcus Claudius
  GE:A&M I-422
March, Peyton
  GE:Am III-1478
Marchais, Georges
  GE:B&C IV-1353, IV-1400
Marchand, Captain Jean Baptiste
  GE:ME II-1113
Marcian
  GE:A&M II-952, 963
Marcion of Sinope
  GE:A&M II-767, 779
Marcius Rex, Quintus. See Rex, Quintus Marcius
Marco Polo. See Polo, Marco
Marco, Fatso
  GE:A&C III-1394
Marconi, Guglielmo
  GE:Am III-1519
  GE:B&C I-363
  GE:HR I-287
  GE:ME II-1080
  GE:S&T I-128, 174, 361, II-669, 751, III-1113
  GL:20 III-1470

Marcos, Ferdinand E.
  GE:HR III-1680, IV-2198, V-2286
  GL:20 III-1475
Marcos, Imelda
  GE:HR III-1680, IV-2198
Marcus Aemilius Lepidus. *See* Lepidus, Marcus
  Aemilius
Marcus Antonius. *See* Antony, Marc
Marcus Atilus Regulus. *See* Regulus, Marcus
  Atilus
Marcus Aurelius
  GE:A&M II-725, 731
  GL:A&M III-1345
Marcus Aurelius Valerius Maxentius. *See*
  Maxentius, Marcus Aurelius Valerius
Marcus Aurelius Valerius Maximianus. *See*
  Maximian
Marcus Caecilius Metellus. *See* Metellus, Marcus
  Caecilius
Marcus Claudius Marcellus. *See* Marcellus,
  Marcus Claudius
Marcus Cornelius Fronto. *See* Fronto, Marcus
  Cornelius
Marcus Cornelius Maluginensis. *See* Cornelius
  Maluginensis, Marcus
Marcus Fabius Quintilianus. *See* Quintilian
Marcus Licinius Crassus. *See* Crassus, Marcus
  Licinius
Marcus Livius Drusus. *See* Drusus, Marcus Livius
Marcus Porcius Cato. *See* Cato the Censor
Marcus Sergius. *See* Sergius, Marcus
Marcus Tullius Cicero (Elder). *See* Cicero,
  Marcus Tullius (the Elder)
Marcus Tullius Cicero (Younger). *See* Cicero
Marcus Ulpius Traianus Augustus. *See* Trajan
Marcus Valerius Laevinius. *See* Laevinius,
  Marcus Valerius
Marcus Valerius Martialis. *See* Martial
Marcus Vipsanius Agrippa. *See* Agrippa, Marcus
  Vipsanius
Marcus, Bernard
  GE:B&C II-603
Mare, André
  GE:A&C II-654
Marei, Sayed Ahmed
  GE:HR IV-1775
Margall, Francisco Pi y
  GE:ME II-945
Margaret of Austria
  GE:ME I-31
Margaret of Denmark, Norway, and Sweden
  GL:A&M III-1350
Marguerite of Navarre
  GE:ME I-116

Marguerite of Provence, Queen
  GE:A&M III-1496, 1533
Marguerite of Valois
  GE:ME I-184, 214
Maria II (of Portugal)
  GE:ME II-675, 722
Maria Anna of Bavaria-Neuburg
  GE:ME I-372
Maria Carlotta, of Spain
  GE:ME II-726
María Cristina (of Spain)
  GE:ME II-726
Maria Theresa, of Austria
  GE:ME I-341, 414, 419, 437, 469, 475
  GL:Ren III-1486
Mariam, Mengistu Haile
  GE:HR IV-1758
  GE:W20 III-1317
Mariam, Wolde
  GE:B&C II-723
Maricourt, Petrus Peregrinus de. *See* Peregrinus
  de Maricourt, Petrus
Marie de France
  GL:A&M III-1355
Marie Louise D'Orléans (of Spain)
  GE:ME I-372
Marinetti, Filippo Tommaso
  GE:A&C I-235
Marion, Frances
  GL:AmW IV-1213
Maritain, Jacques
  GL:20 III-1481
Marius, Gaius
  GE:A&M I-496
  GL:A&M III-1360
Mark Antony. *See* Antony, Marc
Markham, William
  GE:Am I-157
Markkula, Mike
  GE:B&C IV-1611
  GE:S&T V-2073
Markov, Andrey Andreyevich
  GE:S&T I-335
Markus, John
  GE:A&C V-2532
Marlborough, First Duke of
  GE:ME I-390, 400
  GL:B&C IV-1793
Marley, Bob
  GE:A&C V-2344
Marley, Rita
  GE:A&C V-2344
Marlowe, Christopher
  GL:B&C IV-1798

Marmor, Judd
    GE:HR III-1497, IV-1741
Maro, Publius Vergilius. *See* Vergil
Marobe, Mafison
    GE:HR IV-1882
Maroboduus
    GE:A&M II-584
Marovic, Ante
    GE:HR V-2612
Marquand, Richard
    GE:A&C V-2391
Marquet, Albert
    GE:A&C I-140
Marquette, Jacques
    GE:Am I-52, 144
Márquez, Gabriel García. *See* García Márquez,
    Gabriel
Marrero, Alex
    GE:HR IV-2101
Marroquin, José Manuel
    GE:Am II-1339
Marsalis, Branford
    GE:A&C V-2454
Marsalis, Ellis
    GE:A&C V-2454
Marsalis, Wynton
    GE:A&C V-2454
Marsden, Ernest
    GE:S&T II-527
Marsh, Mae
    GE:A&C I-402
Marshall, Garry
    GE:A&C V-2305
Marshall, George C.
    GE:Am III-1686, 1697, 1715, 1764, 1776,
        1783, 1789, 1794
    GE:B&C III-902
    GE:HR II-706, 755, 771, 907
    GE:ME III-1477, 1486, 1491, 1532, 1555
    GE:W20 I-211, 260
    GL:Am III-1479
Marshall, James
    GE:Am I-377
Marshall, James Wilson
    GE:Am II-843
Marshall, John
    GE:Am I-312, 437, 461, 485, 539, 564, 600,
        666
    GE:B&C I-63
    GL:Am III-1484
Marshall, Penny
    GE:A&C V-2443
    GL:AmW IV-1217

Marshall, Richard E.
    GE:S&T IV-1687
Marshall, Robert D.
    GE:B&C I-246
Marshall, Thurgood
    GE:HR II-635, 913, III-1381, 1474
    GL:Am III-1491
Marsiglio of Padua
    GE:A&M III-1608, 1640
Martel, Charles. *See* Charles Martel
Martí, Agustín Farabundo
    GE:HR I-464
Martí, José
    GE:HR II-1026
    GE:ME II-1119
Martial
    GL:A&M III-1366
Martin, Agnes
    GL:AmW IV-1221
Martin, Clyde E.
    GE:W20 II-619
Martin, Dick
    GE:A&C IV-2115
Martin, Edward
    GE:Am II-812
Martin, George
    GE:A&C IV-2098
Martin, Graham Anderson
    GE:W20 III-1227
Martin, Homer
    GE:Am III-1655
Martin, James S., Jr.
    GE:S&T V-2052
    GE:W20 III-1294
Martin, John Stuart
    GE:B&C I-412
Martin, Luther
    GE:Am I-485, 564
Martin, Paul
    GE:HR III-1321
Martin, William McChesney
    GE:B&C IV-1341
Martinet, Louis A.
    GE:Am II-1261
Martínez, Maximiliano Hernández
    GE:HR I-464
Martinez, Seferino
    GE:HR III-1573
Martini, Simone
    GL:A&M III-1371
Martinitz, Count Jaroslav
    GE:ME I-250
Martius, Carl
    GE:S&T III-1107

Martov, Julius (J. O. Zederbaum)
GE:ME II-1105
Marty, Dick
GE:B&C V-2045
Martyn, Benjamin
GE:Am I-182
Marx, Chico
GE:A&C II-822
Marx, Groucho
GE:A&C II-822
Marx, Harpo
GE:A&C II-822
Marx, Karl
GE:ME II-781, 897, 992
GE:W20 I-38
GL:Ren III-1491
Marx, Zeppo
GE:A&C II-822
Mary (mother of Jesus)
GE:A&M I-567
Mary I (of England, Bloody Mary)
GE:ME I-103, 123, 153, 158, 168
GL:B&C IV-1808
Mary II (of Great Britain)
GE:ME I-357, 385
Mary Joseph, Sister. *See* Joseph, Sister Mary
Mary Louise (of Spain)
GE:ME II-581
Mary of Burgundy
GE:A&M III-1733
Mary, Queen of Scots
GE:ME I-162, 174
GL:B&C IV-1803
Masaccio
GE:A&M III-1665, 1691
GL:Ren III-1496
Masaryk, Jan Garrigue
GE:W20 II-626
Masaryk, Tomáš Garrigue
GE:W20 I-158
GL:20 III-1487
Masina, Guilietta
GE:A&C III-1596
Maskelyne, John Nevil
GE:A&C I-57
Mason, Florence
GE:HR II-1062
Mason, George
GE:Am I-367
GL:Am III-1496
Mason, Richard B.
GE:Am II-843
Massey, Vincent
GL:B&C IV-1813

Massey, William Ferguson
GL:B&C IV-1819
Massine, Léonide
GE:A&C III-1088
GL:20 III-1493
Massinissa
GE:A&M I-473
Massu, Jacques
GE:ME III-1607
Mastai-Ferretti, Giovanni Maria. *See* Pius IX
Masters, Edgar Lee
GE:Am III-1399
Mas'udi, al-
GL:A&M III-1376
Masursky, Harold
GE:S&T IV-1825
Mather, Cotton
GE:Am I-169
GL:Am III-1501
Mather, Frank Jewett, Jr.
GE:A&C I-502
Mather, Increase
GE:Am I-127, 163, 169
GL:Am III-1507
Mather, Richard
GE:Am I-127
Mathers, Jerry
GE:A&C III-1470
Mathew, Father Theobald
GE:Am II-754
Mathis, John Samuel
GE:S&T V-2164
Mathison, Melissa
GE:A&C V-2491
Matilda of Tuscany
GE:A&M III-1269
Matisse, Henri
GE:A&C I-140, 156, 204, 320
GE:Am III-1411
GL:20 III-1499
Matlock, Glen
GE:A&C V-2299, 2360
Matlovich, Leonard
GE:HR IV-1801
Matos, Huber
GE:HR II-1026
Matsudaira Takechiyo. *See* Tokugawa Ieyasu
Matsui, Iwane
GE:HR I-539
GE:W20 I-361
Matsuo Bashō
GL:Ren III-1502

Matsuoka, Yosuke
  GE:HR I-474
  GE:W20 I-438
Matsushita, Konosuke
  GE:B&C IV-1573
  GL:20 III-1504
Mattathias
  GE:A&M I-459
Matteotti, Giacomo
  GE:HR I-395
Matteson, Edward E.
  GE:Am II-843
Matthaei, J. H.
  GE:S&T IV-1687
Matthews, Sir Brian Harold Cabot
  GE:S&T II-890
Matthews, Thomas
  GE:W20 II-899
Matthews, Thomas A.
  GE:S&T IV-1757
Matthias
  GE:ME I-250
Matthias I Corvinus
  GL:Ren III-1506
Mauchly, John William
  GE:S&T III-1213, 1347, 1396, IV-1475
  GE:W20 II-535
Maudslay, Henry
  GE:ME I-524
Maulānā. *See* Rumi Jalal al-Din
Maupassant, Guy de
  GL:Ren III-1511
Maura y Montaner, Antonio
  GE:ME III-1259
Mauriac, François
  GE:A&C IV-1700
Maurice
  GE:A&M II-1063
Maurice, Duke of Saxony
  GE:ME I-91
Maurice, Frederick Denison
  GL:B&C IV-1825
Mauroy, Pierre
  GE:B&C V-1793
Maurras, Charles
  GE:ME III-1386
Maurus, Rabanus. *See* Rabanus Maurus
Maury, Antonia
  GL:AmW IV-1225
Maury, Matthew Fontaine
  GE:Am II-895
  GL:Am III-1513
Mauzy, Oscar
  GE:HR V-2512

Max of Baden, Prince (Maximilian Alexander
    Friedrich Wilhelm)
  GE:ME III-1295
Maxentius, Marcus Aurelius Valerius
  GE:A&M II-846
Maxim, Hiram Percy
  GE:S&T II-669
Maximian
  GE:A&M II-829
Maximilian I
  GE:A&M III-1733
  GE:ME I-31, 44, 64
  GL:Ren III-1516
Maximilian II Emanuel, of Three Electors of
    Bavaria
  GE:ME I-390
Maximilian II, Holy Roman Emperor
  GE:ME I-148
Maximilian of Austria (Ferdinand Maximilian
    Joseph, Emperor of Mexico)
  GE:ME II-876
Maximilian of Wittelsbach (Duke of Bavaria)
  GE:ME I-270
Maximus
  GE:A&M II-888
Maximus the Confessor
  GE:A&M II-1011
Maxwell, George
  GE:A&C I-379
  GE:B&C I-252
Maxwell, James Clerk
  GE:S&T I-128, II-625, 669, III-1035
  GE:W20 I-324
  GL:B&C IV-1831
May, Cornelius
  GE:Am I-80
May, George O.
  GE:B&C I-246, 308
Mayakovsky, Vladimir
  GE:A&C II-787
  GL:20 III-1510
Mayer, Carl
  GE:A&C I-486
Mayer, Louis B.
  GE:A&C II-799, 822, 833
Mayer, Maria Goeppert
  GL:AmW IV-1230
Mayhew, Jonathan
  GE:Am I-194, 570
Mayo, Charles H.
  GE:Am II-1178
  GL:Am III-1519
Mayo, George Elton
  GE:B&C II-437, 770

Mayo, William J.
  GE:Am II-1178
  GL:Am III-1519
Mayo, Dr. William Worrall
  GE:Am II-1178
Mazarin, Jules
  GE:ME I-324, 341, 349
  GL:Ren III-1522
Mazowiecki, Tadeusz
  GE:B&C V-2017
  GE:HR IV-2112, V-2477, 2500
Mazzatta, Rose-Marie. See Rose-Marie
Mazzini, Giuseppe
  GE:ME II-697, 775
  GL:Ren III-1528
Mazzoli, Romano
  GE:B&C V-1933
Mboya, Tom
  GE:HR V-2431
Mead, Elwood
  GE:B&C V-1773
  GE:S&T III-1075
Mead, Margaret
  GE:B&C V-1798
  GE:S&T II-869
  GL:AmW IV-1235
Mead, Sidney Earl
  GE:W20 I-507
Mead, Syd
  GE:A&C V-2486
Meade, George Gordon
  GE:Am II-997
Meade, James Edward
  GE:B&C III-914
Meadows, Audrey
  GE:A&C IV-1673
Means, Gardiner C.
  GE:B&C II-619
Means, Russell
  GE:HR IV-1709
  GE:W20 II-865
Meany, George
  GE:B&C III-1064, 1092, 1122
  GE:HR III-1567, 1585
  GE:W20 II-730
Meara, Anne
  GE:A&C V-2239
Meckling, William H.
  GE:B&C II-619
Medici, Cosimo de. See De Medici, Cosimo
Médici, Emílio Garrastazú
  GE:HR III-1468
Medici, Giovanni de'. See Leo X, Pope

Medici, Giuseppe
  GE:HR IV-1775
Medici, Lorenzo de'
  GE:A&M IIIK-1723, 1766
  GE:ME I-35, 44
  GL:Ren III-1533
Médicis, Catherine de. See Catherine de Médicis
Medina, Ernest
  GE:HR III-1555
Medina-Sidonia, Duke of (Don Alonso Pérez de
  Guzmán)
  GE:ME I-193
Medinaceli, Duke of
  GE:A&M III-1756
Medjid, Abdul
  GE:ME II-813
Meduna, Lazlo von
  GE:S&T III-1086
Medvedev, Roy
  GE:W20 II-988
Meer, Simon van der. See Van der Meer, Simon
Mega, Christopher J.
  GE:HR V-2359
Meggers, Betty J.
  GE:S&T IV-1624, 1645
Mehmed II
  GL:Ren III-1538
Meinecke, Friedrich
  GE:W20 I-54
Meinhof, Ulrike
  GE:W20 II-1028
Meir, Golda
  GE:HR IV-1685
  GE:W20 III-1182
  GL:20 III-1515
Meitner, Lise
  GE:S&T III-1135, IV-1557
  GE:W20 I-246
  GL:20 III-1521
Mejía Víctores, Oscar Humberto
  GE:HR IV-1972
Mekas, Jonas
  GE:A&C IV-2053
Melady, Thomas Patrick
  GE:HR III-1668
Melanchthon, Philipp (Philipp Schwarzert)
  GE:ME I-148, 168
  GL:Ren III-1544
Melba, Nellie
  GE:A&C I-69
Melbourne, John
  GE:ME II-737

Melbourne, Viscount (William Lamb)
GE:ME II-737, 764
GL:B&C IV-1836
Melchior, Marcus
GE:HR II-641
Meletus
GE:A&M I-318
Melgares, Don Facundo
GE:Am I-467
Méliès, Gaston
GE:A&C I-57
Méliès, Georges
GE:A&C I-57, 74
GE:Am II-1333
Melin, Arthur
GE:B&C III-1102
Mellon, Andrew
GE:Am III-1542
GE:B&C II-431
GL:Am III-1523
Mellon, William L.
GE:B&C I-24
Melville, Herman
GE:A&C I-502
GE:Am II-848
GL:Am III-1528
Memmi, Simone. See Martini, Simone
Memmius, Gaius
GE:A&M I-511
Menander (dramatist)
GE:A&M I-368
GL:A&M III-1380
Menander (Indian king)
GL:A&M III-1385
Mencius
GL:A&M III-1388
Mencken, H. L.
GE:Am III-1566
GL:Am III-1535
Mendel, Gregor Johann
GE:ME II-908
GE:S&T I-61, 148, 153, 390, II-486
GL:Ren III-1550
Mendeleyev, Dmitry Ivanovich
GE:ME II-1062
GL:Ren III-1555
Mendelsohn, Erich
GL:20 III-1527
Mendelssohn, Felix
GL:Ren III-1563
Mendenhall, Dorothy Reed
GL:AmW IV-1240
Menderes, Adnan
GE:HR II-1084

Mendès-France, Pierre
GE:W20 II-696
GL:20 IV-1533
Mendizábal, Juan Álvarez
GE:ME II-726
Menelaus. See Onias
Menelaus of Alexandria
GE:A&M II-716
Menelik II (of Ethiopia)
GE:ME II-1094
GL:Ren III-1567
Menelik II, Shewa
GE:HR II-607
Menenius Agrippa. See Agrippa, Menenius
Meng-tzu. See Mencius
Menichella, Donato
GE:B&C II-645
Menjou, Adolphe
GE:A&C II-1011
Menno Simons
GL:Ren III-1572
Menotti, Gian Carlo
GE:A&C III-1536
GL:20 IV-1538
Menshikov, Alexander
GE:ME I-364, II-813
Menzies, Robert Gordon
GL:B&C IV-1841
Menzies, William Cameron
GE:A&C III-1154
Merbold, Ulf
GE:S&T V-2256
Mercalli, Giuseppe
GE:S&T III-1050
Mercator, Gerardus
GL:Ren III-1577
Mercer, Charles Fenton
GE:Am I-576
Mercier, Auguste
GE:ME II-1075
Merck, George W.
GE:HR III-1662
Mercoeur, Duke of
GE:ME I-214, 220
Meredith, James
GE:HR III-1167
Merenda, Titus Antonius
GE:A&M I-253
Mergenthaler, Ottmar
GL:Am III-1540
Merhige, Robert, Jr.
GE:HR V-2342
Merleau-Ponty, Maurice
GL:20 IV-1543

Merluzzi, Vincent
  GE:S&T V-2382
Merman, Ethel
  GL:AmW IV-1245
Merneptah
  GE:A&M I-75
Merriam, Charles
  GE:Am I-636
Merriam, Charles Edward
  GE:B&C III-890
Merriam, George
  GE:Am I-636
Merrill, Charles
  GE:B&C II-809
Merritt, William Hamilton
  GE:S&T IV-1608
  GE:W20 II-783
Merry, Anthony
  GE:Am I-461
Merryman, Jerry D.
  GE:B&C IV-1517
  GE:S&T V-1971
Mersenne, Marin
  GE:ME I-294
  GL:Ren III-1582
Merz, Alfred
  GE:S&T II-805
Meservey, Robert Preston. See Preston, Robert
Mesic, Stipe
  GE:HR V-2612
Messiaen, Olivier
  GE:A&C III-1206
  GL:20 IV-1548
Messmer, Pierre
  GE:ME III-1683
Mesta, Perle
  GL:AmW IV-1250
Metalious, Grace
  GE:A&C IV-2017
Metcalf, Eleanor Melville
  GE:A&C I-502
Metchnikoff, Élie
  GE:S&T I-422
Metellus, Marcus Caecilius
  GE:A&M I-432
Methodius, Saint, and Saint Cyril
  GE:A&M II-1173
  GL:A&M II-579
Metternich
  GL:Ren III-1589
Metzinger, Jean
  GE:A&C I-337

Meyer, Eugene
  GE:Am III-1594
  GE:B&C II-630, 717
Meyer, Harry M., Jr.
  GE:S&T IV-1655
Meyergold, Karl Theodor Kasimir. See
  Meyerhold, Vsevolod
Meyerhof, Otto
  GE:S&T III-1390
Meyerhold, Vsevolod
  GE:A&C I-1, II-787
  GL:20 IV-1553
Meynell, Thomas
  GE:ME II-660
Mi Fei
  GL:A&M III-1394
Miaskovski, Nikolai
  GE:A&C III-1388
Miassin, Leonid. See Massine, Léonide
Michael the Scot
  GE:A&M III-1524
Michaels, James
  GE:B&C I-314
Michaels, Lorne
  GE:A&C V-2355
Michejda, Maria
  GE:S&T V-2174
Michel, Helen
  GE:S&T V-2120
Michelangelo
  GE:ME I-26
  GL:Ren III-1594
Michelet, Jules
  GL:Ren III-1599
Michelin, André, and Édouard Michelin
  GL:20 IV-1559
Michelman, Kate
  GE:HR V-2489
Michelsen, Peter Christian Hersleb Kjerschow
  GE:ME III-1164
Michelson, Albert Abraham
  GE:ME III-1160
  GE:S&T I-297, II-700
  GL:Am IV-1545
Michinaga. See Fujiwara Michinaga
Michnik, Adam
  GE:HR V-2500
Micombero, Michel
  GE:HR III-1668
Middleton, John
  GE:Am II-930
Midgley, Thomas, Jr.
  GE:S&T II-916

Mielziner, Jo
  GE:A&C III-1164
Mier y Teran, Manuel
  GE:Am II-736
Mieroslawski, Ludwick
  GE:ME II-886
Mies van der Rohe, Ludwig
  GE:A&C I-181, 463, IV-1716
  GL:Am IV-1552
Mifflin, Thomas
  GE:Am I-377
Mifune, Toshiro
  GE:A&C III-1476
Miguel, King of Portugal
  GE:ME II-675, 722
Mihajlov, Mihajlo
  GE:HR IV-1949
Mikawa, Gunichi
  GE:Am III-1709
Mikhailovich, Lifshitz
  GE:S&T III-1129
Mikoyan, Anastas
  GE:HR II-969
  GE:ME III-1566
  GE:W20 II-736
Mikulski, Barbara
  GL:AmW IV-1255
Miles, Nelson Appleton
  GE:Am II-1284
Miles, Samuel A.
  GE:B&C I-47
Miles, Vera
  GE:A&C IV-1855
Miley, George Kilroy
  GE:S&T V-2367
Miley, James "Bubber"
  GE:A&C II-739
Milhaud, Darius
  GE:A&C I-435
  GL:20 IV-1564
Milinda. See Menander (Indian king)
Miliukov, Paul
  GE:ME III-1169, 1179
Milius, John
  GE:A&C V-2428
Milken, Michael
  GE:B&C IV-1449, 1641, V-1921, 1958
Mill, James
  GE:ME II-629
  GL:B&C IV-1846
Mill, John Stuart
  GE:ME II-843
  GL:B&C IV-1851

Millay, Edna St. Vincent
  GL:AmW IV-1260
Miller, Agatha. See Christie, Agatha
Miller, Arthur
  GE:A&C III-1164
Miller, Arthur Lewis
  GE:B&C II-787
Miller, Barry
  GE:S&T V-2159
Miller, Bernard J.
  GE:S&T III-1024
Miller, Charles R.
  GE:B&C I-69
Miller, Court
  GE:A&C V-2502
Miller, G. William
  GE:B&C V-1763
Miller, Henry
  GE:A&C II-963
Miller, Henry East
  GE:S&T I-320
Miller, J. Irwin
  GE:HR II-1096
Miller, John E.
  GE:B&C II-764
Miller, John F.
  GE:Am II-1123
Miller, Marvin
  GE:B&C IV-1437, 1512
Miller, Paul
  GE:A&C V-2507
Miller, Richard B.
  GE:S&T V-1956
Miller, Robert C.
  GE:S&T V-2025
Miller, Robert S.
  GE:B&C V-1763
Miller, Stanley Lloyd
  GE:S&T IV-1465, 1851
Miller, Thomas W.
  GE:B&C IV-1733
Miller, Wade
  GE:S&T V-2357
Miller, William
  GE:Am I-420
Miller, William Edward
  GE:Am III-1918
Millett, Kate
  GL:AmW IV-1265
Millikan, Robert Andrews
  GE:S&T I-443, II-532, 694, III-983
  GL:Am IV-1558
Millis, Robert
  GE:S&T V-2068

Mills, Caleb
GE:Am I-576
Mills, Darius Ogden
GE:Am II-1135
Mills, Irving
GE:A&C II-739
Mills, Ogden Livingston
GE:Am III-1594
Mills, Wilbur D.
GE:B&C III-1218, 1248
GE:HR III-1206
Milne, John
GE:S&T I-51, II-552, III-1065
Milner, Sir Alfred
GE:HR I-287
GE:ME II-1128
GE:W20 I-87
Milosevic, Slobodan
GE:HR V-2386, 2612
Miltiades
GE:A&M II-857
Miltiades the Younger
GE:A&M III-1398
Milton, John
GE:ME I-317
GL:B&C IV-1860
Milton, Mary Powell
GE:ME I-317
Milunsky, Aubrey
GE:S&T IV-1439
Minasy, Arthur
GE:B&C IV-1421
Min-Chueh Chang
GE:S&T IV-1512
Mindaugas
GE:A&M III-1650
Mindell, Fania
GE:HR I-184
Minedra. See Menander (Indian king)
Miner, Ellis D.
GE:S&T V-2082
Minh, Duong Van (Big)
GE:W20 III-1227
Minh, Ho Chi. See Ho Chi Minh
Minin, Nikita. See Nikon
Mink, Douglas
GE:S&T V-2068
Minkowski, Rudolf
GE:S&T III-1008, 1271
Minnelli, Vincente
GE:A&C III-1432
Minor, Benjamin B.
GE:Am II-725

Minot, George Richards
GE:S&T II-795
Minovitch, Michael A.
GE:S&T V-2003
Minow, Newton
GE:A&C III-1465, IV-1835
GE:W20 II-669
Minto, Lord Gilbert John
GE:HR I-87
Minucius, Lucius
GE:A&M I-253
Minuit, Peter
GE:Am I-80
Mirabeau, Comte de
GL:Ren IV-1603
Miranda, Ernesto
GE:HR III-1343
Miró, Joan
GE:A&C II-604
GL:20 IV-1570
Mises, Richard von
GE:S&T II-664
Mishima, Yukio
GL:20 IV-1576
Mishin, Vasili P.
GE:S&T IV-1797, V-1928, 1950
Mishra
GE:A&M II-807
Mitchell, Arthur
GE:A&C I-161, IV-2110, V-2521
Mitchell, Charles E.
GE:B&C II-574
Mitchell, George
GE:B&C V-2034
Mitchell, John
GE:Am II-1329
GE:B&C I-122
Mitchell, John Newton
GE:HR III-1532
GE:W20 III-1131
Mitchell, Joni
GL:AmW IV-1270
Mitchell, Margaret
GE:A&C III-1154
Mitchell, Maria
GL:AmW IV-1274
Mitchell, Michael
GE:A&C V-2543
Mitchell, Mitch
GE:A&C IV-2092
Mitchell, Parren J.
GE:B&C IV-1595
Mitchell, Thomas
GE:A&C III-1115

Mitchell, William
    GL:Am IV-1563
Mithridates I
    GE:A&M I-427
Mithradates the Great
    GL:A&M III-1404
Mitsuya, Hiroaki
    GE:S&T V-2382
Mitterrand, François
    GE:A&C V-2619
    GE:B&C V-1793, 2051
    GE:HR V-2268
    GE:ME III-1683
    GL:20 IV-1580
Mixter, Samuel Jason
    GE:S&T I-275
Miyazawa, Kiichi
    GE:B&C V-1964
Mobutu, Joseph
    GE:HR II-1068, 1074
    GE:ME III-1613
Mobutu Sese Seko
    GL:20 IV-1586
Mochnacki, Maurycy
    GE:ME II-691
Modrow, Hans
    GE:HR V-2523
Moe, Henry Allen
    GE:A&C III-1279
Mohammed. See Muhammad
Mohammed I Askia
    GL:Ren IV-1608
Mohammed II the Great
    GE:A&M III-1660, 1718
Mohammed Abed Ar'ouf Arafat. See Arafat, Yasir
Mohammad Reza Shah Pahlavi
    GE:B&C IV-1533
    GE:HR I-406, IV-2013, 2045
    GE:W20 II-912, III-1338
    GL:20 IV-1591
Mohammed, Duse
    GE:Am III-1444
Moholy-Nagy, Làszlò
    GE:A&C I-463
Mohorovičić, Andrija
    GE:S&T I-340, II-552, III-1065
Moi, Daniel Arap
    GE:HR IV-2136, V-2431
Mokae, Zakes
    GE:A&C V-2496
Mokhtarian, Patricia Lyon
    GE:B&C IV-1733
Molapo, Mooki V.
    GE:HR IV-1993

Molé, Mathieu
    GE:ME I-324
Moley, Raymond
    GE:Am III-1609, 1615
Molière
    GL:Ren IV-1613
Molina, Mario José
    GE:S&T V-2009, 2285
Mollenhoff, Clark R.
    GE:B&C III-1092, 1213
Mollet, Guy
    GE:HR II-963, III-1137
    GE:ME III-1589, 1683
Molotov, Vyacheslav Mikhailovich (Skryabin)
    GE:Am III-1736
    GE:ME III-1433, 1440, 1501, 1507, 1512,
        1532, 1566
    GE:W20 II-591, 715
Momaday, N. Scott
    GE:W20 II-865
Mommsen, Theodor
    GL:Ren IV-1618
Monash, Paul
    GE:A&C IV-2017
Monck, Baron. See Monck, George
Monck, George
    GE:Am I-121
    GE:ME I-337
    GL:B&C IV-1866
Mond, Sir Alfred
    GE:HR I-429
Mondale, Walter F.
    GE:B&C IV-1364
    GE:HR III-1639, IV-1752, 2209
Mondlane, Eduardo
    GE:ME III-1673
Mondrian, Piet
    GE:A&C I-429, 458
    GL:20 IV-1597
Monet, Claude
    GE:A&C II-718
    GL:Ren IV-1623
    GL:20 IV-1602
Money, John
    GE:HR III-1497
Monge, Gaspard
    GL:Ren IV-1628
Monino, Jose. See De Floridablanca, Conde
Moñino y Redondo, José. See De Floridablanca,
    Conde
Moniz, António Egas
    GE:S&T III-1060
    GL:20 II-608

Monk, Meredith
    GL:AmW IV-1279
Monnet, Jean
    GE:B&C III-875, 1081, 1320
    GE:ME III-1601
    GL:20 IV-1607
Monro, Sir Charles Carmichael
    GE:W20 I-129
Monroe, Bill
    GE:A&C III-1121
Monroe, Charlie
    GE:A&C III-1121
Monroe, Harriet
    GE:A&C I-314
    GE:Am III-1399
Monroe, James
    GE:Am I-389, 443, 522, 552, 558, 593
    GE:HR II-879
    GL:Am IV-1569
Monroe, Marilyn
    GE:A&C III-1567
Monroy Cabra, Marco Gerardo
    GE:HR III-1503
Monson, Sir Herbert
    GE:ME II-1113
Montagu, Ashley
    GE:S&T IV-1808
Montagu, Edward (Earl of Manchester)
    GE:ME I-313
Montagu, Edwin
    GE:HR I-235
Montaigne, Michel de
    GL:Ren IV-1636
Montale, Eugenio
    GL:20 IV-1613
Montaner, Antonio Maura y. See Maura y
    Montaner, Antonio
Montanus from Phrygia
    GE:A&M II-767
Montcorbier, François de. See Villon, François
Montebello, Marquis of. See Lannes, Gustave
    Louis
Monterey, Carlotta
    GE:A&C IV-1726
Montesquieu
    GE:ME I-464
    GL:Ren IV-1640
Montessori, Maria
    GL:20 IV-1618
Monteux, Pierre
    GE:A&C I-373
Monteverdi, Claudio
    GL:Ren IV-1645

Montezuma II
    GE:ME I-59
    GL:Ren IV-1651
Montezuma, Carlos
    GE:HR I-121
Montfort, Simon V de
    GE:A&M III-1441, 1457, 1528
    GL:B&C IV-1872
Montgolfier, Jacques-Étienne
    GE:ME I-496
    GL:Ren IV-1656
Montgolfier, Joseph-Michel
    GE:ME I-496
    GL:Ren IV-1656
Montgomery of Alamein, First Viscount. See
    Montgomery, Bernard Law
Montgomery, Bernard Law
    GE:Am III-1720, 1748
    GE:ME III-1467, 1486, 1491, 1496
    GE:W20 II-557
    GL:B&C IV-1880
Montgomery, Olen
    GE:Am III-1588
Montgomery, Robert H.
    GE:B&C I-246, 308, 319
Montini, Giovanni Battista. See Paul VI, Pope
Montsitsi, Daniel Sechabo
    GE:HR IV-1882
Moody, Dwight L.
    GE:Am II-1173
    GL:Am IV-1575
Moody, Helen Wills
    GL:AmW IV-1284
Moog, Robert
    GE:A&C IV-1785
Moore, A. Y.
    GE:Am II-679
Moore, Charles
    GE:A&C V-2521
Moore, G. E.
    GL:B&C IV-1885
Moore, George S.
    GE:B&C III-1159
Moore, Gordon E.
    GE:S&T V-1938
Moore, Henry
    GE:A&C III-1190
    GL:B&C IV-1892
Moore, Hiram
    GE:Am II-679
Moore, John Bassett
    GE:Am II-1296
Moore, Joseph Hampton
    GE:B&C I-229

Moore, Marianne
GE:B&C III-1087
GL:AmW IV-1289
Moore, Mary Tyler
GE:A&C IV-1908, V-2197, 2218
Moore, Stanford
GE:S&T IV-1459
Moorhead, William
GE:B&C IV-1384
Moorman, Charlotte
GE:A&C IV-1955
Mora, José A.
GE:HR II-1032
Moraga, Alfrérez José Joaquin
GE:Am I-272
Morales, Juan Ventura
GE:Am I-443
Morant, Sir Robert
GE:HR I-109
Mordkin, Mikhail
GE:A&C I-187
More, Hermon
GE:A&C II ‹:·)01
More, Kenneth
GE:A&C IV-2168
More, Sir Thomas
GE:ME I-49, 103
GL:B&C IV-1898
Morehouse, Edward W.
GE:B&C III-1196
Morel, Edmond Dene, George E. P. A.
Morel-de-Ville
GE:HR I-13, 103
Morgan, Arthur E.
GE:Am III-1621
GE:B&C II-650
Morgan, Harcourt
GE:Am III-1621
GE:B&C II-650
Morgan, Harry
GE:A&C III-1531
Morgan, J. P.
GE:A&C I-24
GE:Am II-1110, 1329
GE:B&C I-29, 91, 97, 134, 346
GL:Am IV-1580
Morgan, John T.
GE:Am II-1339
Morgan, Julia
GL:AmW IV-1294
Morgan, Lewis Henry
GL:Am IV-1586
Morgan, M. J. de. See De Morgan, M. J.

Morgan, Terence
GE:A&C III-1378
Morgan, Thomas Hunt
GE:S&T I-153, 407, 433, II-486
GE:W20 I-7
GL:Am IV-1591
Morgenthau, Henry, Sr.
GE:HR I-150
GE:W20 I-107
Morgenthau, Henry J., Jr.
GE:Am III-1680, 1686
GE:B&C II-851
Morin, Claude
GE:W20 II-820
Morínigo, Higinio
GE:HR I-533
Morissey, Frank
GE:B&C IV-1325
Morita, Akio
GE:B&C III-1009, IV-1573, 1710, V-1848, 1996
GE:S&T IV-1528
GL:20 IV-1624
Morita, Ko
GE:B&C V-1964
Morland, T. L. N.
GE:B&C I-196
Morley, Edward Williams
GE:ME III-1160
GE:S&T II-700
Morley, John
GE:HR I-156
Moro, Aldo
GE:W20 II-1028
Moroder, Giorgio
GE:A&C V-2386
Moroka, James
GE:W20 III-1272
Morones, Luis
GE:HR I-196
Morozov, Georgy I.
GE:HR IV-1926
Morricone, Ennio
GE:A&C IV-1984
Morrill, Justin Smith
GE:Am II-962, 974
Morris, Arthur J.
GE:B&C I-180
Morr᾽ ·. Lewis
GE:Am I-188
Morris, Mark
GE:A&C V-2559, 2663
Morris, Robert
GE:A&C IV-1949

GE:Am I-356
GL:Am IV-1597
Morris, Steveland. *See* Wonder, Stevie
Morris, William
GL:B&C IV-1903
Morrisett, Lloyd
GE:A&C V-2185
Morrison, Herbert
GE:B&C II-857
Morrison, Jeanette Helen. *See* Leigh, Janet
Morrison, Marion Michael. *See* Wayne, John
Morrison, Philip
GE:W20 II-827
Morrison, Toni
GL:AmW IV-1300
Morse, Charles W.
GE:B&C I-134
Morse, Sir Christopher
GE:W20 III-1104
Morse, David A.
GE:HR II-985, III-1509
Morse, Jedidiah
GE:Am I-570
Morse, Samuel F. B.
GE:Am II-742, 895
GE:ME II-834
GE:S&T I-128, IV-1502, V-2078
GL:Am IV-1603
Morse, Wayne
GE:B&C III-1185
GE:HR III-1172
Mortenson, Norma Jean. *See* Monroe, Marilyn
Mortimer, John
GE:A&C V-2249
Morton, Ferdinand "Jelly Roll"
GE:A&C I-13
Morton, Joy
GE:W20 I-1
Morton, William Thomas Green
GE:Am II-1791
GL:Am IV-1609
Moryson, Francis
GE:Am I-151
Mosca, Gaetano
GL:20 IV-1629
Mosed de Léon. *See* Moses de Léon
Moseley, Henry
GE:S&T I-118
Moser, Koloman
GE:A&C I-79
Moses
GE:A&M I-75, 84
GL:A&M III-1410
Moses ben Maimon. *See* Maimonides, Moses

Moses de León
GE:A&M III-1559
GL:A&M III-1416
Moses, Grandma
GL:AmW IV-1305
Moses, Phoebe Anne. *See* Oakley, Annie
Moses, Robert (1888-1981)
GE:B&C III-1076
GE:S&T IV-1608, 1782
Moses, Robert (b. 1935)
GE:HR III-1149
Moskowitz, Belle
GL:AmW IV-1310
Mosleh od-Din Saʿdi. *See* Saʿdi
Moss, Frank E.
GE:B&C IV-1443
GE:HR III-1527
Moss, John E.
GE:B&C IV-1522, 1584
Moss, Paula
GE:A&C V-2370
Mossadegh, Mohammad
GE:B&C IV-1533
Mössbauer, Rudolf Ludwig
GE:S&T IV-1640
Mother Teresa, Agnes Gonxha Bojaxhiu
GE:HR IV-2051
Motley, Constance Baker
GE:B&C V-2040
GE:HR III-1167
Mott, John R.
GE:ME III-1550
GL:Am IV-1614
Mott, Lucretia
GE:Am I-642
GL:AmW IV-1316
Moulton, Charles
GE:A&C V-2480
Mounier, Jean-Joseph
GE:ME I-506
Mountbatten, Lord Louis
GE:HR II-731
GE:W20 II-605
GL:B&C IV-1908
Moynihan, Daniel Patrick
GE:Am III-1866
GE:HR III-1267
Mozart, Wolfgang Amadeus
GL:Ren IV-1661
Mubarak, Hosni
GE:HR IV-2003
Mudaliar, Sir Ramaswami
GE:HR II-985

Mueller, Paul Hermann
GE:W20 I-425
Mugabe, Robert
GE:HR III-1224
GE:W20 II-981
GL:20 IV-1634
Muge, Alexander
GE:HR V-2431
Múgica, Francisco J.
GE:HR I-196
Muhammad
GE:A&M II-1075
GL:A&M III-1422
Muhammad adh-Dhib
GE:W20 II-598
Muhammad 'Al Pasha
GL:Ren IV-1668
Muhammad, Elijah
GE:A&C IV-1929, 2022
Muhī-ud-Dīn Muhammad. See Aurangzeb
Muir, John
GL:Am IV-1620
Muldowney, Shirley
GL:AmW IV-1321
Mulholland, William
GE:B&C II-453
Mullenger, Donna Belle. See Reed, Donna
Muller, Alex
GE:S&T III-1414
Müller, Erwin Wilhelm
GE:S&T III-1070, IV-1434
Müller, Hans
GE:ME I-76
Muller, Hermann Joseph
GE:S&T I-407
GE:W20 I-7
GL:Am IV-1624
Müller, Johannes
GE:A&M II-716
Müller, Karl Alexander
GE:S&T V-2311
Müller, Lucas. See Cranach, Lucas, the Elder
Müller, Otto
GE:A&C I-134
Müller, Paul Hermann
GE:B&C IV-1395
GE:HR III-1515
GE:S&T III-1146, V-1982
Mulligan, Gerry
GE:A&C III-1438, 1617
Mullins, Joseph H.
GE:B&C IV-1647
Mullis, Kary B.
GE:S&T V-2362

Mulroney, Brian
GE:HR V-2376
Munch, Edvard
GL:20 IV-1640
Muni, Paul
GE:A&C II-839
Muñoz Marín, Luis
GE:HR II-801
Munro, J. Richard
GE:B&C I-412
Münsterberg, Hugo
GE:B&C I-258
Münter, Gabriele
GE:A&C I-275
Münzer, Thomas
GE:ME I-76
Murad I
GE:A&M III-1660
Muradeli, Vano
GE:A&C III-1388
Murasaki Shikibu
GL:A&M III-1430
Murat, Joachim
GE:A&M II-659
GE:ME II-581
Muravyev, Nikolai M.
GE:ME III-1678
Muravyov, Mikhail Nikolaevich
GE:ME II-886
Muravyov, Nikita
GE:ME II-665
Muravyov-Apostol, Serge
GE:ME II-665
Murchison, Roderick
GE:ME II-678
Murdani, Benny
GE:HR IV-1835
Murdoch, Rupert
GE:A&C V-2652, 2554
GE:B&C IV-1636, V-1928
Murdock, William
GL:B&C IV-1916
Muris, Johannes de
GL:A&M III-1434
Murphy, Edgar Gardner
GE:HR I-131
Murphy, Frank
GE:Am III-1655
GE:HR II-629
Murphy, John
GE:S&T IV-1782
Murphy, Robert Daniel
GE:W20 II-758

Murphy, Thomas
  GE:B&C V-1751
Murphy, William Parry
  GE:S&T II-795
Murray, Andrew W.
  GE:S&T V-2251
Murray, George Evelyn
  GE:B&C I-218
Murray, George Herbert
  GE:B&C I-218
Murray, James E.
  GE:Am III-1770
Murray, Jeanne. *See* Stapleton, Jean
Murray, John Courtney
  GE:ME III-1633
  GE:W20 I-507
Murray, Philip
  GE:Am III-1655
  GE:B&C II-729, III-997, 1064
  GE:W20 II-572
Murray, William. *See* Mansfield, First Earl of
Murray, William Vans
  GE:Am I-408
Murrow, Edward R.
  GE:W20 II-669
  GL:Am IV-1629
Mūsā. *See* Mansa Mūsā
Musa ibn Nusair. *See* Ibn Nusair, Musa
Musa, Salamah
  GE:A&C V-2625
Muskie, Edmund
  GE:Am III-1933
  GE:B&C III-1265
  GE:HR III-1310, 1561
  GE:W20 II-872

Mussolini, Benito
  GE:B&C II-645, 723
  GE:HR I-395, II-607, 695
  GE:ME III-1299, 1319, 1354, 1401, 1416,
    1425, 1429, 1440, 1451, 1486
  GE:W20 I-138, 342, 348, 444, 465
  GL:20 IV-1645
Mussorgsky, Modest
  GL:Ren IV-1673
Mustafa II (Sultan of Turkey)
  GE:ME I-368
Mustafa III (Sultan of the Ottoman Empire)
  GE:ME I-475
Mustafa el-Nahas Pasha
  GE:W20 I-494
Mustafa Kemal Atatürk. *See* Atatürk, Kemal
Mutch, Thomas
  GE:W20 III-1294
Mutesa II
  GE:HR III-1600
Muthesius, Hermann
  GE:A&C I-181
Muto, Akira
  GE:HR I-539
Muwatallish
  GE:A&M I-70
Muzorewa, Abel
  GE:HR III-1224
  GE:W20 II-981
Myer, Dillon S.
  GE:HR II-595, 820, 897
Myers, Ronald
  GE:S&T IV-1635
Myrdal, Gunnar
  GL:20 IV-1651

N

Nabonidus
GE:A&M I-179

Nabu-rimanni
GL:A&M III-1439

Nader, Ralph
GE:B&C III-1265, 1270, IV-1416, 1426, 1561
GE:HR III-1267
GE:W20 II-856

Nadolny, Rudolf
GE:W20 I-276

Nagai, Ryutaro
GE:HR I-417

Nagao, Ariga
GE:W20 I-121

Nagel, Conrad
GE:A&C II-799

Nagumo, Chuichi
GE:W20 I-472

Nagy, Imre
GE:HR II-969, III-1408, V-2421
GE:ME III-1595

Nahmanides
GE:A&M III-1559

Naidu, Sarojini
GL:20 IV-1656

Nakano, Seigo
GE:HR I-417

Nakasone, Yasuhiro
GE:B&C V-1964

Naksznski, Nikolaus. *See* Kinski, Klaus

Nānak
GL:Ren IV-1680

Nance, James J.
GE:B&C III-1190

Nanni di Banco. *See* Di Banco, Nanni

Nansen, Fridtjof
GE:HR I-361, II-918

Napoleon I (Bonaparte)
GE:Am I-443, 505
GE:ME I-538, 547, II-556, 564, 568, 581, 585, 590, 594, 598, 618
GL:Ren IV-1686

Napoleon III
GE:ME II-770, 775, 786, 808, 813, 818, 838, 849, 860, 870, 876, 918, 923, 949, 954, 958
GL:Ren IV-1691

Napoleon, Prince Jerome, of Westphalia
GE:ME II-838

Narasimhan, C. V.
GE:HR IV-1993

Narayeva, Margarita
GE:S&T V-2042

Narazaki, Yanosuke
GE:B&C V-1964

Narcissus
GE:A&M II-621

Nash, Arthur J.
GE:A&C I-34

Nash, John
GL:B&C IV-1921

Nash, Paul
GL:B&C IV-1927

Nash, Philleo
GE:HR II-820

Nasica, Publius Cornelius Scipio. *See* Scipio Nasica Serapio

Nasmyth, James
GE:ME I-524
GL:B&C IV-1932

Naso, Publius Ovidius. *See* Ovid

Nasser, Gamal Abdel
GE:A&C V-2625
GE:B&C IV-1336
GE:HR II-963, III-1131, 1194, 1241
GE:ME III-1589, 1654
GE:W20 II-690, 758
GL:20 IV-1661

Nast, Thomas
GL:Am IV-1635

Nasution, Abdul Haris
GE:HR III-1305

Nathan
GE:A&M I-101

Nathan, Joe
GE:HR V-2256

Nathan, Syd
GE:A&C IV-2059

Nation, Carry
GL:AmW IV-1325

Natta, Giulio
GL:20 IV-1668

Naumann, Friedrich
GE:A&C I-181

Naur, Peter
GE:S&T IV-1475

Navarre, Eugène
GE:ME III-1577

166

Navarro, José Francis de
 GE:B&C I-35
Navratilova, Martina
 GL:AmW IV-1329
Neave, Airey
 GE:HR IV-2024
Nebuchadrezzar. See Nebuchadnezzar II
Nebuchadnezzar II
 GE:A&M I-179
 GL:A&M III-1444
Necham, Alexander. See Neckam, Alexander
Necho
 GE:A&M I-149
Neckam, Alexander
 GE:A&M III-1503
 GL:A&M III-1449
Necker, Anne-Louise-Germaine. See Staël,
 Madame de
Necker, Jacques
 GE:ME I-502, 510
 GL:Ren IV-1696
Necquam. See Neckam, Alexander
Neel, Alice
 GL:AmW IV-1333
Néel, Louis-Eugène-Félix
 GL:20 IV-1673
Ne'eman, Yuval
 GE:S&T IV-1767
Nefertiti
 GE:A&M I-64
Negulesco, John
 GE:A&C III-1567
Nehemiah
 GE:A&M I-189
Nehru, Jawaharlal
 GE:A&C III-1503
 GE:HR I-156, 447, 459, II-731, 743, 837, 924,
  III-1131, IV-1858, V-2426, 2535
 GE:W20 I-175, 605
 GL:20 IV-1678
Nehru, Motilal
 GE:HR I-156, 315, 447
Neidlinger, George
 GE:B&C I-103
Neier, Aryeh
 GE:HR V-2494
Neill, Beverly Louise. See Blake, Amanda
Nelson, Clifford H.
 GE:S&T IV-1825
Nelson, Donald M.
 GE:Am III-1680
 GE:B&C II-820
Nelson, Eugene
 GE:HR III-1161

Nelson, Lord Horatio
 GE:ME I-538
 GL:B&C IV-1937
Nelson, Ozzie
 GE:A&C III-1470
Nelson, Tom
 GE:HR V-2256
Nelson, Willie
 GE:A&C V-2365
Nemiroff, Robert
 GE:A&C IV-1795
Nemirovich-Danchenko, Vladimir
 GE:A&C I-1
Nenni, Pietro
 GE:ME III-1538
Nepos, Julius. See Julius Nepos
Neri, Saint Philip
 GL:Ren IV-1701
Nernst, Walther Hermann
 GE:S&T I-385
 GL:20 IV-1684
Nero Claudius Drusus. See Drusus, Nero Claudius
Nero Claudius Drusus Germanicus
 GE:A&M II-584
Nero, Claudius Caesar Drusus Germanicus
 GE:A&M II-638
Nero, Tiberius Claudius. See Tiberius
Neruda, Pablo
 GL:20 IV-1689
Nerva
 GE:A&M II-675
Nervi, Pier Luigi
 GE:A&C IV-2064
 GL:20 IV-1694
Nesmith, Michael
 GE:A&C V-2475
Nestor
 GE:A&M III-1205
Nestorius
 GE:A&M II-952
Neto, Antonio Augustino
 GE:ME III-1673
 GE:W20 III-1219
Neuberger, Maurine B.
 GE:HR III-1338, 1527
Neuharth, Allen
 GE:A&C V-2507
 GE:B&C V-1842
Neuharth, Christina
 GE:A&C V-2507
Neumann, J. B.
 GE:A&C II-1001
Neumann, John von. See Von Neumann, John

Neurath, Konstantin von
  GE:W20 I-276, 348, 375
Neutra, Richard
  GE:A&C III-1290
Neuville, René Victor
  GE:S&T V-2341
Nevelson, Louise
  GL:AmW IV-1338
Neville, Bill
  GE:HR V-2376
Neville, Richard. See Warwick, Earl of
Nevsky, Alexander. See Alexander Nevsky
New, Harry S.
  GE:B&C II-493
Newbery, John
  GL:B&C IV-1943
Newberry, Truman Handy
  GE:B&C II-476
Newcastle, Duke of. See Pelham-Holles, Thomas
Newcastle, Marquis of. See Cavendish, William
Newcomb, Simon
  GL:Am IV-1646
Newcomen, Thomas
  GE:ME I-460
  GL:B&C IV-1948
Newell, Homer E.
  GE:S&T IV-1825
Newkirk, John B.
  GE:S&T V-2174
Newman, John Henry
  GL:B&C IV-1953
Newman, Max H. A.
  GE:S&T III-1155
Newman, Rosalind
  GE:A&C V-2480
Newmarch, Rosa
  GE:A&C I-292
Newport, Christopher
  GE:Am I-59
Newton, Huey P.
  GE:Am III-1861, 1866
  GE:HR III-1348
Newton, Sir Isaac
  GE:S&T I-297, II-625, 630, IV-1640
  GL:B&C IV-1959
Ney, Michel
  GE:ME II-618
  GL:Ren IV-1706
Neyman, Jerzy
  GE:S&T IV-1454
Nezahualcóyotl
  GL:A&M III-1454

Ngo Dinh Diem
  GE:Am III-1906
  GE:W20 II-696, III-1243
Nguema, Francisco Macias
  GE:HR IV-2136
Nguyen Phuc Anh. See Gia Long
Nguyen That Thanh. See Ho Chi Minh
Nguyen Van Thieu
  GE:HR IV-1691
Niblo, Fred
  GE:A&C II-799
Nicator. See Seleucus I Nicator
Nichiren
  GL:A&M III-1460
Nicholas I (of Russia)
  GE:ME II-665, 691, 813
  GL:Ren IV-1711
Nicholas II, Pope
  GE:A&M III-1243, 1263
Nicholas II (of Russia)
  GE:HR I-70, 92, 212, 225
  GE:ME II-1062, 1123, III-1148, 1156, 1169,
    1179, 1192, 1271
  GE:W20 I-101
Nicholas V, Pope
  GL:Ren IV-1716
Nicholas of Autrecourt
  GL:A&M III-1465
Nicholas of Cusa
  GE:A&M III-1708
  GL:Ren IV-1722
Nicholas the Great
  GL:A&M III-1471
Nichols, J. C.
  GE:B&C I-380
Nichols, John B.
  GE:S&T II-775
Nicholson, Sir Arthur
  GE:ME III-1197
Nicholson, Ben
  GL:B&C IV-1964
Nicholson, Sir Francis
  GE:Am I-132
Nicholson, Jack
  GE:A&C IV-2158, V-2320
Nicias
  GE:A&M I-308
Nickerson, Eugene H.
  GE:HR IV-2106
Nickerson, William Emery
  GE:B&C I-75
Nicola di Lorenzo. See Rienzo, Cola di
Nicolet, Jean
  GE:Am I-52

Nicolette, Thomas A.
  GE:B&C IV-1421
Nicolls, Richard
  GE:Am I-140
Nicolo Polo. *See* Polo, Nicolo
Nidetch, Jean
  GL:AmW IV-1344
Niebuhr, Barthold Georg
  GL:Ren IV-1728
Niebuhr, Helmut Richard
  GE:Am III-1604
  GE:W20 I-507
Niebuhr, Reinhold
  GE:Am III-1604
  GL:Am IV-1650
Nielsen, A. C., Jr.
  GE:B&C I-401
Nielsen, A. C., Sr.
  GE:B&C I-401
Niemeyer, Oscar
  GL:20 IV-1699
Niemöller, Martin
  GL:20 IV-1704
Niépce, Isidore
  GE:ME II-747
Niépce, Nicéphore
  GE:ME II-747
  GL:Ren IV-1733
Nietzsche, Friedrich Wilhelm
  GE:A&C I-85, II-890, III-1573, IV-1829,
    2075, V-2464
  GE:ME II-1024
  GE:W20 I-38
  GL:Ren IV-1741
Nightingale, Florence
  GL:B&C IV-1969
Nijinsky, Vaslav
  GE:A&C I-241, 247, 332, 373
  GL:20 IV-1710
Nikolay Pavlovich. *See* Nicholas I (of Russia)
Nikon
  GL:Ren IV-1747
Nikonov, Aleksandr
  GE:HR V-2471
Nilles, Jack M.
  GE:B&C IV-1733
Nimitz, Chester W.
  GE:Am III-1709, 1731
  GE:W20 I-472
  GL:Am IV-1655
Nimoy, Leonard
  GE:A&C V-2260
Nin, Anaïs
  GE:A&C II-963

Nipkow, Paul Gottlieb
  GE:S&T II-751
Nirenberg, Marshall W.
  GE:S&T III-1363, IV-1687
Nishida, Kitarō
  GL:20 IV-1715
Nivelle, Robert Georges
  GE:ME III-1262
Niven, John Ballantine
  GE:B&C II-608
Nixon, E. D.
  GE:HR II-947
Nixon, Richard M.
  GE:Am III-1843, 1866, 1871, 1906, 1933
  GE:B&C II-442, 851, III-1241, IV-1431,
    1460, 1466, 1477, 1483, 1489, 1506, 1522,
    1555, 1561, 1699
  GE:HR I-520, II-897, 997, III-1177, 1521,
    1532, 1537, 1561, 1573, 1579, 1585, 1595,
    1628, 1650, 1662, IV-1691, 1731, 1747,
    1769, 1786, 1791
  GE:W20 I-513, II-865, 872, 988, 1050, 1054,
    1083, 1091, III-1097, 1104, 1110, 1124,
    1131, 1161, 1188, 1193, 1200, 1212
  GL:Am IV-1660
Nizam al-Mulk
  GL:A&M IV-1477
Nkomo, Joshua
  GE:HR III-1224
  GE:ME III-1642
  GE:W20 II-981
Nkrumah, Kwame
  GE:HR II-980, III-1194
  GL:20 IV-1721
Nobel, Alfred
  GE:A&C I-45, V-2423, 2594, 2668
  GE:HR II-907
  GL:Ren IV-1752
Nobile, Federico. *See* Niblo, Fred
Nobiling, Dr. Karl
  GE:ME II-1013
Noble, David F.
  GE:B&C III-1202
Noble, Edward J.
  GE:A&C III-1211
  GE:B&C II-827
Nochlin, Linda
  GE:A&C V-2608
Noel-Baker, Philip J.
  GE:HR I-361
Noether, Emmy
  GE:S&T II-650, 716
Noguchi, Isamu
  GE:A&C III-1284
Nol, Lon. *See* Lon Nol

Nolde, Emil
    GE:A&C I-134, III-1083, 1217
Nomura, Kichisaburo
    GE:Am III-1697
Nonomura, Sōtatsu. *See* Sōtatsu
Nordau, Max Simon
    GE:ME II-1089
Nordhoff, Heinz
    GE:B&C IV-1664
Norfolk, Duke of
    GE:ME II-669
Norman, Jessye
    GL:AmW IV-1349
Norman, Marsha
    GL:AmW IV-1354
Norman, Montagu
    GE:B&C II-613
Normand, Mabel
    GE:A&C I-230
    GL:AmW IV-1359
Normanus. *See* Muris, Johannes de
Norris, Clarence
    GE:Am III-1588
Norris, Frank
    GE:A&C I-39
Norris, George W.
    GE:Am III-1621
    GE:B&C II-635, 650
North, Lord (Earl of Guilford)
    GE:Am I-225, 241
    GL:B&C IV-1976
Northcliffe, Alfred Harmsworth, First Viscount.
    See Harmsworth, Alfred, First Viscount
    Northcliffe
Northcote, Sir Stafford Henry
    GE:ME II-1038
Norton, Eleanor Holmes
    GE:B&C III-1185
Nott, Josiah
    GE:Am I-648

Nourse, Edwin G.
    GE:Am III-1770
Novak, David
    GE:HR V-2262
Novatian
    GE:A&M II-812
Novotný, Antonín
    GE:A&C IV-1967
    GE:HR III-1441
    GE:ME III-1666
Noyce, Robert Norton
    GE:B&C IV-1721
    GE:S&T V-1938
Noyes, John Humphrey
    GE:Am I-420
Noyes, Nicholas
    GE:Am I-169
Nujoma, Sam
    GE:HR V-2409
Nureyev, Rudolf
    GE:A&C IV-1962, V-2559
Nuri, Sheikh Fazlullah
    GE:HR I-52
Nuri as-Said
    GE:W20 I-494
Nusair, Musa ibn. *See* Ibn Nusair
Nuttall, John Mitchell
    GE:S&T II-851
Nutzhorn, Dorothea Margaretta. *See* Lange,
    Dorothea
Nuwas, Abu-. *See* Abu-Nuwas
Nye, Gerald P.
    GE:Am III-1649
Nyerere, Julius
    GE:HR III-1194, 1491, 1668, IV-1736
    GL:20 IV-1727
Nyquist, Harry
    GE:S&T V-2200
Nyun, U
    GE:B&C III-1276

O

Oakley, Annie
  GL:AmW IV-1364
Oastler, Richard
  GE:ME II-730, 741
Obasanjo, Olusegun
  GE:B&C IV-1589
  GE:HR III-1365
Oberth, Hermann
  GE:Am III-1555
  GE:S&T IV-1545, V-2377
  GE:W20 II-751
  GL:20 IV-1732
Obote, Milton
  GE:HR III-1600
Obregón, Álvaro
  GE:Am III-1438
  GE:W20 I-69
  GL:20 IV-1737
O'Brian, Hugh
  GE:A&C IV-1768
O'Brien, Lawrence
  GE:B&C IV-1506
O'Brien, William Smith
  GE:ME II-757
Obruchev, Nikolai
  GE:ME II-1070
Ochoa, Severo
  GE:S&T III-1363
Ockels, Wubbo
  GE:S&T V-2256
Ockham, William of
  GE:A&M III-1564, 1640
  GL:B&C IV-1981
O'Connell, Daniel
  GE:ME II-669, 741, 757
  GL:B&C IV-1988
O'Connor, Basil
  GE:Am III-1835
O'Connor, Carroll
  GE:A&C V-2234
O'Connor, Feargus Edward
  GE:ME II-730, 741, 764
O'Connor, Flannery
  GE:A&C IV-1645
  GL:AmW IV-1369
O'Connor, Sir Nicholas
  GE:ME II-1133
O'Connor, Sandra Day
  GE:HR IV-2141, V-2320, 2506

GL:Am IV-1665
  GL:AmW IV-1374
Octavian. *See* Augustus
Octavianus, Gaius Julius Caesar. *See* Augustus
Octavius, Gaius. *See* Augustus
Octavius, Marcus
  GE:A&M I-481
Oda Nobunaga
  GL:Ren IV-1757
Odell, Charles Robert
  GE:S&T V-2377
Odets, Clifford
  GE:A&C II-874, 1006
Odilo
  GE:A&M II-1184
Odinga, Oginga
  GE:HR V-2431
Odo
  GE:A&M II-1184
Odo of Lagery. *See* Urban II
O'Donnell, May
  GE:A&C III-1284
Odovacar
  GE:A&M II-980
O'Dwyer, Sir Michael
  GE:HR I-264
Oersted, Hans Christian
  GE:ME II-649
O'Feeney, Sean Aloysius. *See* Ford, John
Offenbach, Jacques
  GL:Ren IV-1763
Officer, Charles
  GE:S&T V-2120
Ogadai
  GE:A&M III-1462
Ogata Kōrin
  GL:Ren IV-1769
Ogden, Aaron
  GE:Am I-600
Oglesby, Carl
  GE:Am III-1861
Oglethorpe, James Edward
  GE:Am I-182
  GL:Am IV-1670
Oh, Sadaharu
  GL:20 IV-1743
Ohain, Hans Pabst von
  GE:S&T III-1187
  GE:W20 I-355

Ohga, Norio
  GE:B&C IV-1710, V-1996
O'Higgins, Bernardo
  GL:Ren IV-1773
Ohnishi, Vice Takijiro
  GE:Am III-1731
Ohno, Taiichi
  GE:B&C IV-1716
O'Horgan, Tom
  GE:A&C IV-2121, V-2254
Ojukwu, Chukwuemeka Odumegwu
  GE:HR III-1365
  GE:W20 II-1003
O'Keeffe, Georgia
  GL:Am IV-1677
  GL:AmW IV-1379
Okyar, Ali Fethi
  GE:W20 I-225
Olaf V
  GE:HR IV-2051
Olaf, Saint
  GL:A&M IV-1484
Oland, Warner
  GE:A&C II-734
Oldenbarnevelt, Johan van
  GL:Ren IV-1778
Oldham, Andrew Loog
  GE:A&C IV-2027
Oldham, Richard Dixon
  GE:S&T I-340, III-1065
Olga
  GE:A&M III-1205
Olgerd
  GE:A&M III-1650
Oliphant, Marcus Laurence
  GE:S&T III-978
Olivares, Count-Duke of. See De Guzmán, Gaspar
Oliveira, John Carlos (Duke of Saldanha)
  GE:ME II-675, 722
Oliver, King
  GE:A&C II-670
Olivier, Sir Laurence
  GE:A&C III-1378, IV-1924
  GL:B&C IV-1994
Ollivier, Émile
  GE:ME II-808
Olmsted, Frederick Law
  GE:Am II-1231
  GL:Am IV-1684
Olney, Richard
  GE:Am II-1206, 1237
Olney, Warren
  GE:B&C II-640

Olsen, George
  GE:S&T II-735
Olson, Harry F.
  GE:A&C IV-1785
Olson, Maynard Victor
  GE:S&T V-2251
O'Malley, Walter
  GE:B&C III-1076
Omar
  GE:A&M II-1075
Omar Khayyám
  GL:A&M IV-1490
Onassis, Jacqueline Kennedy
  GE:Am III-1899
  GL:AmW IV-1384
O'Neal, Ryan
  GE:A&C IV-2017
O'Neill, Edmond
  GE:S&T I-320
O'Neill, Eugene
  GE:A&C I-343, IV-1726
  GL:Am IV-1688
O'Neill, Terence
  GE:HR III-1485
Onesimus
  GE:A&M II-696
Ong, Walter J.
  GE:A&C IV-1973
Onias (Menelaus)
  GE:A&M I-459
Onias III
  GE:A&M I-459
Onnes, Heike Kamerlingh
  GE:S&T IV-1533, V-2311
Oort, Jan Hendrik
  GE:S&T II-830, III-1379, 1414
  GL:20 IV-1748
Opal, Chet
  GE:S&T V-1992
Oparin, Aleksandr Ivanovich
  GE:S&T IV-1465
  GL:20 IV-1753
Opel, John
  GE:S&T V-2169
Oppenheimer, J. Robert
  GE:A&C IV-1939
  GE:Am III-1692
  GE:S&T III-1150, 1265, IV-1434, 1881
  GE:W20 II-683, 835, 1009
  GL:Am IV-1695
Oppenheimer, Jess
  GE:A&C III-1525
Oppius Cornicen, Spurius
  GE:A&M I-253

Orange, Prince of the Netherlands. *See* William I
(of the Netherlands)
Orcagna, Andrea
  GL:A&M IV-1495
Ordaz, Gustavo Díaz
  GE:B&C III-1241
Oresme, Nicole
  GE:A&M III-1614
Orff, Carl
  GE:A&C II-816
Orfila, Alejandro
  GE:W20 III-1251
Orgel, Leslie Eleazer
  GE:S&T IV-1662
Origen
  GE:A&M I-418, II-731, 757, 762, 773, 779,
    795, 801
  GL:A&M IV-1499
Orkun, Serge
  GE:B&C I-401
Orlando, Vittorio Emanuele
  GE:Am III-1484
  GE:HR I-270
  GE:ME III-1283
Orléans, Charles D'. *See* Charles D'Orléans
Orléans, Duke of. *See* Baptiste, Gaston Jean
Orlov, Count Aleksei
  GE:ME I-475
Orlov, Count Grigori Grigorievich
  GE:ME I-464
Orlov, Yuri
  GE:HR IV-1915
Oró, Juan
  GE:S&T IV-1662
Orowitz, Eugene Maurice. *See* Landon, Michael
Orozco, José Clemente
  GE:A&C II-957
  GL:20 IV-1758
Orr-Cahall, Christina
  GE:A&C V-2636
Orsini, Felice
  GE:ME II-838
Ortega, Katherine Davalos
  GL:AmW IV-1389
Ortega Saavedra, Daniel
  GE:HR IV-2035, V-2336, 2564
Ortega y Gasset, José
  GE:ME II-1119
  GL:20 IV-1764
Ortiz, Roberto
  GE:HR II-673
Ortoli, François-Xavier
  GE:ME III-1683

Orwell, George
  GE:A&C III-1421
  GL:B&C IV-2004
Osborn, Henry Fairfield
  GE:S&T II-735
Osborne, John
  GE:A&C III-1454, IV-1721
Osborne, Thomas. *See* Leeds, First Duke of
Osborne, Thomas Burr
  GE:S&T II-725
Oscar II (of Sweden and Norway)
  GE:ME III-1164
Osiander, Andreas
  GE:ME I-138
Osler, Sir William
  GL:B&C IV-2012
Osman
  GL:A&M IV-1504
Ossietzky, Carl von
  GE:HR V-2292
Ossoli, Marchioness. *See* Fuller, Margaret
Österling, Anders
  GE:A&C IV-2147
Ostwald, Wilhelm
  GE:S&T I-385
  GL:20 IV-1769
O'Sullivan, William J., Jr.
  GE:S&T IV-1677
Osumare, Halifu
  GE:A&C V-2370
Oswald
  GE:A&M II-1081
Oswald, Lee Harvey
  GE:Am III-1899
Oswald, Richard
  GE:Am I-300
Oswald, Russell G.
  GE:HR III-1633
Othman. *See* Osman
Otis, Elisha Graves
  GE:S&T II-906
Otis, Harrison Gray
  GE:Am I-414, 517
Otis, Samuel
  GE:Am I-341
Ottaviani, Alfredo Cardinal
  GE:ME III-1633, 1659
Otto the Great
  GE:A&M III-1195
  GL:A&M IV-1510
Otto, Nikolaus August
  GE:ME II-1033
  GL:Ren IV-1783

Oud, Jacobus Johannes Pieter
  GE:A&C I-429
  GL:20 IV-1774
Oueddei, Goukouni
  GE:HR III-1273
Ouko, Robert
  GE:HR V-2431
Outram, Sir James
  GL:B&C IV-2017
Ou-yang Hsiu
  GL:A&M IV-1515
Overton, George
  GE:ME II-660
Ovid
  GE:A&M II-573
  GL:A&M IV-1520
Owen, Robert
  GE:Am I-511

GE:HR III-1290
GL:B&C IV-2022
Owen, Robert Dale
  GE:Am I-511
Owen, Robert Latham
  GE:Am III-1432
  GE:B&C I-240
Owens, Frances Marion. *See* Marion, Frances
Owens, Jesse
  GL:Am IV-1699
Oxenstierna, Axel
  GE:ME I-290, 308
  GL:Ren IV-1788
Ozal, Turgut
  GE:HR V-2397
Ozil, J. P.
  GE:S&T V-2273

P

Paar, Jack
GE:A&C III-1623
Paarlberg, Don
GE:B&C III-1052
Paasikivi, Juho Kusti
GE:HR I-212
Pacelli, Eugenio. *See* Pius XII
Pacelli, Francesco
GE:ME III-1354
Pach, Walter
GE:A&C I-361
Pachacuti
GL:A&M IV-1525
Pacino, Al
GE:A&C V-2265
Padín Rodríguez, José
GE:HR II-801
Paes, Sidonio Barnadino Cardosa da Silva
GE:ME III-1219
Page, David
GE:S&T V-2346
Page, Geraldine
GL:AmW IV-1394
Page, Jimmy
GE:A&C V-2228
Page, Robert M.
GE:W20 I-324
Page, Walter Hines
GE:Am III-1450
Paget, Henry William (Marquis of Anglesey)
GE:ME II-669
Pahlavi, Mohammad Reza Shah. *See* Mohammad
Reza Shah Pahlavi
Pahlavi, Princess Ashraf
GE:HR III-1430, IV-1796
Pahlavi, Reza Shah
GE:HR I-406
Paik, Nam June
GE:A&C IV-1955
Paine, Thomas
GE:Am I-194, 261
GL:Am IV-1704
Painlevé, Paul
GE:ME III-1359
Painter, William
GE:B&C I-75
Paisley, Reverend Ian
GE:HR III-1485
GE:W20 III-1117

Pakenham, Sir Edward Michael
GE:Am I-533
Pakenham, Richard
GE:Am II-778
Paki, Lydia Kamekaeha. *See* Liliuokalani
Palade, George Emil
GE:W20 I-501
Palaeologus, Sophia (Zöe)
GE:A&M III-1738
Palavicini, Felix Fulgencio
GE:HR II-985
Paléologue, Maurice
GE:W20 I-181
Paley, William S.
GE:A&C III-1211, 1383
GE:B&C I-363, IV-1578
GE:S&T III-1166
GE:W20 II-669
Palin, Michael
GE:A&C IV-2174
Palladio, Andrea
GL:Ren IV-1793
Pallas
GE:A&M II-621
Palmela, Duke of. *See* De Sousa, Pedro
Palmer, Alexander Mitchell
GE:Am III-1491
GE:B&C II-459
GE:HR I-258
Palmer, Alice Freeman
GL:AmW IV-1399
Palmer, Dewey
GE:HR I-527
Palmer, Herbert
GE:ME I-317
Palmer, Ingrid
GE:HR IV-2057
Palmer, Patrick Edward
GE:W20 II-827
Palmerston, Lord
GE:ME II-686, 722, 794, 813, 818, 998
GL:B&C IV-2027
Palmiter, Richard
GE:S&T V-2154
Palóu, Francisco
GE:Am I-272
Pan, Hermes
GE:A&C II-984

175

Pan Ku
  GL:A&M IV-1530
Panaetius of Rhodes
  GE:A&M I-453, 541
Panagiotopolous, Hermes. *See* Pan, Hermes
Panainos
  GE:A&M I-297
Panchen Lama
  GE:HR II-826
Pandit, Vijaya Lakshmi
  GL:20 IV-1779
Panin, Count Nikita
  GE:ME I-464
Pankhi. *See* Piankhi
Pankhurst, Christabel
  GE:HR I-19, 247
Pankhurst, Emmeline
  GE:HR I-19, 247
  GL:B&C IV-2034
Pankhurst, Sylvia
  GE:HR I-19, 247
Pannartz, Arnold
  GE:A&M III-1713
Pantaenus
  GE:A&M II-795
Papadopoulos, George
  GE:HR III-1359, IV-1747
  GE:W20 III-1193
Papandreou, Andreas
  GE:HR III-1359
Papandreou, George
  GE:HR III-1359
Papanek, Victor J.
  GE:A&C V-2208
Papanicolaou, George N.
  GE:S&T II-864
Papen, Franz von
  GE:W20 I-311
  GL:20 IV-1784
Papin, Denis
  GL:Ren IV-1799
Papirofsky, Yosl. *See* Papp, Joseph
Papkoff, Harold
  GE:S&T III-1358
Papp, Joseph
  GE:A&C IV-1967, V-2571
Pappus
  GL:A&M IV-1536
Paracelsus
  GL:Ren IV-1804
Paredes y Arrillaga, Mariano
  GE:Am II-825
Parentucelli, Tommaso. *See* Nicholas V, Pope

Pareto, Vilfredo
  GE:B&C II-770
Paris, Jerry
  GE:A&C IV-1908
Parizeau, Jacques
  GE:W20 II-820
Park, Keith R.
  GE:W20 I-430
Park, Maud Wood
  GE:HR I-339
Park, Mungo
  GL:B&C IV-2040
Park, Robert E.
  GE:Am III-1357
Parker, Arthur C.
  GE:HR I-121
Parker, Charles Christopher "Bird"
  GE:A&C III-1318, 1617
Parker, Dorothy
  GL:AmW IV-1404
Parker, Eleanor
  GE:A&C IV-2033
Parker, Eugene N.
  GE:S&T IV-1577
Parker, Fess
  GE:A&C III-1612
Parker, Francis Wayland
  GE:Am II-1301
Parker, George F.
  GE:B&C I-122
Parker, John
  GE:Am I-251
Parker, Matthew
  GE:ME I-168
  GL:B&C IV-2045
Parker, Robert A.
  GE:S&T V-2256
Parker, Samuel D.
  GE:Am II-785
Parker, Theodore
  GE:Am I-654
  GL:Am IV-1710
Parker, Colonel Tom
  GE:A&C IV-1705
Parkes, Sir Henry
  GE:W20 I-14
  GL:B&C IV-2050
Parkes, Joseph
  GE:ME II-737
Parkman, Francis
  GL:Am IV-1716
Parkman, Paul D.
  GE:S&T IV-1655

Parks, Robert J.
GE:S&T IV-1734
Parks, Rosa
GE:Am III-1855
GE:HR II-947, III-1257, 1419
GL:Am IV-1724
GL:AmW IV-1409
Parmenides
GE:A&M I-231
GL:A&M IV-1541
Parmenion
GE:A&M I-358
Parnell, Charles Stewart
GE:ME II-1038
GL:B&C IV-2056
Parr, Catherine
GE:ME I-123
Parri, Ferruccio
GE:ME II-1538
Parrington, Vernon L.
GE:W20 I-205
GL:Am IV-1728
Parris, Samuel
GE:Am I-169
Parsons, Sir Charles
GE:S&T II-547
Parsons, Ed
GE:B&C III-953
Parsons, Elsie Clews
GL:AmW IV-1414
Parsons, John
GE:B&C III-1128
Parsons, Robert
GE:ME I-174, 224
Partch, Harry
GE:A&C III-1279
Parton, Dolly
GL:AmW IV-1419
Pascal, Blaise
GL:Ren IV-1809
Pasch, Moritz
GE:S&T I-31
Paschasius Radbertus. *See* Radbertus, Paschasius
Paschen, Friedrich
GE:S&T II-800
Pasha, Ahmed Djemal
GE:HR I-150
Pasha, Ali (of Turkey)
GE:ME I-180
Pasha, Mehmet Talaat
GE:HR I-150
Pasha, Midhat
GE:HR I-98

Pasha, Mohammed Said (of Egypt)
GE:ME II-818
Pasha, Omar (of Turkey)
GE:ME II-813
Pasha, Zagan
GE:A&M III-1718
Pashitch, Nikola (Pasic)
GE:ME III-1340
Paskevich-Erivanski, Count Ivan
GE:ME II-691
Pasquier, Étienne
GE:A&C III-1206
Passidomo, John A.
GE:HR IV-2220
Pasternak, Boris
GE:A&C IV-1747
GL:20 IV-1789
Pasteur, Louis
GE:ME II-935, III-1174
GL:Ren IV-1814
Pate, Maurice
GE:HR II-689
Patel, Vallabhbhai Jhaverbhai
GL:20 IV-1795
Pater, Walter
GL:B&C IV-2061
Paterson, William
GE:Am I-330
GL:B&C IV-2066
Pathé, Charles
GE:A&C I-57
Pati, Jogesh
GE:S&T V-2014
Patik
GE:A&M II-807
Patman, Wright
GE:B&C II-746, III-1014, 1107
Patolichev, Nikolai
GE:B&C III-1287
Patout, Pierre
GE:A&C II-654
Päts, Konstantin
GE:HR I-207
Patterson, Daniel T.
GE:Am I-533
Patterson, Haywood
GE:Am III-1588
Patterson, Robert Porter
GE:Am III-1783
Patterson, W. E.
GE:B&C II-752
Patton, George S.
GE:Am III-1715
GL:Am IV-1734

177

Paul III, Pope
  GE:ME I-91, 96, 143
  GL:Ren IV-1820
Paul IV, Pope
  GE:ME I-96, 153
Paul V, Pope
  GE:ME I-285
Paul VI, Pope
  GE:HR IV-1988
Paul VI, Pope (Giovanni Battista Montini)
  GE:ME III-1633, 1659
  GL:20 IV-1800
Paul of Aegina
  GL:A&M IV-1553
Paul of Tarsus. *See* Paul, Saint
Paul, Prince (Karageorgevich)
  GE:W20 I-444
Paul, Saint
Paul the Deacon
  GE:A&M II-1136
Paul, Alice
  GE:Am III-1513
  GE:HR I-339
  GL:AmW IV-1423
Paul, Les
  GE:A&M II-607, 632, 638
  GE:B&C III-919
  GL:A&M IV-1547
Paulding, James Kirke
  GE:Am I-481
Pauley, Jane
  GL:AmW IV-1428
Pauli, Wolfgang
  GE:S&T II-590, 800, III-992
  GE:W20 I-166
  GL:20 IV-1805
Pauling, Linus
  GE:B&C IV-1416
  GE:S&T II-926, III-1406
  GL:Am IV-1739
Paulinus
  GE:A&M II-1081
Paull, Lawrence G.
  GE:A&C V-2486
Paullada, Pedro Ojeda
  GE:HR IV-1796
Paulus, Friedrich
  GE:ME III-1472
Pauncefote, Sir Julian
  GE:ME II-1123
Pausanias
  GE:A&M I-237

Pavlov, Ivan Petrovich
  GE:S&T I-163, 179, 243
  GL:20 IV-1809
Pavlova, Anna
  GE:A&C I-187, 247
  GL:20 IV-1814
Paxson, Lowell W. "Bud"
  GE:B&C V-1909
Paxton, Joseph
  GE:ME II-799
Payne, Sereno Elisha
  GE:B&C I-168
Paz, Octavio
  GE:A&C III-1268, IV-1995
Peabody, Elizabeth Palmer
  GL:AmW IV-1433
Peale, Charles Willson
  GL:Am IV-1745
Peano, Giuseppe
  GE:S&T I-31, 143, 465
Pearl, Raymond
  GE:S&T I-433
Pears, Peter
  GE:A&C III-1296
Pearse, Padhraic (Patrick Henry)
  GE:HR I-178
  GE:ME III-1233
Pearson, Gerald Leondus
  GE:S&T IV-1487
Pearson, Lester Bowles
  GE:HR II-1079, III-1321
Peary, Robert Edwin
  GE:W20 I-63
  GL:Am IV-1750
Pease, Edward
  GE:ME II-660
Pease, Francis Gladhelm
  GE:S&T II-815
Pease, Joseph Albert, Lord Gainford
  GE:A&C II-712
Pease, William
  GE:B&C III-1128
Pecci, Vincenzo Gioacchino. *See* Leo XIII, Pope
Pecham, John
  GL:B&C IV-2071
Peche, Dagobert
  GE:A&C I-79
Pechstein, Max
  GE:A&C I-134
Peck, James
  GE:HR II-718
Peck, John
  GE:Am I-485

Peckham, Rufus Wheeler
    GE:B&C I-112
    GE:HR I-36
Pecora, Ferdinand
    GE:B&C II-656, 679
Pedersen, Knut. *See* Hamsun, Knut
Pedro I (of Brazil)
    GE:ME II-675, 722
Pedro III (of Aragon)
    GE:A&M III-1514
Pedro IV (of Portugal). *See* Pedro I (of Brazil)
Pedro Alfonso. *See* Alfonso, Pedro
Peebles, Mario Van
    GE:A&C V-2565
Peel, Lord Earl
    GE:W20 I-411
Peel, Sir Robert
    GE:Am II-778
    GE:ME II-669, 704, 737, 757, 764
    GL:B&C IV-2077
Peer, Ralph S.
    GE:A&C II-729
Peers, William R.
    GE:HR III-1555
Pei, I. M.
    GE:A&C V-2619
Pei, Mario A.
    GE:A&C IV-1898
Peirce, Charles Sanders
    GE:Am II-1077, III-1363
    GL:Am IV-1757
Peisistratus
    GL:A&M IV-1557
Pelagius
    GE:A&M II-946
Pelé
    GL:20 IV-1819
Pelham, Henry
    GL:B&C IV-2083
Pelham-Holles, Thomas (Duke of Newcastle)
    GE:ME I-437
Pelikan, Jaroslav
    GE:Am III-1604
Pelissier, Jean-Jacques (Duke of Malakoff)
    GE:ME II-813
Pellicioli Mauro
    GE:A&M III-1761
Pelloux, Luigi
    GE:ME II-1109
Pelz, Paul Johannes
    GE:Am II-1279
Pemberton, Israel
    GE:Am I-157

Pemberton, John Clifford
    GE:Am II-997
Peña-Irala, Americo Norberto
    GE:HR IV-2106
Peñaranda, Enrique Costillo
    GE:W20 I-289
Penck, A. R.
    GE:A&C V-2464
Penda
    GE:A&M II-1081
Pendlebury, John
    GE:S&T I-67
Pendleton, George
    GE:Am II-1128
Peng Dehuai
    GE:B&C III-1003
    GE:HR II-1015
    GL:20 IV-1824
P'eng Te-huai. *See* Peng Dehuai
Peng Zhen
    GE:HR IV-1983
Penn, William
    GE:Am I-157
    GL:Am IV-1763
Pennewill, Simeon
    GE:B&C I-69
Pennock, George A.
    GE:B&C II-437
Penrose, Boies
    GE:B&C II-476
Penry, Johnny Paul
    GE:HR V-2506
Penzias, Arno A.
    GE:S&T IV-1762
Peoples, David
    GE:A&C V-2486
Peoples, John
    GE:S&T V-2301
Pepe, Guglielmo
    GE:ME II-638
Pepin I
    GE:A&M II-1158
Pepin III
    GE:A&M II-1121, 1131
Pepin the Short. *See* Pepin III
Pepo, Bencivieni di. *See* Cimabue
Pepper, Claude
    GE:B&C III-1185
    GE:HR III-1172
Perceval, Sir John
    GE:Am I-182
Percival, Arthur Ernest
    GE:W20 I-457

Percival, Thomas
    GE:HR IV-2169
Percy, Charles
    GE:B&C IV-1522
Percy, Henry
    GE:A&M III-1640
Peregrinus de Maricourt, Petrus
    GL:A&M IV-1563
Perelman, S. J.
    GE:A&C II-648
Pérez, Juan
    GE:A&M III-1756
Pérez de Cuéllar, Javier. See Cuéllar, Javier
    Pérez de
Pérez-Minguez, Rafael
    GE:A&C V-2203
Pericles
    GE:A&M I-158, 226, 242, 276
    GL:A&M IV-1569
Perkin, Sir William Henry
    GE:S&T I-98
Perkin, William Henry
    GE:S&T V-1918
Perkins, Anthony
    GE:A&C IV-1855
Perkins, Frances
    GE:Am III-1643
    GE:B&C II-711, 792
    GE:HR I-486, 508, 514
    GL:Am IV-1769
    GL:AmW IV-1438
Perkins, George W.
    GE:B&C I-52
Perkins, Maxwell
    GE:A&C II-696
Perl, Martin
    GE:S&T V-2031
Perón, Eva
    GE:HR II-673
Perón, Juan
    GE:HR II-673, IV-1864, V-2280
    GL:20 IV-1829
Pérotin
    GE:A&M III-1410
    GL:A&M IV-1575
Peroz
    GE:A&M II-807
Perpich, Rudy
    GE:HR V-2256
Perret, Auguste
    GL:20 IV-1834
Perrin, Claude Victor. See Victor, Claude
Perry, Fred
    GL:B&C IV-2088

Perry, Matthew C.
    GE:Am II-884
    GL:Am IV-1775
Perry, Oliver Hazard
    GL:Am IV-1781
Persephone
    GE:A&M I-158
Pershing, John J.
    GE:Am III-1438, 1466, 1478
    GL:Am IV-1785
Perske, Betty Joan. See Bacall, Lauren
Persky, Bill
    GE:A&C IV-1908
Personick, Stewart D.
    GE:B&C IV-1647
Pertschuk, Michael
    GE:B&C IV-1658
Pescara, Marquis of
    GE:ME I-82
Peshkov, Aleksey Maksimovich. See Gorky,
    Maxim
Pestalozzi, Johann Heinrich
    GL:Ren IV-1825
Pestel, Paul
    GE:ME II-665
Pétain, Philippe
    GE:Am III-1715
    GE:ME III-1262, 1359, 1452
    GL:20 IV-1839
Peter I (of Russia). See Peter the Great
Peter II of Aragon
    GE:A&M III-1441
Peter II of Yugoslavia (Karageorgevich)
    GE:W20 I-444
Peter III (of Russia)
    GE:ME I-414, 464
Peter of Murrone. See Celestine V
Peter of Spain
    GE:A&M III-1524
Peter, Prince of Portugal
    GE:A&M III-1686
Peter, Saint
    GE:A&M II-589, 607, 638, 643, 681
    GL:A&M IV-1580
Peter the Great
    GE:A&M II-1173
    GE:ME I-364, 376, 432, 464
    GL:Ren IV-1830
Peter the Hermit
    GE:A&M III-1276
Peter the Lombard
    GE:A&M III-1338, 1400
Peter the Venerable
    GE:A&M II-1184

Peters, Curtis Arnoux, Jr. *See* Arno, Peter
Peters, Jane Alice. *See* Lombard, Carole
Peters, Jon
    GE:B&C V-1996
Peters, Thomas J.
    GE:B&C V-1815
Peters, William Wesley
    GE:A&C II-902
Peterson, Oscar
    GE:A&C III-1617
Peterson, Ottis G.
    GE:S&T V-2025
Peterson, Randy
    GE:HR V-2256
Petrarca, Francesco. *See* Petrarch
Petrarch
    GL:A&M IV-1585
Petree, Richard
    GE:HR IV-1993
Petren, Broc Arvid Sture
    GE:HR II-843
Petrov, Vasily Ivanovich
    GE:W20 III-1317
Petrus Helias
    GE:A&M II-1023
Petrus Peregrinus de Maricourt. *See* Peregrinus de
    Maricourt, Petrus
Pettigrew, Thomas F.
    GE:HR IV-1786
Petty, William. *See* Marquess of Lansdowne
Petty-Fitzmaurice, Henry Charles Keith. *See*
    Lansdowne, Fifth Marquess of
Peymann, Klaus
    GE:A&C IV-2126
Pfeiffer, Jane Cahill
    GL:AmW IV-1443
Pfitzner, Hans
    GE:A&C I-166
Pfleumer, Fritz
    GE:S&T IV-1746
Pflimlin, Pierre
    GE:ME III-1607
Pham Hung
    GE:W20 III-1243
Pham Van Dong
    GE:HR II-573
    GE:W20 III-1243
Phan Boi Chau
    GE:W20 II-696
Phelan, Edward J.
    GE:HR I-281, III-1509
Phelon, John
    GE:B&C V-1953

Pher, Alain
    GE:ME III-1683
Phidias
    GE:A&M I-276, 297
    GL:A&M IV-1592
Philadelphus. *See* Ptolemy Philadelphus
Philagathus, John
    GE:A&M III-1215
Philemon
    GE:A&M I-368
Philibert, Daniel
    GE:S&T V-2185
Philip (the Deacon)
    GE:A&M II-607
Philip I of Spain
    GE:ME I-40
Philip II (of France)
    GE:A&M III-1323, 1400
    GL:A&M IV-1598
Philip II of Macedonia
    GE:A&M I-338
    GL:A&M IV-1603
Philip II (of Spain)
    GE:ME I-153, 158, 162, 174, 180 189, 193,
        202, 220
    GL:Ren IV-1835
Philip IV (of Spain)
    GE:ME I-299, 304, 341
Philip IV the Fair
    GE:A&M III-1421, 1581, 1592
    GL:A&M IV-1609
Philip V (of Spain)
    GE:ME I-372, 400
Philip VI of Valois
    GE:A&M III-1620
Philip Augustus. *See* Philip II (of France)
Philip of Hesse
    GE:ME I-76, 91, 148
Philip of Swabia
    GE:A&M III-1436
Philip the Good
    GE:A&M III-1697
    GL:A&M IV-1614
Philip the Magnanimous
    GL:Ren IV-1840
Philippa
    GE:A&M III-1686
Philippe Emmanuel. *See* Duke of Mercoeur
Phillip, Arthur
    GL:B&C IV-2093
Phillips, John
    GE:A&C IV-2104
Phillips, Sam
    GE:A&C IV-1705

Phillips, Wendell
GL:Am IV-1790
Philo of Alexandria
GE:A&M I-210, II-612
GL:A&M IV-1619
Philolaus of Croton
GE:A&M I-194
Phips, Sir William
GE:Am I-169
Phleger, Herman
GE:W20 II-798
Phocas, Bardas
GE:A&M III-1215
Phung Thi Le Ly. See Hayslip, Le Ly
Piaget, Jean
GL:20 IV-1843
Piankhi
GL:A&M IV-1624
Piano, Renzo
GE:A&C V-2402
Picabia, Francis
GE:A&C I-349, 513
Picard, Émile
GL:20 IV-1848
Picasso, Pablo
GE:A&C I-156, 204, 337, II-1062, IV-1742
GE:Am III-1411
GL:20 IV-1852
Piccard, Auguste
GE:S&T III-963
Piccolomini, Enea Silvio. See Pius II
Pickens, Slim
GE:A&C IV-1989
Pickering, Edward Charles
GE:S&T II-557
Pickering, Timothy
GE:Am I-324, 350, 403, 408, 414
Pickering, William H.
GE:S&T IV-1583, 1734
Pickering, William Henry
GE:S&T I-291
Pickford, Mary
GE:A&C I-224
GE:Am III-1501
GL:AmW IV-1447
Pico Della Mirandola. See Della Mirandola, Pico
Picotte, Susan La Flesche
GL:AmW IV-1451
Picquart, Georges
GE:ME II-1075
Pierce, Franklin
GE:Am II-871, 884, 889
GL:Am IV-1796

Pierce, John R.
GE:S&T IV-1677, 1728
Piercy, Marge
GL:AmW IV-1456
Piero della Francesca
GL:Ren IV-1845
Pietro D'Abano. See Abano, Pietro D'
Pigafetta, Antonio
GE:ME I-68
Piguet, Robert
GE:A&C III-1346
Pike, Zebulon Montgomery
GE:Am I-467
Pilate, Pontius
GE:A&M II-601
Pilgrim
GE:A&M III-1210
Pilling, James Constantine
GE:Am II-1104
Pilyugin, Nikolai A.
GE:S&T V-1950
Pinchot, Gifford
GE:Am III-1374, 1390
GE:B&C II-464
Pinckney, Charles Cotesworth
GE:Am I-426
Pinckney, Thomas
GE:Am I-396, 456
Pincus, Gregory
GE:HR III-1290
GE:S&T IV-1512
Pindar
GE:A&M I-215
GL:A&M IV-1630
Pine, David A.
GE:B&C III-997
Pine, Seymour
GE:HR III-1479
Pinel, Philippe
GE:A&C IV-1877
Piñero, Emilio Pérez
GE:A&C V-2310
Pinkham, Lydia Estes
GL:AmW IV-1461
Pinkney, William
GE:Am I-564
Pinochet, Augusto
GE:HR IV-1725, 1747, 2186, V-2540
Pinola, Joseph
GE:B&C IV-1739
Pinsker, Leo
GE:ME II-1089
Pinter, Harold
GE:A&C III-1454, IV-1861, 1871

Pinzón, Martín Alonso
   GE:ME I-16
Pirandello, Luigi
   GE:A&C I-534
   GL:20 IV-1858
Pire, Dominique
   GL:20 IV-1863
Pire, Georges
   GE:HR II-1020
Pirelli, Alberto. *See* Pirelli family, The
Pirelli, Giovanni Battista. *See* Pirelli family, The
Pirelli, Piero. *See* Pirelli family, The
Pirelli family, The
   GL:20 IV-1867
Pirenne, Henri
   GL:20 IV-1872
Pires, Mario Lemos
   GE:HR IV-1835
Pisano, Andrea
   GL:A&M IV-1635
Pisano, Leonardo. *See* Leonardo of Pisa
Pisano, Nicola, and Giovanni Pisano
   GL:A&M IV-1639
Piscator, Erwin
   GE:A&C III-1410
Pisistratus
   GE:A&M I-158
Pissarro, Camille
   GL:Ren IV-1851
Piston, Walter
   GE:A&C I-508
Pitcairn, Major John
   GE:Am I-251
Pitoëff, Georges
   GE:A&C I-534
Pitofsky, Robert
   GE:B&C IV-1410
Pitt, William (the Elder)
   GE:Am I-200, 225
   GE:ME I-451
   GL:B&C IV-2098
Pitt, William (the Younger)
   GE:Am I-389
   GE:ME I-485, II-551
   GL:B&C IV-2103
Pittacus of Mytilene
   GL:A&M IV-1644
Pittman, Robert
   GE:A&C V-2475
Pitts, ZaSu
   GE:A&C II-593
Pius II
   GL:Ren IV-1856

Pius III
   GE:ME I-26
Pius IV
   GE:ME I-174
Pius V
   GE:ME I-174, 180
   GL:Ren IV-1861
Pius VI
   GE:ME I-516, 520
Pius VII
   GE:ME II-564
Pius IX (Giovanni Maria Mastai-Ferretti)
   GE:ME II-770, 775, 808, 892, 902, 923, 958,
      969, 978, III-1143
   GL:Ren IV-1866
Pius X (Giuseppe Melchiorre Sarto)
   GE:ME III-1143
Pius XI (Ambrogio Damiano Achille Ratti)
   GE:HR III-1113
   GE:ME III-1354
   GL:20 IV-1877
Pius XII (Eugenio Maria Giuseppe Pacelli)
   GE:ME III-1659
   GL:20 IV-1882
Pizarro, Francisco
   GL:Ren IV-1871
Pizarro Leongómez, Carlos. *See* Leongómez,
   Carlos Pizarro
Place, Francis
   GE:ME II-704, 741
   GL:B&C IV-2109
Placidia, Galla. *See* Galla
Planck, Max
   GE:S&T I-83, 260, III-1293
   GL:20 IV-1886
Planetta, Otto
   GE:ME III-1395
Plant, Robert
   GE:A&C V-2228
Plaskett, John Stanley
   GE:S&T II-815, 830
Plath, Sylvia
   GE:A&C IV-1850
   GL:AmW IV-1465
Plato
   GE:A&M I-318, 323, 328, 383, II-612
   GL:A&M IV-1650
Platt, Orville Hitchcock
   GE:Am II-1325
Plautus
   GL:A&M IV-1656
Player, Gary
   GL:20 IV-1891

Pleasant, Richard
  GE:A&C II-1036
Pleasence, Donald
  GE:A&C IV-1861
Plekhanov, Geori Valentinovich
  GE:ME II-1105
Plessis, Armand-Jean du. *See* Richelieu,
  Cardinal de
Plessy, Homer Adolph
  GE: Am II-1261
Pletho, Gemistus
  GE:A&M III-1723
Pliny the Elder
  GE:A&M II-653, 659
  GL:A&M IV-1660
Pliny the Younger
  GE:A&M II-659, 692
Plotinus
  GE:A&M II-823
  GL:A&M IV-1665
Plotius Tucca. *See* Tucca, Plotius
Plücker, Julius
  GE:S&T I-108
Plumer, Lord (Herbert Charles Onslow)
  GE:W20 I-231
Plumet, Charles
  GE:A&C II-654
Plummer, Christopher
  GE:A&C IV-2033
Plummer, Henry S.
  GE:Am II-1178
Plutarch
  GE:A&M II-686
  GL:A&M IV-1670
Poage, William R.
  GE:B&C II-840, IV-1567
Pobedonostsev, Konstantin Petrovich
  GE:ME III-1156
  GL:Ren IV-1875
Pocahontas
  GL:Am IV-1802
  GL:AmW IV-1469
Podhoretz, Norman
  GE:A&C IV-1929, 2163
Podrabinek, Alexander
  GE:HR IV-1909
Poe, Edgar Allan
  GE:Am II-725
  GL:Am IV-1807
Poetelius, Quintus
  GE:A&M I-253
Poff, Richard H.
  GE:B&C IV-1358

Poggio
  GL:Ren IV-1881
Pogosyan, Henry
  GE:HR V-2348
Pogue, William R.
  GE:S&T V-1997
Poincaré, Henri
  GE:S&T I-184
  GL:Ren IV-1886
Poincaré, Raymond
  GE:ME III-1340
  GL:20 IV-1896
Poindexter, William, IV
  GE:B&C V-1788
Poiret, Paul
  GE:A&C I-263
Poirier, Richard
  GE:A&C V-2283
Poisson, Siméon-Denis
  GE:S&T I-340
Poitier, Sidney
  GE:A&C IV-1650, 1795
Pol Pot
  GE:HR IV-1791, V-2459
  GE:W20 III-1212, 1346
Polanyi, Michael
  GE:S&T IV-1703
Polfuss, Lester William. *See* Paul, Les
Polge, C.
  GE:S&T V-2273
Polglase, Van Nest
  GE:A&C II-984
Poli, Robert E.
  GE:B&C V-1803
Polignac, Prince of. *See* De Polignac, Prince
Polk, Frank Lyon
  GE:HR I-287
Polk, James K.
  GE:Am II-748, 778, 818, 825, 831
  GL:Am IV-1812
Polk, Leonidas LaFayette
  GE:Am II-1225
Pollack, James Barney
  GE:S&T V-1944
Pollio, Alberto
  GE:ME III-1228
Pollock, Jackson
  GE:A&C III-1239, 1557
  GL:Am IV-1819
Polo, Maffeo
  GE:A&M III-1550
Polo, Marco
  GE:A&M III-1550
  GL:A&M IV-1675

Polo, Nicolo
  GE:A&M III-1550
Polybius
  GE:A&M I-453
  GL:A&M IV-1681
Polycarp
  GE:A&M II-681, 696
Polygnotus
  GL:A&M IV-1685
Pomare, Eleo
  GE:A&C V-2521
Pomeranchuk, Isaak Yakovlevich
  GE:S&T III-1129
Pomeroy, Wardell B.
  GE:W20 II-619
Pompaedius, Silo
  GE:A&M I-506
Pompeius Magnus, Gnaeus. *See* Pompey
Pompey (Gnaeus Pompeius Magnus)
  GE:A&M I-516
  GL:A&M IV-1689
Pompidou, Georges Jean Raymond
  GE:A&C V-2402
  GE:B&C IV-1353
  GE:HR III-1425
  GE:ME III-1648, 1683
  GE:W20 III-1146
  GL:20 IV-1902
Ponce de León, Juan
  GE:Am I-33
Poniatowski, Stanislas
  GE:ME I-469
Pontadera, Andrea da. *See* Pisano, Andrea
Pontiac
  GL:Am IV-1825
Pontius Pilate. *See* Pilate, Pontius
Ponzi, Charles
  GE:B&C I-324
Poole, Elijah. *See* Muhammad, Elijah
Poorten, Hein ter
  GE:W20 I-457
Pope, Alexander
  GL:B&C IV-2115
Popenoe, Charles B.
  GE:A&C I-469
Popham, Sir John
  GE:Am I-59
Popov, Aleksandr Stepanovich
  GE:ME II-1080
  GL:Ren IV-1891
Popper, Sir Karl Raimund
  GE:S&T II-664
Poquelin, Jean-Baptiste. *See* Molière

Porphyry
  GE:A&M II-731, 834
  GL:A&M IV-1695
Portal, Sir Charles Frederick Algernon
  GE:ME III-1461
Porter, Cole
  GE:A&C III-1404
Porter, Edwin S.
  GE:A&C I-57, 74
  GE:Am II-1333
Porter, Eric
  GE:A&C IV-2168
Porter, Katherine Anne
  GL:AmW IV-1474
Porter, Keith R.
  GE:W20 I-501
Porter, Nyree Dawn
  GE:A&C IV-2168
Porter, Paul
  GE:B&C II-833
Porter, Steven
  GE:B&C I-75
Pory, John
  GE:Am I-65
Posidonius
  GL:A&M IV-1700
Postumius, Spurius
  GE:A&M I-253
Poujade, Pierre
  GE:B&C III-1035
Poulenc, Francis
  GE:A&C I-435
  GL:20 IV-1907
Poulson, Norris
  GE:B&C III-1076
Pound, Sir Alfred Dudley Pickman Rogers
  GE:ME III-1446
Pound, Ezra
  GE:A&C I-314, 326, 445, II-539, 555, III-1443
  GE:Am III-1399, 1560
Pound, Robert Vivian
  GE:S&T IV-1640
Poussin, Nicolas
  GL:Ren IV-1897
Povey, Thomas
  GE:Am I-121
Powazinik, William
  GE:B&C IV-1647
Powderly, Terence V.
  GE:Am II-1152
Powell, Anthony
  GE:A&C III-1509
Powell, Dick
  GE:A&C II-925

Powell, John Wesley
    GE:Am II-1104
    GE:B&C V-1773
    GL:Am IV-1831
Powell, Lewis Franklin, Jr.
    GE:HR IV-1697, V-2320
    GE:W20 III-1279
Powell, Maud
    GL:AmW IV-1480
Powell, Ozie
    GE:Am III-1588
Powers, Francis Gary
    GE:W20 II-906
Powhatan
    GE:Am I-59
    GL:Am IV-1836
Pozsgay, Imre
    GE:HR V-2421
Prabhakaran, Vellupillai
    GE:HR IV-2068
Praeger, Otto
    GE:B&C I-357, II-493
Prandtl, Ludwig
    GL:20 IV-1913
Pratella, Francesco Balilla
    GE:A&C I-235
Prats, Carlos
    GE:HR IV-1725
Pratt, Orson
    GE:Am II-812
Pratt, Parley P.
    GE:Am II-812
Pratt, Richard T.
    GE:B&C V-1788
Pratt, Wallace
    GE:B&C I-385
Pratt, William Henry. See Karloff, Boris
Praxiteles
    GL:A&M IV-1706
Prebisch, Raul
    GE:W20 III-1206
Predock, Antoine
    GE:A&C V-2646
Preece, Sir William Henry
    GE:ME II-1080
Premadasa, Ranasinghe
    GE:HR IV-2068, 2174, V-2315
Prendergast, Maurice Brazil
    GE:A&C I-361
Preobrajenska, Olga
    GE:A&C I-247
Preobrazhensky, Yevgeny
    GE:B&C II-563

Prescott, William Hickling
    GL:Am IV-1842
Presley, Elvis
    GE:A&C IV-1705
    GL:Am IV-1847
Preston, Ann
    GL:AmW IV-1484
Preston, James E.
    GE:B&C V-2012
Preston, Robert
    GE:A&C IV-1752
Preston, Thomas
    GE:Am I-231
Preuss, Charles
    GE:Am II-795
Preuss, Hugo
    GE:ME III-1295
Price, Byron
    GE:Am III-1703
Price, Cecil Ray
    GE:HR III-1246
Price, Derek de Solla
    GE:S&T IV-1588
Price, Leontyne
    GL:AmW IV-1488
Price, Lonny
    GE:A&C V-2496
Price, Robert E.
    GE:B&C IV-1621
Price, Sol
    GE:B&C IV-1621
Price, Victoria
    GE:Am III-1588
Priestley, Joseph
    GL:B&C IV-2120
Priestly Writer, The
    GE:A&M I-96
Prieto, Indalecio
    GE:ME III-1368
Prieto, Manual Garcia. See De Alhuemas, Marquis
Prim y Prats, Juan (Marqués de los Castillejos)
    GE:ME II-945
Primo de Rivera, José Antonio
    GE:HR II-695
Primrose, Archibald Philip. See Rosebery, Earl of
Primus, Pearl
    GL:AmW IV-1493
Prince, Hal
    GE:A&C V-2213, 2433
Principal, Victoria
    GE:A&C V-2418
Prins, Marthinus
    GE:HR IV-1887

Prior, William E.
    GE:B&C V-1898
Priscian
    GE:A&M II-1023
    GL:A&M IV-1712
Priscilla
    GE:A&M II-632
Priscillian
    GL:A&M IV-1717
Pritzker, Jay A.
    GE:B&C V-1826
Proclus
    GE:A&M I-383
    GL:A&M IV-1722
Procter, William Cooper
    GE:B&C I-330
Prodbelsek, Frank
    GE:B&C V-1943
Prodicus of Ceos
    GE:A&M I-286
Prokhorov, Aleksandr Mikhaylovich
    GE:W20 II-881
Prokofiev, Sergei
    GE:A&C II-914, III-1388
    GL:20 IV-1918
Propertius, Sextus
    GL:A&M IV-1727
Prophet, The. See Tenskwatawa
Protagoras
    GE:A&M I-286
    GL:A&M IV-1732
Prothero, George Walter
    GE:W20 I-24
Protogenes
    GE:A&M II-872
Proudhon, Pierre-Joseph
    GE:ME II-897
    GL:Ren IV-1902
Proust, Marcel
    GE:A&C I-355
    GL:20 IV-1924
Prout, William
    GE:S&T II-471, 660
Prouvé, Jean
    GE:A&C II-1021
Proxmire, William
    GE:B&C IV-1358, 1384, 1454, 1595
Prunskiene, Kazimiera
    GE:HR V-2577
Psammetichus I. See Psamtik I
Psamtik I
    GL:A&M IV-1737
Psappho. See Sappho

Psellus, Michael
    GL:A&M IV-1741
Pseudo-Dionysius
    GE:A&M II-1011
Ptolemaeus, Claudius. See Ptolemy
Ptolemy
    GE:A&M II-712, 716
    GL:A&M IV-1747
Ptolemy Philadelphus
    GE:A&M I-353, 403, 413, 418
    GL:A&M IV-1752
Ptolemy Soter
    GE:A&M I-353, 403, II-924
    GL:A&M IV-1757
Publius Cornelius Scipio Aemilianus. See Scipio
    Aemilianus
Publius Cornelius Scipio Africanus Major. See
    Scipio Africanus Major, Publius Cornelius
Publius Cornelius Scipio Nasica. See Scipio
    Nasica, Publius Cornelius
Publius Cornelius Scipio Nasica Serapio. See
    Scipio Nasica Serapio, Publius Cornelius
Publius Curiatius. See Curiatius, Publius
Publius Quintilius Varus. See Varus, Publius
    Quintilius
Publius Sestius. See Sestius, Publius
Publius Sulpicius. See Sulpicius, Publius
Publius Terentius Afer. See Terence
Publius Vergilius Maro. See Vergil
Puccini, Giacomo
    GE:A&C I-29
    GL:20 IV-1929
Pucelle, Jean
    GL:A&M IV-1763
Pudovkin, Vsevolod Illarionovich
    GE:A&C II-701
Pufendorf, Samuel von
    GL:Ren IV-1908
Pugin, Augustus Welby Northmore
    GL:B&C IV-2125
Pujo, Arsène
    GE:B&C I-275
Pujo, Maurice
    GE:ME III-1386
Pulcheria
    GE:A&M II-963
Pulitzer, Joseph
    GE:A&C I-407
    GE:Am II-1243, 1284
    GL:Am IV-1853
Pullman, George Mortimer
    GE:Am II-1237
Puni, Ivan
    GE:A&C I-413

Punnett, Reginald Crundall
  GE:S&T I-270, 314
Purbach, Georg
  GE:A&M II-716
Purcell, Edward Mills
  GE:S&T IV-1496
Purcell, Henry
  GL:B&C IV-2131
Purdy, Jean M.
  GE:S&T V-2099
Pusey, E. B.
  GL:B&C IV-2137
Pushkin, Alexander
  GL:Ren IV-1914
Putnam, Howard
  GE:B&C V-1826
Putnam, Israel
  GE:Am I-267
Putnam, Rufus
  GE:Am I-306

Pu-yi, "Henry" (Hsüan T'ung)
  GE:HR I-474
  GE:W20 I-92
Puzo, Mario
  GE:A&C V-2265
Pyatakov, Grigori L.
  GE:ME III-1329
Pym, John
  GL:B&C IV-2144
Pynchon, Thomas
  GE:A&C V-2283
Pyrrhon of Elis
  GE:A&M I-471
  GL:A&M IV-1769
Pythagoras
  GE:A&M I-194, 383
  GL:A&M IV-1773
Pytheas
  GL:A&M IV-1779

Q

Qahtani, Muhammad ibn Abdullah al-
  GE:HR IV-2095
Qasim, Malik
  GE:HR IV-1898
Quadratus
  GE:A&M II-707
Quant, Mary
  GE:A&C IV-1824
Quesnay, François
  GE:ME I-485
Quinn, Anthony
  GE:A&C III-1596
Quiñones, José María Gil Robles
  GE:ME III-1368
Quintero, José
  GE:A&C IV-1726

Quintilian
  GE:A&M I-531
Quintilianus, Marcus Fabius. *See* Quintilian
Quintilius Varus, Publius. *See* Varus, Publius
  Quintilius
Quintín Lame, Manuel
  GE:HR II-737
Quintus Ennius. *See* Ennius, Quintus
Quintus Fabius Vibulanus. *See* Fabius Vibulanus,
  Quintus
Quintus Hortensius. *See* Hortensius
Quintus Marcius Rex. *See* Rex, Quintus Marcius
Quintus Poetelius. *See* Poetelius, Quintus
Quisling, Vidkun
  GE:ME III-1446
Quwatli, Shukri al-. *See* Kuwatli, Shukri al-

R

Raab, Kirk
  GE:B&C IV-1616
Rab
  GE:A&M II-985
Rabanus Maurus
  GL:A&M IV-1784
Rabbina II
  GE:A&M II-985
Rabelais, François
  GL:Ren IV-1919
Rabi, Isidor Isaac
  GL:Am IV-1858
Rabin, Yitzhak
  GE:HR V-2331
Rabinowitz, Jerome. *See* Robbins, Jerome
Rabuka, Sitiveni
  GE:HR V-2309
Rabuleus, Manius
  GE:A&M I-253
Rachmaninoff, Sergei
  GL:20 IV-1935
Racine, Jean
  GL:Ren IV-1924
Radbertus, Paschasius
  GE:A&M II-1164
Radek, Karl
  GE:A&C II-914
Radice, Anne-Imelda
  GE:A&C V-2608
Radner, Gilda
  GE:A&C V-2355
Rado, James
  GE:A&C IV-2121
Raeburn, Sir Henry
  GL:B&C IV-2149
Raeder, Erich
  GE:ME III-1446, 1467
  GE:W20 I-430
Ragni, Gerome
  GE:A&C IV-2121
Rahman I, Abd-al-. *See* Abd-al-Rahman I
Rahman II, Abd-al-. *See* Abd-al-Rahman II
Rahman III, Abd-al-. *See* Abd-al-Rahman III
  al-Nasir
Rahman, Sheikh Mujibur
  GE:HR III-1611, IV-2018
  GE:W20 II-1091
Rāi Bhoi dī Talvandī. *See* Nānak

Raiffeisen, Friedrich Wilhelm
  GE:B&C II-690
Raimundo
  GE:A&M III-1524
Rainey, Ma
  GE:A&C I-252, II-572
Rainolds, John
  GE:ME I-241
Rains, Claude
  GE:A&C III-1245
Raistrick, Harold
  GE:ME III-1335
Raitt, Bonnie
  GL:AmW IV-1499
Rajah, Rao Bahadur M. C.
  GE:HR I-469
Rakosi, Matyas
  GE:HR II-969
  GE:ME III-1595
Rakowski, Mieczysaw
  GE:HR V-2477
Ralegh, Sir Walter
  GE:Am I-46
  GL:B&C IV-2154
Ralph of Beauvais
  GE:A&M II-1023
Ralph of Royaumont
  GE:A&M III-1533
Ralston, Vera. *See* Miles, Vera
Ramachandran, Arcot
  GE:HR IV-2174
Raman, Sir Chandrasekhara Venkata
  GL:20 IV-1940
Rāmānuja
  GL:A&M IV-1790
RaMBaM. *See* Maimonides, Moses
Rambert, Marie
  GE:A&C II-1036
Rameau, Jean-Philippe
  GL:Ren IV-1930
Ramón y Cajal, Santiago
  GE:S&T I-1, 243, 380
Ramos, Fidel
  GE:HR V-2286
Ramsay, Sir Bertram H.
  GE:ME III-1456
Ramses II
  GE:A&M I-70, 75
  GL:A&M IV-1795

Ramsey, Frank Plumpton
GE:A&C I-518
Ramsey, James Andrew Broun. *See* Dalhousie,
First Marquess of
Randall, Clarence
GE:B&C III-1052
Randall, Jesse W.
GE:B&C III-964
Randall, Ruth
GE:HR V-2256
Randall, Vischer A.
GE:B&C I-396
Randolph, Asa Philip
GE:B&C IV-1495
GE:HR II-578, 601, 777, III-1200
GL:Am IV-1863
Randolph, Edward
GE:Am I-163
Randolph, John
GE:Am I-485, 539
Randolph, Peyton
GE:Am I-246
Ranke, Leopold von
GE:Am II-1184
GE:W20 I-54
GL:Ren IV-1935
Rankin, Jeannette
GE:HR I-190
GL:AmW IV-1504
Rankin, John
GE:B&C II-845
Rankin, William H.
GE:B&C I-396
Ransom, John Crowe
GE:A&C III-1169
Rantoul, Robert, Jr.
GE:Am II-785
Raphael
GL:Ren IV-1940
Rapp, George
GE:Am I-511
Rashad, Phylicia
GE:A&C V-2532
Rashid, Harun al-. *See* Al-Rashid, Harun
Rask, Grete
GE:S&T V-2149
Raskob, John Jacob
GE:A&C II-880
GE:Am III-1566, 1577
GE:B&C I-368, III-1164
Rasmussen, Knud Johan Victor
GL:20 IV-1945
Rathbone, Basil
GE:A&C III-1131

Rathbone, Eleanor
GE:HR I-442
Rathbone, Monroe "Jack"
GE:B&C III-1154
Rathenau, Walther
GE:A&C I-219
Ratramnus
GE:A&M II-1164
GL:A&M IV-1801
Ratti, Achille Ambrogio Damiano. *See* Pius XI
Ratti, Ambrogio Damiano Achille. *See* Pius XI
Ratu Ganilau, Sir Penaia
GE:HR V-2309
Ratu Mara, Sir Kamisese
GE:HR V-2309
Rauh, Joseph L., Jr.
GE:HR II-578
Raulston, John T.
GE:Am III-1549
Raup, David Malcolm
GE:S&T V-2120
Rauschenberg, Robert
GE:A&C III-1590, IV-2011
Rauschenbusch, Walter
GE:Am II-1195
GL:Am IV-1870
Rauschenbush, Paul
GE:Am III-1643
Ravaillac, François
GE:ME I-214
Ravel, Maurice
GE:A&C I-90
GL:20 IV-1950
Ravidat, Monsieur
GE:S&T III-1176
Rawlings, Jerry
GE:HR IV-2180
Ray, James Earl
GE:Am III-1927
GE:HR III-1419
Ray, Man
GE:A&C I-349, 513
Ray, Nicholas
GE:A&C IV-1640
Ray, Rammohan
GL:Ren IV-1946
Ray, Satyajit
GL:20 IV-1954
Rayburn, Sam
GE:B&C II-679, III-1122
GE:HR II-997
Raymond IV of Toulouse
GE:A&M III-1276

Raymond VI of Toulouse
  GE:A&M III-1441
Raymond VII of Toulouse
  GE:A&M III-1441
Raymond Lull. *See* Lull, Raymond
Raymond of Peñafort
  GE:A&M III-1491, 1544
  GL:A&M IV-1806
Razi, al-
  GE:A&M II-1179
  GL:A&M IV-1810
Read, Herbert
  GE:A&C III-1190, 1239
Read, William A.
  GE:B&C I-97
Reagan, John H.
  GE:Am II-1157
Reagan, Ronald
  GE:B&C III-1030, IV-1431, 1483, 1555,
    1727, V-1751, 1757, 1782, 1803, 1893,
    1933
  GE:HR III-1595, 1656, IV-2084, 2090, 2141,
    2152, 2209, V-2244, 2326, 2336, 2397,
    2443
  GE:S&T V-2372
  GE:W20 III-1302
  GL:Am IV-1875
Réard, Louis
  GE:A&C III-1324
Reasoner, Harry
  GE:A&C IV-2136
Rebay, Hilla
  GE:A&C IV-1806
Reber, Grote
  GE:S&T II-934, III-1113, 1193, IV-1539
Reberioux, Madeleine
  GE:A&C V-2588
Rebeur-Paschwitz, Ernst von
  GE:S&T I-340
Rebka, Glen A.
  GE:S&T IV-1640
Recceswinth
  GE:A&M II-1005
Red Cloud
  GL:Am IV-1882
Redding, Noel
  GE:A&C IV-2092
Redding, Otis
  GE:A&C IV-2104
Redl, Wolf R.
  GE:A&C IV-2126
Redmond, John Edward
  GE:ME III-1233

Reece, Gordon
  GE:HR IV-2024
Reed, David A.
  GE:B&C II-459
Reed, Donna
  GE:A&C III-1335, 1470
Reed, James A.
  GE:Am III-1507
Reed, Thomas Brackett
  GE:Am II-1273
Reed, Walter
  GE:Am II-1313
  GE:S&T I-73, 223, 249
  GL:Am IV-1887
Reenstra, Will A.
  GE:B&C IV-1647
Rees, Martin John
  GE:W20 II-835
Reeves, William Pember
  GE:W20 I-14
Refshauge, William Dudley
  GE:HR III-1644
Regan, Donald
  GE:B&C II-809
Reginald of Piperno
  GE:A&M III-1544
Regulus, Marcus Atilus
  GE:A&M I-408
Rehm, Albert
  GE:S&T IV-1588
Rehnquist, William H.
  GE:B&C IV-1449, 1704, V-1915
  GE:HR IV-1703, 2029
  GE:W20 III-1154
Rehoboam
  GE:A&M I-106
Reich, Steve
  GE:A&C IV-1979
Reichenbach, Henry M.
  GE:B&C I-11
Reid, Fergus
  GE:B&C I-180
Reid, Sir George Houston
  GE:W20 I-14
Reilly, William
  GE:B&C V-2034
Reimann, Walter
  GE:A&C I-486
Reiner, Carl
  GE:A&C IV-1908
Reiner, Rob
  GE:A&C V-2234
Reinhardt, Max
  GE:A&C I-145, 534

Reinsch, Paul Samuel
GE:W20 I-121
Reis, Johann Philipp
GE:Am II-1089
Reith of Stonehaven, First Baron
GL:B&C IV-2160
Reith, John Charles
GE:A&C II-712
GE:B&C II-758
Reitherman, Wolfgang
GE:A&C II-1053
Reitz, Dana
GE:A&C V-2480
Remark, Erich Paul. *See* Remarque, Erich Maria
Remarque, Erich Maria
GE:A&C II-767
Rembrandt
GL:Ren IV-1952
Remington, Frederic
GE:A&C I-304
GE:Am II-1243
GL:Am IV-1892
Remsen, Ira
GE:S&T V-2226
Renan, Ernest
GE:ME II-892
GL:Ren IV-1957
Renfrew, Colin
GE:S&T IV-1718
Renkin, Jules
GE:HR I-103
Rennenkampf, Pavel Karlovich
GE:W20 I-101
Reno, Janet
GE:HR IV-2101
GL:AmW IV-1509
Reno, Marcus
GE:Am II-1094
Reno, Milo
GE:Am III-1582
Renoir, Jean
GE:A&C II-1073
GL:20 IV-1960
Renoir, Pierre-Auguste
GL:Ren IV-1963
Renzetti, Nicholas A.
GE:S&T IV-1734
Resnick, Idrian N.
GE:HR IV-2130
Retherford, Robert C.
GE:S&T III-1293
Reuss, Henry Schoellkopf
GE:W20 II-872

Reuter, Ernst
GE:ME III-1543
Reuther, Walter P.
GE:B&C II-729, III-943, 1064, 1092
GE:HR II-766
GE:W20 II-572, 730
GL:Am IV-1897
Revere, Paul
GE:Am I-251
Rex, Quintus Marcius
GE:A&M II-626
Rey, Charles F.
GE:HR I-304
Reyes Basoalto, Neftalí Ricardo. *See* Neruda, Pablo
Reynaud, Paul
GE:ME III-1451
Reynolds, Burt
GE:A&C IV-1668
Reynolds, Gene
GE:A&C V-2271
Reynolds, George
GE:B&C I-385
Reynolds, Joseph J.
GE:Am II-1094
Reynolds, Sir Joshua
GL:B&C IV-2166
Reynolds, Richard, II
GE:B&C I-212
Reynolds, Richard Joshua "Josh"
GE:B&C I-57
Reynolds, Russel B.
GE:HR II-662
Rhazes, abū Bakr Muhammad ibn-Zakarīyāʾ al-Rāzi. *See* Razi, al-
Rhee, Syngman
GE:Am III-1823
GE:W20 II-676
GL:20 IV-1966
Rheticus
GE:ME I-138
Rhett, Robert Barnwell
GE:Am II-941
Rhoads, Charles J.
GE:HR I-497
Rhodes, Cecil John
GE:ME II-1128
GE:W20 II-981
GL:B&C V-2173
Rhodes, James A.
GE:HR III-1532
Rhondda, Lady Margaret
GE:HR I-442

Ribault, Jan
    GE:Am I-33
Ribbentrop, Joachim von
    GE:ME III-1433, 1440, 1522
    GE:W20 I-375
Ribeiro, Angelo D'Almeida
    GE:HR IV-2146
Ribicoff, Abraham A.
    GE:HR III-1206, 1267
    GE:S&T IV-1740
    GE:W20 II-856
Ricardo, David
    GE:ME II-629
    GL:B&C V-2180
Rice, Betsy
    GE:HR V-2256
Rice, Edwin W.
    GE:B&C I-17
Rice, John Ap
    GE:ME I-110
Rice, Joseph Mayer
    GE:Am II-1301
Rice, Tim
    GE:A&C V-2254
Rice-Wray, Edris
    GE:S&T IV-1512
Rich, Matty
    GE:A&C V-2565
Rich, Robert (Second Earl of Warwick)
    GE:Am I-91
Richard I (of England)
    GL:B&C V-2185
Richard II (of England)
    GL:B&C V-2189
Richard III (of England)
    GE:ME I-6
    GL:B&C V-2194
Richards, Ann
    GE:HR V-2512
    GL:AmW IV-1514
Richards, I. A.
    GE:A&C III-1169
Richards, James P.
    GE:W20 II-709
Richards, Keith
    GE:A&C IV-2027
Richards, Lloyd
    GE:A&C IV-1795
Richards, Willard
    GE:Am II-812
Richardson, Elliot Lee
    GE:W20 III-1188
Richardson, Henry Hobson
    GL:Am IV-1903

Richardson, Tony
    GE:A&C IV-1721
Richarte
    GE:S&T II-491
Richberg, Donald
    GE:Am III-1637
    GE:B&C II-516
Richelieu, Cardinal de
    GE:Am I-52
    GE:ME I-259, 270, 274, 278, 290, 299, 304,
        308, 353
    GL:Ren IV-1968
Richmond, David
    GE:HR II-1056
Richmond, Julius
    GE:HR III-1284
Richter, Burton
    GE:S&T V-2031
Richter, Charles
    GE:S&T III-1050
Richter, Hans Werner
    GE:A&C I-7, 214, III-1357
Rickenbacker, Edward (Eddie)
    GE:B&C II-752
Ricketts, Ed
    GE:A&C III-1138
Ricketts, Howard T.
    GE:S&T II-921
Ricketts, John Bill
    GE:Am II-1066
Rickey, Branch
    GE:HR II-712
Rickover, Hyman G.
    GE:B&C III-1196
    GE:S&T IV-1557
    GL:Am IV-1909
Ride, Sally
    GL:AmW IV-1519
Ridgway, Matthew Bunker
    GE:W20 II-584
Rienzo, Cola di
    GL:A&M IV-1815
Riesz, Frigyes
    GE:S&T I-325
Rietveld, Gerrit Thomas
    GE:A&C I-429, 458
Rifkin, Joshua
    GE:A&C V-2350
Rijn, Rembrandt van. See Rembrandt
Rikabi, Sabah al-
    GE:HR IV-1967
Riley, Charles Valentine
    GE:S&T II-640

Riley, Terry
    GE:A&C IV-1979
Rilke, Rainer Maria
    GE:A&C I-281, 396
    GL:20 IV-1971
Rimbaud, Arthur
    GL:Ren IV-1975
Rimsky-Korsakov, Nikolay
    GL:Ren IV-1980
Rinde, Herman
    GE:S&T II-775
Rinehart, Mary Roberts
    GE:A&C I-496
Ringer, Barbara
    GE:B&C IV-1626
Ringwald, Molly
    GE:A&C V-2527
Rintelen, Dr. Anton
    GE:ME III-1395
Ríos Montt, Efraín
    GE:HR III-1503, IV-1972
Ripley, George
    GE:Am I-654
Riqueti, Honoré-Gabriel. See Mirabeau, Comte de
Risberg, Charles "Swede"
    GE:Am III-1497
Risher, Carol
    GE:B&C V-2040
Risshō Daishi. See Nichiren
Ritchey, George Willis
    GE:S&T II-645
Ritchie, John Simon. See Vicious, Sid
Ritschl, Albrecht
    GL:Ren IV-1985
Rittau, Günther
    GE:A&C II-707
Ritter, Gerhard
    GE:W20 II-918
Rivera, Diego
    GE:A&C II-957
    GL:20 IV-1976
Rivers, Joan
    GE:B&C V-1928
Rivers, L. Mendel
    GE:B&C IV-1384
Rivette, Jacques
    GE:A&C IV-1710
Rivlin, Alice
    GL:AmW IV-1523
Riza, Ahmed
    GE:HR I-98
Rizzo, Paul
    GE:S&T V-2169

Roa y Garcia, Raul
    GE:W20 III-1251
Robards, Jason
    GE:A&C IV-1984
Robb, Charles S.
    GE:HR V-2517
Robbe-Grillet, Alain
    GE:A&C III-1481
Robbins, Jerome
    GE:A&C III-1274, IV-1731
Robbins, Lionel Charles
    GE:B&C III-914
Robeck, John de
    GE:W20 I-129
Roberson, Willie
    GE:Am III-1588
Robert de Courçon. See De Courçon, Robert
Robert de Luzarches. See De Luzarches, Robert
Robert of Arbrissel
    GE:A&M III-1276
Robert of Artois
    GE:A&M III-1496
Robert of Molesme
    GE:A&M II-1029
Robert, Aine
    GE:ME I-496
Robert, Cadet
    GE:ME I-496
Roberto, Holden
    GE:ME III-1673
Roberts, Evelyn
    GE:B&C III-925
Roberts, Frederick Sleigh
    GE:ME II-1128
Roberts, George R.
    GE:B&C IV-1641
Roberts, Kenneth
    GE:HR I-350
Roberts, Oral
    GE:B&C III-925
Roberts, Owen J.
    GE:HR III-1182
Roberts, Pernell
    GE:A&C IV-1800
Roberts, Richard
    GE:B&C III-925
Roberts, Thomas
    GE:ME III-1659
Robertson, A. Willis
    GE:B&C IV-1358
Robertson, Anna Mary. See Moses, Grandma
Robertson, Dale
    GE:A&C IV-1768

Robertson, D. H.
    GE:ME III-1406
Robeson, Paul
    GL:Am IV-1916
Robespierre, Augustin
    GE:ME I-529
Robespierre, Maximilien
    GE:ME I-529
    GL:Ren IV-1991
Robins, E. Claiborne, Jr.
    GE:HR V-2342
Robins, E. Claiborne, Sr.
    GE:HR V-2342
Robinson, Charles
    GE:Am II-889
Robinson, Edward G.
    GE:A&C II-839
Robinson, Edwin Arlington
    GE:Am III-1399
Robinson, Henry M.
    GE:Am III-1537
Robinson, Jackie
    GE:HR II-712
    GL:Am IV-1924
Robinson, Joan
    GE:B&C II-740
Robinson, John Hamilton
    GE:Am I-467
Robinson, Joseph Taylor
    GE:Am III-1667
Robinson, Kent
    GE:HR IV-1741
Robinson, Smokey
    GE:A&C IV-1790
Robinson, Wayne
    GE:B&C III-925
Robison, John
    GE:ME I-460
Robledo, Francisco Romero
    GE:ME II-1119
Robscheit-Robbins, Frieda S.
    GE:S&T II-795
Robusti, Jacopo. See Tintoretto
Rocco, Alfredo
    GE:ME III-1299
Roche, Kevin
    GE:A&C IV-1716
Rochefort, Joseph J., Jr.
    GE:W20 I-472
Rochefort, Victor Henri (Marquis de
        Rochefort-Lucay)
    GE:ME II-1053
Rochow, Eugene G.
    GE:S&T I-123

Rock, John
    GE:S&T IV-1512
Rock, John C.
    GE:ME III-1659
Rockefeller, Abby Aldrich
    GE:A&C II-782
    GL:AmW IV-1528
Rockefeller, James Stillman
    GE:B&C III-1159
Rockefeller, John D.
    GE:Am II-1116, 1206
    GE:B&C I-24, 206, II-551
    GL:Am IV-1930
Rockefeller, John D., Jr.
    GE:A&C III-1149
Rockefeller, John D., III
    GE:HR III-1579
Rockefeller, Laurance Spelman
    GE:B&C III-1254
Rockefeller, Nelson A.
    GE:A&C II-957, III-1149
    GE:Am III-1918, 1933
    GE:HR IV-1633
Rockefeller, William
    GE:Am II-1116, 1135
Rockhill, William Woodville
    GE:Am II-1296
Rockingham, Marquis of. See Wentworth,
    Charles Watson
Rodchenko, Alexander
    GE:A&C II-787
Roddenberry, Gene
    GE:A&C V-2260
Roddis, Louis H., Jr.
    GE:B&C III-1196
Roderick
    GE:A&M II-1105
Rodgers, Jimmie
    GE:A&C II-729
Rodgers, Nile
    GE:A&C V-2386
Rodgers, Richard
    GE:A&C III-1256
    GL:Am IV-1936
Rodgers, William F.
    GE:S&T II-573
Rodin, Auguste
    GL:Ren IV-1997
Rodino, Peter
    GE:B&C III-1229, V-1933
    GE:HR IV-1812, 1817
    GE:W20 III-1200
Rodney, George
    GL:B&C V-2203

Rodriguez, Fray Augustín
GE:Am I-40
Rodríguez, Jorge Alessandri
GE:B&C III-1207
Rodríguez, Simon
GE:ME I-96
Rodríguez de Francia, José Gaspar
GE:HR I-533
Roe, Jane
GE:HR IV-1703
GE:W20 III-1154
Roebling, Emily
GE:Am II-1060
Roebling, John Augustus
GE:Am II-1060
GE:S&T IV-1782
GL:Am IV-1940
Roebling, Washington Augustus
GE:Am II-1060
Roebuck, Alvah C.
GE:B&C I-6, II-487
Roebuck, John
GE:ME I-460
GL:B&C V-2209
Roentgen, Wilhelm Conrad. See Röntgen,
Wilhelm Conrad
Roerich, Nikolay Konstantinovich
GE:A&C I-241, 373
Roethke, Theodore
GE:A&C IV-1850
Roethlisberger, Fritz Jules
GE:B&C II-437
Rogan, Ralph F.
GE:B&C I-330
Roger of York
GE:A&M III-1375
Rogers, Ginger
GE:A&C II-984
GL:AmW IV-1532
Rogers, Harrison G.
GE:Am I-619
Rogers, Howard G.
GE:S&T III-1331
Rogers, Paul G.
GE:HR III-1561
Rogers, Richard
GE:A&C V-2402
Rogers, Ruby
GE:HR IV-2226
Rogers, Samuel Shepard. See Shepard, Sam
Rogers, Wayne
GE:A&C V-2271
Rogers, Will
GL:Am IV-1944

Rogers, William P.
GE:HR II-935
Röhm, Ernst
GE:HR I-491
GE:ME III-1391
GE:W20 I-311
Rohmer, Eric
GE:A&C IV-1710
Rohrer, Heinrich
GE:S&T V-2093
Röhrig, Walter
GE:A&C I-486
Rojas Pinilla, Gustavo
GE:HR II-737, V-2465
Roker, Roxie
GE:A&C V-2339
Rokossovski, Konstantin
GE:ME III-1472
GE:W20 II-577
Roland. See Cid, El
Roller, Alfred
GE:A&C I-7
Rolls, Charles Stewart, and Sir Frederick Henry
Royce
GL:B&C V-2216
Romanenko, Yuri
GE:S&T V-2316
Romanov, Alexander Nikolayevich. See
Alexander II (of Russia)
Romanov, Alexis
GE:ME I-364
Romanov, Michael
GE:ME I-247
Romanus IV Diogenes
GE:A&M III-1253
Romilius, Titus
GE:A&M I-253
Rommel, Erwin
GE:Am III-1720
GE:ME III-1467, 1491
GL:20 IV-1980
Romney, George
GE:HR III-1376
GL:B&C V-2221
Romulus Augustulus
GE:A&M II-980
Roncalli, Angelo Giuseppe. See John XXIII, Pope
Rönquist, Anders
GE:HR V-2529
Ronsard, Pierre de
GL:Ren IV-2002
Ronstadt, Linda
GL:AmW IV-1537

Röntgen, Wilhelm Conrad
  GE:ME II-1084
  GE:S&T I-118, 309, 356, 412, II-517, III-1336
Roos, John
  GL:Am IV-1973
Roosevelt, Eleanor
  GE:A&C III-1126
  GE:HR II-578, 783, 789, 918, III-1353, 1462,
    IV-1847
  GL:Am IV-1951
  GL:AmW IV-1542
Roosevelt, Franklin D.
  GE:A&C II-828
  GE:Am III-1472, 1566, 1582, 1609, 1615,
    1621, 1627, 1632, 1637, 1643, 1649, 1661,
    1667, 1674, 1680, 1686, 1692, 1697, 1703,
    1715, 1725, 1736, 1741, 1748
  GE:B&C I-146, 396, II-650, 662, 668, 679,
    685, 701, 706, 711, 781, 787, 792, 803,
    815, 820, 833, 845, 851
  GE:HR I-486, 497, 508, 514, 520, 545, II-567,
    578, 584, 595, 612, 635, 657
  GE:ME III-1406, 1477, 1486, 1491, 1501,
    1507
  GE:W20 I-260, 319, 368, 389, 404, 418, 438,
    465, 487
  GL:Am IV-1955
Roosevelt, Nicholas J.
  GE:Am I-471
Roosevelt, Theodore
  GE:A&C I-24
  GE:Am II-831, 1201, 1284, 1325, 1329, 1339,
    III-1353, 1374, 1390, 1399, 1405
  GE:B&C I-35, 86, 91, 107, 122, 128, 134, 146,
    264, 269, 275, 297, II-476
  GE:HR I-7, 25, 41, 46, 64, 81, 92, 126, 520,
    III-1573
  GE:ME III-1148, 1192
  GE:W20 II-790
  GL:Am IV-1963
Root, Elihu
  GE:Am II-1329, III-1531
  GE:HR I-7, 81
  GE:ME III-1192
  GL:Am IV-1968
Root, Elisha King
  GE:S&T II-542
Root, John Wellborn
  GE:Am II-1231
Roper, Daniel C.
  GE:B&C II-685
Rorem, Clarence Rufus
  GE:B&C II-557
Rorschach, Hermann
  GL:20 IV-1986

Rose, Fred
  GE:A&C III-1415
Rose, Sir John
  GE:Am II-1072
Rose, William Cumming
  GE:S&T I-46
Rosebery, Earl of (Archibald Philip Primrose)
  GE:ME III-1214
Rose-Marie
  GE:A&C IV-1908
Rosenberg, Alfred
  GE:A&C III-1217
  GE:HR I-389, II-667
  GE:ME III-1363, 1522
Rosenberg, Harold
  GE:A&C III-1557
Rosenberg, Lev. See Bakst, Léon
Rosenberg, R.
  GE:S&T V-2025
Rosenblum, Ralph
  GE:A&C V-2381
Rosenblum, Robert
  GE:A&C V-2608
Rosenfeld, Lev. See Kamenev, Lev Borisovich
Rosenstock, Sami. See Tzara, Tristan
Rosenthal, Ida
  GL:AmW IV-1547
Rosenwald, Julius
  GE:B&C I-6, II-487, III-1020
Ross, Diana
  GE:A&C IV-1790
Ross, Edward A.
  GE:Am III-1357
Ross, Fred
  GE:W20 II-842
Ross, John
  GE:Am I-666
  GL:Am IV-1973
Ross, Harold
  GE:A&C II-648
Ross, Marion
  GE:A&C V-2305
Ross, Nellie Tayloe
  GE:HR I-412
  GL:AmW IV-1551
Ross, Robert
  GE:Am I-533
Ross, Sir Ronald
  GE:S&T I-223
  GL:B&C V-2226
Ross, Roy G.
  GE:HR II-1096
Ross, Susan C.
  GE:B&C IV-1682

Ross, William Bradford
    GE:HR I-412
Rossby, Carl-Gustav Arvid
    GE:S&T II-675
Rossel, Louis
    GE:ME II-984
Rossellini, Roberto
    GE:A&C III-1228, 1596
Rossi, Bruno
    GE:S&T IV-1708
Rossi, Count Pellegrino
    GE:ME II-770
Rossini, Gioacchino
    GL:Ren IV-2007
Roth, Philip
    GE:A&C IV-2163
Rothchild, Paul
    GE:A&C IV-2038
Rothenberg, Susan
    GL:AmW IV-1556
Rothermere, First Viscount. *See* Harmsworth, Harold
Rothschild, Amschel Mayer. *See* Rothschild family, The
Rothschild, Carl Mayer. *See* Rothschild family, The
Rothschild, James Mayer. *See* Rothschild family, The
Rothschild, Lionel
    GE:B&C II-613
    GE:HR I-235
Rothschild, Mayer Amschel. *See* Rothschild family, The
Rothschild, Nathan Mayer. *See* Rothschild family, The
Rothschild, Salomon Mayer. *See* Rothschild family, The
Rothschild family, The
    GL:Ren IV-2012
Rothstein, Arnold
    GE:Am III-1497
Rotislav
    GE:A&M II-1173
Rotten, Johnny
    GE:A&C V-2299, 2360
Rouaix, Pastor
    GE:HR I-196
Rouault, Georges
    GE:A&C I-140
    GL:20 IV-1991
Rouhani, Fuad
    GE:B&C III-1154
    GE:W20 II-912

Rouher, Eugène
    GE:ME II-808
Rous, Peyton
    GE:S&T I-459
Rouse, James W.
    GE:HR IV-2174
Rousseau, Jean-Jacques
    GE:ME I-446
    GL:Ren IV-2019
Roux, Pierre-Paul-Émile
    GE:S&T I-6, II-567
Rowan, Dan
    GE:A&C IV-2115
Rowland, F. Sherwood
    GE:S&T V-2009, 2285
Rowland, Henry Augustus
    GE:S&T I-417
Roy, Raja Ram Mohan
    GE:HR I-401, II-731
Royce, Sir Frederick Henry, and Charles Stewart Rolls
    GL:B&C V-2216
Royce, Josiah
    GL:Am IV-1978
Rozelle, Alvin Ray "Pete"
    III-1298
Rozhdestvenski, Zinovi Petrovich
    GE:ME III-1148
Rubbia, Carlo
    GE:S&T V-2230, 2301
Rubens, Peter Paul
    GL:Ren IV-2024
Rubenstein, Jacob. *See* Ruby, Jack
Rubin, Jerry
    GE:Am III-1861
Rubinstein, Arthur
    GE:A&C IV-1818
Rublee, George
    GE:B&C I-269
Rubruquis, Guillaume. *See* William of Rubrouck
Ruby, Jack (Jacob Rubinstein)
    GE:Am III-1899
Ruckelshaus, William D.
    GE:S&T V-1982
Rüdenberg, Reinhold
    GE:S&T III-958
Rudkin, Margaret
    GL:AmW V-1561
Rudolf I
    GL:A&M IV-1820
Rudolf II, Holy Roman Emperor
    GE:ME I-148, 236, 250
Rudolf of Hapsburg
    GE:A&M III-1603

Rudolf, Karl August. *See* Steinmetz, Charles
  Proteus
Rudolph, Wilma
  GL:AmW V-1566
Ruegger, Paul
  GE:HR II-808
Ruether, Rosemary Radford
  GL:AmW V-1571
Ruffin, Edmund
  GE:Am I-371
Rufino, Brother
  GE:A&M III-1447
Rufinus
  GE:A&M II-752
Rufus, Tineius
  GE:A&M II-702
Rufus, Varius
  GE:A&M I-556
Rufus, William
  GE:A&M III-1291
Rugg, Harold Ordway
  GE:Am II-1301
Rugger, Paul
  GE:HR II-985
Ruhlmann, Jacques Émile
  GE:A&C II-654
Rukeyser, Muriel
  GL:AmW V-1576
Rulfo, Juan
  GE:A&C IV-1689
Rumford, Count (Benjamin Thompson)
  GE:ME II-560
Rumi, Jalal al-Din
  GL:A&M IV-1825
Runciman, Walter
  GE:ME III-1429
Rundstedt, Gerd von
  GE:Am III-1720
  GE:ME III-1451, 1456, 1491, 1496
  GE:W20 I-450, II-577
  GL:20 V-1996
Runge, P. K.
  GE:S&T V-2025
Runyon, Damon
  GE:A&C II-1011
Rupert, Prince
  GE:ME I-313
Ruppa, Wencelaus
  GE:ME I-250
Ruppert, Jacob "Jake"
  GE:B&C I-341
Rush, Benjamin
  GE:Am I-194

GE:HR IV-2169
GL:Am IV-1983
Rush, Richard
  GE:Am I-593
Rushdie, Salman
  GE:A&C V-2630
Rusk, Dean
  GE:Am III-1888
  GE:W20 II-955, 1036
Ruska, Ernst
  GE:S&T III-958, V-2093
Ruskin, John
  GE:A&C I-257
  GL:B&C V-2232
Russell, Sir Archibald
  GE:B&C IV-1606
Russell, Bertrand
  GE:A&C I-518
  GE:S&T I-184, 233, 465
  GE:W20 I-79
  GL:B&C V-2238
Russell, Bill
  GL:Am IV-1987
Russell, Charles Taze
  GE:HR II-629
Russell, Henry Norris
  GE:S&T I-265, 370, II-496, 585, 785
Russell, John
  GE:A&C V-2608
Russell, John. *See* Bedford, Duke of
Russell, Jonathan
  GE:Am I-522
Russell, Lord John
  GE:ME II-669, 704, 737, 757, 764, 929
  GL:B&C V-2243
Russell, Richard B.
  GE:HR II-997, III-1231, 1251
Russell, William Hepburn
  GE:Am II-925
Russolo, Luigi
  GE:A&C I-235
Rusticus, Junius
  GE:A&M II-725
Rustin, Bayard
  GE:HR II-601, 618, 718, 974
Rutan, Burt
  GE:S&T V-2336
Rutan, Dick
  GE:S&T V-2336
Ruth, George Herman "Babe"
  GE:Am III-1497
  GE:B&C I-341
  GL:Am IV-1993

Rutherford, Ernest
  GE:S&T I-93, 199, 285, 412, II-471, 507, 527,
    590, 660, 746, 851, III-973, 978, 1129
  GE:W20 I-246, 283
  GL:B&C V-2248
Rutledge, John
  GE:Am I-345
Ryazanskiy, Mikhail S.
  GE:S&T IV-1819, V-1928, 1950
Rydberg, Johannes Robert
  GE:S&T II-800
Ryder, Donald
  GE:B&C IV-1347

Rye, George
  GE:ME I-424
Rykov, Aleksei Ivanovich
  GE:ME III-1329
Ryle, Sir Martin
  GE:S&T III-1271, IV-1496, 1902
  GE:W20 II-899
Ryleiev, Kondraty
  GE:ME II-665
Ryzhkov, Nikolai I.
  GE:B&C V-2022

S

Saarinen, Eero
  GE:A&C II-610, IV-1716
Saarinen, Eliel
  GE:A&C II-610, IV-1716
Sabah, Jabir as-
  GE:HR V-2600
Sabath, Adolph
  GE:HR I-350, 383
Sabin, Albert Bruce
  GE:Am III-1835
  GE:S&T IV-1522
Sabin, Florence
  GL:AmW V-1580
Sacagawea
  GE:Am I-450
  GL:Am IV-1999
  GL:AmW V-1584
Sachs, Alexander
  GE:W20 I-389
Sachs, Henry
  GE:B&C I-75
Sachs, Nelly
  GL:20 IV-2001
Sachs, Paul
  GE:A&C II-782
Sackheim, Maxwell
  GE:A&C II-686
  GE:B&C II-504
Sackville, Viscount. See Germain, Lord George
Sadat, Anwar el-
  GE:A&C V-2625
  GE:B&C IV-1544
  GE:HR IV-1943, 2003
  GE:W20 I-145, III-1182
  GL:20 IV-2006
Saʿdi
  GL:A&M IV-1830
Safdie, Moshe
  GE:A&C IV-2081
Saffiotti, Umberto
  GE:B&C IV-1390
Sagan, Carl
  GE:S&T III-1245, V-1944
  GE:W20 II-827, III-1311
Sagasta, Práxedes Mateo
  GE:ME II-1003, 1119
Sagredo, Giovanni Francesco
  GE:ME I-285
Sahle Mariam. See Menelik II

Saigh, Patriarch Maximos IV
  GE:ME III-1633
Saigō Takamori
  GL:Ren IV-2028
Saint Bernard. See Bernard of Clairvaux, Saint
Saint Clare
  GE:A&M III-1447
Saint Colman
  GE:A&M II-969
Saint Columba
  GE:A&M II-969
Saint Columban
  GE:A&M II-969
Saint Finnian
  GE:A&M II-969
Saint Francis of Assisi. See Francis of Assisi,
  Saint
Saint Patrick
  GE:A&M II-969
Saint, Thomas
  GE:Am II-837
St. Clair, Arthur
  GE:Am I-324, 383
St. Clair, James D.
  GE:W20 III-1200
St. Denis, Ruth
  GE:A&C I-390
  GL:AmW V-1589
Saint-Gaudens, Augustus
  GL:Am IV-2003
St. Germain, Fernand J.
  GE:B&C IV-1595, V-1757
St. John, Henry. See Bolingbroke, First Viscount
Saint-Just, Louis de
  GL:Ren IV-2034
Saint-Phalle, Jacques de
  GE:B&C III-1102
Sainteny, Jean
  GE:HR II-683
Saionji, Kinmochi
  GE:HR I-81
Saito, Ryoei
  GE:A&C V-2603
Sakharov, Andrei
  GE:HR III-1177, 1549, IV-1847, 1852
  GE:W20 II-988
  GL:20 IV-2011
Saks, Gene
  GE:A&C V-2537

Śākyamuni. *See* Buddha
Saladin
   GL:A&M IV-1835
Salam, Abdus
   GE:S&T V-2014
Salamanca, Daniel
   GE:W20 I-289
Salan, Raoul
   GE:ME III-1607
Salandra, Antonio
   GE:W20 I-138
Salas, Octaviano Campos
   GE:B&C III-1241
Salazar, António de Oliveira
   GE:HR II-1119
   GE:ME III-1673
Saldanha, Duke of. *See* Oliveira, John Carlos
Salim, Salim Ahmed
   GE:HR IV-1736
Salimbene
   GL:A&M IV-1840
Salinas de Gortari, Carlos
   GE:B&C V-2072
Salinger, J. D.
   GE:A&C III-1493
   GL:Am IV-2007
Salisbury, Earl of. *See* William, Earl of Salisbury
Salisbury, First Earl of
   GE:ME I-224
   GL:B&C V-2254
Salisbury, Lord. *See* Salisbury, Third Marquess of
Salisbury, Third Marquess of
   GE:B&C I-41
   GE:ME II-1038, 1057, 1113
   GL:B&C V-2259
Salk, Jonas Edward
   GE:Am III-1835
   GE:HR IV-1998
   GE:S&T IV-1444
   GL:Am IV-2012
Sallust
   GL:A&M IV-1845
Salmerón, Alphonse
   GE:ME I-96
Salmon, André
   GE:A&C I-337
Salomon, Albert
   GE:S&T II-562
Salpeter, Mechel. *See* Gordon, Max
Saltzman, Harry
   GE:A&C IV-1913
Salviati, Filippo
   GE:ME I-285

Samarin, Yurii
   GE:ME II-866
Samish, Adrian
   GE:A&C IV-2017
Samoset
   GE:Am I-74
Samphan, Khieu
   GE:W20 III-1212
Sampson, Nikos
   GE:W20 III-1193
Sampson, William Thomas
   GE:Am II-1284
Samsonov, Aleksandr Vasilievich
   GE:W20 I-101
Samuel (prophet)
   GE:A&M I-90
   GL:A&M IV-1851
Samuel (rabbi)
   GE:A&M II-985
Samuel (tsar)
   GE:A&M III-1215
Samuel, Archbishop Athanasius Yeshue
   GE:W20 II-598
Samuel, Sir Herbert
   GE:B&C I-218
   GE:HR I-429
   GE:ME III-1324
   GE:W20 I-231
Samuel, Mar Athanasius Yeshue
   GE:S&T III-1298
Samuel, Marcus
   GE:B&C IV-1336
Samuel ibn-Tibbon. *See* Ibn-Tibbon, Samuel
Samuelson, Paul
   GE:B&C II-740
San Martín, José de
   GL:Ren IV-2045
Sanballat
   GE:A&M I-189
Sanborn, Franklin Benjamin
   GE:Am II-918
Sanchez, Ilitch Ramirez ("Carlos")
   GE:W20 II-1028
Sánchez, Oscar Arias. *See* Arias Sánchez, Oscar
Sanctorius, Sanctorius. *See* Santorio, Santorio
Sand, George
   GL:Ren IV-2040
Sandage, Allan Rex
   GE:S&T IV-1449, 1757
   GE:W20 II-899
Sandburg, Carl
   GE:Am III-1399
Sanders, Harland
   GE:B&C IV-1406

Sanders, Otto Liman von. *See* Liman von
  Sanders, Otto
Sandifer, Durward V.
  GE:HR II-1032
Sandino, Augusto César
  GE:HR I-137
Sandoz, Mari
  GL:AmW V-1594
Sandrich, Mark
  GE:A&C II-984
Sands, Diana
  GE:A&C IV-1795
Sandstrøm, J. W.
  GE:S&T I-21
Sandys, Sir Edwin
  GE:Am I-65
Sanford, Isabel
  GE:A&C V-2339
Sanford, John F. A.
  GE:Am II-900
Sanger, Frederick
  GE:S&T IV-1459, 1567, V-2115
Sanger, Margaret
  GE:HR I-184, 356, III-1290, 1579
  GE:S&T IV-1512
  GL:Am IV-2017
  GL:AmW V-1599
Sanguinetti, Julio María
  GE:HR IV-1715
Sanjurjo, José
  GE:ME III-1368
Sanness, John
  GE:HR IV-2051
Sansovino, Jacopo
  GL:Ren IV-2050
Santa Coloma, Count of
  GE:ME I-299
Santayana, George
  GL:Am IV-2023
Santorio, Santorio
  GL:Ren IV-2055
Santos, José Eduardo dos
  GE:HR V-2409
Santos-Dumont, Alberto
  GL:20 IV-2017
Sanzio, Raffaello. *See* Raphael
Sappho
  GL:A&M IV-1856
Saragat, Giuseppe
  GE:ME III-1538
Sardou, Victorien
  GE:A&C I-29
Sargent, John Singer
  GL:Am IV-2027

Sargent, Winthrop
  GE:Am I-306
Sargon II
  GL:A&M IV-1861
Sarich, Vincent M.
  GE:S&T V-2267
Sarkisian, Cherilyn. *See* Cher
Sarnoff, David
  GE:A&C I-469, III-1143, 1149, 1211, 1362,
    1383
  GE:Am III-1519, 1674
  GE:B&C I-363, 396, II-522, 640, 803, 827
  GE:S&T II-939, 1166
  GE:W20 II-669
Sarokin, H. Lee
  GE:HR V-2381
Sarraute, Nathalie
  GE:A&C III-1481
  GL:20 IV-2022
Sarson, Christopher
  GE:A&C IV-2168
Sarto, Andrea del. *See* Andrea del Sarto
Sarto, Giuseppe Melchiorre. *See* Pius X, Pope
Sartre, Jean-Paul
  GE:A&C III-1174, 1262, 1449, 1573, 1812
  GE:ME III-1482
  GE:W20 I-252
  GL:20 IV-2026
Satie, Erik
  GE:A&C I-435
  GL:20 IV-2031
Sato, Eisaku
  GE:B&C III-1276
  GL:20 V-2038
Satre, Pierre
  GE:B&C IV-1606
Satyapal, Doctor
  GE:HR I-264
Saul
  GE:A&M I-90
Saul of Tarsus. *See* Paul, Saint
Saulnier, Raymond
  GE:S&T II-600
Saunders, Clarence
  GE:B&C I-302
Saunders, LaVerne (Blondie)
  GE:W20 I-487
Saunders, Peter
  GE:A&C III-1551
Saunders, Robert
  GE:S&T IV-1608
Saunders, Stuart Thomas
  GE:W20 I-520

Saunders, William
GE:Am II-1043
Sauser, Frédéric. *See* Cendrars, Blaise
Saussure, Ferdinand de
GE:A&C IV-2075
GL:20 V-2043
Sauvage, Jean
GE:ME I-72
Sauvé, Jeanne
GL:AmW V-1604
Savage, Augusta
GL:AmW V-1609
Savage, Blair DeWillis
GE:S&T V-2164
Savić, Pavle Petar
GE:S&T III-1135
Savigny, Friedrich Karl von
GL:Ren IV-2061
Savimba, Joseph
GE:ME III-1673
Savimbi, Jonas
GE:W20 III-1219
Savio, Mario
GE:Am III-1912
Savonarola, Girolamo
GE:ME I-21
GL:Ren IV-2066
Savoretti, Piero
GE:B&C III-1293
Savoye, M. and Mme. Pierre
GE:A&C II-869
Sawyer, Charles
GE:B&C III-997
Sawyer, Roger
GE:HR II-902
Sawyer, Wilbur Augustus
GE:S&T III-1091
Saxbe, William
GE:B&C V-1821
Saxo Grammaticus
GL:A&M IV-1866
Sayan, Enrique Garcia
GE:HR II-985
Sayer, Gerry
GE:S&T III-1187
Sayers, Dorothy L.
GE:A&C I-496
Sazonov, Sergei Dmitrievich
GE:ME III-1240, 1245, 1340
Scalero, Rosario
GE:A&C III-1536
Scali, John
GE:Am III-1888

Scalia, Antonin
GE:B&C V-1915
GE:HR IV-2124, V-2506
Scaliger, Joseph Justus
GL:Ren IV-2072
Scalonge, Daniel
GE:ME I-405
Scalonge, Moses
GE:ME I-405
Scanlon, Terrence
GE:B&C IV-1426
Scarlatti, Alessandro
GL:Ren IV-2078
Scarritt, Winthrop E.
GE:B&C I-47
Scelba, Mario
GE:ME III-1538
Schacht, Horace Greeley Hjalmar
GE:ME III-1522
Schaefer, Vincent Joseph
GE:S&T III-1276
Schaeffer, Pierre
GE:A&C III-1629
Schaffert, R. M.
GE:S&T III-1013
GE:W20 I-382
Scharnhorst, Gerhard Johann David von
GE:ME II-472
GL:Ren IV-2084
Schaub, Johannes
GE:A&C V-2548
Schaudinn, Fritz
GE:S&T II-476
Schawlow, Arthur L.
GE:S&T IV-1672
GE:W20 II-881
Scheele, Leonard Andrew
GE:Am III-1835
Scheer, Reinhard
GE:ME III-1266
Scheidemann, Philipp
GE:HR I-241
GE:ME III-1295
Scheil, Vincent
GE:S&T I-169
Scheler, Max
GL:20 V-2049
Schelling, Friedrich Wilhelm Joseph
GL:Ren V-2089
Schempp, Edward
GE:W20 II-949
Schempp, Sidney
GE:W20 II-949

Schenck, Joseph M.
  GE:A&C II-691
Schenov, Ivan Mikhaylovich
  GE:S&T I-163
Scherer, Lee R.
  GE:S&T IV-1825
Scherman, Harry
  GE:A&C II-686
  GE:B&C II-504
Scheuer, James H.
  GE:HR III-1402
Scheyer, Emmy "Galka"
  GE:A&C II-583
Schiaparelli, Elsa
  GE:A&C II-979
Schiaparelli, Giovanni Virginio
  GE:S&T I-291
Schick, Béla
  GE:S&T II-567
Schiff, Dorothy
  GE:B&C IV-1636
Schiff, Jacob
  GE:B&C I-97
Schiller, Friedrich
  GL:Ren V-2095
Schiller, Karl
  GE:ME III-1690
  GE:W20 III-1097
Schippers, Thomas
  GE:A&C III-1536
Schirra, Walter ("Wally") M.
  GE:S&T IV-1723, 1803
Schlafly, Phyllis
  GE:HR III-1656
Schlamm, William S.
  GE:A&C IV-1683
Schlatter, George
  GE:A&C IV-2115
Schlatter, James M.
  GE:S&T V-2226
Schleicher, Kurt von
  GE:W20 I-311
Schleiermacher, Friedrich
  GL:Ren V-2100
Schlesinger, Bruno. See Walter, Bruno
Schlesinger, James R.
  GE:B&C IV-1555
Schliemann, Heinrich
  GL:Ren V-2105
Schlink, Frederick J.
  GE:HR I-527
Schloezer, Tatiana
  GE:A&C I-286

Schmertz, Herbert
  GE:A&C IV-2168
Schmidheiny, Stephan
  GE:B&C V-2061
Schmidt, Bernhard Voldemar
  GE:S&T II-884
  GL:20 V-2055
Schmidt, Helmut
  GE:W20 III-1257
Schmidt, Maarten
  GE:S&T IV-1757
  GE:W20 II-899
Schmidt, Paul
  GE:S&T III-1235
Schmidt, Walter A.
  GE:S&T I-320
Schmidt-Rottluff, Karl
  GE:A&C I-134
  GL:20 V-2059
Schmitz, Eugene
  GE:HR I-81
Schmüecker, Toni
  GE:B&C IV-1664
Schnitzler, William F.
  GE:W20 II-730
Schnabel, Julian
  GE:A&C V-2438
Schneider, Franz
  GE:S&T II-600
Schneider, Stephen Henry
  GE:S&T IV-1840
Schneider, William C.
  GE:S&T V-1997
Schneiderman, Dan
  GE:S&T IV-1734
Schneiderman, Rose
  GE:B&C I-191
Schoeffer, Peter
  GE:A&M III-1713
Schoenberg, Arnold
  GE:A&C I-166, 193, 367, 528, II-680, 816
  GL:20 V-2064
Schoenmaekers, M. H. J.
  GE:A&C I-429
Scholl, Roland
  GE:S&T I-98
Scholz, Georg
  GE:A&C II-631
Schönbein, Christian Friedrich
  GE:S&T I-280
Schopenhauer, Arthur
  GL:Ren V-2110
Schopf, J. William
  GE:S&T IV-1851

Schorr, Richard
    GE:S&T II-884
Schramm, Tex
    GE:B&C III-1298
Schreiber, Marc
    GE:HR III-1430
Schrieffer, John Robert
    GE:S&T IV-1533
Schrimpf, Georg
    GE:A&C II-631
Schrödinger, Erwin
    GE:S&T II-590, 741, 851, III-1030
    GE:W20 I-166
    GL:20 V-2071
Schroeder, Patricia (Pat)
    GE:B&C IV-1595
    GE:HR IV-1752
    GL:AmW V-1614
Schubert, Franz
    GL:Ren V-2115
Schuch, Ernst von
    GE:A&C I-151
Schüfftan, Eugen
    GE:A&C II-707
Schulhof, Michael
    GE:B&C V-1996
Schuller, Gunther
    GE:A&C V-2350
Schulze-Delitzsch, F. Hermann
    GE:B&C II-690
Schumacher, Kurt
    GE:ME III-1690
Schuman, Robert
    GE:B&C III-1081
    GE:HR II-873
    GE:ME III-1601
    GL:Ren V-2120
Schumer, Charles
    GE:B&C V-1933
Schumpeter, Joseph
    GE:B&C III-1020
Schur, Edwin
    GE:HR III-1497
Schurz, Carl
    GE:Am III-754, 1128, 1140, 1161
    GL:Am IV-2033
Schütz, Heinrich
    GL:Ren V-2126
Schwab, Charles M.
    GE:B&C I-29, 346
Schwann, Theodor
    GE:S&T I-380
Schwartz, Fred C.
    GE:Am III-1861

Schwartz, Herman
    GE:HR III-1633
Schwartz, Morton I.
    GE:B&C IV-1647
Schwartze, E. W.
    GE:W20 II-942
Schwarz, Berthold (Black Berthold)
    GE:A&M III-1509
Schwarzenberg, Karl Philipp
    GE:ME II-590
Schwarzert, Philipp. See Melanchthon, Philipp
Schwarzschild, Karl
    GE:S&T I-370, II-630, 884, III-1150, IV-1881
    GE:W20 II-835
    GL:20 V-2077
Schweitzer, Albert
    GE:HR II-907
    GL:20 V-2082
Schweitzer, Pierre-Paul
    GE:W20 III-1097
Schwerner, Michael Henry
    GE:HR III-1149, 1246
Schwinger, Julian Seymour
    GE:S&T III-1293
Scipio Aemilianus, Publius Cornelius
    GE:A&M I-453, 531
    GL:A&M IV-1871
Scipio Africanus Major, Publius Cornelius
    GE:A&M I-437, 448, 453
    GL:A&M IV-1876
Scipio Nasica, Publius Cornelius
    GE:A&M I-432
Scipio Nasica Serapio, Publius Cornelius
    GE:A&M I-481
Scleros, Bardas
    GE:A&M III-1215
Scopas
    GL:A&M IV-1881
Scopes, John Thomas
    GE:Am III-1549
Scott, Allan
    GE:A&C II-984
Scott, Dred
    GE:Am II-900
Scott, Elizabeth Leonard
    GE:S&T IV-1454
Scott, F. A.
    GE:Am III-1460
Scott, George C.
    GE:A&C IV-1989
Scott, Sir George Gilbert
    GL:B&C V-2265
Scott, Hazel
    GE:A&C III-1159

Scott, Hugh L.
GE:Am III-1438
Scott, James
GE:A&C I-13
Scott, Michael
GE:B&C IV-1611
GE:S&T V-2073
Scott, Oz
GE:A&C V-2370
Scott, Ridley
GE:A&C V-2486
Scott, Robert Falcon
GE:W20 I-63
Scott, Thomas A.
GE:Am II-1099
Scott, Sir Walter
GL:B&C V-2270
Scott, Walter Dill
GE:B&C I-80
Scott, Winfield
GE:Am II-825
GL:Am IV-2038
Scotus Erigena, Johannes. *See* Johannes Scotus, Erigena
Scotus, Johannes Duns. *See* Duns Scotus, John
Scotus, John Duns. *See* Duns Scotus, John
Scranton, William W., III
GE:B&C IV-1693
Screvane, Paul
GE:B&C IV-1472
Scriabin, Aleksandr
GE:A&C I-286
Scripps, William E.
GE:Am III-1519
Scruggs, Earl
GE:A&C III-1121
Scruggs, Mary Elfrieda. *See* Williams, Mary Lou
Scrugham, James C.
GE:HR I-373
Sculley, John
GE:B&C IV-1611
Seaborg, Glenn T.
GE:B&C III-1046
GE:S&T III-1181
GL:Am IV-2045
Seale, Bobby
GE:HR III-1348
Seaman, Elizabeth Cochrane. *See* Bly, Nellie
Sears, Richard W.
GE:B&C I-6, II-487
Sebastian
GE:A&M II-898
Sebastian I (of Portugal)
GE:ME I-189

Seberg, Jean
GE:A&C IV-1845
Sebokhut, Severus
GE:A&M III-1282
Secondat, Charles-Louis de. *See* Montesquieu
Seddon, Richard John
GE:W20 I-14
GL:B&C V-2276
Sedgwick, Adam
GE:ME II-678
Sedgwick, Theodore, III
GE:Am II-673
Sedgwick, William Thompson
GE:S&T I-401
Seeckt, Hans von
GL:20 V-2088
Seeger, Pete
GE:A&C II-810
Segni, Ugo of. *See* Gregory IX, Pope
Segovia, Andrés
GL:20 V-2093
Segrè, Emilio Gino
GE:S&T III-1101, 1181
Séguy, Georges
GE:HR III-1425
Seidelman, Susan
GE:A&C V-2443
GL:AmW V-1619
Seidensticker, Edward
GE:A&C IV-2147
Seidman, L. William
GE:B&C V-1991
Seko, Mobutu Sese
GE:W20 III-1219
Selassie, Haile. *See* Haile Selassie
Seleucus I Nicator
GL:A&M IV-1885
Self, Jim
GE:A&C V-2480
Selikoff, Irving J.
GE:HR V-2274
Selivanov, Arnold
GE:S&T V-2042
Seljuk
GE:A&M III-1253
Sellars, Peter
GE:A&C IV-1989, V-2599
Sellin, Johan Thorstein
GE:HR II-935
Sells, Elijah W.
GE:B&C I-308
Selznick, David O.
GE:A&C III-1154

Semmelweis, Ignaz Philipp
  GE:ME II-935
  GL:Ren V-2131
Sempronius Gracchus, Tiberius. *See* Gracchi, The
Sendic, Raul
  GE:HR IV-1715
Seneca the Younger
  GE:A&M I-531
  GL:A&M IV-1890
Senefelder, Alois
  GE:ME I-542
Senghor, Léopold
  GE:B&C IV-1589
  GE:HR III-1194
  GL:20 V-2099
Senior, Nassau
  GE:ME II-730
Sennett, Mack
  GE:A&C I-230
Serber, Robert
  GE:S&T IV-1767
Serebrov, Felix
  GE:HR IV-1909
Sergius
  GE:HR II-561
Sergius I, Patriarch of the Russian Orthodox
    Church
  GL:A&M IV-1895
Sergius I, Saint
  GL:A&M IV-1901
Sergius, Marcus
  GE:A&M I-253
Seripando, Jerome
  GE:ME I-143
Serra, Junípero
  GE:Am I-272
Serrano y Dominguez, Francisco
  GE:ME II-945, 1003
Sert, Misia
  GE:A&C I-474
Servatius, Robert
  GE:HR II-1108
Servetus, Michael
  GL:Ren V-2137
Sesostris III
  GL:A&M IV-1906
Sesshū
  GL:Ren V-2143
Sestius, Publius
  GE:A&M I-253
Seton, Elizabeth Ann (Saint)
  GL:Am IV-2052
  GL:AmW V-1623

Seurat, Georges
  GL:Ren V-2148
Severini, Gino
  GE:A&C I-235
Severinsen, Doc
  GE:A&C III-1623
Severus, Sextus Julius
  GE:A&M II-702, 1011
Sevier, John
  GE:Am I-396
Sewall, Arthur
  GE:Am II-1268
Sewall, Henry
  GE:S&T I-6
Sewall, Samuel
  GE:Am I-169
Seward, William H.
  GE:Am II-754, 877, 946, 980, 1037
  GL:Am IV-2057
Sexton, Anne
  GL:AmW V-1628
Sextus Julius Africanus. *See* Africanus, Sextus
    Julius
Sextus Julius Frontinus. *See* Frontinus, Sextus
    Julius
Sextus Julius Severus. *See* Severus, Sextus Julius
Seyewetz, Alphonse
  GE:S&T I-375
Seymour, Horatio
  GE:Am II-991
Seymour, Jane
  GE:ME I-123
Seynes, Philippe de
  GE:HR III-1212
Seysenegg, Erich Tschermak von. *See* Tschermak
    von Seysenegg, Erich
Sforza, Ludovico
  GE:A&M III-1761
  GE:ME I-21
  GL:Ren V-2154
Shabazz, Betty
  GE:A&C IV-2022
Shackleton, Baron
  GE:HR II-902
Shackleton, Ernest Henry
  GE:W20 I-63
Shafter, William Rufus
  GE:Am II-1284
Shaftesbury, First Earl of
  GE:Am I-132
  GL:B&C V-2282
Shagari, Alhaji Shehu
  GE:HR IV-2180
Shah of Iran. *See* Mohammad Reza Shah Pahlavi

Shah, Mohammad Ali
GE:HR I-52
Shah, Mohammad Zahir
GE:HR IV-2062
Shah, Mozaffar od-Din
GE:HR I-52
Shaka
GL:Ren V-2159
Shakespeare, William
GE:A&C III-1404
GE:ME I-208
GL:B&C V-2288
Shakura, Nikolai
GE:W20 II-835
Shalala, Donna
GL:AmW V-1632
Shamir, Yitzhak
GE:HR V-2331
Shammai
GE:A&M I-477
Shams al-Din Muhammed. *See* Hafiz
Shane, Charles Donald
GE:S&T IV-1454
Shange, Ntozake
GE:A&C V-2370
Shank, Charles Vernon
GE:S&T V-2020
Shankar, Ravi
GE:A&C IV-2104
Shannon, Claude Elwood
GE:S&T V-2200
Shapiro, Irwin
GE:S&T IV-1902
Shapiro, Karl
GE:A&C III-1443
Shapiro, Mel
GE:A&C V-2239
Shapley, Harlow
GE:S&T I-218, II-496, 502, 557, 655, 766,
790, III-1193, IV-1449
Shapp, Milton J.
GE:B&C IV-1664
Shapur I
GE:A&M II-807
Shapur II
GL:A&M IV-1910
Sharon, Ariel
GE:W20 III-1182
Sharp, Granville
GL:B&C V-2294
Sharp, Walter B.
GE:S&T I-396
Sharpey-Schafer, Sir Edward Albert
GE:S&T IV-1459

Shatalin, Stanislav S.
GE:B&C V-2022
Shatalov, Vladimir A.
GE:S&T IV-1891
Shatner, William
GE:A&C V-2260
Shaw, Anna Howard
GE:HR I-339
GL:AmW V-1637
Shaw, Arch W.
GE:B&C I-157
Shaw, Brewster H.
GE:S&T V-2256
Shaw, George Bernard
GE:A&C I-85, 534
GL:B&C V-2299
Shaw, Howard Van Doren
GE:B&C I-380
Shaw, John
GE:Am I-121
Shaw, Lemuel
GE:Am II-785
Shaw, Louis
GE:S&T II-895
Shaw, Theodore. *See* Wilson, Teddy
Shawn, Ted
GE:A&C I-390
Shcharansky, Anatoly
GE:HR IV-1915
Sheba
GE:A&M I-106
Shehab, Fuad
GE:W20 II-758
Shehan, Lawrence Cardinal Joseph
GE:ME III-1659
Shelburne, Earl of (William Petty). *See*
Lansdowne, Marquess of
Sheldon, Edward
GE:A&C I-343
Shelley, Mary Wollstonecraft. *See*
Wollstonecraft, Mary
Shelley, Percy Bysshe
GL:B&C V-2307
Shelton, Ian
GE:S&T V-2351
Shepard, Alan B.
GE:S&T IV-1698, 1723
GE:W20 II-934
Shepard, Sam
GE:A&C V-2413
Shepherd, Mark, Jr.
GE:B&C IV-1517
Sheppard, Morris (Sam)
GE:B&C I-357

Sherley, Joseph Swager
    GE:B&C I-229
Sherman, Forrest Percival
    GE:W20 II-676
Sherman, John
    GE:Am II-985, 1206
    GE:B&C I-206, 212
Sherman, Roger
    GL:Am IV-2062
Sherman, William Tecumseh
    GE:Am II-997, 1010
    GL:Am IV-2068
Sherrington, Sir Charles Scott
    GE:S&T I-243
Shertok, Moshe
    GE:HR II-814
Sherwood, Robert E.
    GE:A&C I-343
Shestack, Jerome Joseph
    GE:HR II-590
Shevardnadze, Eduard
    GE:HR V-2589
Shidehara, Baron Kijuro
    GE:Am III-1531
Shigeru, Yoshida
    GE:HR II-725
Shih Huang Ti. See Ch'in Shih Huang Ti
Shihab, Fuad. See Shehab, Fuad
Shingo, Shigeo
    GE:B&C IV-1716
Shinto, Hisashi
    GE:B&C V-1964
Shinwell, Emanuel
    GE:B&C II-857
Shipherd, John J.
    GE:Am II-708
Shirakawa, Hideki
    GE:S&T V-2063
Shire, Talia
    GE:A&C V-2265
Shirley, William
    GE:Am I-200
Shkolnik. See Eshkol, Levi
Shockley, William B.
    GE:B&C III-1009
    GE:S&T III-1304, IV-1528, V-1938
    GE:W20 II-612
Shoemaker, Eugene Merle
    GE:S&T V-2120
Shoemaker, Robert
    GE:HR V-2437
Shook, Karel
    GE:A&C IV-2110

Short, Walter Campbell
    GE:Am II-1697
Short, William
    GE:Am I-396
Shorter, Wayne
    GE:A&C IV-2153
Shostakovich, Dmitri
    GE:A&C II-787, 914, 1042, III-1388
    GL:20 V-2104
Shōtoku Taishi
    GL:A&M IV-1918
Shreve, Henry Miller
    GE:Am I-471
Shriver, David, Jr.
    GE:Am I-491
Shriver, R. Sargent
    GE:Am III-1877
    GE:HR III-1102, 1284
Shugart, Alan
    GE:S&T V-1923, 2240
Shuisky, Vasily Ivanovich
    GE:ME I-231
Shukairy, Ahmed
    GE:HR III-1241
Shultz, George P.
    GE:B&C IV-1466, 1489
    GE:HR V-2397
Shumway, Norman Edward
    GE:W20 II-1016
Shuskevich, Stanislav
    GE:HR V-2618
Shuttlesworth, Fred L.
    GE:HR II-974, III-1188
Shuvalov, I. I.
    GE:ME I-432
Siad Barre, Muhammad
    GE:W20 III-1317
Sibelius, Jean
    GE:A&C I-292
    GL:20 V-2109
Sibley, Charles Gald
    GE:S&T V-2267
Sibley, Hiram
    GE:Am II-930
Sibthorp, Colonel Charles
    GE:ME II-799
Sicinius
    GE:A&M I-221
Siddhārtha. See Buddha
Sidgwick, Henry
    GL:B&C V-2315
Sidney, Sir Philip
    GL:B&C V-2320

Siedentopf, H. F. W.
  GE:S&T I-159
Siegel, Martin
  GE:B&C V-1876
Siemens, Carl Friedrich von
  GE:B&C III-1035
Siemens, Ernst Werner. *See* Siemens family, The
Siemens, Friedrich. *See* Siemens family, The
Siemens, Karl. *See* Siemens family, The
Siemens, Sir William. *See* Siemens family, The
Siemens family, The
  GL:Ren V-2164
Sièyes, Abbé Emmanuel Joseph
  GE:ME I-506, 547, II-564
Siger of Brabant
  GE:A&M III-1564
  GL:A&M IV-1922
Sigismund
  GE:A&M III-1675, 1680
Sihanouk, Norodom
  GE:HR IV-1791, V-2459
  GE:W20 II-1083, III-1212, 1346
  GL:20 V-2115
Silcox, Ferdinand A.
  GE:Am III-1627
Silliman, Benjamin, Jr.
  GE:Am III-912
Sillitoe, Alan
  GE:A&C III-1454, V-2244, 2330, 2397, 2470
Sills, Beverly
  GL:AmW V-1642
Silo Pompaedius. *See* Pompaedius, Silo
Siloé, Diego de
  GL:Ren V-2170
Silone, Ignazio
  GE:W20 I-241
Silva, Colin de
  GE:HR III-1590
Silver, Albert De
  GE:HR I-327
Silverman, Belle Miriam. *See* Sills, Beverly
Silverman, Fred
  GE:A&C V-2244, 2330, 2397, 2470
  GE:B&C IV-1578
Silverman, Sydney
  GE:HR III-1316
Simenon, Georges
  GE:A&C I-496
Simeon Stylites, Saint
  GL:A&M IV-1927
Simmons, Jean
  GE:A&C III-1378
Simmons, Joseph
  GE:A&C V-2582

Simmons, Russell
  GE:A&C V-2582
Simmons, William J.
  GE:HR I-298
Simon. *See* Peter, Saint
Simon bar Kokhba. *See* Bar Kokhba, Simon
Simon ben Giora. *See* Ben Giora, Simon
Simon de Montfort. *See* Montfort
Simon Peter. *See* Peter, Saint
Simon, Herbert A.
  GE:B&C III-890
Simon, Sir John Allsebrook
  GE:W20 I-276
Simon, Melvin
  GE:B&C I-380
Simon, Neil
  GE:A&C V-2537
Simon, Paul
  GE:HR V-2364
Simon, Sam
  GE:A&C V-2652
Simonides of Ceos
  GE:A&M I-215
Simons, Elwyn L.
  GE:S&T IV-1814
Simons, Henry C.
  GE:B&C III-931
Simović, Dušan
  GE:W20 I-444
Simplicius
  GE:A&M II-989
Simpson, Alan
  GE:B&C V-1933
Simpson, James Y.
  GE:ME II-935
Simpson, John A.
  GE:S&T IV-1577, V-1956
Simpson, Wallis Warfield
  GE:ME III-1420
Sin, Jaime
  GE:HR III-1680, IV-2198
Sinatra, Dolly
  GE:A&C III-1250
Sinatra, Frank
  GE:A&C III-1250
Sinclair, Sir Archibald
  GE:ME III-1461
Sinclair, Harry F.
  GE:Am III-1525
  GE:B&C II-464
Sinclair, Upton
  GE:Am III-1353
  GE:B&C I-107, 128

GE:HR I-46, 64
GE:W20 I-241, II-942
Sinegal, James D.
  GE:B&C IV-1621
Singer, Alma
  GE:A&C V-2423
Singer, Isaac Bashevis
  GE:A&C V-2423
Singer, Isaac Merrit
  GE:Am III-837
Singer, Israel Joshua
  GE:A&C V-2423
Singer, Saul
  GE:B&C II-603
Singh, Beant
  GE:HR IV-2232
Singh, Satwant
  GE:HR IV-2232
Singh, Udham
  GE:HR I-264
Singh, Vishwanath Pratap
  GE:HR V-2426
Singleton, John
  GE:A&C V-2565
Sinnott, Michael. *See* Sennett, Mack
Sinsheimer, Robert L.
  GE:S&T IV-1857
Sipes-Metzler, Paige
  GE:HR V-2437
Sipila, Helvi
  GE:HR II-885, III-1391, IV-1796, 2057
Siqueiros, David Alfaro
  GE:A&C II-957
Sirhan, Sirhan Bishara
  GE:Am III-1927
Sirica, John Joseph
  GE:W20 III-1131, 1200
Siricius, Saint
  GE:A&M II-914, III-1257
  GL:A&M IV-1933
Sirota, Beate
  GE:HR II-725
Sisulu, Walter
  GE:HR V-2559
Sithole, Ndabaningi
  GE:HR III-1224
  GE:ME III-1642
  GE:W20 II-981
Sitter, Willem de
  GE:S&T II-684, 766
Sitting Bull
  GE:Am II-1094
  GL:Am V-2075

Śivajī
  GL:Ren V-2175
Sjostrand, Osten
  GE:A&C V-2594
Skellett, Albert Melvin
  GE:S&T II-934
Skelton, Red
  GE:A&C III-1520
Skidmore, Thomas
  GE:Am I-582
Skinner, Hugh. *See* Laing, Hugh
Skinner, B. F.
  GL:Am V-2080
Skolem, Thoralf Albert
  GE:S&T I-233
Skouras, Spyros
  GE:A&C III-1307
Skryabin. *See* Molotov, Vyacheslav
Skrzynecki, Jan
  GE:ME II-691
Slater, John C.
  GE:S&T II-926
Slater, Montagu
  GE:A&C III-1296
Slater, Samuel
  GE:Am I-362
  GL:Am V-2086
Slattery, Harry A.
  GE:Am III-1525
Slavata, Count Wilhelm
  GE:ME I-250
Slayton, Donald K. (Deke)
  GE:S&T IV-1723
Sledd, James
  GE:A&C IV-1898
Slidell, John
  GE:Am II-825
Slim, First Viscount
  GL:B&C V-2326
Slipher, Earl Carl
  GE:S&T I-291
Slipher, Vesto Melvin
  GE:S&T I-213, 291, II-502, 689, 878
Sloan, Alfred P., Jr.
  GE:B&C I-368, II-419, 533, III-943, 1020
Sloan, David
  GE:S&T III-953
Sloan, John French
  GE:A&C II-885
Sloane, Sir Hans
  GE:ME I-424
Slocum, Henry Warner
  GE:Am II-1010

Slovo, Joe
  GE:HR V-2304
Sluter, Claus
  GL:A&M IV-1938
Sly and the Family Stone
  GE:A&C IV-2180
Small, Albion W.
  GE:Am III-1357
Smalls, Charlie
  GE:A&C V-2334
Smeal, Eleanor
  GE:HR III-1656
Smedley, Agnes
  GL:AmW V-1647
Smetona, Antanas
  GE:HR I-207
Smith, Adam
  GE:ME I-424, 485, II-629
  GL:B&C V-2332
Smith, Alfred E.
  GE:A&C II-880
  GE:Am III-1566
  GE:B&C I-191
  GE:HR I-486
  GE:S&T II-906
  GL:Am V-2091
Smith, Bessie
  GE:A&C I-252, II-572, 670
  GL:AmW V-1652
Smith, Bradford Adelbert
  GE:S&T V-1944, 2082, 2104
Smith, Bradford, Jr.
  GE:B&C III-964
Smith, C. R.
  GE:B&C II-752
Smith, David
  GE:A&C II-1001
Smith, E. Graham
  GE:S&T III-1271
Smith, Edward J.
  GE:S&T V-1956
Smith, Francis
  GE:Am I-251
Smith, Francis Ormand Jonathan
  GE:Am II-742
Smith, Fred
  GE:B&C IV-1538
Smith, Geoffrey L.
  GE:S&T V-2326
Smith, George
  GE:S&T I-169
Smith, Gerrit
  GE:Am II-918
Smith, Gladys Louise. See Pickford, Mary

Smith, H. Alexander
  GE:W20 II-703
Smith, Harold V.
  GE:B&C III-964
Smith, Harrison
  GE:A&C II-805
Smith, Henry Babington
  GE:B&C I-218
Smith, Herbert
  GE:B&C II-510
  GE:HR I-429
Smith, Howard K.
  GE:Am III-1871
  GE:HR III-1479
Smith, Hugh
  GE:S&T III-1091
Smith, Hugh Oliver
  GE:S&T V-1987
Smith, Ian
  GE:HR III-1224
  GE:ME III-1642
  GE:W20 II-981
Smith, Jedediah Strong
  GE:Am I-619
Smith, John
  GE:Am I-59
  GL:Am V-2096
Smith, Joseph
  GL:Am V-2101
Smith, June Edith
  GE:A&C II-963
Smith, Kate
  GE:A&C II-828
Smith, Lula Carson. See McCullers, Carson
Smith, Mamie
  GE:A&C II-572
Smith, Margaret Chase
  GE:Am III-1817
  GL:Am V-2106
  GL:AmW V-1657
Smith, Oliver
  GE:A&C III-1234, 1274
Smith, Oliver P.
  GE:W20 II-676
Smith, Raymond W.
  GE:B&C V-2066
Smith, Robert L.
  GE:S&T IV-1645
Smith, Ron
  GE:B&C III-925
Smith, Solomon
  GE:ME I-405
Smith, Theobald
  GL:Am V-2111

Smith, W. A. "Uncle Billy"
  GE:Am II-912
Smithmeyer, John L.
  GE:Am II-1279
Smithson, James
  GE:Am II-831
Smoot, Reed
  GE:B&C II-591
Smouluchowski, Max von
  GE:S&T I-159
Smuts, Jan Christian
  GE:HR I-270, 453, II-861
  GE:ME III-1289
  GE:W20 I-87
  GL:B&C V-2338
Smyer, Sidney
  GE:HR III-1188
Smythe, Sir Thomas
  GE:Am I-59
Snaith, William T.
  GE:A&C II-777
Snellman, Johan Vilhelm
  GE:HR I-70, 212
Snezhnevsky, Andrei
  GE:HR IV-1909, 1926
Snorri Sturluson
  GL:A&M IV-1943
Snyder, Gary
  GE:A&C III-1460
Snyder, Hartland S.
  GE:S&T III-1150
Snyder, Howard
  GE:S&T II-453
Snyder, John W.
  GE:Am III-1759
Snyder, Mitch
  GE:HR V-2326
Snyder, Ralph
  GE:B&C III-959
Soares, Mario
  GE:ME III-1673
Sobieski. See John III Sobieski
Sobukwe, Robert
  GE:W20 III-1272
Socarides, Charles
  GE:HR IV-1741
Socrates
  GE:A&M I-318, 323, 328
  GL:A&M V-1949
Soddy, Frederick
  GE:S&T I-199, II-590
Soderblom, Laurence
  GE:S&T V-2082

Söderblom, Nathan
  GE:ME III-1550
  GL:20 V-2120
Soffen, Gerald A.
  GE:S&T V-2052
Solomon
  GE:A&M I-101, 106
  GL:A&M V-1956
Solomon, Anthony M.
  GE:B&C IV-1670
Solomon, Aubrey. See Eban, Abba
Solomon ibn-Gabirol. See Ibn Gabirol, Solomon
Solon
  GE:A&M I-168
  GL:A&M V-1962
Solovyov, Vladimir
  GE:A&C I-286
  GE:S&T V-2316
Solzhenitsyn, Aleksandr
  GE:A&C V-2277
  GE:HR IV-1764
  GE:W20 II-988
  GL:20 V-2124
Sombart, Werner
  GE:W20 I-38
Somers, Sir George
  GE:Am I-59
Sommerfeld, Arnold
  GE:S&T II-800
Somoza Debayle, Anastasio
  GE:HR I-137, IV-2035
Somoza Debayle, Luis
  GE:HR I-137
Somoza García, Anastasio
  GE:HR I-137
Son Sann
  GE:HR V-2459
Sondheim, Stephen
  GE:A&C IV-1731, V-2213, 2433
Sones, F. Mason
  GE:S&T IV-1835
Sontag, Susan
  GL:AmW V-1662
Soong, Tsu-wên
  GE:Am III-1764
Sophia, Electress of Hanover
  GE:ME I-385
Sophia (Zöe) Palaeologus. See Palaeologus, Sophia
Sophocles
  GL:A&M V-1967
Sorel, Georges
  GL:20 V-2130

Sorensen, Charles E.
  GE:Am III-1421
  GE:B&C I-234
Sorokin, Peter P.
  GE:S&T V-2025
Soschka, Cyrill
  GE:A&C II-767
Sosigenes
  GE:A&M I-536
  GL:A&M V-1972
Sostratus of Cnidus
  GE:A&M I-353
Sōtatsu
  GL:Ren V-2181
Sotelo, José Calvo
  GE:ME III-1416
Soter. See Ptolemy Soter
Soto, Hernando de
  GE:Am I-33
  GL:Am V-2116
Sousa, John Philip
  GL:Am V-2122
Sôustelle, Jacques
  GE:ME III-1607
Southampton, Fourth Earl of (Thomas
    Wriothesley)
  GE:Am I-121
Soyinka, Wole
  GE:A&C V-2594
  GL:20 V-2135
Spaak, Charles
  GE:A&C II-1073
Spaak, Paul-Henri
  GE:B&C III-1081
  GE:HR II-678, 849
  GE:ME III-1601, 1648
  GL:20 V-2140
Spadafora, Skip
  GE:B&C V-1854
Spallanzani, Lazzaro
  GE:S&T I-113
  GL:Ren V-2186
Spargo, John
  GE:HR I-131
Sparkman, John Jackson
  GE:B&C III-1107
Sparks, Jared
  GE:Am I-570, II-673, 801
Speer, Albert
  GE:HR II-667
Speer, Edgar B.
  GE:B&C IV-1670
Speer, Roy
  GE:B&C V-1909

Speke, John Hanning
  GL:B&C V-2343
Spelling, Aaron
  GE:A&C V-2330
Spencer, George John (Viscount Althorp)
  GE:ME II-730
Spencer, Herbert
  GE:A&C I-161
  GE:Am II-1167
  GE:B&C I-80, 112
  GL:B&C V-2347
Spender, Stephen
  GE:A&C II-857
Spengler, Murray
  GE:S&T I-88
Spengler, Oswald
  GE:ME III-1279
Spenser, Edmund
  GL:B&C V-2352
Speransky, Mikhail Mikhaylovich
  GL:Ren V-2192
Sperrle, Hugo
  GE:W20 I-430
Sperry, Elmer Ambrose
  GE:S&T I-303
Sperry, Roger W.
  GE:S&T IV-1635
Spewack, Bella
  GE:A&C III-1404
Spewack, Samuel
  GE:A&C III-1404
Spiech, John A.
  GE:B&C V-1898
Spielberg, Steven
  GE:A&C V-2491
Spinoza, Baruch
  GL:Ren V-2196
Spitzer, Robert L.
  GE:HR IV-1741
Spitzmüller, Alexander
  GE:B&C II-613
Spofford, Ainsworth Rand
  GE:Am II-1279
Spooner, John
  GE:Am II-1325, 1339
Sprague, Thomas L.
  GE:Am III-1731
Springsteen, Bruce
  GE:A&C V-2325
Spruance, Raymond Ames
  GE:W20 I-472
Spurius Postumius. See Postumius, Spurius
Squadrille, Edward F.
  GE:HR II-1020

Squanto
GE:Am I-74
Squier, George O.
GE:B&C II-674
Ssu-ma Ch'ien
GL:A&M V-1977
Ssu-ma Kuang
GL:A&M V-1983
Stadtman, Kenneth L.
GE:S&T V-2357
Staël, Madame de
GL:Ren V-2202
Stafford, Robert T.
GE:HR IV-2084
Stafford, Thomas P.
GE:S&T IV-1803
Stagg, Francis
GE:HR IV-1870
Stahl, Georg Ernst
GL:Ren V-2208
Ståhlberg, Kaarlo Juho
GE:HR I-212
Stainer, Leslie. See Howard, Leslie
Stais, Spyridon
GE:S&T IV-1588
Stalin, Joseph
GE:A&C II-544, 908, 914, 1042, III-1388,
V-2277
GE:Am III-1736, 1741, 1748, 1794, 1806
GE:B&C I-374, II-563
GE:HR I-218, 503, 561, II-567, 612, 657, 771,
795, 952, III-1177, V-2249, 2298, 2348
GE:ME III-1271, 1329, 1347, 1411, 1416,
1433, 1440, 1472, 1477, 1491, 1501, 1507,
1512, 1566, 1583
GE:W20 I-319, 336, 444, 450, 479, II-577,
626, 640, 736
GL:20 V-2145
Stanford, Kevin N.
GE:HR V-2506
Stanford, Leland
GE:Am II-969
GL:Am V-2129
Stang, Arnold
GE:A&C III-1394
Stangeland, Roger
GE:B&C V-1943
Stanhope, First Earl
GL:B&C V-2357
Stanislavsky, Konstantin
GE:A&C I-1
GL:20 V-2150
Stanley, Edward George Geoffrey Smith. See
Derby, Fourteenth Earl of
Stanley, Edward Henry Smith. See Derby, Earl of

Stanley, Henry Morton
GE:HR I-13, 436
GL:B&C V-2363
Stanton, Edwin M.
GE:Am I-980, 991, 1026
GL:Am V-2137
Stanton, Elizabeth Cady
GE:Am III-1513
GE:HR I-190, 339
GL:Am V-2143
GL:AmW V-1666
Stanton, Frank
GE:A&C III-1211, 1465
Stapleton, Jean
GE:A&C V-2234
Stark, Harold R.
GE:Am III-1697
GE:W20 I-368, 404
Stark, Johannes
GL:20 V-2156
Stark, John
GE:A&C I-13
Starkey, Richard, Jr. See Starr, Ringo
Starling, Ernest Henry
GE:S&T I-179
GL:B&C V-2370
Starr, Ringo. See also Beatles, the
GE:A&C IV-1944, 2098
Staudinger, Hermann
GL:20 V-2161
Staupitz, John
GE:ME I-54
Stavisky, Serge Alexandre
GE:ME III-1386, 1411
Stead, William Thomas
GE:Am II-1167
GE:HR I-30
GE:ME II-1057
Steagall, Henry Bascom
GE:B&C II-656, 781
Steele, Charles Kenzie
GE:HR II-974
Steelman, John Roy
GE:B&C III-880
Steenbock, Harry
GE:S&T II-771
Stefan Dušan
GL:A&M V-1987
Stefanich, Juan
GE:HR I-533
Stefano, Joseph
GE:A&C IV-1855
Steffens, Lincoln
GE:Am III-1353

Steichen, Edward
GE:A&C I-63
GL:Am V-2150

Stein, Baron Heinrich Friedrich Karl vom und zum. *See* Stein, Freiherr vom

Stein, Edith
GL:20 V-2167

Stein, Freiherr vom
GE:ME II-572, 602
GL:Ren V-2215

Stein, Gertrude
GE:A&C I-129, II-696
GE:Am III-1560
GL:AmW V-1672

Stein, Herbert
GE:B&C IV-1489

Stein, Leo
GE:A&C I-129

Stein, Michael
GE:A&C I-129

Stein, Sarah Samuels
GE:A&C I-129

Stein, William H.
GE:S&T IV-1459

Steinbeck, Carol Henning
GE:A&C III-1138

Steinbeck, John
GE:A&C III-1138
GE:W20 I-418
GL:Am V-2155

Steinem, Gloria
GL:AmW V-1677
GE:HR III-1327

Steiner, Jakob
GL:Ren V-2220

Steiner, Rudolf
GE:A&C I-320

Steinhardt, Paul J.
GE:S&T V-2125

Steinitz, Ernst
GE:S&T I-438

Steinmetz, Charles Proteus
GE:B&C I-17
GE:S&T I-401
GL:Am V-2161

Stella, Frank
GE:A&C IV-1949

Stendhal
GL:Ren V-2225

Stephen. *See* Estebanico

Stephen (Deacon). *See* Stephen, Saint

Stephen (of England)
GL:B&C V-2375

Stephen I (of Hungary)
GE:A&M III-1210
GL:A&M V-1998

Stephen II, Pope
GE:A&M II-1121, 1131

Stephen, Bishop of Rome
GE:A&M II-818

Stephen, Saint
GE:A&M II-607
GL:A&M V-1993

Stephen, Virginia. *See* Woolf, Virginia

Stephens, Alexander Hamilton
GE:Am II-871, 941

Stephens, John Lloyd
GE:S&T V-2145

Stephens, J. R.
GE:ME II-741

Stephenson, David C.
GE:HR I-298

Stephenson, George
GE:ME II-608, 660
GL:B&C V-2382

Stephenson, Robert
GE:ME II-608, 660

Stephenson, Ward
GE:HR V-2274

Steptoe, Patrick Christopher
GE:S&T V-2099
GE:W20 III-1324

Sterling, Ford
GE:A&C I-230

Stern, Robert A. M.
GE:A&C V-2646

Sterne, Simon
GE:Am II-1157

Sterrett, Joseph E.
GE:B&C I-319

Stettinius, Edward R., Jr.
GE:Am III-1736, 1741
GE:B&C II-820
GE:HR II-657
GE:ME III-1501, 1507

Stevens, Isaac I.
GE:Am II-865

Stevens, John Frank
GE:S&T I-223, 249

Stevens, John Paul
GE:HR IV-1697
GE:W20 III-1279

Stevens, Nettie Maria
GE:S&T I-148

Stevens, Roger L.
GE:A&C IV-2048

Stevens, Ross, III
    GE:B&C V-2061
Stevens, Thaddeus
    GE:Am I-576, II-760, 985, 1003, 1026, 1049
    GL:Am V-2166
Stevens, Theodore "Ted"
    GE:B&C IV-1331, 1653
Stevenson, Adlai E.
    GE:Am III-1843
    GE:HR III-1212
    GE:W20 II-926
    GL:Am V-2170
Stevenson, Derek Paul
    GE:HR IV-1829
Stevenson, McLean
    GE:A&C V-2271
Steward, Balfour
    GE:S&T I-174
Stewart, Alice
    GE:S&T IV-1562
Stewart, A. T.
    GE:Am III-1549
Stewart, Edward J.
    GE:B&C I-75
Stewart, Homer J.
    GE:S&T IV-1583
Stewart, Jimmy
    GE:A&C III-1335
Stewart, Martha
    GL:AmW V-1682
Stewart, Philo P.
    GE:Am II-708
Stewart, Potter
    GE:B&C IV-1364, V-1882
    GE:HR III-1474
    GE:W20 II-949, III-1154, 1279
Stewart, Robert. See Castlereagh, Viscount
Stewart, Timothy A.
    GE:B&C V-1970
Stewart, William M.
    GE:Am II-1083
Steyn, Martinus Theunis
    GE:ME II-1128
Stibitz, George
    GE:S&T III-1396
Sticht, J. Paul
    GE:B&C V-1976
Stieglitz, Alfred
    GE:A&C I-63, II-885, 1001
    GL:Am V-2177
Stigler, George J.
    GE:B&C III-931
Stigwood, Robert
    GE:A&C V-2254

Stilicho, Flavius
    GE:A&M II-935
    GL:A&M V-2002
Stillman, James
    GE:B&C I-134
Stimson, Henry L.
    GE:Am III-1599, 1686, 1753
    GE:HR II-595
    GE:W20 I-465
    GL:Am V-2184
Stine, Charles M. A.
    GE:B&C II-798
    GE:S&T III-1055
Stingl, Josef
    GE:B&C IV-1549
Stitch, George Ford. See Sterling, Ford
Stockard, Charles
    GE:S&T II-864
Stockhausen, Karlheinz
    GE:A&C I-528
    GL:20 V-2175
Stockton, Robert Field
    GE:Am II-818
Stoclet, Adolphe
    GE:A&C I-124
Stoecker, Adolf
    GE:ME II-1028
Stokes, Donald
    GE:B&C IV-1347
Stokes, Sir George Gabriel
    GE:S&T I-309, III-1080
Stokes, T. L.
    GE:S&T III-1024
Stokowski, Leopold
    GE:A&C I-425, III-1195
Stoll, Arthur
    GE:S&T I-345, III-1123
Stoll, Werner
    GE:S&T III-1123
Stolypin, Pëtr Arkadevich
    GE:ME III-1179, 1202
Stone, Edward C.
    GE:S&T V-2104
Stone, Harlan Fiske
    GE:B&C II-792
    GE:HR II-629
    GL:Am V-2190
Stone, Lucy
    GE:Am III-1513
    GL:AmW V-1687
Stone, Milburn
    GE:A&C IV-1668
Stone, Oliver
    GE:A&C V-2576

Stone, Robert
GE:A&C V-2315
Stone, Sid
GE:A&C III-1394
Stone, William A.
GE:Am II-1329
Stone, William J.
GE:Am III-1450
Stoneham, Horace
GE:B&C III-1076
Stoner, Edmund C.
GE:S&T II-800
Stonorov, Oscar
GE:A&C IV-1919
Stopes, Marie
GL:B&C V-2388
Stoph, Willi
GE:W20 III-1167
Stoppard, Tom
GE:A&C IV-1967
Storey, David
GE:A&C III-1454
Story, Joseph
GE:B&C I-163
GL:Am V-2196
Stotts, Carl
GE:B&C V-1882
Stoughton, William
GE:Am I-169
Stowe, Calvin Ellis
GE:Am II-859
Stowe, Harriet Beecher
GE:Am II-859
GL:Am V-2202
GL:AmW V-1692
Str...
GE:A&M I-506
GL:A&M V-2007
Strachey, James
GE:A&C I-19
Strachey, Rachel (Ray)
GE:HR I-247
Stradivari, Antonio
GL:Ren V-2231
Strafford, First Earl of
GE:ME I-263
GL:B&C V-2393
Straight, Willard
GE:A&C I-385
Strange, Glenn
GE:A&C IV-1668
Strasberg, Lee
GE:A&C II-874, 1006
Strassberg, Isreal. See Strasberg, Lee

Strasser, Adolf
GE:Am II-1152
Strasser, Gregor
GE:ME III-1391
Strassman, Fritz
GE:S&T III-1135
Stratton, Charles Sherwood. See Thumb, "General" Tom
Stratton, Samuel
GE:HR IV-1823
Strauss, David Friedrich
GE:ME II-892
Strauss, Baron George R.
GE:A&C IV-2131
Strauss, Johann
GL:Ren V-2236
Strauss, Levi
GE:B&C IV-1400
Strauss, Lewis L.
GE:B&C III-1196
GE:S&T IV-1557
GE:W20 II-683
Strauss, Richard
GE:A&C I-151, 193, 292
GL:20 V-2183
Straussler, Tomas. See Stoppard, Tom
Stravinsky, Igor
GE:A&C I-269, 373, 528, II-561, 816, III-1301, 1514
GL:Am V-2207
Streep, Meryl
GL:AmW V-1697
Street, George Edmund
GL:B&C V-2399
Streisand, Barbra
GE:A&C V-2443
GL:AmW V-1701
Stresemann, Gustav
GE:B&C I-406
GE:HR I-423
GE:W20 I-197, 342
GL:20 V-2188
Strindberg, August
GE:A&C I-199
GL:20 V-2193
Stringfellow, Thornton
GE:Am I-648
Stroessner, Alfredo
GE:HR I-533, IV-2106
Strong, Benjamin
GE:B&C I-134, 406, II-717
Strong, Caleb
GE:Am I-517

Strong, Maurice
  GE:B&C V-2061
Strowger, Almon Brown
  GE:S&T I-11, V-1934
Strugnell, John
  GE:S&T III-1298
Struthers, Sally
  GE:A&C V-2234
Strutt, Jedediah
  GE:Am I-362
Struve, Otto
  GE:S&T II-815
Stuart, Ackroyd
  GE:ME II-1100
Stuart, Arabella
  GE:ME I-224
Stuart, Charles
  GE:Am II-708
Stuart, Gilbert
  GL:Am V-2212
Stuart, James Francis Edward (the "Old
  Pretender")
  GE:ME I-357
Stuart, John (Earl of Bute)
  GE:Am I-200
  GE:ME I-451
Stuart, John Leighton
  GE:Am III-1764
Stuart, Mary. See Mary, Queen of Scots
Stuart, Robert
  GE:Am I-476
Stuart-Wortley, Edward James Montague
  GE:ME III-1207
Stuchka, Peteris (P. I.)
  GE:HR I-207
Studebaker, John W.
  GE:Am III-1725
Stults, Walter B.
  GE:B&C III-1107
Sturge, Joseph
  GE:ME II-715
Sturgeon, Theodore
  GE:A&C III-1094
Sturluson, Snorri. See Snorri Sturluson
Sturtevant, Alfred Henry
  GE:S&T I-407, II-486
  GE:W20 I-7
Stuyvesant, Peter
  GE:Am I-80, 140
  GL:Am V-2219
Su Shih. See Su Tung-p'o
Su Tung-p'o
  GL:A&M V-2014

Suárez, Adolfo
  GE:HR IV-1921, 2079
  GE:W20 II-1043
Subandrio
  GE:HR III-1305
SubbaRow, Yellapragada
  GE:S&T III-1255
Suchocka, Hanna
  GE:B&C V-2017
Sudbury, Archbishop
  GE:A&M III-1640
Süe, Louis
  GE:A&C II-654
Suenens, Leo-Joseph Cardinal
  GE:ME III-1659
Suess, Theodor
  GE:B&C III-991
Suetin, Nikolai
  GE:A&C I-413
Suger
  GE:A&M III-1416
  GL:A&M V-2020
Suharto
  GE:HR III-1305, IV-1835
Sukarno
  GE:HR III-1305
  GL:20 V-2199
Sukenik, Eliezer
  GE:S&T III-1298
  GE:W20 II-598
Süleyman the Magnificent
  GE:ME I-87
  GL:Ren V-2241
Sulla, Lucius Cornelius
  GL:A&M V-2026
Sullivan, Sir Arthur, and W. S. Gilbert
  GL:B&C III-1134
Sullivan, Ed
  GE:A&C III-1383
Sullivan, Eugene G.
  GE:S&T II-605
Sullivan, Eugene J.
  GE:HR I-412
Sullivan, Harry Stack
  GL:Am V-2224
Sullivan, John
  GE:S&T V-2382
Sullivan, John Florence. See Allen, Fred
Sullivan, Leonor
  GE:B&C IV-1358
Sullivan, Louis
  GE:Am II-1231
  GE:S&T II-906
  GL:Am V-2229

Sulpicius, Publius
  GE:A&M I-253
Summer, Donna
  GE:A&C V-2386
Sumner, Charles
  GE:Am II-871, 980, 1003, 1037, 1049, 1072
  GL:Am V-2234
Sumner, William Graham
  GE:Am II-1167, III-1357
Sun Yat-sen
  GE:HR I-116
  GE:W20 I-92, 211, II-654
  GL:20 V-2206
Sunday, Billy
  GL:Am V-2241
Sundjata
  GL:A&M V-2032
Sung Chiao-jen
  GE:W20 I-92
Sung, Kim Il. See Kim Il Sung
Sunyaev, Rashid
  GE:W20 II-835
Suslov, Mikhial Andreevich
  GE:W20 II-974
Sutherland, George
  GE:B&C II-426
  GE:HR III-1182
Sutherland, Graham Vivian
  GL:B&C V-2405
Sutter, John Augustus
  GE:Am II-807, 843
Suttner, Bertha von
  GE:A&C I-45
  GL:Ren V-2246
Sutton, Walter S.
  GE:S&T I-148, 153
Suvorov, Aleksandr Vasilyevich
  GE:ME I-475
  GL:Ren V-2251
Sveda, Michael
  GE:S&T III-1368, V-2226
Svedberg, Theodor
  GE:S&T II-775, III-1336
Sverdrup, Johan
  GE:ME III-1164
Svinhufvud, Pehr Evind
  GE:HR I-212
Svirbely, Joseph L.
  GE:S&T II-857
Svoboda, Ludvík
  GE:HR III-1441
  GE:ME III-1666
Svoronos, Joannes N.
  GE:S&T IV-1588

Swados, Elizabeth
  GL:AmW V-1706
Swain, Mack
  GE:A&C II-659
Swan, Joseph Wilson
  GE:ME II-753
  GL:B&C V-2409
Swanson, Robert
  GE:B&C IV-1616
Swarts, Frédéric
  GE:S&T II-916
Swartz, Edward M.
  GE:B&C IV-1426
Sweanor, David
  GE:HR V-2376
Swedenborg, Emanuel
  GL:Ren V-2257
Sweeney, James Johnson
  GE:A&C IV-1806
Sweinheim, Konrad
  GE:A&M III-1713
Swift, Gustavus F.
  GE:B&C I-107
Swift, Jonathan
  GE:ME I-424
  GL:B&C V-2413
Swineshead, Richard
  GE:A&M III-1614
Swinton, Alan A. Campbell
  GE:B&C II-758
  GE:S&T II-751
Swit, Loretta
  GE:A&C V-2271
Syagrius
  GE:A&M II-995
Sydenham, Thomas
  GL:B&C V-2419
Sydnes, William L.
  GE:S&T V-2169
Sydney, Basil
  GE:A&C III-1378
Sydow, Max von
  GE:A&C IV-1742
Sykes, E. O.
  GE:B&C II-685
Sykes, Sir Mark
  GE:B&C I-351
Sylvester II
  GE:A&M II-857, 1121, III-1200, 1210, 1231
  GL:A&M V-2037
Sylvester, James Joseph
  GE:Am II-1077
Symmes, John Cleves
  GE:Am I-306

T

Taback, Israel
GE:S&T V-2052
Tabari, al-
GL:A&M V-2043
Tacitus, Cornelius
GE:A&M I-531
GL:A&M V-2047
Tack, Juan Antonio
GE:W20 III-1331
Tadashi, Hanaya
GE:W20 I-269
Tafel, Edgar
GE:A&C II-902
Taft, Julia Vadala
GE:HR V-2354
Taft, Robert A.
GE:Am III-1759, 1800, 1843
GE:B&C III-880, 908
GL:Am V-2248
Taft, William Howard
GE:Am II-1290, III-1379, 1390, 1405, 1415
GE:B&C I-146, 168, II-426
GE:HR I-41, 172, 231
GL:Am V-2254
Tagore, Rabindranath
GL:20 V-2211
T'ai Tsung
GL:A&M V-2053
Taieb, Maurice
GE:S&T V-2037
Tailleferre, Germaine
GE:A&C I-435
Taine, Hippolyte-Adolphe
GL:Ren V-2261
Taira Kiyomori
GL:A&M V-2059
Tai-shang Hsüan-yüan Huang-ti. See Lao-tzu
Takaishi, Kunio
GE:B&C V-1964
Takamine, Jokichi
GE:S&T I-16
Takauji. See Ashikaga Takauji
Takei, Kei
GE:A&C V-2480
Takeshita, Noboru
GE:B&C V-1964
Talaat Pasha, Mehmet
GE:W20 I-107

Talabani, Jalal al-
GE:HR II-1050
Talbot, Marion
GL:AmW V-1715
Talib, Abu. See Abu Talib
Tallard, Marshal Camille D'Hostun
GE:ME I-390
Tallchief, Maria
GL:AmW V-1720
Talley, Lynn P.
GE:B&C II-668
Talleyrand
GE:Am I-408
GE:ME I-516, 547, II-598, 612, 623
GL:Ren V-2265
Tallmadge, James, Jr.
GE:Am I-552
Tally, Thomas L.
GE:Am II-1333
Talmadge, Herman E.
GE:B&C IV-1495, 1567
Talon, Jean Baptiste (The Great Intendant)
GE:Am I-52, 144
Talon, Omer
GE:ME I-324
Tamberlaine. See Tamerlane
Tambo, Oliver
GE:HR III-1143
Tamerlane
GL:A&M V-2065
Tamm, Igor Yevgenyevich
GE:S&T III-1003
Tan, Amy
GL:AmW V-1725
Tandy, Jessica
GL:AmW V-1730
Taney, Roger Brooke
GE:Am II-696, 900, 946
GL:Am V-2260
T'ang San-tsang. See Hsüang-tsang
Tanguy, Yves
GE:A&C II-604
Tanizaki, Jun'ichirō
GL:20 V-2217
Tannenbaum, Stanley
GE:B&C IV-1410
T'ao Ch'ien
GL:A&M V-2070
T'ao Yüan-ming. See T'ao Ch'ien

Tapa, Sione
  GE:HR IV-1893
Tappan, Arthur
  GE:Am I-642, II-708, 719
Tappan, Lewis
  GE:Am I-642, II-708, 719
Taraki, Nur Mohammad
  GE:HR IV-2062, V-2449
Tarasov, Aleksandr
  GE:B&C III-1293
Tarbell, Ida
  GE:Am III-1353
  GL:AmW V-1735
Tardieu, André Pierre Gabriel Amédée
  GE:W20 I-276
Tardini, Domenico Cardinal
  GE:ME III-1633
Tarik ibn Ziyad. See Ibn Ziyad, Tarik
Tariki, Abdullah
  GE:B&C III-1154
  GE:W20 II-912
Tarlton, Robert J.
  GE:B&C III-953
Tarquinius Superbus
  GE:A&M I-200
Tartikoff, Brandon
  GE:A&C V-2532
Tashunca-uitko. See Crazy Horse
Tassel, James Van. See Van Tassel, James
Tasso, Torquato
  GL:Ren V-2271
Tatanka Iyotake. See Sitting Bull
Tate, Allen
  GE:A&C III-1169, 1443
Tatian
  GE:A&M II-707
Tatlin, Vladimir
  GE:A&C I-413, II-544
Tatsumi, Masao
  GE:B&C V-1964
Tattersall, Ian
  GE:S&T V-2279
Tatti, Jacopo. See Sansovino, Jacopo
Tatum, Howard
  GE:S&T IV-1629
Taubman, Alfred
  GE:A&C V-2603
Taussig, Frank William
  GE:B&C I-157, 297
Taussig, Helen Brooke
  GE:B&C III-1180
  GE:S&T III-1250
Tawaraya, Sōtatsu. See Sōtatsu

Taylor, Deems
  GE:A&C III-1195
Taylor, Dwight
  GE:A&C II-984
Taylor, Frank Bursley
  GE:S&T II-522
Taylor, Frederick Winslow
  GE:B&C I-258, 287, II-770, III-890
  GE:S&T II-542
  GL:Am V-2268
Taylor, John (Mormon Leader)
  GE:Am II-812
Taylor, John (Senator from Virginia)
  GE:Am I-456
Taylor, John W. (Senator from New York)
  GE:Am I-552
Taylor, Myron C.
  GE:Am III-1655
Taylor, Nathaniel William
  GE:Am I-420
Taylor, Paul
  GE:A&C III-1602
Taylor, Richard E.
  GE:S&T IV-1871
Taylor, William C.
  GE:S&T II-605
Taylor, Zachary
  GE:Am II-825, 854
  GL:Am V-2274
Tchaikovsky, Peter Ilich
  GL:Ren V-2276
Teagle, Walter Clark
  GE:B&C II-551
Teague, Walter Dorwin
  GE:A&C II-777, 1057
Teasdale, Sara
  GL:AmW V-1740
Tecosky, Morton. See Da Costa, Morton
Tecumseh
  GE:Am I-498
  GL:Am V-2280
Tee-Van, John
  GE:S&T III-1018
Teilhard de Chardin, Pierre
  GE:S&T III-1096
  GL:20 V-2222
Teisserenc de Bort, Léon
  GE:S&T I-26
Teitgen, Pierre-Henri
  GE:HR II-843
Teleki, Paul
  GE:W20 I-181
Telemann, Georg Philipp
  GL:Ren V-2282

Telford, Thomas
  GL:B&C V-2424
Teller, Edward
  GE:S&T III-1401
  GE:W20 II-683
  GL:Am V-2285
Teller, Henry M.
  GE:Am II-1161
Temin, Howard M.
  GE:S&T I-459
Tempier, Étienne
  GE:A&M III-1544, 1564
Temple, Henry John. *See* Palmerston, Lord
Temple, Shirley. *See also* Black, Shirley Temple
  GE:A&C II-1011
Temple, Sir William
  GE:ME III-1550
Templeton, Fay
  GE:A&C I-108
Temüjin. *See* Genghis Khan
Teng Hsiao-p'ing
  GE:W20 III-1264
  GL:20 V-2230
Tennent, Gilbert
  GE:Am I-176
Tennent, William
  GE:Am I-176
Tenney, Jack
  GE:HR II-624
Tennyson, Alfred, Lord
  GL:B&C V-2430
Tenskwatawa, The Prophet
  GE:Am I-498
Terceira, Duke of. *See* De Sousa, Antonio
Terence
  GE:A&M I-453
  GL:A&M V-2075
Terentius Afer, Publius. *See* Terence
Teresa, Mother
  GL:20 V-2235
Teresa of Ávila, Saint
  GL:Ren V-2288
Terkel, Studs
  GE:A&C III-1329
Terry, Alfred
  GE:Am II-1094
Terry, Ellen
  GL:B&C V-2435
Terry, Luther L.
  GE:B&C IV-1443
  GE:HR III-1338, 1527
Terry, Megan
  GL:AmW V-1745

Terry, Randall
  GE:HR V-2443
Tertullian
  GE:A&M II-742, 757, 762, 767, 818, III-1338
  GL:A&M V-2081
Tesla, Nikola
  GL:Am V-2292
Tetzel, John
  GE:ME I-54
Teutsch, Georges
  GE:S&T V-2185
Thacher, Peter O.
  GE:Am II-785
Thalberg, Irving G.
  GE:A&C II-833
Thales of Miletus
  GE:A&M I-173, 383
  GL:A&M V-2086
Thant, U. *See* U Thant
Tharp, Twyla
  GE:A&C V-2288
  GL:AmW V-1750
Thatcher, Margaret
  GE:B&C V-1831, 1887
  GE:HR IV-2024, 2073
  GL:B&C V-2441
Thayendanega. *See* Brant, Joseph
Thayendanegea. *See* Brant, Joseph
Thayer, Harry B.
  GE:B&C I-396
Thayer, Sylvanus
  GE:Am I-432
Theiler, Max
  GE:S&T III-1091
Thein, Swee Lay
  GE:S&T V-2296
Themistocles
  GE:A&M I-226, 237
  GL:A&M V-2092
Theobald
  GE:A&M III-1375
Theodora
  GE:A&M II-1152
Theodore
  GE:A&M II-1152
Theodore I (of Russia)
  GE:ME I-198
Theodore of Mopsuestia
  GL:A&M V-2098
Theodoret of Cyrrhus
  GL:A&M V-2104
Theodoric
  GE:A&M II-975

Theodoric II
    GE:A&M II-1052
Theodoric the Great
    GE:A&M II-1018
    GL:A&M V-2108
Theodosius I. *See* Theodosius the Great
Theodosius II
    GE:A&M II-952, 963
Theodosius, Russian Patriarch
    GE:A&M III-1205
Theodosius the Great
    GE:A&M II-852, 904, 920, 924
    GL:A&M V-2115
Theodotion
    GE:A&M I-418
Theodulph
    GE:A&M II-1136
Theoleptus of Philadelphia
    GL:A&M V-2122
Theophanes the Confessor
    GL:A&M V-2128
Theophilus
    GE:A&M II-707, 924
Theophrastus
    GE:A&M I-348
    GL:A&M V-2132
Theopompus
    GE:A&M I-134
Theorell, Axel Hugo Teodor
    GL:20 V-2245
Theotokópoulos, Doménikos. *See* Greco, El
Thiel, F. A.
    GE:S&T V-2159
Thierry of Chartres
    GE:A&M III-1231
Thiers, Adolphe
    GE:ME II-974, 984
    GL:Ren V-2293
Thieu, Nguyen Van
    GE:W20 III-1161, 1227
Thimonnier, Barthélemy
    GE:Am II-837
Thiong'o, Ngugi wa
    GE:HR V-2431
Tho, Le Duc
    GE:W20 III-1161, 1212
Thomas à Becket. *See* Becket, Thomas
Thomas à Kempis
    GE:A&M III-1670
    GL:A&M V-2145
Thomas Aquinas, Saint
    GE:A&M III-1395, 1519, 1544, 1564
    GL:A&M V-2152

Thomas Didymus, Saint
    GL:A&M V-2138
Thomas of Celano
    GE:A&M III-1349
Thomas, Albert
    GE:HR I-281, III-1509
Thomas, Danny
    GE:A&C III-1470
Thomas, Émile
    GE:ME II-786
Thomas, Evan
    GE:Am I-624
Thomas, Frank
    GE:A&C II-1053
Thomas, George Henry
    GE:Am II-997
Thomas, George Holt
    GE:Am II-807
Thomas, J. H.
    GE:HR I-429
Thomas, J. Parnell
    GE:A&C III-1340
    GE:HR I-550, II-701
Thomas, Jesse B.
    GE:Am I-552
Thomas, Martha Carey
    GL:AmW V-1754
Thomas, Norman
    GE:Am III-1609
    GE:HR I-327
    GL:Am V-2297
Thomas, Philip Evan
    GE:Am I-624
Thomas, Rowland
    GE:HR I-298
Thomas, Theodore
    GL:Am V-2304
Thomas, Vivien
    GE:S&T III-1250
Thomaz, Americo Deus
    GE:ME III-1673
Thompsom, Hugh
    GE:HR III-1555
Thompson, Almond H.
    GE:Am II-1104
Thompson, Benjamin. *See* Rumford, Count
Thompson, Dorothy
    GL:AmW V-1759
Thompson, Uncle Jimmy
    GE:A&C II-675
Thompson, John Griggs
    GE:S&T V-2130
Thompson, John Reuben
    GE:Am II-725

Thompson, Morris
  GE:B&C IV-1631
Thompson, William Coleridge
  GE:HR III-1451
Thomson, Elihu
  GE:S&T III-1325
Thomson, Sir Joseph John
  GE:S&T I-199, 260, 309, 356, II-471, 507,
  527, 660, 746, III-973
Thomson, Tom
  GL:B&C V-2447
Thomson, Virgil
  GE:A&C I-508
Thomson, Sir William, Lord Kelvin. *See* Kelvin,
  Sir William Thomson, Lord
'T Hooft, W. A. Visser
  GE:ME III-1550
Thorburn, Richard
  GE:A&C V-2283
Thoreau, Henry David
  GE:Am I-654, II-848
  GL:Am V-2310
Thorez, Maurice
  GE:B&C II-735
Thornburgh, Dick
  GE:B&C IV-1693
Thorndike, Edward L.
  GE:Am II-1301
  GE:S&T I-163
  GL:Am V-2315
Thorpe, Jim
  GL:Am V-2320
Thothmes III. *See* Thutmose III
Thucydides
  GE:A&M I-242, 292
  GL:A&M V-2159
Thumb, "General" Tom (Charles Sherwood
  Stratton)
  GE:Am II-1066
Thurber, F. B.
  GE:Am II-1157
Thurber, James
  GE:A&C II-648
Thurmond, Strom
  GE:Am III-1800
  GE:HR III-1262, 1381
Thurn, Count Mattias
  GE:ME I-250
Thutmose III
  GL:A&M V-2164
Tib, Tippu
  GE:HR I-13
Tibald of Champagne, Count
  GE:A&M III-1436

Tibbon, Samuel ibn-. *See* Ibn-Tibbon, Samuel
Tiberius
  GE:A&M II-584
  GL:A&M V-2169
Tiberius Claudius Drusus Nero Germanicus. *See*
  Claudius I
Tiberius Sempronius Gracchus. *See* Gracchi, The
Tiepolo, Giovanni Battista
  GL:Ren V-2299
Tiffany, Charles Louis
  GE:A&C I-34
Tiffany, Louis Comfort
  GE:A&C I-34
Tigranes the Great
  GL:A&M V-2175
Tikamthi. *See* Tecumseh
Tikhon, Vasily Belavin
  GE:HR I-202
Tikhonov, Vladimir
  GE:HR V-2471
Tilak, Bal Gangadhar
  GE:HR I-156
  GL:20 V-2249
Tilden, Samuel
  GE:Am II-1099
Tillett, Ben
  GE:HR I-58
Tillich, Paul
  GE:Am III-1604
  GE:W20 I-295, 507
  GL:Am V-2326
Tillstrom, Burr
  GE:A&C III-1400
Timerman, Jacobo
  GE:HR IV-1864
Timur Lenk. *See* Tamerlane
Tinbergen, Nikolaas
  GE:S&T IV-1808
Tineius Rufus. *See* Rufus, Tineius
Ting, Samuel C. C.
  GE:S&T V-2031
Tinker, Grant
  GE:A&C V-2218, 2470
Tintoretto
  GL:Ren V-2305
Tiridates
  GE:A&M I-427
Tiroff, Romain de. *See* Erté
Tirpitz, Alfred von
  GL:20 V-2255
Tissaphernes
  GE:A&M I-313
Tissé, Éduard
  GE:A&C II-615

Titchener, Edward Bradford
    GE:B&C I-80
Titian
    GE:ME I-133
    GL:Ren V-2310
Tito (Josip Broz)
    GE:HR III-1131, 1408, IV-1949, V-2386, 2612
    GE:ME III-1595
    GE:W20 II-640
    GL:20 V-2261
Titov, Vladimir
    GE:S&T V-2316
Tittoni, Tommaso
    GE:HR I-287
Tituba
    GE:Am I-169
Titus
    GE:A&M II-648
Titus Antonius Merenda. See Merenda, Titus
    Antonius
Titus Flavius Clemens. See Flavius Clemens, Titus
Titus Flavius Sabinus Vespasianus. See Vespasian
Titus Genucius. See Genuscius, Titus
Titus Livius. See Livy
Titus Lucretius Carus. See Lucretius
Titus Manlius Torquatus. See Torquatus, Titus
    Manlius
Titus Romilius. See Romilius, Titus
Tizard, Henry Thomas
    GE:W20 I-324
Tobin, Daniel J.
    GE:B&C III-1213
Tobin, James
    GE:B&C II-740
Tocker, Phillip
    GE:B&C III-1254
Tocqueville, Alexis de
    GL:Ren V-2314
Todd, Reginald Stephen Garfield
    GE:W20 II-981
Todd, Samuel C. T.
    GE:Am II-1116
Toeplitz, Giuseppe
    GE:B&C II-645
Toffler, Alvin
    GE:B&C IV-1733
Toftoy, H. N.
    GE:S&T III-1342
Togliatti, Palmiro
    GE:B&C III-1293
    GE:ME III-1538
Toit, Alexander Logie Du
    GE:S&T II-522

Tojo, Hideki
    GE:Am III-1697
Toklas, Alice B.
    GE:A&C I-129
Tokugawa Ieyasu
    GL:Ren V-2319
Toland, Gregg
    GE:A&C III-1200
Tolbert, William Richard, Jr.
    GE:B&C IV-1589
Toledano, Vicente Lombardo
    GE:HR I-196
Tolkien, Christopher
    GE:A&C III-1607
Tolkien, John Ronald Reul
    GE:A&C III-1607
Tolstoy, Leo
    GE:Am II-1184
    GL:Ren V-2324
Tomás de Torquemada. See De Torquemada,
    Tomás
Tomás, Manuel Fernandes
    GE:ME II-645
Tombalbaye, François
    GE:HR III-1273
Tombaugh, Clyde William
    GE:S&T I-291, II-944
Tomlin, Lily
    GL:AmW V-1764
Tommaso di Giovanni di Simone Guidi. See
    Masaccio
Tomochichi
    GE:Am I-182
Tomonaga, Shin'ichirō
    GE:S&T III-1293
Tomsky, Mikhail
    GE:B&C I-374
    GE:ME III-1329
Tone, Wolfe
    GE:ME II-551
Tongorara, Josiah
    GE:HR III-1224
Tönnies, Ferdinand Julius
    GL:20 V-2266
Toombs, Robert Augustus
    GE:Am II-941
Torgler, Ernst
    GE:HR I-480
    GE:ME III-1377
Toro, David
    GE:W20 I-289
Torquatus, Titus Manlius
    GE:A&M I-333

Torrance, Jared Sidney
    GE:Am III-1811
Torres, Esteban Edward
    GE:B&C IV-1454
Torres, Niceto Alcalá Zamora y. *See* Zamora y
    Torres, Niceto Alcalá
Torrey, Reuben A.
    GE:Am II-1173
Torricelli, Evangelista
    GL:Ren V-2330
Torrijos Herrera, Omar
    GE:W20 III-1331
Torrington, Earl of. *See* Monck, George
Torstenson, Lennart
    GL:Ren V-2335
Tosh, Peter
    GE:A&C V-2344
Tosorthros. *See* Zoser
Totheroh, Roland H.
    GE:A&C II-659
Totleben, Count Edward Ivanovitch
    GE:ME II-813
Touche, George A.
    GE:B&C II-608
Toule, Katherine
    GE:Am III-1912
Toulouse-Lautrec, Henri de
    GL:Ren V-2340
Touré, Ahmed Sékou
    GE:HR III-1194
    GL:20 V-2272
Tourgée, Albion Winegar
    GE:Am II-1261
Toussaint-Louverture
    GE:Am I-443
    GE:HR II-1009
    GL:Ren V-2346
Tower, John
    GE:B&C IV-1495
Townes, Charles Hard
    GE:S&T IV-1672
    GE:W20 II-881
Townsend, Francis
    GE:Am III-1582, 1643
    GE:HR I-514
Townsend, James M.
    GE:Am II-912
Townsend, Sir John Sealy Edward
    GE:S&T I-412
Townsend, Robert
    GE:A&C V-2565
Townshend, Charles
    GE:Am I-225

Toynbee, Arnold
    GE:W20 I-107
    GL:B&C V-2453
Toyoda, Eiji
    GL:20 V-2278
Toyoda, Kiichirō
    GE:B&C IV-1716
Toyotomi Hideyoshi
    GL:Ren V-2351
Traianus Augustus, Marcus Ulpius. *See* Trajan
Train, Russell E.
    GE:B&C IV-1460
Trajan (Marcus Ulpius Traianus Augustus)
    GE:A&M I-373, II-675, 692, 696
Trammel, Park
    GE:W20 I-368
Trapp, Martin E.
    GE:HR I-367
Traut, Herbert
    GE:S&T II-864
Travanti, Daniel J.
    GE:A&C V-2470
Travis, William Barret
    GE:Am II-736
Trenchard, Sir Hugh Montague
    GE:ME III-1461
Tressler, Donald K.
    GE:S&T II-635
Trevelyan, Charles Edward
    GE:ME III-757
Trevelyan, Sir George Otto
    GE:ME II-1038
Trevelyan, John
    GE:A&C IV-2131
Trevithick, Richard
    GE:ME II-608
    GL:B&C V-2458
Trevor, Claire
    GE:A&C III-1115
Tripitaka. *See* Hsüang-tsang
Trippe, Juan T.
    GE:B&C III-1112
    GE:S&T IV-1897
Triptolemus
    GE:A&M I-158
Trist, Nicholas Philip
    GE:Am II-825
Tristam, Nuno
    GE:A&M III-1686
Tristano, Lennie
    GE:A&C III-1617
Trochu, Louis
    GE:ME II-954

Troeltsch, Ernst
GL:20 V-2283
Troitsky, Vsevolod
GE:W20 II-827
Trojan
GL:A&M V-2180
Tromp, Maarten, and Cornelis Tromp
GL:Ren V-2357
Trotsky, Leon
GE:B&C II-563
GE:HR I-218, 225, 503
GE:ME III-1169, 1271, 1304, 1329, 1347
GE:W20 I-152, 336
GL:20 V-2289
Trotter, William Monroe
GE:Am III-1384
GE:HR I-41
Troyes, Chrétien de. *See* Chrétien de Troyes
Trubetskoy, Prince Serge
GE:ME II-665
Truche, Pierre
GE:HR IV-2193
Trudeau, Garry
GE:A&C V-2223
Trudeau, Pierre Elliott
GE:HR III-1543, IV-1876, 2158
GE:W20 II-820
GL:B&C V-2464
Truffaut, François
GE:A&C IV-1710, 1845
GL:20 V-2294
Truitt, Anne
GE:A&C IV-1949
Truly, Richard H.
GE:B&C IV-1727
GE:S&T V-2180
Truman, Harry S
GE:Am III-1680, 1741, 1748, 1753, 1759,
1770, 1776, 1783, 1789, 1794, 1800, 1806,
1817, 1823, 1829, 1843
GE:B&C II-668, 833, III-880, 902, 908, 970,
975, 997
GE:HR II-701, 706, 771, 777, 795
GE:ME III-1512, 1526, 1532, 1543, 1555,
1561
GE:W20 I-260, II-572, 584, 683, 783
GL:Am V-2331
Trumbo, Dalton
GE:A&C III-1340
Trumbull, Douglas
GE:A&C IV-1989, V-2486
Trumbull, Jonathan
GE:Am I-267

Trumbull, Lyman
GE:Am II-906
GE:B&C IV-1364
Trump, Donald
GE:B&C IV-1600
Truong Chinh
GE:HR II-573
GE:W20 III-1243
Truscott, Lucien, IV
GE:HR III-1479
Truth, Sojourner
GL:Am V-2337
GL:AmW V-1769
Tryon, William
GE:Am I-213
Tsai Feng. *See* Ch'un, Prince
Ts'ai Yuan-p'ei
GE:HR I-276
Tschermak von Seysenegg, Erich
GE:S&T I-61, 270
Tseng Kuo-fan
GL:Ren V-2362
Tse-tung, Mao. *See* Mao Tse-tung
Tshombe, Moise
GE:HR II-1068, 1074
GE:ME III-1613
GL:20 V-2300
Tsiolkovsky, Konstantin
GE:S&T I-189, IV-1545
GL:20 V-2306
Tsui-weng. *See* Ou-yang Hsiu
Tsuji, Masanobu
GE:W20 I-457
Tsvetayeva, Marina
GL:20 V-2311
Tu Fu
GL:A&M V-2186
Tubman, Harriet
GL:Am V-2342
GL:AmW V-1774
Tubman, William V. S.
GE:HR III-1194
GL:20 V-2317
Tucca, Plotius
GE:A&M I-556
Tuchinda, Prakorb
GE:HR IV-1893
Tuchman, Barbara
GL:AmW V-1778
Tucker, Sophie
GL:AmW V-1783
Tudjman, Franjo
GE:HR V-2612

Tudor, Antony
  GE:A&C II-1036
Tudor, Mary. *See* Mary I
Tufts, Eleanor
  GE:A&C V-2608
Tughril
  GE:A&M III-1253
Tugwell, Rexford Guy
  GE:Am III-1609, 1615
  GE:B&C II-662, 787
Tuke, Samuel
  GE:A&C IV-1877
Tull, Jethro
  GL:B&C V-2473
Tully, R. Brent
  GE:S&T V-2306
Tunnell, Ebe
  GE:B&C I-69
Tunner, William H.
  GE:Am III-1794
  GE:ME III-1543
Tunney, John
  GE:HR IV-1817
Tupolev, Andrei Nikolayevich
  GL:20 V-2322
Tupper, Earl S.
  GE:B&C II-863
Turati, Filippo
  GE:ME II-1109
Turco, El
  GE:Am I-40
Turgenev, Ivan
  GL:Ren V-2368
Turgot, Anne-Robert-Jacques
  GL:Ren V-2373
Turing, Alan Mathison
  GE:S&T III-1045, 1155, 1347
  GE:W20 II-535
  GL:B&C V-2478
Turner, Frederick Jackson
  GE:Am II-1077
  GL:Am V-2348
Turner, J. M. W.
  GL:B&C V-2482
Turner, Nat
  GE:Am II-685
Turner, Richmond K.
  GE:Am III-1709
Turner, Ted
  GE:A&C V-2554
  GE:B&C III-953, V-1768
Turner, Tina
  GL:AmW V-1787

Turner-Jones, A.
  GE:S&T III-1240
Turok, Neil
  GE:S&T V-2047
Turoldus
  GE:A&M III-1308
Tutankhamen
  GE:S&T II-730
Tuttle, Roger
  GE:HR V-2342
Tutu, Desmond
  GE:HR IV-1882, V-2244
  GL:20 V-2328
Tvardovskii, Aleksandr
  GE:HR IV-1764
Tverdokhlebov, Andrei
  GE:HR III-1549
Tvrtko I
  GE:A&M III-1660
Twain, Mark
  GE:Am II-1146
  GL:Am V-2354
Tweed, William Marcy
  GE:Am II-1054
Twelve Disciples of Jesus, The
  GE:A&M II-595
Tydings, Joseph
  GE:HR III-1579
Tydings, Millard
  GE:Am III-1817
  GE:B&C II-764
Tye, Henry
  GE:S&T V-2125
Tyler, John
  GE:Am II-748, 760, 766, 772, 801, 825
  GL:Am V-2360
Tyler, Stanley Allen
  GE:S&T IV-1481
Tynan, Kenneth Peacock
  GE:A&C IV-1721, 1924
Tyndale, William
  GL:B&C V-2488
Tyrtaeus
  GE:A&M I-134
Tyrtamus. *See* Theophrastus
Tyson, Cicely
  GL:AmW V-1792
Tzara, Tristan
  GE:A&C I-419, 513
Tz'u-hsi
  GE:HR I-1
  GE:W20 I-92

U

U Thant
GE:HR II-808, III-1212, 1236, 1391, 1430,
1457, 1644
GE:ME III-1654
GL:20 V-2240

Uchida, Yoshiko
GL:AmW V-1797

Uchtenhagen, Lilian
GE:HR III-1605

Udall, Morris
GE:B&C IV-1331, 1653

Udall, Stewart L.
GE:B&C IV-1374

Ugo of Segni. *See* Gregory IX, Pope

Ugolino, Cardinal
GE:A&M III-1447

Ugolino of Orvieto
GE:A&M III-1410

Ulam, Stanislaw
GE:S&T III-1401
GE:W20 II-683

Ulbricht, Walter
GE:HR II-795, III-1125
GE:ME III-1624, 1666
GE:W20 II-647
GL:20 V-2333

Ullah, Khwaja Salim
GE:HR I-87

Ulman, Douglas. *See* Fairbanks, Douglas, Sr.

Ulmanis, Karlis
GE:HR I-207

Ul-Mulk, Nawab Mohsin, Sayyid Mahdi Ali
GE:HR I-87

Ulpian (Domitius Ulpianus)
GE:A&M II-784

Ulpianus, Domitius. *See* Ulpian

Ulrich
GE:ME I-76

Ulyanov, Vladimir Ilich. *See* Lenin, Vladimir Ilich

Unamuno y Jugo, Miguel de
GL:20 V-2338

Underwood, Oscar Wilder
GE:Am III-1405, 1531
GE:B&C I-297

Unkei
GL:A&M V-2192

Unwin, Rayner
GE:A&C III-1607

Updike, John
GE:A&C IV-2163

Uquaili, Nabi Baksh Mohammed Sidiq
GE:B&C III-1276

Urban II
GE:A&M III-1257, 1276, 1354
GL:A&M V-2197

Urban VI
GE:A&M III-1644

Urban VIII
GE:ME I-285

Ure, Mary
GE:A&C IV-1721

U'Ren, William
GE:Am II-1307

Urey, Harold Clayton
GE:S&T IV-1465
GL:Am V-2366

Ussachevsky, Vladimir
GE:A&C IV-1785

Utaibi, Juhaiman ibn Muhammad
GE:HR IV-2095

V

Vadim, Roger
  GE:A&C IV-1710
Vaid, Urvashi
  GE:HR V-2364
Vail, Alfred
  GE:Am II-742
Vail, Theodore N.
  GE:B&C II-470
  GE:S&T II-615
Vaillant, Édouard
  GE:ME II-1044
Valdemar II
  GL:A&M V-2202
Valdez, R.
  GE:HR IV-1993
Valens
  GE:A&M II-893, 898
Valenti, Jack
  GE:B&C IV-1573
Valentinian II
  GE:A&M II-904
Valentinus
  GE:A&M II-747
  GL:A&M V-2206
Valenzuela, Pablo
  GE:S&T V-2326
Valera, Eamon De
  GE:HR I-309
Valerian
  GE:A&M II-812
Valerius, Licinius. See Licinius, Valerius
Valerius, Manius
  GE:A&M I-221
Valerius Constantius Chlorus, Flavius. See
  Constantius
Valerius Diocletianus, Gaius Aurelius. See
  Diocletian
Valerius Laevinius, Marcus. See Laevinius,
  Marcus Valerius
Valerius Maxentius, Marcus Aurelius. See
  Maxentius
Valerius Maximianus, Gaius Galerius. See
  Galerius
Valerius Maximianus, Marcus Aurelius. See
  Maximian
Valéry, Paul
  GL:20 V-2343
Valla, Lorenzo
  GL:Ren V-2378

Valladas, Hélène
  GE:S&T V-2341
Vallee, Rudy
  GE:A&C II-828
Valletta, Vittorio
  GE:B&C III-1293
Valois, Louis de. See Louis XI
Van. See also entry under family name
Van Aeken, Jeroen. See Bosch, Hieronymus
Van Allen, James A.
  GE:S&T IV-1572, 1583, V-1956
  GE:W20 II-764
Van Breugel, Willem Johannes
  GE:S&T V-2367
Vanbrugh, Sir John
  GL:B&C V-2493
Van Brunt, Henry
  GE:Am II-1231
Van Buren, Martin
  GE:Am I-607, II-690, 696, 748, 760, 772
  GL:Am V-2371
Van Buren, Paul Matthews
  GE:W20 I-507
Van Calcar, Stephen
  GE:ME I-133
Vance, Cyrus Roberts
  GE:HR III-1376, IV-1903, 1943, 2045
  GE:W20 II-1054, III-1331
Vance, Harold S.
  GE:B&C III-1190
Vance, Vivian
  GE:A&C III-1525
Van Cleef, Lee
  GE:A&C IV-1984
Van Couvering, John
  GE:S&T V-2279
Van Deerlin, Lionel
  GE:B&C II-685
Van de Graaff, Robert Jemison
  GE:S&T III-1336
Vandegrift, Alexander A.
  GE:Am III-1709
Van de Hulst, Hendrik Christoffel
  GE:S&T IV-1414, 1496
Vandenberg, Arthur Hendrick
  GE:Am III-1741, 1800, 1806
  GE:B&C II-656
  GE:ME III-1555

Vandenberg, Hoyt
  GE:W20 II-683
Van den Bruck, Mueller
  GE:ME III-1363
Vanderbilt, Cornelius
  GL:Am V-2377
Vanderbilt, Gloria
  GL:AmW V-1801
Vanderbilt, William H.
  GE:Am II-1135
Van der Lubbe, Marinus
  GE:HR I-480
  GE:ME III-1377
Van der Meer, Simon
  GE:S&T V-2230
Vandermeersch, Bernard
  GE:S&T V-2341
Van der Weyden, Rogier. See Weyden, Rogier
  van der
Vanderwier, Gerald
  GE:HR IV-2124
Van Doesburg, Theo. See Doesburg, Theo van
Van Doren, Carl
  GE:A&C I-502
Van Dyke, Dick
  GE:A&C IV-1908
Van Dyke, Fred
  GE:W20 II-842
Vane, Sir Henry
  GE:Am I-103
Vanga, Epifanio Fernández
  GE:HR II-801
Van Gogh, Vincent. See Gogh, Vincent van
Van Hengel, Adrianus Johannes
  GE:B&C II-613
Van Heuven Goedhart, Gerrit Jan
  GE:HR II-855, 867
Van Kuijk, Andreas Cornelius. See Parker,
  Colonel Tom
Van Leeuwenhoek, Antoni
  GE:S&T V-2093
  GL:Ren III-1280
Van Maanen, Adriaan
  GE:S&T II-502, 655, 790
Vannikov, Boris Lvovich
  GE:ME III-1561
Van Ronk, Dave
  GE:HR III-1479
Van Steenwyk, Elmer Arnold (E. A.)
  GE:B&C II-557
Van Sweringen, Mantis James
  GE:Am III-1811
Van Sweringen, Oris Paxton
  GE:Am III-1811

Van Tassel, James
  GE:S&T V-1971
Van Twiller, Wouter
  GE:Am I-91
Varas, Emilio C.
  GE:Am II-1190
Vardhamāna
  GL:A&M V-2213
Varèse, Edgard
  GE:A&C III-1629
  GL:20 V-2348
Vargas, Virgilio Barco
  GE:HR V-2465
Vargas Llosa, Mario
  GE:A&C IV-1689, 2086
Varius Rufus. See Rufus, Varius
Varro, Marcus Terentius
  GL:A&M V-2217
Varus, Publius Quintilius
  GE:A&M II-578, 584
Vasa, Sigismund III (of Sweden)
  GE:ME I-247
Vasa, Wladyslav
  GE:ME I-247
Vasari, Giorgio
  GL:Ren V-2384
Vasilyevich, Ivan
  GE:ME I-231
Vásquez de Coronado, Francisco. See Coronado,
  Francisco Vásquez de
Vassian, Bishop
  GE:A&M III-1742
Vassiliou, George
  GE:HR III-1218
Vauban, Sébastien Le Prestre de
  GL:Ren V-2390
Vaucouleurs, Gérard Henri de. See
  De Vaucouleurs, Gérard Henri
Vaughn, Jack Hood
  GE:Am III-1870
Vaughan, Sarah
  GL:AmW V-1806
Vaughan Williams, Ralph
  GE:A&C I-90
  GL:B&C V-2500
Vaughan Williams, Ursula Wood
  GE:A&C I-90
Vaux, Roland de
  GE:S&T III-1298
Vauxcelles, Louis
  GE:A&C I-204
Vavilov, Nikolai Ivanovich
  GL:20 V-2353

Vavilov, Sergei
    GE:ME III-1561
Veblen, Thorstein
    GL:Am V-2382
Vecellio, Tiziano. *See* Titian
Vega, Frank
    GE:B&C V-1842
Vega Carpio, Lope de
    GL:Ren V-2395
Veidt, Conrad
    GE:A&C I-486, III-1245
Veksler, Vladimir Iosifovich
    GE:S&T III-1282
Velásquez Rodríguez, Angel Manfredo
    GE:HR III-1503
Velázquez, Diego
    GE:ME I-59
    GL:Ren V-2400
Velde, Henry van de
    GE:A&C I-181
Venette, Jean de
    GL:A&M V-2223
Venizélos, Eleuthérios
    GL:20 V-2358
Ventris, Michael
    GE:S&T I-67
Ver, Fabian
    GE:HR III-1680, IV-2198
Vercingetorix
    GE:A&M I-516
Verdi, Giuseppe
    GL:Ren V-2405
Verdon, Gwen
    GL:AmW V-1810
Vereen, Ben
    GE:A&C V-2254, 2397
Verges, Jacques
    GE:HR IV-2193
Vergil
    GE:A&M I-556
    GL:A&M V-2228
Vergilius Maro, Publius. *See* Vergil
Verkuil, Paul R.
    GE:B&C I-47
Vermeer, Jan
    GL:Ren V-2410
Verne, Jules
    GE:Am III-1555
Vernon, James
    GE:Am I-182
Vernov, Sergei
    GE:S&T IV-1614
Veronese, Paolo
    GL:Ren V-2415

Verrius Flaccus, Marcus
    GL:A&M V-2233
Verrocchio, Andrea del
    GL:Ren V-2419
Verschuur, Gerrit L.
    GE:W20 II-827
Vertov, Dziga
    GE:A&C II-701
Verus, Marcus Annius. *See* Marcus Aurelius
Verwoerd, Hendrik Frensch
    GE:HR II-861
Vesalius, Andreas
    GE:ME I-133
    GL:Ren V-2424
Vespasian
    GE:A&M II-648
    GL:A&M V-2237
Vespucci, Amerigo
    GL:Ren V-2429
Veturius, Lucius
    GE:A&M I-253
Veuillot, Louis François
    GE:ME III-1143
Vibulanus, Quintus Fabius. *See* Fabius Vibulanus, Quintus
Vicious, Sid
    GE:A&C V-2299, 2360
Vico, Giambattista
    GL:Ren V-2435
Victor, Claude (Claude Victor Perrin)
    GE:ME II-556
Victor Emmanuel II (of Italy)
    GE:ME II-770, 838, 849, 860, 870, 923, 958
Victor Emmanuel III
    GE:HR I-395
    GE:ME III-1319, 1354, 1486
Victoria, (of England)
    GE:ME II-799
    GE:W20 I-14
    GL:B&C V-2505
Videla, Jorge Rafael
    GE:HR V-2280
Vidor, King
    GE:A&C II-772
Viegas Carrascaloã. *See* Carrascaloã, Mário Viegas
Vigée-Lebrun, Élisabeth
    GL:Ren V-2440
Vigilantius
    GE:A&M II-929
Vikár, Béla
    GE:A&C I-102
Vilas, George H.
    GE:Am II-1116

Villa, Francisco "Pancho." *See* Villa, Pancho
Villa, Pancho
  GE:Am III-1438
  GE:W20 I-69
  GL:20 V-2363
Village People, the
  GE:A&C V-2386
Villa-Lobos, Heiter
  GE:A&C IV-1818
  GL:20 V-2368
Villa-Lobos, Lucilia Guimarães
  GE:A&C IV-1818
Villalta, Guillermo Pérez
  GE:A&C V-2203
Villani, Giovanni
  GL:A&M V-2242
Villanova, Arnold of. *See* Arnold of Villanova
Villard, Oswald Garrison
  GE:Am III-1384
  GE:HR I-327
Villehardouin, Geoffroi de
  GL:A&M V-2247
Villeneuve, Arnaud de. *See* Arnold of Villanova
Villiers, Charles
  GE:ME II-764
Villiers, George. *See* Buckingham, First Duke of
Villius, Lucius
  GE:A&M I-448
Villon, François
  GL:A&M V-2254
Villon, Jacques
  GE:A&C I-349
Vincent de Paul, Saint
  GL:Ren V-2445
Vincent of Beauvais
  GE:A&M II-1533
  GL:A&M V-2261
Vincent of Lérins, Saint
  GL:A&M V-2265
Vinci, Leonardo da. *See* Leonardo da Vinci
Vinogradov, Alexander
  GE:S&T V-2042
Vinson, Carl
  GE:W20 I-368
Vinson, Frederick Moore
  GE:Am III-1849
  GE:B&C III-997
Viola, Roberto Eduardo
  GE:HR V-2280
Violaki-Paraskeva, Meropi
  GE:HR IV-1893
Violette, Maurice
  GE:HR II-651

Viollet-le-Duc, Eugène-Emmanuel
  GE:A&C I-257
Vipsanius Agrippa, Marcus. *See* Agrippa, Marcus
  Vipsanius
Virchow, Rudolf
  GE:ME II-822
  GE:S&T I-428
  GL:Ren V-2450
Virgil. *See* Vergil
Visconti-Venosta, Emilio
  GE:ME II-978
Vishtaspa
  GE:A&M I-163
Vitale, Faliero I
  GE:A&M III-1354
Vitale, Michieli
  GE:A&M III-1354
Viten
  GE:A&M III-1650
Vitold
  GE:A&M III-1650
Vitoria, Francisco de
  GL:Ren V-2455
Vitry, Philippe de
  GL:A&M V-2270
Vivaldi, Antonio
  GL:Ren V-2460
Vivar, Rodrigo Díaz de. *See* Cid, El
Viviani, René Raphaël
  GE:Am III-1531
Vladimir I
  GL:A&M V-2274
Vladimir of Kiev
  GE:A&M III-1205, 1215
Vladislav II Jagiello. *See* Jadwiga and Władysław
  II Jagiełło
Vlaminck, Maurice de
  GE:A&C I-140, 156
Vlasi, Azem
  GE:HR V-2386
Vo Nguyen Giap
  GE:HR II-573, 683
  GE:ME III-1577
  GE:W20 II-696, III-1243
  GL:20 V-2373
Voelkel, Steven A.
  GE:S&T V-2273
Voeller, Bruce
  GE:HR IV-1741
Vogel, Orville A.
  GE:B&C III-1133
Vogel, Phillip
  GE:S&T IV-1635

Vogel, W.
    GE:S&T II-562
Vogelweide. See Walther von der Vogelweide
Vogt, A. E. van
    GE:A&C III-1094
Volcker, Paul A.
    GE:B&C V-1757, 1870
    GE:W20 III-1104
Volkoff, George Michael
    GE:S&T III-1150
Vollmer, August
    GE:S&T II-711
Volonté, Gian Maria
    GE:A&C IV-1984
Voloshanovich, Alexander
    GE:HR IV-1909
Volpe, John A.
    GE:B&C IV-1431
Volta, Count Alessandro
    GE:ME II-560
    GL:Ren V-2466
Voltaire
    GE:ME I-446, 456
    GL:Ren V-2471
Volterra, Vito
    GE:S&T I-325
Volynov, Boris V.
    GE:S&T IV-1891
Von. See also entry under family name
Von Aehrenthal, Count Alois Lexa
    GE:ME III-1202, 1228
Von Alvensleben, Albrecht
    GE:ME II-711
Von Baeyer, Adolf. See Baeyer, Adolf von
Von Behring, Emil Adolf. See Behring, Emil
    Adolf von
Von Benedek, Ludwig
    GE:ME II-912
Von Berchtold, Count Leopold
    GE:ME III-1240, 1245, 1340
Von Bethmann-Hollweg, Theobald. See
    Bethman-Hollweg, Theobald von
Von Beust, Count Friedrich Ferdinand. See Beust,
    Friedrich von
Von Bieberstein, Baron Adolf Herman Marschall
    GE:ME II-1133
Von Bismarck-Schönhausen, Count Otto Eduard
    Leopold. See Bismarck, Otto von
Von Blomberg, Werner. See Blomberg, Werner
    von
Von Blücher, Gebhard Leberecht. See Blücher,
    Gebhard Leberecht von
Von Bodelschwingh, Ernst
    GE:ME II-711

Von Boyen, Hermann
    GE:ME II-572
Von Brandenburg, Count Friedrich Wilhelm
    GE:ME II-790
Von Braun, Wernher. See Braun, Wernher von
Von Brockdorff-Rantzau, Count Ulrich
    GE:ME III-1283
Von Bülow, Prince Bernhard. See Bülow,
    Bernhard von
Von Bülow, Karl
    GE:ME III-1249
Von Döllinger, Johann Joseph Ignaz
    GE:ME II-902, 969
Von Falkenhayn, Erich
    GE:ME III-1262
Von Falkenhorst, Nikolaus
    GE:ME III-1446
Von Gneisenau, August Neithardt. See
    Gneisenau, August von
Von Grumbkow, Frederick William
    GE:ME I-396
Von Hardenberg, Prince Karl August. See
    Hardenberg, Karl von
Von Helmholtz, Hermann Ludwig Ferdinand. See
    Helmholtz, Hermann von
Von Herder, Johann Gottfried
    GE:Am II-730
    GE:ME I-480
Von Hindenburg, Paul (Paul Ludwig Hans von
    Beneckendorff und von Hindenburg). See
    Hindenburg, Paul von
Von Hipper, Franz
    GE:ME III-1266
Von Hohenheim, Philippus Aureolus
    Theophrastus Bombast. See Paracelsus
Von Hötzendorf, Count Franz Conrad
    GE:ME III-1228
Von Humboldt, Wilhelm. See Humbolt, Wilhelm
    von
Von Kaunitz-Rietberg, Prince Wenzel Anton
    GE:ME I-437, 469, 480
Von Ketteler, Bishop Wilhelm Emmanuel
    GE:ME II-1028
Von Kiderlen-Waechter, Alfred. See
    Kiderlen-Waechter, Alfred von
Von Klitzing, Klaus
    GE:S&T V-2136
Von Kluck, Alexander
    GE:ME III-1249
Von Knobelsdorf, Schmidt
    GE:ME III-1262
Von Krismaníc, Gideon
    GE:ME II-912

Von Leiberich, Baron Karl Mack
  GE:ME II-568
Von Maassen, Karl Georg
  GE:ME II-711
Von Manstein, Erich
  GE:ME III-1451, 1472
Von Manteuffel, Hasso
  GE:ME III-1496
Von Mantueffel, Baron Otto
  GE:ME II-790
Von Melas, Baron Michael Friedrich Benedikt
  GE:ME II-556
Von Metternich, Prince Klemens
  GE:Am I-593
  GE:ME II-598, 602, 612, 623, 634, 638, 654,
    775, 794
Von Moltke, Count Helmuth
  GE:ME II-880, 912, 949, 954, III-1249
Von Nägeli, Karl Wilhelm
  GE:ME II-908
Vonnegut, Bernard
  GE:S&T III-1276
Vonnegut, Kurt, Jr.
  GE:A&C IV-1939
Von Neumann, John
  GE:S&T III-1045, 1213, 1347, 1396, IV-1475
  GE:W20 II-535, 683
  GL:Am IV-1640
Von Ranke, Leopold. See Ranke, Leopold von
Von Roon, Count Albrecht Theodor Emil
  GE:ME II-880, 949
Von Rundstedt, Karl Rudolf Gerd. See Runstedt,
  Gerd von
Von Salis-Soglio, Johann Ulrich
  GE:ME II-794
Von Salza, Hermann
  GE:A&M III-1472
Von Scharnhorst, Gerhard Johann. See
  Scharnhorst, Gerhard Johann David von
Von Schlieffen, Alfred
  GE:ME III-1249
Von Schoen, Baron Wilhelm Eduard
  GE:ME III-1207

Von Schön, Theodor
  GE:ME II-572
Von Schuschnigg, Kurt
  GE:ME III-1425
Von Schweitzer, Johann Baptist
  GE:ME II-992
Von Seyss-Inquart, Artur
  GE:ME III-1425
Von Siemens, Georg
  GE:ME II-1133
Von Sonnenfels, Joseph
  GE:ME I-480
Von Stemrich, Wilhelm
  GE:ME III-1207
Von Sternberg, Josef
  GE:A&C II-845
Von Stroheim, Erich
  GE:A&C II-593, 1073
Von Sydow, Oscar
  GE:HR I-345
Von Tirpitz, Alfred
  GE:S&T I-350
Von Trauttmansdorff, Count Maximilian
  GE:ME I-308
Von Truchsess, George
  GE:ME I-76
Von Waechter, Karl Georg
  GE:ME III-1395
Von Weizsäcker, Carl Friedrich
  GE:S&T III-1208
Von Werther, Baron Karl
  GE:ME II-949
Vorster, Balthazar Johannes (John)
  GE:HR IV-1882, 1887, 2008, V-2244
  GE:W20 III-1272
Voskresensky, Vasily. See Basil, Colonel
  Wassili de
Vreeland, Diana
  GL:AmW V-1815
Vries, Hugo de. See De Vries, Hugo
Vuillard, Édouard
  GL:20 V-2379
Vyshinsky, Andrei
  GE:W20 I-336

W

Wach, Joachim
  GL:20 V-2384
Wachtel, Stephen
  GE:S&T V-2346
Wadati, Kiyoo
  GE:S&T III-1050
Waddell, William B.
  GE:Am II-925
Waddy, Joseph C.
  GE:HR IV-1780
Wade, Henry
  GE:HR IV-1703
  GE:W20 III-1154
Wade, Jeptha H.
  GE:Am II-930
Wagner, Adolf
  GE:ME II-1028
Wagner, Otto
  GE:A&C I-79
Wagner, Richard
  GL:Ren V-2476
Wagner, Robert F.
  GE:Am III-1637
  GE:B&C I-191, II-662, 706, 781
  GE:HR I-508, 514
Wagner, Robin
  GE:A&C V-2254
Wagoner, Dan
  GE:A&C III-1602
Wagstaff, Sam
  GE:A&C V-2636
Wahl, Arthur C.
  GE:S&T III-1181
Wain, John
  GE:A&C III-1454
Wai-shih. *See* Mi Fei
Wait, Isaac
  GE:Am II-785
Wakefield, Edward Gibbon
  GL:B&C V-2511
Waksman, Selman Abraham
  GE:S&T III-1224
  GL:Am V-2387
Walcott, Charles Dolittle
  GE:S&T IV-1481
Wald, Lillian D.
  GE:HR I-131
  GL:AmW V-1820

Waldeck-Rousseau, Pierre Marie René
  GE:ME II-1044, III-1143
Waldemar II. *See* Valdemar II
Waldersee, Count Alfred von
  GE:HR I-1
Waldeyer, Wilhelm von
  GE:S&T II-476
Waldheim, Kurt
  GE:HR III-1457, IV-1775, 1841, 1893, 1993,
    2008, 2040
Waldo, Peter
  GE:A&M III-1381
Waldock, Sir Humphrey
  GE:HR II-843
Walensky, Sir Roy
  GE:ME III-1642
Walentynowicz, Anna
  GE:HR IV-2112
Wałęsa, Lech
  GE:B&C V-2017
  GE:HR IV-2112, 2152, V-2477, 2500
  GL:20 V-2390
Walewski, Count
  GE:ME II-838
Walker, Alice
  GL:AmW V-1825
Walker, Madam C. J.
  GL:AmW V-1830
Walker, David
  GE:Am II-719
Walker, Edwin
  GE:Am II-1237
Walker, Frank
  GE:Am III-1632
Walker, Joseph R.
  GE:Am II-795
Walker, Maggie Lena
  GL:AmW V-1835
Walker, Robert John
  GE:Am II-772, 889, 1037
  GE:B&C I-297
Walker, William H.
  GE:B&C I-11
Wall, Danny C.
  GE:B&C V-1991
Wallace, Alfred Russel
  GE:ME II-855

Wallace, DeWitt
  GE:A&C II-549
  GE:B&C I-390
Wallace, George
  GE:Am III-1933
  GE:HR III-1278
Wallace, George J.
  GE:W20 II-942
Wallace, Henry A.
  GE:Am III-1615, 1800
  GE:B&C II-668
  GE:HR I-555, III-1515
  GE:W20 II-572
  GL:Am V-2393
Wallace, Lila Bell Acheson
  GE:A&C II-549
Wallace, Mike
  GE:A&C IV-2136
Wallace, Ruby Ann. See Dee, Ruby
Wallach, Eli
  GE:A&C IV-1984
Wallach, Meier Moiseevich. See Litvinov,
  Maksim Maksimovich
Wallenstein, Albrecht Wenzel von
  GE:ME I-236, 270, 274
  GL:Ren V-2482
Waller, Augustus D.
  GE:S&T I-41
Wallia
  GE:A&M II-958
Walling, William English
  GE:Am III-1384
Wallis, W. Allen
  GE:B&C III-931
Walpole, Sir Robert
  GE:Am I-182
  GL:B&C V-2516
Walras, Léon
  GL:20 V-2395
Walsh, Raoul
  GE:A&C I-402
Walsh, Thomas J.
  GE:Am III-1525
  GE:B&C II-464, 792
  GE:HR I-172
Walter, Bruno
  GE:A&C I-298
Walter, John, II
  GE:ME II-730
  GL:B&C V-2523
Walters, Barbara
  GL:AmW V-1840
Walthall, Henry B.
  GE:A&C I-402

Walther von der Vogelweide
  GL:A&M V-2279
Walton, Ernest Thomas Sinton
  GE:S&T III-978
Walton, John "Jack"
  GE:HR I-367
Walton, Samuel M.
  GE:B&C IV-1621
Walton, William
  GE:A&C III-1378
Walton, Sir William
  GL:B&C V-2529
Walwyn, William
  GE:ME I-317
Wang An-shih
  GL:A&M V-2284
Wang Ching-wei
  GL:20 V-2400
  GE:W20 I-361
Wang Ch'ung
  GL:A&M V-2289
Wang Hongwen
  GE:HR III-1332
Wang Hsi-chih
  GL:A&M V-2294
Wang Hung-wen
  GE:W20 III-1264
Wang Mo-ch'i. See Wang Wei
Wang Pi
  GL:A&M V-2299
Wang Wei
  GL:A&M V-2304
Wang Yang-ming
  GL:Ren V-2487
Wangenheim, Hans von
  GE:W20 I-107
Wanger, Walter
  GE:A&C III-1115
Wankel, Felix
  GL:20 V-2406
Waraka
  GE:A&M II-1075
Warburg, Edward
  GE:A&C II-974
Warburg, Fredric
  GE:A&C III-1421
Warburg, Otto Heinrich
  GE:S&T III-1390
Warburg, Paul Moritz
  GE:B&C I-240
Ward, Aaron Montgomery
  GE:B&C I-6
Ward, Sir Adolphus William
  GE:W20 I-24

Ward, Geoffrey C.
  GE:A&C V-2657
Ward, Sir Joseph George
  GE:W20 I-14
Ward, Julia. *See* Howe, Julia Ward
Ward, Lester Frank
  GE:Am III-1357
  GL:Am V-2400
Ward, Montgomery
  GL:Am V-2405
Ward, Theodora
  GE:A&C IV-1662
Wardhana, Ali
  GE:W20 III-1104
Ware, Henry
  GE:Am I-570
Wärendorf, Fritz
  GE:A&C I-79
Warhol, Andy
  GE:A&C IV-2053
  GL:Am V-2412
Warhola, Andrew. *See* Warhol, Andy
Warm, Hermann
  GE:A&C I-486
Warne, Colston E.
  GE:HR I-527, II-1062
Warner, Albert
  GE:A&C II-761
  GE:S&T II-820
Warner, Harry
  GE:A&C II-734, 761
  GE:S&T II-820
Warner, Jack L.
  GE:A&C II-734, 833
  GE:B&C II-545
  GE:S&T II-820
Warner, John W.
  GE:W20 III-1287
Warner, Samuel
  GE:A&C II-734, 761
  GE:B&C II-545
  GE:S&T II-820
Warner, William Lloyd
  GE:B&C II-437
Warren, Earl
  GE:Am III-1800, 1849, 1883
  GE:HR II-595, 624, 913, 1003, III-1182, 1343
  GE:W20 I-513, II-893, 949
  GL:Am V-2417
Warren, Joseph
  GE:Am I-241
Warren, Mercy Otis
  GL:AmW V-1845

Warren, Stafford L.
  GE:S&T II-562
Warwick, Earl of
  GL:B&C V-2535
Warwick, Second Earl of. *See* Rich, Robert
Washington, Booker T.
  GE:Am II-1249, III-1384, 1444
  GE:HR I-41
  GL:Am V-2424
Washington, Denzel
  GE:A&C V-2565
Washington, George
  GE:Am I-256, 294, 330, 341, 345, 350, 356,
    377, 383, 389, 396, 403, 432
  GL:Am V-2430
Washington, Lula
  GE:A&C V-2521
Washkansky, Louis
  GE:S&T IV-1866
  GE:W20 II-1016
Wassermann, August von
  GE:S&T II-756
Wasson, Ben
  GE:A&C II-805
Watanabe, Takeshi
  GE:B&C III-1276
Waterhouse, Keith
  GE:A&C III-1454
Waterman, Robert H., Jr.
  GE:B&C V-1815
Waters, Walter W.
  GE:Am III-1582
Watson, Forbes
  GE:A&C II-885
Watson, James D.
  GE:ME III-1572
  GE:S&T III-1406
  GL:Am V-2436
Watson, John B.
  GE:A&C II-896
Watson, Thomas A.
  GE:Am II-1089
  GE:S&T II-595
Watson, Thomas Edward
  GE:Am II-1225, 1268
Watson, Thomas J., Jr.
  GE:B&C II-447
  GE:S&T V-2240
Watson, Thomas J., Sr.
  GE:B&C II-447
  GE:S&T III-1024, V-2169
Watson-Watt, Sir Robert
  GE:S&T III-1040
  GE:W20 I-324

Watt, James
  GE:Am I-371
  GE:ME I-460
  GL:B&C V-2541
Watt, Margaret
  GE:HR I-167
Watteau, Antoine
  GL:Ren V-2492
Wattenberg, Hermann
  GE:S&T II-805
Watters, Robert Lisle
  GE:S&T III-1101
Watterson, Mark
  GE:B&C II-453
Watterson, Wilfred
  GE:B&C II-453
Wattleton, Faye
  GE:HR V-2489
Watts, Charlie
  GE:A&C IV-2027
Watts, Michael
  GE:HR IV-2101
Watts, Sir Philip
  GE:ME III-1187
Wauneka, Annie Dodge
  GL:AmW V-1849
Wavell, Sir Archibald Percival
  GE:ME III-1467
  GE:W20 I-457
Waxman, Henry A.
  GE:B&C V-2034
Wayne, John
  GE:A&C III-1115, 1313
Wayne, "Mad" Anthony
  GE:Am I-383
We Xueqian
  GE:B&C V-1887
Weaver, Dennis
  GE:A&C IV-1668
Weaver, George "Buck"
  GE:Am III-1497
Weaver, Harriet Shaw
  GE:A&C II-555
Weaver, James Baird
  GE:Am II-1225
Weaver, Raymond M.
  GE:A&C I-502
Weaver, Sylvester "Pat"
  GE:A&C III-1465, 1623
Webb, Beatrice
  GE:B&C III-885
  GE:HR I-75
Webb, Beatrice, and Sidney Webb
  GL:B&C V-2546

Webb, Frank C.
  GE:B&C I-47
Webb, Jack
  GE:A&C III-1531
Webb, Sidney
  GE:HR I-75
Webb, William H.
  GE:Am II-807
Webber, Andrew Lloyd
  GE:A&C V-2254
Weber, Brian
  GE:B&C IV-1704
  GE:HR IV-2029
Weber, Carl Maria von
  GL:Ren V-2497
Weber, Heinrich
  GE:S&T I-438
Weber, Lois
  GL:AmW V-1854
Weber, Max
  GE:W20 I-38
  GL:20 V-2411
Weber, Susan
  GE:HR III-1386
Webern, Anton von
  GE:A&C I-193, 367, 528
  GL:20 V-2416
Webster, Daniel
  GE:Am I-539, 564, 600, 607, 660, II-690, 696,
    778, 801, 854
  GL:Am V-2441
Webster, Noah
  GE:Am I-636
  GL:Am V-2446
Wedderburn, Joseph
  GE:S&T I-438
Weddigen, Otto
  GE:ME III-1254
Weddington, Sarah
  GL:AmW V-1859
Wedekind, Frank
  GE:A&C II-1078
Wedgwood, Josiah
  GL:B&C V-2553
Weed, Thurlow
  GE:Am I-607, II-760, 877
Weems, Charlie
  GE:Am III-1588
Wegelius, Martin
  GE:A&C I-292
Wegener, Alfred Lothar
  GE:S&T II-522, IV-1508, 1650, 1876
  GL:20 V-2423

Weglyn, Michiko Nishiura
  GE:HR V-2392
Wehner, Herbert
  GE:ME III-1690
Wei Jingsheng
  GE:HR IV-1983
Weidenreich, Franz
  GE:S&T II-761, III-1096
Weidman, Charles
  GE:A&C I-390
Weigel, Helene
  GE:A&C III-1410
Weil, André
  GE:S&T III-1140
Weil, Simone
  GL:20 V-2429
Weill, Kurt
  GE:A&C II-724
  GL:20 V-2435
Weinberg, Jack
  GE:Am III-1912
Weinberg, Wilhelm
  GE:S&T I-390
Weinberger, Caspar
  GE:B&C IV-1727
Weiner, Alexander S.
  GE:S&T I-56
Weininger, Otto
  GE:A&C I-518
Weisenfreund, Muni. See Muni, Paul
Weisman, Joel
  GE:S&T V-2149
Weismann, August
  GL:Ren V-2503
Weiss, Charles S.
  GE:B&C V-1939
Weiss, Peter
  GE:A&C IV-2005
Weitz, Paul J.
  GE:S&T V-1997
Weizman, Ezer
  GE:HR IV-1943
Weizmann, Chaim
  GE:HR I-235, II-749, 761
  GE:W20 I-231, II-634
  GL:20 V-2441
Welch, Robert
  GE:Am III-1861
Weld, Theodore Dwight
  GE:Am I-642, II-708, 719
Wellens, Joe
  GE:S&T V-2245
Welles, Julia Elizabeth. See Andrews, Julie

Welles, Orson
  GE:A&C II-989, III-1103, 1200
Welles, Sumner
  GE:HR II-584
  GE:W20 I-260, II-743
Wellesley, Arthur. See Wellington, Duke of
Wellington, Duke of
  GE:ME II-594, 618, 623, 654, 669, 704
  GL:B&C V-2560
Wellman, William
  GE:A&C II-839
Wells, Frank
  GE:B&C V-2056
Wells, Gideon
  GE:Am II-957
Wells, Horace
  GE:Am II-791
Wells-Barnett, Ida B.
  GL:AmW V-1864
Wels, Otto
  GE:ME III-1382
Welsh, Herbert
  GE:Am II-1161
Welsh, John
  GE:A&C IV-1721
Welyer y Nicolau, Valeriano
  GE:Am II-1243
Wenceslaus
  GE:A&M III-1675
Wen-chung. See Ou-yang Hsiu
Weng Chung Pei
  GE:S&T II-761, III-1096
Wentworth, Charles Watson (Marquis of
    Rockingham)
  GE:Am I-219
Wentworth, John
  GE:Am II-906
Wentworth, Thomas. See Strafford, First Earl of
Wentworth, W. C.
  GL:B&C V-2565
Werner, Thomas
  GE:A&C V-2532
Wertheimer, Max
  GL:20 V-2447
Wertheimer, Pie
  GE:A&C I-474
Wesley, Charles
  GE:ME I-409
Wesley, John
  GE:ME I-409
  GL:B&C V-2570
Wesley, Susanna
  GE:ME I-409

West, Mae
  GL:AmW V-1868
West, Thomas (Lord de La Warr)
  GE:Am I-59
Westinghouse, George
  GL:Am V-2451
Westminster, Duke of. *See* Grosvenor, Hugh
  "Bend'or"
Westmoreland, William Childs
  GE:W20 II-1036
Weston, George M.
  GE:Am II-1083
Weston, Thomas
  GE:Am I-74
Westwood, Vivienne
  GE:A&C V-2299
Wetherald, Richard
  GE:S&T IV-1840
Wexler, Harry
  GE:S&T IV-1667
Weyden, Rogier van der
  GL:Ren V-2508
Weydenhammer, Rudolf
  GE:ME III-1395
Weygand, Maxime
  GE:ME III-1451
Weyl, Walter
  GE:A&C I-385
Weyler, Valeriano Nicolau
  GE:ME II-1119
Whale, James
  GE:A&C II-863
Whalen, Robert P.
  GE:HR IV-1961
Wharton, Edith
  GL:Am V-2457
  GL:AmW V-1873
Whately, Thomas
  GE:Am I-219
Wheatstone, Charles, and William Fothergill
  Cooke
  GL:B&C II-683
Wheeler, Burton Kendall
  GE:Am III-1667
  GE:B&C II-775
Wheeler, Earle Gilmore
  GE:W20 II-1036
Wheeler, John Archibald
  GE:S&T IV-1881
Wheeler, William Morton
  GE:S&T I-148
Wheelwright, George, III
  GE:B&C III-896

Whipple, Amiel Weeks
  GE:Am II-865
Whipple, Fred
  GE:S&T III-1379
Whipple, George Hoyt
  GE:S&T II-795
Whistler, James McNeill
  GL:Am V-2462
Whitaker, Martin D.
  GE:S&T III-1230
White, Andrew Dickson
  GE:Am II-1077
White, Burton L.
  GE:HR IV-2118
White, Byron
  GE:B&C V-1773, 1882
  GE:HR III-1343
  GE:W20 III-1154
White, Clarence H.
  GE:A&C I-63
White, E. B.
  GE:A&C II-648
White, E. E.
  GE:Am II-1031
White, Edward A.
  GE:B&C IV-1517
White, Edward Douglass
  GE:Am II-1318
  GE:B&C I-206, 212
White, Ellen G.
  GL:AmW V-1878
White, Harry Dexter
  GE:B&C II-851
White, John
  GE:Am I-46
White, Katharine Sergeant
  GE:A&C II-648
White, Mary Ovington
  GE:Am III-1384
White, Robert I.
  GE:HR III-1532
White, Thomas W.
  GE:Am II-725
White, Tim
  GE:S&T V-2037
White, Walter
  GE:A&C II-755, III-1159
  GE:HR II-578, 777
Whitefield, George
  GE:Am I-176
  GE:ME I-409
Whitehead, Alfred North
  GE:S&T I-465

GE:W20 I-79
GL:B&C V-2477
Whitehead, Sir Edgar
GE:ME III-1642
Whitehead, T. North
GE:B&C II-437
Whitelaw, William
GE:HR IV-1720
GE:W20 III-1117
Whiteman, Paul
GE:A&C II-598
Whitfield, Norman
GE:A&C IV-1790
Whitman, Walt
GE:A&C I-90, II-851, III-1179
GE:Am II-848
GL:Am V-2467
Whitney, Alexander Fell
GE:Am III-1759
GE:B&C III-880
Whitney, Courtney
GE:HR II-725
Whitney, Eli
GE:Am I-371
GE:S&T II-542
GL:Am V-2474
Whitney, Gertrude Vanderbilt
GE:A&C II-885
GL:AmW V-1884
Whitney, Richard
GE:Am III-1577
GE:B&C II-574, 679
Whitney, William Collins
GE:B&C I-57
Whitney, Willis R.
GE:B&C I-17
Whittle, Sir Frank
GE:S&T III-1187
GE:W20 I-355
GL:B&C V-2584
Who, the
GE:A&C IV-2104, 2180
Wickard, Claude R.
GE:B&C II-840
Wicker, Thomas Gray
GE:HR III-1633
Wickersham, George Woodward
GE:Am III-1507
GE:B&C I-29
Wiechert, Emil
GE:S&T I-51
Wielopolski, Count Aleksander
GE:ME II-886
Wiene, Robert
GE:A&C I-486

Wiener, Norbert
GL:Am V-2479
Wiesel, Elie
GE:A&C IV-1700
GE:HR V-2292
GL:20 V-2453
Wiesel, Shlomo
GE:A&C IV-1700
Wiesenthal, Simon
GL:20 V-2457
Wiggins, Marianne
GE:A&C V-2630
Wigginton, Randy
GE:S&T V-2073
Wightman, Hazel Hotchkiss
GL:AmW V-1888
Wigley, Mark
GE:A&C V-2614
Wigner, Eugene Paul
GE:S&T III-1230
Wijeratna, Ranjan
GE:HR V-2315
Wijeweera, Rohana
GE:HR III-1590, V-2315
Wilberforce, William
GE:ME II-715
GL:B&C V-2589
Wilde, Oscar
GE:A&C I-151
GE:HR II-991
Wilder, Billy
GE:A&C III-1567
Wilder, L. Douglas
GE:HR V-2517
Wilder, Thornton
GE:A&C III-1099, 1164
Wildgruber, Ulrich
GE:A&C IV-2126
Wiley, Calvin
GE:Am I-576
Wiley, Harvey Washingon
GE:B&C I-128
GE:HR I-46, 64
Wilhelmina
GE:HR I-92
Wilhelmus Rubruquis. *See* William of Rubrouck
Wilkes, Charles
GL:Am V-2484
Wilkes, John
GL:B&C V-2595
Wilkes, Maurice Vincent
GE:S&T IV-1475
Wilkie, William
GE:B&C IV-1410

Wilkins, Arnold F.
GE:S&T III-1040
Wilkins, Sir George Hubert
GL:B&C V-2601
Wilkins, Heath
GE:HR V-2506
Wilkins, Maurice H. F.
GE:ME III-1572
GE:S&T III-1406
GL:B&C V-2606
Wilkins, Robert Wallace
GE:S&T III-1353, IV-1429
Wilkins, Roy
GE:HR III-1370
Wilkinson, James
GE:Am I-396, 461, 467
Wilkinson, John
GL:B&C V-2612
Willadsen, Steen M.
GE:S&T V-2273
Willard, Daniel
GE:Am III-1460
Willard, Emma
GL:Am V-2488
GL:AmW V-1893
Willard, Frances
GL:Am V-2494
GL:AmW V-1898
Willard, Henry
GE:Am II-1110
Willem van Ruysbroeck. *See* William of
Rubrouck
Willem, Frederik. *See* William I (of The
Netherlands)
William I (of The Netherlands)
GE:ME II-686, 880, 912, 918, 949, 954, 963,
988, 993, 1013, 1028
William II (of Germany and Prussia)
GE:Am II-1201
GE:B&C I-293
GE:HR I-75
GE:ME II-1013, 1070, 1123, III-1148, 1192,
1207, 1262, 1295
GE:S&T I-350
GE:W20 I-46
GL:20 V-2464
William III (of England, Scotland, and Ireland)
GE:Am I-163
GE:ME I-357, 385
GL:B&C V-2623
William IV (of Great Britain and Ireland)
GE:ME II-704
GL:B&C V-2628

William, Crown Prince of Germany (Friedrich
Wilhelm Viktor August Ernst)
GE:ME III-1262
William, Duke of Normandy
GE:A&M III-1248
William, Earl of Salisbury
GE:A&M III-1496
William of Auvergne
GL:A&M V-2311
William of Auxerre
GE:A&M III-1338
GL:A&M V-2318
William of Beaujeau
GE:A&M III-1574
William of Conches
GE:A&M III-1231
William of Moerbeke
GE:A&M III-1544
GL:A&M V-2325
William of Nogaret
GE:A&M III-1592
William of Ockham. *See* Ockham, William of
William of Paris. *See* William of Auvergne
William of Rubrouck
GL:A&M V-2328
William of Saint-Amour
GL:A&M V-2333
William of Saint-Thierry
GL:A&M V-2339
William the Conqueror
GL:B&C V-2618
William the Pious, Duke of Aquitaine
GE:A&M II-1184
William the Silent
GL:Ren V-2512
Williams, Audrey Sheppard
GE:A&C III-1415
Williams, Betty
GE:HR IV-1932
Williams, Clarence
GE:A&C II-572
Williams, Claude "Lefty"
GE:Am III-1497
Williams, Eugene
GE:Am III-1588
Williams, George Washington
GL:Am V-2499
Williams, Hank
GE:A&C III-1415
Williams, Harrison A., Jr.
GE:B&C IV-1466, 1561
GE:HR III-1650
Williams, Hosea
GE:HR III-1278

Williams, Mary Lou
GL:AmW V-1903
Williams, Matt
GE:A&C V-2532
Williams, Paulette. *See* Shange, Ntozake
Williams, Ralph Vaughan. *See* Vaughan
Williams, Ralph
Williams, Roger
GE:Am I-85, 97, 318
GL:Am V-2504
Williams, Talcott
GE:A&C I-407
Williams, Tennessee
GE:A&C III-1164, 1487
GL:Am V-2509
Williams, Wendy
GE:B&C IV-1682
Williams, William Appleman
GE:W20 II-663
Williams, William Carlos
GE:A&C I-445
Williams, Sir William Emrys
GE:B&C II-696
Williamson, R. S.
GE:Am II-865
Willibrord
GE:A&M II-1126
Willie, James G.
GE:Am II-812
Willis, Frances E.
GE:HR III-1605
Willis, Gordon
GE:A&C V-2381
Willis, Henry Parker
GE:Am III-1432
GE:B&C I-240
Willkie, Wendell
GE:A&C III-1159
GE:Am III-1621
Wills, Helen Newington. *See* Moody, Helen Wills
Wills, William Henry
GE:B&C I-57
Willson, Meredith
GE:A&C IV-1752
Willstätter, Richard
GE:S&T I-345
Wilmot, David
GE:Am II-854
Wilson, Allan C.
GE:S&T V-2267
Wilson, Charles Erwin
GE:B&C III-943, 997
GE:HR II-766

Wilson, Charles Thomson Rees
GE:S&T I-356, II-746
Wilson, Sir David
GE:HR IV-2073
Wilson, Edmund
GE:A&C II-626
GL:Am V-2515
Wilson, Edmund Beecher
GE:S&T I-148
Wilson, Edward O.
GE:S&T IV-1808
Wilson, Sir Harold
GE:B&C IV-1347
GE:HR III-1316, 1485, IV-1870
GE:ME III-1642
GE:W20 III-1146
GL:B&C V-2634
Wilson, Henry
GE:Am II-991
Wilson, J. Tylee
GE:B&C V-1976
Wilson, Jackie
GE:B&C III-1143
Wilson, James
GE:Am I-330, 345, 367
GL:Am V-2521
Wilson, James Harold. *See* Wilson, Sir Harold
Wilson, Joseph C.
GE:S&T III-1013
GE:W20 I-382
Wilson, Kemmons
GE:B&C III-1138
Wilson, Richard
GE:HR IV-1709
GE:W20 II-865
Wilson, Robert M.
GE:A&C V-2375
Wilson, Robert Rathbun
GE:S&T V-2301
Wilson, Robert W.
GE:S&T IV-1762
Wilson, Teddy
GE:A&C II-930, 968
Wilson, Victoria
GE:S&T V-2296
Wilson, Woodrow
GE:A&C I-24
GE:Am II-1077, III-1390, 1405, 1432, 1438,
1450, 1454, 1460, 1466, 1472, 1478, 1484,
1491, 1507, 1513, 1560
GE:B&C I-35, 69, 246, 269, 275, 282, 297,
357, II-775
GE:HR I-172, 231, 241, 252, 270, 339, 350
GE:ME III-1283, 1289

GE:W20 I-107, 121, 158
GL:Am V-2529
Winant, John G.
GE:HR III-1509
Winchell, Walter
GE:A&C II-828
Winckelmann, Johann Joachim
GL:Ren V-2517
Windaus, Adolf
GE:S&T II-771
Windsor, Duke of
GE:ME III-1420
GL:B&C V-2639
Windthorst, Ludwig
GE:ME II-1013
Winfrey, Oprah
GL:AmW V-1909
Wingfield, Edward Maria
GE:Am I-59
Winkler, Henry
GE:A&C V-2305
Winnemucca, Sarah
GL:AmW V-1914
Winslow, Edward
GE:Am I-91, 109
Winter, Mildred
GE:HR IV-2118
Winthrop, John
GE:Am I-85, 103, 109
GL:Am V-2535
Winthrop, John, Jr.
GE:Am I-91
Wirt, William
GE:Am I-564
Wirtanen, Carl Alvan
GE:S&T IV-1454
Wirtz, Willard
GE:B&C II-840
GE:HR III-1397
Wise, Brownie
GE:B&C II-863
Wise, Henry Alexander
GE:Am II-918
Wise, Isaac Mayer
GL:Am V-2540
Wise, Robert
GE:A&C IV-2033
Witiza
GE:A&M II-1105
Witte, Edwin
GE:B&C II-711
GE:HR I-514
Witte, Count Sergei Yelievich. *See* Witte, Sergey
  Yulyevich

Witte, Sergey Yulyevich
GE:HR I-70
GE:ME II-1062, III-1148, 1169, 1179
Witten, Edward
GE:S&T V-2047
Wittgenstein, Ludwig
GE:A&C I-518
GL:20 V-2470
Wittich, Marie
GE:A&C I-151
Wiyayabahu, Keerthi. *See* Fernando, S. Saman
  Piyasiri
Władysław II Jagiełło and Jadwiga
GL:A&M V-2344
Wofford, Chloe Anthony. *See* Morrison, Toni
Wöhler, Friedrich
GE:ME III-1174
GL:Ren V-2522
Wojtyła, Karol Jozef. *See* John Paul II, Pope
Wolf, Max
GL:20 V-2475
Wolfe, James
GE:Am I-200
GL:B&C V-2644
Wolfe, Kenneth B.
GE:W20 I-487
Wolfe, Thomas
GE:A&C I-343
GE:W20 I-241
GL:Am V-2545
Wolfenden, Sir John
GE:HR II-991
Wolff, Antonio Navarro
GE:HR V-2465
Wolff-Metternich, Paul
GE:W20 I-107
Wolfram von Eschenbach
GL:A&M V-2349
Woll, Joseph Albert
GE:W20 II-730
Wollstonecraft, Mary
GL:B&C V-2650
Wolpe, Howard
GE:HR V-2354
Wolper, David
GE:A&C V-2397
Wolsey, Cardinal Thomas
GE:ME I-6, 103
GL:B&C V-2656
Wonder, Stevie
GE:A&C IV-1790, V-2294
Wong, Anna May
GL:AmW V-1919
Wong Liu Tson. *See* Wong, Anna May

Wood, Annie. *See* Besant, Annie
Wood, Arthur
  GE:Am III-1582
Wood, Arthur M.
  GE:B&C IV-1631
Wood, Edward Frederick Lindley. *See* Irwin, Lord
Wood, Jethrow
  GE:Am II-679
Wood, John S.
  GE:A&C III-1340
Wood, Natalie
  GE:A&C IV-1640
Wood, Nicholas
  GE:ME II-608
Wood, Robert D.
  GE:A&C V-2197, 2234
Wood, Robert E.
  GE:B&C II-487
Woodbridge, John, Jr.
  GE:Am I-127
Woodhead, Sir John Ackroyd
  GE:W20 I-411
Woodmason, Charles
  GE:Am I-213
Woodrow, O. B.
  GE:S&T I-453
Woodruff, Robert (1889-1985)
  GE:B&C V-1904
Woodruff, Robert (b. 1946?)
  GE:A&C V-2413
Woods, Mark
  GE:B&C II-827
Woodthorpe, Peter
  GE:A&C IV-1861
Woodward, Joanne
  GL:AmW V-1923
Woodward, Robert Burns
  GL:Am V-2550
Woodworth, John M.
  GE:Am III-1394
Woolf, Leonard S.
  GE:A&C II-637
Woolf, Virginia
  GE:A&C II-637
  GL:B&C V-2660
Wordsworth, William
  GL:B&C V-2664
Workman, Fanny Bullock
  GL:AmW V-1928
Worley, Jo Anne
  GE:A&C IV-2115
Wozniak, Stephen
  GE:B&C III-1138, IV-1611
  GE:S&T V-2073

Wrangel, Pëtr Nikolaevich
  GE:W20 I-152
Wrede, Stuart
  GE:A&C V-2614
Wren, Sir Christopher
  GL:B&C V-2669
Wright, Almroth Edward
  GE:ME III-1335
Wright, Andy
  GE:Am III-1588
Wright, Carroll D.
  GE:B&C I-86
Wright, Chauncey
  GE:Am III-1363
Wright, Elizur
  GE:Am II-719
Wright, Frank Lloyd
  GE:A&C II-902, 1067, IV-1806, V-2208
  GL:Am V-2556
Wright, Jim
  GE:HR V-2455
Wright, Olgivanna Lloyd
  GE:A&C II-902
Wright, Orville
  GE:Am II-1346
  GE:B&C II-499
  GE:S&T I-203
  GL:Am V-2562
Wright, Paul S.
  GE:HR II-929
Wright, Richard
  GE:A&C III-1185
Wright, Roy
  GE:Am III-1588
Wright, Sewall
  GE:W20 I-7
Wright, Silas
  GE:Am II-748
Wright, Wilbur
  GE:Am II-1346
  GE:S&T I-203
  GL:Am V-2562
Wriothesley, Thomas. *See* Southampton, Fourth Earl of
Wriston, Walter B.
  GE:B&C III-1159, IV-1739
Wu, Chien-Shiung
  GL:AmW V-1933
Wundt, Wilhelm
  GE:B&C I-80
  GL:20 V-2478
Württemberg, Duke Albrecht von
  GE:HR I-161

Wüst, Georg
   GE:S&T II-805
Wyclif, John
   GE:A&M III-1640, 1675
   GL:B&C V-2674
Wyeth, Henriette
   GL:AmW V-1937
Wyman, Bill
   GE:A&C IV-2027

Wyndham, Charles. *See* Egremont, Earl of
Wynen, André
   GE:HR IV-1829
Wynfrith. *See* Boniface, Saint
Wynn, Steve
   GE:B&C IV-1600
Wynn-Williams, C. E.
   GE:S&T III-1155

X

X, Malcolm. *See* Malcolm X
Xavier, Saint Francis
  GE:ME I-96
  GL:Ren V-2527
Xenakis, Yannis (Iannis)
  GE:A&C III-1629
  GL:20 V-2483
Xenophanes
  GE:A&M I-173
  GL:A&M V-2354

Xenophanes (Atenophanes)
  GE:A&M I-153
Xenophon
  GE:A&M I-313
  GL:A&M V-2359
Xerxes I
  GE:A&M I-237
  GL:A&M V-2364
Xuma, Alfred B.
  GE:W20 III-1272

Y

Yadin, Yigael
GE:W20 II-598
Yakovlev, Aleksandr N.
GE:B&C V-2022
Yalow, Rosalyn S.
GL:AmW V-1942
Yamagata, Prince Aritomo
GE:W20 I-121
Yamaguchi, Kristi
GL:AmW V-1947
Yamamoto, Isoroku
GE:Am III-1697
GE:W20 I-472
Yamani, Ahmad Zaki
GE:B&C IV-1533
GL:20 V-2490
Yamashita, Tomoyuki
GE:HR II-662
GE:W20 I-457
Yanayev, Gennady
GE:HR V-2618
Yáñez, Pedro Castillo
GE:HR IV-2186
Yao Wenyuan
GE:HR III-1332
GE:W20 III-1264
Yaqut
GL:A&M V-2370
Yarborough, Barton
GE:A&C III-1531
Yarborough, J. M.
GE:S&T V-2025
Yarborough, Ralph W.
GE:Am III-1899
GE:HR III-1402
Yard, Molly
GE:HR V-2489
Yawist, The
GE:A&M I-96
Yeager, Jeana
GE:S&T V-2336
Yeamans, Sir John
GE:Am I-132
Yeardley, Sir George
GE:Am I-65
Yearian, Mason Russell
GE:S&T III-1384
Yeats, William Butler
GE:A&C I-119, 176, 309, 440, 445

GE:Am III-1399
GL:B&C V-2679
Yeh Chien-ying
GE:W20 III-1264
Yehuda ben Shemuel ha-Levi. See Judah ha-Levi
Yeliseyev, Alexei S.
GE:S&T IV-1891
Yellen, Ben
GE:B&C V-1773
Yeltsin, Boris
GE:B&C V-2022
GE:HR V-2249, 2471, 2618
Yen Li-pen
GL:A&M V-2374
Yepes y Álvarez, Juan de. See John of the Cross, Saint
Yeremeko, Andrei Ivanovich
GE:ME III-1472
Yersin, Alexandre
GE:S&T I-6, II-567
Yevtushenko, Yevgeny
GE:W20 II-988
Yezhov, Nikolai
GE:HR I-503
GE:W20 I-336
Yo Fei
GL:A&M V-2379
Yoelson, Asa. See Jolson, Al
Yohannis IV. See John IV, of Ethiopia
Yolles, Stanley F.
GE:HR III-1497
York, Duke of. See James II
Yorke, Francis R. S.
GE:A&C IV-2064
Yorkin, Bud
GE:A&C V-2197, 2234
Yorty, Samuel
GE:HR III-1301
Yoshida, Shigeru
GE:W20 II-584
Yoshino, Sakuzo
GE:HR I-417
Yost, Charles
GE:B&C IV-1501
Young, A. Thomas
GE:S&T V-2052
Young, Andrew
GE:HR IV-1903, 1937, 2040

Young, Brigham
   GE:Am II-812
   GL:Am V-2568
Young, Frank E.
   GE:B&C V-1986
Young, John Russell
   GE:Am II-1279
Young, John W.
   GE:S&T V-2180, 2256
Young, La Monte
   GE:A&C IV-1979
Young, Leo C.
   GE:W20 I-324
Young, Lester
   GE:A&C II-930, III-1617
Young, Owen D.
   GE:Am III-1537
   GE:B&C I-363, 396, II-522, 640
Young, Robert (actor)
   GE:A&C III-1470

Young, Robert (businessman)
   GE:W20 I-520
Young, Terence
   GE:A&C IV-1913
Young, Walker
   GE:S&T III-1075
Young, William Henry
   GE:S&T I-36
Yuan Shih-kai
   GE:HR I-116
   GE:W20 I-92, 121
Yüan Tsang. See Hsün-tsang
Yüan-chang. See Mi Fei
Yuderich, Nikolai Nikolaevich
   GE:W20 I-152
Yukawa, Hideki
   GE:S&T III-992, 1030
   GL:20 V-2495
Yung-lo
   GL:A&M V-2383
Yung-shu. See Ou-yang Hsiu

Z

Zacharias
GE:A&M II-1121, 1131
Zadok
GE:A&M I-477
Zaghlūl, Sa'd
GL:20 V-2500
Zaharias, "Babe" Didrikson
GL:Am V-2573
GL:AmW V-1952
Zahīr-ud-Dīn Muhammad. *See* Bābur
Zakkai, Johanan ben. *See* Ben Zakkai, Johanan
Zambona, Jutta Ilse
GE:A&C II-767
Zamora y Torres, Niceto Alcalá
GE:ME III-1368
Zamoyski, Andrei
GE:ME II-886
Zanardelli, Giuseppe
GE:ME II-1109
Zane, Ebenezer
GE:Am I-491
Zane, Edward R.
GE:HR II-1056
Zanuck, Darryl F.
GE:A&C II-1011, III-1131
GL:Am V-2578
Zapata, Emiliano
GE:W20 I-69
GL:20 V-2505
Zápolya, John
GE:ME I-87
Zarathustra. *See* Zoroaster
Zaret, Milton M.
GE:S&T IV-1714
Zaslavsky, David
GE:A&C IV-1747
Zaug, Arthur J.
GE:S&T V-2190
Zawinul, Joe
GE:A&C IV-2153
Zdansky, Otto
GE:S&T II-761
Zeami Motokiyo
GL:A&M V-2390
Zecca, Ferdinand
GE:A&C I-57
Zechariah
GE:A&M I-189

Zedekiah
GE:A&M I-149
Zederbaum, J. O. *See* Martov, Julius
Zedong, Mao. *See* Mao Tse-tung
Zeeman, Pieter
GE:S&T I-417, II-800
Zehntbauer, John
GE:A&C I-491
Zehntbauer, Roy
GE:A&C I-491
Zehrfuss, Bernard
GE:A&C II-1021, IV-2064
Zeidler, Othmar
GE:W20 I-425
Zelaya, José Santos
GE:HR I-137
Zemlinsky, Alexander von
GE:A&C I-193
Zenawi, Meles
GE:HR IV-1758
Zenger, John Peter
GE:Am I-188
GL:Am V-2583
Zeno, Byzantine Emperor
GE:A&M II-980, 989
Zeno of Citium
GE:A&M I-210, 388, 403
GL:A&M V-2397
Zeno of Elea
GE:A&M I-231
GL:A&M V-2403
Zeno the Isaurian. *See* Zeno, Byzantine Emperor
Zenshōbō Renchō. *See* Nichiren
Zeppelin, Ferdinand von
GE:S&T I-78
GL:20 V-2510
Zermelo, Ernst
GE:S&T I-233
Zerubbabel
GE:A&M I-189
Zetkin, Clara
GL:20 V-2516
Zhang Chunqiao
GE:HR III-1332
Zhao Ziyang
GE:B&C V-1887
GE:HR V-2483
Zhdanov, Andrei Aleksandrovich
GE:A&C II-908, 914, III-1388

255

Zhou Enlai
    GE:B&C III-1003, 1281, IV-1477
    GE:HR II-837, 958, 1015
Zhu De
    GE:HR II-958
Zhukov, Georgy Konstantinovich
    GE:ME III-1472
    GE:W20 I-479, II-577
    GL:20 V-2522
Zhuyovich-Tsrni, Streten
    GE:W20 II-640
Zia Ul-Haq, General Mohammad
    GE:HR IV-1898, 2018, V-2403
Ziedler, Othmar
    GE:S&T III-1146
Ziegfeld, Florenz
    GE:A&C II-745
Ziegler, Adolf
    GE:A&C III-1083
Ziegler, Henri
    GE:B&C III-1303
Zilva, Sylvester Solomon
    GE:S&T II-857
Zimmerman, Ethel Agnes. See Merman, Ethel
Zimmerman, Robert. See Dylan, Bob
Zimmerman, William F., Jr.
    GE:HR I-497, II-897
Zinn, Walter Henry
    GE:S&T III-1198, 1419
Zinoviev, Grigori
    GE:B&C I-374, II-563
    GE:HR I-503
    GE:ME III-1347
    GE:W20 I-336
Zinsser, Hans
    GE:S&T II-921
Zinzendorf, Graf von
    GL:Ren V-2532
Ziolkovsky, Konstantin Eduardovich
    GE:Am III-1555
    GE:W20 II-751, 776
Zipper, Jaime A.
    GE:S&T IV-1629
Ziyad, Tarik ibn. See Ibn Ziyad, Tarik
Žižka, Count Jan
    GL:A&M V-2407
Zohn, Barbara
    GE:HR V-2256
Zola, Émile
    GE:A&C II-890

GE:ME II-1075
GL:Ren V-2537
Zook, George F.
    GE:Am III-1725
Zorilla, Manuel Ruíz
    GE:ME II-945
Zoroaster
    GE:A&M I-163
    GL:A&M V-2411
Zoser
    GL:A&M V-2416
Zosimas
    GE:A&M II-946, III-1738
Zsigmondy, Richard
    GE:S&T I-159
Zubaidha
    GE:A&M II-1142
Zubatov, Sergei
    GE:ME III-1156
Zucker, Joseph
    GE:B&C IV-1647
Zuckerman, Arie J.
    GE:S&T V-2326
Zuckerman, Benjamin Michael
    GE:W20 II-827
Zukor, Adolph
    GE:A&C I-224, II-567
    GE:B&C I-117
Zumalacárregui, Tomas
    GE:ME II-726
Zvi, Shabtay
    GE:HR II-832
Zweig, George
    GE:S&T IV-1767
Zweng, H. Christian
    GE:S&T IV-1714
Zwicky, Fritz
    GE:S&T III-1008
    GE:W20 II-1009
Zwilich, Ellen Taaffe
    GL:AmW V-1957
Zwingli, Huldrych
    GE:ME I-116
    GL:Ren V-2542
Zworykin, Vladimir
    GE:A&C III-1143, 1211
    GE:Am III-1674
    GE:B&C II-803
    GE:S&T II-751
    GL:Am V-2589